Stephen Poliakoff

Close to the Enemy

With an introduction by the author

Bloomsbury Methuen Drama
An imprint of Bloomsbury Publishing Plc

B L O O M S B U R Y
LONDON • OXFORD • NEW YORK • NEW DELHI • SYDNEY

Bloomsbury Methuen Drama
An imprint of Bloomsbury Publishing Plc
Imprint previously known as Methuen Drama

50 Bedford Square	1385 Broadway
London	New York
WC1B 3DP	NY 10018
UK	USA

BLOOMSBURY, METHUEN DRAMA and the Diana logo
are trade mark of Bloomsbury Publishing Plc

First published 2016

© Amor Road Films Limited 2016

Stephen Poliakoff has asserted his rights under the Copyright,
Designs and Patents Act 1988 to be identified as the author of this work

All rights whatsoever in this publication are strictly reserved.
Requests to reproduce the text in whole or in part should be addressed
to the publisher. Application for performance etc. by professionals or amateurs
in any medium and in any language throughout the world should be made
in writing before rehearsals begin to Judy Daish Associates Limited,
2 St Charles Place, London, W10 6EG. No performance may be given
unless a licence has been obtained and no alteration may be made
in the title or text of the work without the author's prior written consent.

No rights in incidental music or songs or illustrations contained in the publication
are hereby granted and performance rights for any performance/presentation
whatsoever must be obtained from the respective copyright owners.

No responsibility for loss caused to any individual or organisation acting
on or refraining from action as a result of the material in this publication
can be accepted by Bloomsbury or the author

British Library Cataloguing-in-Publication Data
A catalogue record for this book is available from the British Library.

ISBN: HB: 978-1-3500-1604-0
PB: 978-1-3500-1600-2
ePDF: 978-1-3500-1601-9
ePub: 978-1-3500-1602-6

Library of Congress Cataloging-in-Publication Data
A catalog record for this book is available from the Library of Congress.

All photographs © Little Island (Poliakoff) Productions
Photographer: Adrian Rogers

Cover design: Olivia D'Cruz Cover image: Adrian Rogers

Typeset by Country Setting, Kingsdown, Kent CT14 8ES
Printed and bound in Great Britain

Close to the Enemy

Stephen Poliakoff, born in December 1952, was appointed writer in residence at the National Theatre for 1976 and the same year won the *Evening Standard*'s Most Promising Playwright Award for *Hitting Town* and *City Sugar*. He has also won a BAFTA Award for Best Single Play for *Caught on a Train* in 1980, the *Evening Standard*'s Best British Film Award for *Close My Eyes* in 1992, the Critics' Circle Best Play Award for *Blinded by the Sun* in 1996 and the Prix Italia and the Royal Television Society Best Drama Award for *Shooting the Past* in 1999.

His plays and films include *Clever Soldiers* (1974), *The Carnation Gang* (1974), *Hitting Town* (1975), *City Sugar* (1975), *Heroes* (1975), *Strawberry Fields* (1977), *Stronger than the Sun* (1977), *Shout Across the River* (1978), *American Days* (1979), *The Summer Party* (1980), *Bloody Kids* (1980), *Caught on a Train* (1980), *Favourite Nights* (1981), *Soft Targets* (1982), *Runners* (1983), *Breaking the Silence* (1984), *Coming in to Land* (1987), *Hidden City* (1988), *She's Been Away* (1989), *Playing with Trains* (1989), *Close My Eyes* (1991), *Sienna Red* (1992), *Century* (1994), *Sweet Panic* (1996), *Blinded by the Sun* (1996), *The Tribe* (1997), *Food of Love* (1998), *Talk of the City* (1998), *Remember This* (1999) and *Shooting the Past* (1999). *Perfect Strangers* (2001) won the Dennis Potter Award at the 2002 BAFTAs and Best Writer and Best Drama at the Royal Television Society Awards, and *The Lost Prince* (2003) was the winner of three Emmy Awards in 2005 including Outstanding Mini Series. *Friends and Crocodiles* (2006) and *Gideon's Daughter* (2006) won two Golden Globes and a Peabody Award in 2007. His most recent work for the BBC includes *Joe's Palace*, *Capturing Mary*, *A Real Summer* (all 2007) and Golden Globe-winning *Dancing on the Edge* (2013). His latest feature film, *Glorious 39*, was released in 2009 and his latest stage play, *My City*, was staged at the Almeida in 2011.

Works by Stephen Poliakoff published by Methuen Drama

PLAYS AND SCREENPLAYS

Dancing on the Edge
Friends and Crocodiles *and* Gideon's Daughter
Glorious 39
Joe's Palace *and* Capturing Mary
The Lost Prince
Perfect Strangers
Remember This
Shooting the Past
Sienna Red
Sweet Panic
Sweet Panic *and* Blinded by the Sun
Talk of the City
My City

COLLECTED WORKS

POLIAKOFF PLAYS: 1
(Clever Soldiers, Hitting Town, City Sugar, Shout Across the River, American Days, Strawberry Fields)

POLIAKOFF PLAYS: 2
(Breaking the Silence, Playing with Trains, She's Been Away, Century)

POLIAKOFF PLAYS: 3
(Caught on a Train, Coming in to Land, Close My Eyes)

SEE ALSO

Poliakoff on Stage and Screen by Robin Nelson

Contents

Introduction vii
Cast and Credits xiii

Close to the Enemy 1

Introduction

One of my earliest memories is of sitting next to my father in the front seat of his car and staring out of the window at a shattered bomb-devastated city as we drove together across London. This was at least ten years after the end of the war and yet there were still bombsites everywhere you looked, houses sliced in half with their wallpaper, fireplaces, bathrooms and sometimes even pianos exposed to the elements. They stood like a series of jagged enormous doll's houses peering at you from the end of the street.

As I got a little older, I realised that many of the adults I encountered still seethed with a sense of danger and grievance about the war. Just below the surface lurked real anger about what they had experienced and how their lives had been changed by it for ever.

I think this is the reason I have always been fascinated by the immediate post-war period and why I have decided to set the most ambitious drama I have attempted in the particular years of 1946 and 1947. It was a time of startling contrasts: people's lives were continually blighted by intense austerity and draconian food rationing (bread was rationed for the first time when it had been freely available during the war), but it was also the moment the National Health Service was being born and the Welfare State was being truly established. What's more, this was all accompanied by a tremendous burst of activity in the arts, which saw one of the finest periods in British cinema, the founding of the Edinburgh Festival and an outpouring of new British classical music.

The adrenaline that had been released by the war, either through the experience of actual combat or the terrifying sensation of being bombed from the air, could not just be switched off like a tap in 1945. The country was still semi-militarised and yet the black market was doing vigorous business in every community. Children swarmed over dangerous bombsites totally unsupervised or hid guns in their desks at school. The atmosphere on the streets was raw and edgy as everybody wondered, 'Now what happens?' And yet we were the victors; we had supposedly triumphed. It seemed inexplicable to many that life could have become even tougher than during wartime. A series of savagely cold winters made existence even more intensely vivid and gruelling. In summer, the light was blindingly bright because of the great many buildings that were missing, completely transforming familiar landscapes so that they seemed totally alien. There was also a widely shared sense of bewilderment once the joy of victory and the realisation that the war had finally ended began to fade. People stared at the ruined cities across Britain and wondered how this could have all been allowed to happen in the first place. Why wasn't the rise of fascism in Germany confronted earlier? Who, apart from Hitler, was really to blame?

I wanted to tell some of the stories from this time, and there were several that had haunted me for years. For a start, how the British (along with the Americans and the Russians) seized any German nationals they thought could be of use to them and compelled them to work for them, whether they wanted to or not. Some of these people were literally kidnapped from the streets of Europe, plucked off the pavements, for they were the human spoils of war. They were brought in considerable numbers to Britain, America and Russia. Those that came to the UK did not just include scientists, but also perfume manufacturers, experts on making plastics – anybody, in fact, who could give the British an advantage over their competitors, especially the Americans.

Another story that intrigued me was how the British secret service often thwarted the attempts by various individuals and organisations to bring people guilty of war crimes to justice. If these potential war criminals were deemed useful – if they had information on the Soviet Union or had important strategic knowledge – they were given new identities or even had their deaths faked. In the US, there was a special secret initiative, called Operation Paperclip, which gave literally hundreds of German scientists new identities. Many of these scientists had enjoyed very close relations with the Nazi regime and some had used slave labour in the course of their work.

And, above all, there was the story that really obsessed me: how the British missed crucial chances that might have helped shorten the war or indeed may have averted it altogether. The most striking examples of this were how we let our lead in jet-engine technology evaporate because we refused to renew a patent for the cost of five pounds and how we ignored an approach from members of the German military who stated they intended to stage a coup against Hitler just weeks before the Munich Agreement in 1938. At this pivotal moment, a year before the outbreak of war, there was no appetite for conflict among the German public, nor was the German army ready for war – for one thing, many of their tanks were not functioning properly. A very serious and highly secret initiative was instigated by several senior German military commanders and diplomats to get rid of Hitler before it was too late. They just needed certain assurances from the British government. These assurances, tragically, were not forthcoming.

In *Close to the Enemy*, I set out to entwine these stories together in one narrative and this drew me back to the hotel setting I had used in *Dancing on the Edge*, my last drama, which told the story of a black jazz band mixing with the aristocracy in the 1930s. The hotel in *Close to the Enemy* is a very different place, however, for it has been seriously damaged during the war. Large portions of its interior are held up by scaffolding, its exterior stares out across a massive bombsite and on its attic floor there are secret rooms being used by military intelligence to listen in to various guests whose bedrooms they have bugged. Furthermore, the hotel's ballroom is not a gilded space populated by the wealthy, but a room sunk deep in the basement where all sorts of characters let off energy by dancing as they try to escape the hardship that lies outside.

As in nearly everything I write, I wanted to tell *Close to the Enemy* through the eyes of just one character so it became a first-person narrative. In this way, the audience can travel with the central character through the story, enter the hotel for the first time at the same moment that he does and then initially meet all of the other characters at the point that he encounters them. By this method, I try to make the past seem to be happening in the present tense – it is as if we are experiencing it, too.

In this story, we see a lot of the action through the eyes of Callum, the young officer working for military intelligence. He has been assigned the job of making the jet-engine scientist Dieter and his daughter Lotte a little happier about being in England after they have been seized from their beds in the middle of the night in Germany. It is to be Callum's last job in the army before he goes back into civilian life and he thinks it will only last a few days. In the event, Callum becomes consumed by his task and it begins to have a profound effect on him, both emotionally and intellectually, changing his whole outlook on life.

As Callum finds himself being drawn deeper and deeper into the Connington Hotel (it has, in fact, become his home), he meets the other main characters who will alter his destiny. These include the mysterious Foreign Office official Harold; the wealthy, seemingly golden couple Rachel and Alex; the combative and very determined war crimes investigator Kathy; the American singer Eva; and the displaced and absolutely terrifying Frau Bellinghausen. At the same time as all these new relationships are forming, Callum also has to deal with the responsibility he feels towards his younger brother, Victor, who has been deeply scarred by his experiences during the war. The two brothers are alone in the world for both their parents are dead and Callum is constantly concerned about his brother's health and general wellbeing. Like many returning servicemen, Victor is desperate to re-enter civilian life and have a proper job, but his volatile moods have made this difficult. He wants his brother to solve this, but Callum's life at the Connington has become increasingly intense, causing their relationship to undergo a dramatic shift.

As the narrative of *Close to the Enemy* unfolds, all these characters either live in, or frequently visit, the crumbling world of the Connington Hotel. When they do venture outside, it is into a city that is not just full of bombsites, ruined churches and rationing, but is being gradually enveloped by paranoia as the Cold War descends and begins to affect everything.

During the seven parts of the drama, I trace what happens to each of these characters and, at the same time, I attempt to illuminate the wider landscape at this crucial moment in history.

All the characters are trying to rebuild their lives after the trauma of the war, but they are also faced by a constant dilemma: how far can one turn a blind eye to what has happened in the immediate past so one can move more easily into the future?

Stephen Poliakoff
September 2016

Close to the Enemy was first screened on BBC2 in November 2016 in a production by Little Island Productions. The cast was as follows:

Callum	Jim Sturgess
Victor	Freddie Highmore
Lotte	Lucy Ward
Dieter	August Diehl
Harold Lindsay-Jones	Alfred Molina
Rachel	Charlotte Riley
Kathy	Phoebe Fox
Alex	Sebastian Armesto
Brigadier Wainwright	Robert Glenister
Salter	Julian Bleach
Ringwood	Alfie Allen
Julia	Charity Wakefield
Eva	Angela Bassett
Frau Bellinghausen	Lindsay Duncan
Miss Clarkson	Emma Fielding
Lucy	Ciara Charteris
Ruth	Carly Bawden
Mr Emmanuel	James Bradshaw
Anna	Sai Bennett
Rita	Vinette Robinson
Horst Kleinow	Aleksander Jovanovic
Birgit Mentz	Antje Traue
Mrs Tooley	Jacqueline Tong
Leonard	Duncan Wisbey
Sharp-faced Woman	Debra Baker
Doctor	Simon Shackleton
Club Desk Clerk	Nick Wilton
Petrol Attendant	Michael Ballard
Hotel Desk Clerk	Peter Prentice
Male Hotel Guest	Ian Swan
Stern-faced Woman	Raewyn Lippert
Sleeping Man Pete	Robert Cawsey
Maître d'	Andrew Price

Attic Room Cleaner	Lacey Bond
Psychiatric Nurse	Hannah Taylor Gordon
Fuller's Waitress	Sophie Bleasdale
Psychiatrist	Laurence Kennedy
Portly Young Poet	James Dryden
Head of the Foreign Office	William Chubb
Kleinow's Nurse	Catherine Skinner
Chubby Minder	Lee Long
Male Party Guest	Lyndon Ogbourne
Mentz's Minder	Kirsty Hoiles
Waste Disposal Man	Barry Aird

Writer/Director   Stephen Poliakoff
Producer   Helen Flint
Music and Lyrics   Adrian Johnston
Director of Photography   Ashley Rowe
Line Producer   Jean Holdsworth
Film Editor   Chris Wyatt
Casting Director   Andy Pryor
Production Designer   Rob Harris
Costume Designer   Nic Ede

Close to the Enemy

Part One

EXT. A SHIP COMING IN TO PORT. NIGHT

A close-up of a small girl, **Lotte**. *She is seven years old, dressed in a battered overcoat that seems too big for her. It is night. The wind is blowing her hair; her face is very tense. She glances sideways; military policemen are standing either side of her, staring ahead, not engaging with her. We cut back to* **Lotte**. *We see from her point of view the approaching shore, a port at night. There are arc lights staring down, military vehicles moving along the shoreline as the ship moves close.*

We cut wide on **Lotte** *and see she is in the bow of the ship, guarded by the two military policemen, as if she is under escort. We cut back to her face; we now see everything from her point of view. The other passengers in the bow of the ship are straining to get a first look at the shore. There is a whole babble of languages being spoken behind her: French, Dutch, German. She sees anxious faces all around her, uncertainty in their eyes, wondering what awaits them.*

Lotte *is holding a battered toy animal in one hand, a misshapen grey donkey with one of its eyes missing. Her hand tightens on her toy as the ship moves closer to the port. She glances at the military police next to her, their impassive faces, and, seeing they are not looking at her, she turns suddenly and pushes back among the passengers.*

Her father, **Dieter**, *is standing a few feet behind her, a man in his late thirties. He is staring ahead, watching the port come into view, his expression very tense. He squeezes her hand, and* **Lotte** *holds on tightly to him. Her father is surrounded by a military escort.*

We stay on **Lotte**, *as she stares at the buildings, looming into view now, and the silhouette of a large naval ship towering above them. The lights from the shore are bright, intense, and the noise suddenly overwhelming, as the ship's engines begin to manoeuvre.*

We cut to the dark water, with the arc lights reflected in it, and then the military vehicles moving along the shore.

A caption comes up over the image.

ENGLAND. 1946.

INT. IMMIGRATION HALL. NIGHT

We cut to **Lotte**, *moving with the military police into the vast immigration hall. It is a building that has several levels. A narrow entrance through which everybody is funnelled, opening out into a general processing area which stretches into the distance, as far as* **Lotte** *can see.*

Her father, who is carrying a single suitcase, is just ahead of her, being moved fast through the hall by the military police. **Lotte** *has to run to keep up.*

All around the hall she sees signs and arrows pointing to different checkpoints: for UK Citizens, for British Commonwealth Subjects, and then an arrow for the rest of the world. Above her head loudspeakers are crackling out, a rasping voice, telling people to find their correct area.

Lotte *catches up with her father and the military police, who have paused for a moment at the bottom of a flight of stairs.* **Lotte** *can see across the hall, to where the swarm of passengers are being separated. The British queue, a short one, is standing opening their suitcases for customs. At the front of the queue is an aristocratic-looking woman wearing a large hat. She appears very impatient when she starts being questioned about what exactly she has brought aboard.*

A couple of men from the British queue stare with detached curiosity at **Lotte**, *in her big coat, with her bedraggled donkey.*

Lotte *looks away from them, across to the other side of the hall, where the much longer queue of refugees is forming. All different ages and shapes. Their faces looking disoriented and very nervous, some of them dragging large trunks behind them; others just have bundles of possessions.*

A **Sharp-faced Woman** *in uniform suddenly appears down the stairs and summons the military escort. Now they are moving fast again, up the stairs, with officials brushing past them in the opposite direction.*

They emerge on to the first floor. Desks line the vast space. At each one an official is sitting, questioning some refugees. And there is a row of passengers sitting waiting their turn, looking gaunt and frightened under the harsh lights. A powerful sense of need on their faces, people desperately wanting the chance to rebuild their lives.

Lotte *has to run again to keep up with the escort. Her father is looking back all the time, checking where she is. Suddenly the military police stop and take her father into a small office off the main area. Two of the police follow him into the office. The other two move further down the passage to have a smoke.*

Lotte *can see a large man in a suit sitting at the desk in the office. Just before the door closes, her father calls out to her in German, as if giving her instructions.*

The **Sharp-faced Woman** *immediately turns to* **Lotte**.

SHARP-FACED WOMAN
What did he say to you?

Lotte *stares back at the woman, giving her nothing. Her expression tense, defiant. The* **Sharp-faced Woman**'s *tone becomes more insistent:*

What did your father say to you?

LOTTE
I don't speak English.

The woman stares at **Lotte** *for a moment, giving her a searching look, trying to work out whether she is lying.*

SHARP-FACED WOMAN
Well, you have to sit still here until they've finished with your father.

Just as she is saying this there are raised voices from the little office. **Lotte**'s *father's voice, clearly very agitated. We can hear shouts of protest. Then the door opens for a brief moment as one of the military police leaves.* **Lotte** *glimpses her father for a second before the door closes, his face flushed with fury.*

We move in on **Lotte** *as the shouting continues. She starts to shake, the faces staring at her, the frightening noise. The sound begins to blur as we see the real shock on the young girl's face at finding herself here.*

The door suddenly bursts open, and the sound comes back with a rush, as the military policeman is escorting **Dieter** *out of the office. As he leaves,* **Dieter** *turns to the large man, and says in English.*

DIETER
I have made my position clear again and again. However many times you ask me, it makes no difference. It will not change anything.

The military escort has now re-formed around **Dieter**. *The four men are moving him back the way they came.* **Dieter** *calls to* **Lotte** *in German.*

DIETER
Keep up! You must keep up!

The police are now almost frogmarching **Dieter** *down the stairs and back towards the entrance of the building.*

At the bottom of the stairs the refugee queue has bulged chaotically, people clamouring to be processed. The Tannoy announcements have become harsher and more urgent, telling people they have to queue in an orderly fashion.

Lotte *is running after the military escort, who are pushing their way through the swirl of people. Her father is frantically glancing back at her.*

Suddenly **Lotte**'s *stuffed animal is knocked out of her hand. She stops instantly to look for it. We see a shot through the crowd of her father and the military escort disappearing towards the exit.*

Lotte *is oblivious to this; she is on all fours, looking for the donkey, among the forest of legs and luggage. People are almost treading on her, cigarette butts falling around her.*

Suddenly she catches sight of the toy, about ten feet away from her, but as she gets closer, people knock into it, kicking it further along the floor.

Lotte *does not stop, she is absolutely focused on retrieving it. We see the real determination on her face as she forces her way through the legs to get it. Just as she is about to touch it, a plump hand reaches down from somewhere, grabs it, and begins to move off with it.*

Lotte *stands up, searching the crowd wildly. She sees a small round man with glinting glasses disappearing across the hall with her toy. She fights her way through the throng, bumping into people, being cursed by people, and catches the man by his arm.*

The man turns. He has a moon-shaped face, almost childlike in its smoothness. But he has a very beady look in his eyes. Before **Lotte** *can even speak, he addresses her in French:*

MAN

So this is yours?

Lotte *nods and makes a grab for it but the man holds it out of her reach.*

Is it very special? Do you carry it always?

Lotte *shakes her head to indicate she does not understand, and she jumps to grab it, but the man continues to hold it just out of her reach. He seems to want to prolong the moment. He switches to English:*

Tell me its name. (*His beady eyes watching her.*) Do you understand me now?

Lotte *stares at him.*

Not going to talk to me? Even though I found it for you, my little sweet? My name is Mr Emmanuel . . . Still not going to talk to me?

That's not very polite! But then I understand, some things must never be lost.

He hands her the donkey. **Lotte** *turns to go but he catches her hand and holds her.*

You didn't thank me . . .

Lotte *mouths an inaudible 'thank you'.*

Goodbye little one . . .

He takes her hand and kisses it, holds it for a moment, very tight, and then lets her go.

Lotte *runs off, desperately looking for her father. There is no sign. She pushes as hard as she can to get out, forcing her way through the bottleneck of people coming towards her in the narrow entrance.*

EXT. THE HARBOUR. NIGHT

Lotte *comes out of the entrance of the building to be greeted by the sight of a jeep and a large saloon car waiting with their headlights on. The military police are standing facing the entrance, and her father is shouting in relief, in German:*

DIETER

There you are, Lotte! Where on earth have you been?!

INT. SALOON CAR. HARBOUR. NIGHT

Lotte *is sitting in the front of the saloon car, her father on the back seat, with one of the military escorts next to him. The driver of the car is another military policeman.*

They are driving along the dock, being escorted by a jeep ahead of them. We see everything through the windscreen, from **Lotte**'s *point of view, people being scattered in front of the cars, as they move fast along the harbour. Somebody's suitcase comes open as they dodge out of the way, their belongings strewn across the road.*

The convoy of two vehicles pause at a barrier with a sentry. The military police in the jeep in front start bantering with the sentry. **Lotte** *can hear her father cursing on the back seat, getting more and more agitated. She turns to look at him but he is staring at the driver.*

DIETER

Are you at least going to tell me where you are taking us?

There is just the sound of the engine running; the soldiers in the car do not even acknowledge the question.

Lotte *stares at the intense arc lights which are pointed straight at the car and at the lens.*

INT. SMALL ROOM. MILITARY CAMP. MORNING

We cut from the blinding arc lights to some curtains moving gently in the breeze, sharp morning sun filtering through them. **Lotte**'s *eyes open, she finds herself in a small, bare room. She is wearing a shabby white nightdress.*

There is the heavy sound of military vehicles rumbling past, very close to the window, and voices shouting from the outside.

She suddenly realises she is not alone. Sitting at the end of the bed, staring at her is a man in uniform, **Callum**. *He is in his early thirties, and has sharp, fearless eyes. He has a London accent. He is looking at her with quite a friendly gaze, as if he has been waiting for her to wake.*

Lotte *instinctively moves back in the bed, pulling the sheets up round her.*

CALLUM
No need to be afraid. (*He smiles.*) I've come to take you to breakfast.

Lotte *just stares back at him.* **Callum** *repeats the word 'breakfast' in German.* **Lotte** *shakes her head.*

Come on, you must be starving . . .

He repeats 'starving' in German. **Lotte** *stares at him with cold hostility.*

My German's not very good, I know . . . (*He smiles.*) But I think you understand English, don't you? A little, anyway?

Their eyes meet.

LOTTE
Prison?

CALLUM
No. You're not in prison.

INT. LARGE HUT. DAY

We cut to **Callum** *and* **Lotte** *sitting in a large hut with wooden tables, an army canteen. They are almost alone, a couple of soldiers are watching from the shadows.* **Lotte**, *now back in her travelling clothes, is staring at the plate in front of her, which has two untouched sausages on it. She is refusing to eat.*

CALLUM
Come on, there's a lot of rations on that plate!

Lotte *ignores the sausages. She stares at* **Callum** *with intense hostility.*

Eat one of them, and I'll tell you where you are!

Lotte *just stares back at him.*

CALLUM
Well I'll tell you anyway. You're in London, on the edge of London – in Enfield, to be exact!

He turns her plate round and points at the sausages.

If these are the centre of London! (*He taps the outer rim of the plate.*) Then we are here. And your father, in case you were worrying, will join you in a couple of hours.

Callum *repeats the last phrase in his faltering German but* **Lotte** *is giving him nothing. She instead looks out of the window, through its filthy yellow glass, to where she can see a huge bombed house, the remains of a stately home, now totally destroyed.*

Its gaunt, roofless walls, staring down at the army camp.

There are a handful of soldiers with weapons and in camouflage uniform moving among the ruins. For a moment, as **Lotte** *sees the soldiers, real fear comes into her eyes.* **Callum** *follows her gaze.*

CALLUM
Don't worry, they're not coming over here!

We see the silhouetted figures of the soldiers staring down from the ruins.

They're just using it for training.

A young **Second Lieutenant** *calls to* **Callum** *from the doorway.*

SECOND LIEUTENANT
The Brigadier wants to see you, sir.

CALLUM
(*turning to* **Lotte**)
Have a good breakfast! *Auf wiedersehen!*

Callum *reaches the* **Second Lieutenant** *who is staring across at this small girl, alone in the canteen.*

SECOND LIEUTENANT
We're really scraping the barrel now, sir. What's she? Spying for the Russians is she?!

CALLUM
(*breezily*)
She understands English, so watch what you say!

We stay on **Lotte***, sitting bolt upright in the canteen, watched over by two soldiers.*

EXT. JEEP. SUBURBAN STREETS. DAY

We cut to **Callum** *being driven by the* **Second Lieutenant** *in a military jeep, through suburban streets. The lieutenant is driving furiously fast and they are passed by two jeeps going in the opposite direction, also driving really fast. It is as if they are an occupying army in their own suburbs.*

Callum *looks into the gardens of the houses as they pass. Some rubble is piled up in the otherwise neat front gardens. A couple of the houses are boarded up from bomb damage. A few children are standing in the gardens watching the jeeps roar past, their pale undernourished faces expressionless.*

Suddenly an old woman steps out into the road, directly in the path of the jeep.

The jeep screeches to a halt, almost hitting her.

The old lady remains standing stock still, staring shocked at the soldiers. The **Second Lieutenant** *mutters angrily, swerves round her and roars off.*

CALLUM
Blimey! How many people have you killed, Rogers, driving like that?!

We stay on his face for a moment.

Time we got out of here! Gave Enfield back to them!

EXT. LARGE HOUSE. MILITARY HQ. DAY

We cut to the jeep driving up to a mansion. There is a duck pond and a substantial garden, but there are army vehicles parked along the drive and notices everywhere, the atmosphere of a military headquarters.

Smoke is climbing from two bonfires in the garden.

INT. WAINWRIGHT'S HQ. DAY

We cut to the interior of a large outbuilding to the main house. It has the feel of a converted barn. It is stacked full of box files and huge piles of loose paper. Seven women in uniform are typing amongst the paper. A makeshift partition separates them from the Brigadier's office.

Callum *is standing opposite* **Wainwright**, *who is in uniform. A large jowly man, with a seemingly affable manner, but very cold eyes.*

Wainwright *is opening a file on his desk and peering at it.*

Callum *surveys the clutter along the walls. The great collection of box files.*

And then he moves to the window and sees smoke climbing into the air from somewhere in the garden; men in uniform are trundling trollies piled with files towards the smoke.

CALLUM

Burning stuff already?

WAINWRIGHT

We've got to start getting rid of some of it. We're drowning in files. Thought you of all people would be glad to see the back of it, having had to spend so much time reading the bloody stuff!

Callum *watches more files being moved towards the smoke. His tone is breezy, almost insolent. There's a familiarity between them.*

CALLUM

And if we miss something interesting?

WAINWRIGHT
(*chuckles*)

Too bad!

He suddenly fixes **Callum** *with his cold eyes.*

So you've seen the little girl?

CALLUM

Yes, I've done the babysitting for you.

WAINWRIGHT

Good! (*His tone more formal.*) I know you're meant to be going on leave this week, and it's very overdue, so this is not an order, but I want you to do a little more babysitting of a rather important kind – (*He shuts the file.*) instead.

CALLUM

I don't think so! (*After slight beat.*) Sir.

We nearly killed a woman coming over here! I can't wait to get out!

WAINWRIGHT
(*a sly smile*)
I didn't say this was happening here, did I?

CALLUM

Who do you want me to babysit?

WAINWRIGHT

Her father, and the little girl of course. He could be *very* important to us. He's a scientist or engineer – never know what the correct term is when you're talking about high speed – a jet plane man anyway! Brilliant apparently.

But *you* can find out more about all that can't you? He speaks quite good English, shouldn't be difficult.

CALLUM

So what's the problem?

WAINWRIGHT

He doesn't like us. Doesn't want to work with us . . . We had to move fast before the Russians got him, they've grabbed nearly a thousand scientists already . . . The Americans are grabbing them too, and so are we . . . we snatched him out of bed in the middle of the night in fact – though I'm sure we did it in as civilised a way as possible!

CALLUM

Of course . . .

Callum *looks down through the window; he now sees a man in a dark suit and hat (***Salter***), sitting on a bench in the shadows watching the trollies trundling past him. He is smoking a slender cigar.*

WAINWRIGHT
But he's a little bit irritated with us nonetheless, maintains he'll never cooperate with us under any circumstances. (*Seeing* **Callum** *staring out.*) Ferguson!

Callum *turns.*

You've got to make him change his mind.

CALLUM
I'm getting demobbed in six weeks, as I'm sure you haven't forgotten, and that's definitely going to happen . . . so I don't think . . .

WAINWRIGHT
This will only take six days.

CALLUM
Six days?! It will definitely *not* take six days!

WAINWRIGHT
It has to. It's urgent.

EXT. THE GARDEN. MILITARY HEADQUARTERS DAY

We cut outside into the garden. **Salter** *gets up from the bench and moves off, following the trollies towards where the smoke is climbing from behind a wall. He still has his small cigar.*

INT. WAINWRIGHT'S OFFICE. DAY

We cut back to the office. **Callum** *is now seated in front of* **Wainwright** *who has leant back in his chair. His tone is now warmer; his fleshy face more benign.*

WAINWRIGHT
I know you're not going to refuse to do this, for reasons we both know!

Callum's *expression remains impassive.*

> So it is totally unnecessary for me to flatter you, but obviously you're the ideal candidate for the job, what with your technical background!
>
> None of the intelligence boys know the first thing about science, and all the boffins are hopeless about intelligence. Believe absolutely everything they're told!

He lights a cigarette.

> It's not easy to fool you.

CALLUM

If I were to do it, it would be under one condition.

WAINWRIGHT

Of course! But you don't know where you're going to be doing it yet, do you?

He leans close again.

> We're using the Connington Hotel, a funny old dump. (*He gives a lascivious smile.*) But with some surprisingly good perks! I want you to take this German and get him wining and dining, and whatever else he shows a real liking for! . . . and completely turn him around, using this hotel.
>
> And find out just how brilliant he is –

CALLUM

In six days?!

WAINWRIGHT

Yes! I managed to stop him going to the Cage, the morons from MI19 are eager to get their hands on him and give him their full treatment – as if shining lights in his eyes and not letting him sleep is going to make him like us! I've told him they can't have him for a few days . . . Six! So it's up to you Ferguson.

EXT. WALLED GARDEN. MILITARY HEADQUARTERS. DAY

We cut outside. **Salter** *is moving into the walled garden. He is greeted by the sight of five bonfires spread across the garden. Men in uniform are throwing the files onto the flames. He watches them, smoking his cigar.*

INT. WAINWRIGHT'S OFFICE. DAY

> WAINWRIGHT
> I imagine your condition is – you want to run it exactly how you like?

> CALLUM
> Yes, with nobody breathing down my neck, from MI5 or CDISC.

> WAINWRIGHT
> Or any other bloody outfit, naturally!

> CALLUM
> When do I have to start?

> WAINWRIGHT
> Four o'clock today, *back* entrance of the hotel, a chap called Ringwood.

Callum *gets up.*

> We don't use uniforms in the hotel . . . (*Indicates his clothes.*) so you'll need to get out of that.

As **Callum** *reaches the door.*

> Only one thing matters.

> CALLUM
> Get him to work for us – doesn't matter how I do it?

> WAINWRIGHT
> That too, of course. But most of all, don't *lose* them . . . Or let them slip away to the Russians, or the Americans.

EXT. MILITARY CAMP. DAY

We see **Lotte** *being escorted by a young soldier past parked military vehicles in the camp and towards the black saloon car that is waiting for her with its engine running.*

She is holding her donkey and her nightdress is bundled up in a paper bag.

She joins her father on the back seat of the car. **Dieter** *greets her with a kiss.*

He is still extremely tense.

A military policeman climbs into the front seat next to the driver and the car sets off.

Lotte *glances behind her; she sees a receding shot of the wrecked stately home, the soldiers moving in the ruins, watching them drive away.*

EXT. BOMBSITE/CONNINGTON HOTEL. AFTERNOON

We cut to a bombsite, a large area of rubble and domestic debris where once a whole street stood. The guts of the houses that have been destroyed are strewn across the site; exposed fireplaces, pieces of beds and baths and basins, burnt-out chairs, chunks of walls with their flowery wallpaper still visible.

There is a deep crater on one side of the bombsite around which a barrier has been erected to try to keep people out, but it has been pulled down in several places.

On the bombsite an old man and his son are scavenging among the wreckage. Children are running along the pathways they have created in the rubble, and are climbing some of the jagged pieces of wall that are still standing.

We follow three particular children running and whooping among the dust and the rubble and then glimpse beyond them the shape of the Connington for the first time. A large rambling Victorian building standing on the edge of the bombsite, with a row of smaller buildings behind it.

Some of the windows on the upper floors of the hotel are still boarded up.

We then cut to a taxi stopping on the edge of the bombsite.

Callum *gets out. He is in civilian clothes and is carrying a battered suitcase.*

The taxi driver is muttering, 'Can get you much closer round the front, sir.'

CALLUM

No, no, this is fine.

He pays the driver.

This is the entrance I need.

We move with **Callum** *towards the back entrance of the Connington, passing the rim of the crater.*

A skinny boy, eating a toffee apple, watches him pass.

We see **Callum** *noticing the boy, he calls out to him, pointing at the toffee apple.*

CALLUM

Where on earth did you get that?

The boy grins and points through the clouds of dust towards some buildings on the other side of the bombsite.

Must be the only toffee apples in London!

Callum *approaches the back entrance of the Connington. It looms above him.*

As he gets close, he sees four chambermaids are sitting on a low wall by the back entrance, smoking and gossiping. They watch him approach with curiosity.

Callum *smiles at them as he moves into the hotel.*

INT. GROUND FLOOR PASSAGE. AFTERNOON

We cut to **Callum** *entering one of the dark ground-floor passages of the Connington.*

It is a faded, shabby, sepulchral world.

The curtains are drawn on all the windows that face the bombsite.

The hotel has clearly suffered some bomb damage itself; there are patched walls and one of the only windows which has its curtains open has tape running across the glass.

As **Callum** *enters this dark interior, an old lady with an extraordinarily lined face moves past him muttering to herself and disappears into the shadows.*

Callum *watches her go. A voice calls from behind him.*

RINGWOOD
People get dumped here for all sorts of reasons, sir, but they don't all look like that!

A man in his late twenties is approaching **Callum***. He has fair hair, an upper-class voice, a humorous look in his eyes.*

Hello, sir, you must be Captain Ferguson, or at least I hope you are?! I was given a very loose description . . .

CALLUM
Yes, and you must be Ringwood.

RINGWOOD
Indeed, that's me sir. (*Indicating* **Callum***'s single suitcase.*) Do you want me to call somebody to help you with your luggage?

CALLUM
(*has no time for such formality*)
That's hardly necessary, is it?!

He picks up his suitcase himself.

Callum *glances back down the dark passage, taking everything in.*

RINGWOOD
Yes, it's all a bit gloomy down here! (*He indicates the curtains and shutters across the windows.*) Because of the bombsite, they keep these closed . . . (*Grins.*) Very different upstairs though! The dust doesn't reach there . . .

I'll show you our operation shall I, sir?

INT. BEDROOM PASSAGE. DAY

We cut to **Ringwood** *and* **Callum** *moving along the bedroom passage on the second floor. Brilliant sunshine is stabbing through the windows; the curtains are all open.*

RINGWOOD
You see? Quite a difference, isn't it? Every building has gone on this side, so it's bloody bright . . . (*He grins.*) All this sun reminds me of the Riviera sometimes . . .

Just at that moment, two girls in their twenties walk past them.

One of them, **Julia**, *is strikingly pretty. They both have a provocative, fearless air about them, as if they may be prostitutes cruising the passages.*

RINGWOOD
(*just after the girls have passed*)
Yes . . .

Not the only thing that reminds one of the Riviera round here sir!

Callum *watches the girls disappear down the passage.*

Ringwood *is fiddling with a large bunch of keys.*

RINGWOOD
Now if I can find the right key . . . (*He unlocks the door.*) This is your bedroom, 246.

The door opens to reveal a plain, small, shabby room.

Callum *hardly bothers to look at it. He throws his suitcase on the bed and turns.*

CALLUM
Right? Where next?

RINGWOOD
And your office is directly across the way here, sir . . .

Ringwood *opens a door on the other side of the passage. There is a small room with one table, a chair and some box files.*

Callum *takes in everything with a sharp, practised eye; it is like he is biding his time.*

RINGWOOD
Except of course it is not your office really.

CALLUM
(*giving him a sharp look*)
You're going to have to explain that to me Ringwood.

RINGWOOD
Ah! . . . Yes!

INT. STAIRS/LANDING. UPPER FLOOR. AFTERNOON

We cut to **Ringwood** *and* **Callum** *emerging from a back staircase on to a high landing. They are confronted by a notice:*

> NO ENTRY BEYOND THIS POINT.
> DANGER. UNSAFE CEILING!

Ringwood *blithely leads* **Callum** *past the notice.*

RINGWOOD
So you see this is our real operation . . . The other office is just for show, for anybody who is pestering us . . . we let them look at that one –

CALLUM
Who are these people who are pestering you?

RINGWOOD
Well somebody from the War Crimes Unit was poking around, but hopefully we've got rid of them. Fingers crossed! They've got rather different priorities to us haven't they sir?! We were told not to let them stick their noses into our files under any account, and I'm glad to say they've never made it up here!

Ringwood *opens a door labelled* NO ENTRY *and reveals the secret floor.*

INT. SECRET FLOOR. AFTERNOON

Ringwood *leads* **Callum** *into a large attic room, full of files, and with four women with headphones listening and transcribing. At the far end of the room a young man is sitting at a desk being passed the transcriptions.*

We see **Callum** *taking it all in with a professional gaze.* **Ringwood** *smiles proudly.*

> RINGWOOD
>
> It's our secret floor! I think I can safely say nobody in the hotel knows about it – except for the two or three that *have* to know, of course! (*He grins.*) And the cleaners too, naturally . . . but they are completely reliable.

He indicates the women on headphones.

> And we have the capacity to listen in to several rooms where we park people we're interested in . . . can monitor who they're talking to, what they say . . . what they're thinking . . .

> CALLUM
>
> Yes . . .

He picks up one of the headphones.

> We did a lot of that in Enfield, at Trent Park, with captured German officers . . .

> RINGWOOD
>
> The old methods are usually the best, aren't they, sir . . .

Callum *ignores this; he stares around the room.*

> CALLUM
>
> You've got a hell of a lot of files in here . . .

> RINGWOOD
>
> Yes, they dumped a lot of stuff on us, loads of interviews from Germany. Now we've just been told to get rid of most of it!

> CALLUM
>
> Has anybody read them?

> RINGWOOD
>
> Good question . . . not quite sure about that, sir!

Ringwood *picks up headphones at a desk in the corner where a woman in a tweed skirt is listening and transcribing.*

RINGWOOD
Here are your people, sir. Want to have a listen . . .?

Callum *lifts the headphones to his ear. He can hear* **Dieter** *speaking German softly to* **Lotte**. *As he listens, he turns to* **Ringwood**.

CALLUM
Just a couple of things I need to make clear, Ringwood.

Dieter's *voice speaking German is running softly in the background through the headphones.*

Stop calling me 'sir'.

RINGWOOD
Really . . .? Are you sure . . .?

CALLUM
Yes, especially in front of the Germans . . . And secondly – (*He puts the headphones down.*) I will be doing some things you don't like, I might be wrong about that, of course, you might not mind at all – but whatever happens, I don't want any questions. Clear?

Ringwood *is very taken aback. He nods. Then he indicates the headphones, we can just hear* **Dieter**'s *voice.*

RINGWOOD
He's very important is he, sir?

CALLUM
He's a jet plane man. Whoever gets the best jet engine, Ringwood, wins whatever is going to happen next . . . We've got to make sure he designs it for us – not the Americans or the Russians!

He picks up the headphones, listens for a second, then turns.

Let's go and meet him, shall we?

INT. THIRD-FLOOR PASSAGE. LATE AFTERNOON

We cut to the third-floor passage, one floor higher than **Callum**'s *bedroom.*

The light is bright here too, stabbing through windows that nevertheless have not been cleaned for years. A man in his pyjamas and dressing gown is moving along the passage even though it is only afternoon.

Callum *knocks on* **Dieter***'s bedroom door.* **Ringwood** *is standing just behind.*

Dieter *opens the door and stares at* **Callum***. His manner is icy, as if his deep anger has now turned into steely resolve.*

DIETER

Yes?

CALLUM

Hello, I'm Callum Ferguson, this is Mr Ringwood. Can we come in for a moment?

INT. DIETER'S ROOM. LATE AFTERNOON

Callum *and* **Ringwood** *enter* **Dieter***'s bedroom, a sparsely furnished room, but of a decent size. An adjoining door leads to* **Lotte***'s separate bedroom.*

Lotte *is standing in this doorway staring at* **Callum** *with fierce hostility.*

Callum *looks at them both. His manner is breezily charming, but not over-polite.*

DIETER

So you're our jailors, are you?

CALLUM

I hope that's not what's going to happen . . . (*He grins.*) For both our sakes.

We see **Callum** *taking in the space, looking for where the listening devices are hidden, but his actions are casual, as if he is evaluating the comfort of the room.*

CALLUM

It's not too bad in here is it . . .? (*He runs his finger along the side table.*) At least it's clean . . . no smell of damp . . . (*He sits on the bed.*) And no springs sticking up through the mattress, not on a first feel anyway . . .

He looks across at **Lotte**.

Hello again . . . did you manage to eat one of those sausages?

Lotte *just stares at him.*

DIETER
Was there something particular you wanted to say to me?

CALLUM
Yes, as it happens. I was hoping you both might have dinner with me tonight.

DIETER
I don't think so, no.

CALLUM
(*unfazed*)
No?

DIETER
Apart from everything, we have nothing to wear. We were only allowed to bring one suitcase.

CALLUM
One suitcase, that's ridiculous . . . ! But I'm sure they don't all dress for dinner in this old place, do they, Ringwood?

RINGWOOD
Not all of them . . . no.

DIETER
My daughter has only one change of dress, how is she expected to manage?

CALLUM
(*to* **Lotte**)
Well, we must see to that, mustn't we?! Mr Ringwood will go shopping for you very soon . . . (*To* **Ringwood**.) Won't he?

LOTTE
I hate my other dress. I will not wear it tonight.

INT. WAINWRIGHT'S OFFICE. LATE AFTERNOON

We cut to the Brigadier, **Wainwright**, *moving through the outer area of his office, among the typists. As he nears the door, he catches sight through the window of a young woman in civilian clothes,* **Kathy**, *standing waiting outside the main building.*

She is staring directly at his office.

Wainwright *mutters angrily; he turns to one of the women typing.*

WAINWRIGHT
She's here again! Bloody woman from the War Crimes Unit!

EXT. T-FORCE HQ. LATE AFTERNOON

Wainwright *is moving purposefully towards* **Kathy**, *who watches his approach with a determined look in her eye.*

Kathy *has a contained, watchful manner, but also a sudden warm, anarchic smile, that suggests a less conventional personality underneath.*

KATHY
Brigadier Wainwright . . . Remember me . . .?

WAINWRIGHT
I most certainly do, Miss Griffiths.

KATHY
I've sent you rather a lot of messages, so I thought –

WAINWRIGHT
You would try to snatch a quick word with me?

KATHY
Exactly . . .

Wainwright *is heading straight for a jeep that is parked in front of the main building.*

WAINWRIGHT
Well, jump in, Miss Griffiths . . . this is perfect timing for a very quick word – I have an appointment down at the camp, which I'm just a trifle late for.

The Brigadier is driving himself. **Kathy** *climbs into the jeep next to him. As she does so,* **Kathy** *looks across at the smoke rising from the bonfires and a wheelbarrow of papers being trundled towards them.*

KATHY

I see you're getting rid of some paperwork, sir?

WAINWRIGHT

Oh that's nothing . . . just a little housekeeping, a few bills from the canteen!

They roar off in the jeep.

EXT. SUBURBAN STREETS/APPROACH TO THE MILITARY CAMP. LATE AFTERNOON

We cut to **Wainwright** *driving fast down the suburban streets.* **Kathy** *has to hold on tight to stop herself from being thrown out of the vehicle. The engine is making so much noise, it is very difficult for her to make herself heard.*

WAINWRIGHT

I always try to drive myself, Miss Griffiths . . . then I've only got myself to blame for anything that happens.

He swerves around a corner at great speed.

So what is it you want?

KATHY

We sent you some names . . .

Wainwright *is staring ahead. She raises her voice.*

Some names . . . a lot of names . . .

WAINWRIGHT

Did you indeed?!

The jeep hurtles down the street. And then we cut to it travelling at speed down the long drive that leads to the military camp.

EXT. THE MILITARY CAMP. LATE AFTERNOON

We cut to the jeep travelling fast, past the ruins of the stately home and into the bustling stable block and other outbuildings, which are one of the main areas of the camp. It is full of uniformed men moving briskly, and military vehicles passing them.

Wainwright *is still driving fast, scattering people in his wake.*

He pulls up sharply outside one of the buildings.

WAINWRIGHT
Here we are.

He gets out of the jeep.

I'm sorry but I have a meeting waiting for me now . . . You must send me your list of names again, Miss Griffiths. I'm afraid I don't recall getting it . . .

He starts to head for the entrance, adding drily.

A pleasure to see you.

Kathy *calls after him loudly:*

KATHY
Sir . . .

Wainwright *turns.*

I know you are dealing with all sorts of people who are of interest to you . . .

Wainwright *staring at her.*

Not just scientists and engineers but also German agents who know a lot about the Russians . . . and you need their cooperation.

I do realise that, sir –

WAINWRIGHT
I'm glad to hear that, Miss Griffiths . . .

KATHY

And nobody in the War Crimes Unit wants to get in the way of that, sir.

*We can see disbelief in **Wainwright**'s eyes.*

Or make it more difficult.

Kathy *stares straight back at him.*

But you may be bringing people over here who did things during the war they need to answer for . . . who are on our list.

WAINWRIGHT

You have your job to do, Miss Griffiths, I understand . . .

KATHY

Good. Thank you, sir –

WAINWRIGHT

But our job here concerns matters of national security. Getting the information we need to protect this country. That is our number one priority, Miss Griffiths. Now if you'll excuse me . . .

He moves off. **Kathy** *refuses to back down. She calls after him.*

KATHY

And one other thing, sir . . .

Wainwright *turns, his manner very terse.*

Excuse me sir, but with all the resources you've got, all those files you've compiled, you may have information on certain other names who are of interest to us, people who are still at large, and maybe those files could help us track them down.

WAINWRIGHT

That couldn't be clearer, Miss Griffiths . . . (*Very tersely.*) What I suggest you do is this – send your list again and we will do our best to be of help.

He disappears inside the building. We stay on **Kathy**. *We see the determination in her eyes.*

INT. MAIN DINING ROOM, CONNINGTON. EVENING

Dieter *and* **Lotte**, **Callum** *and* **Ringwood** *are standing in the doorway of the dining room of the hotel.* **Lotte** *is wearing, over her dress, the heavy overcoat that doesn't fit her properly. She looks distinctly odd. Many of the diners are glancing in her direction.*

There is an atmosphere of hushed gloom in the room. A whole mixture of people amongst the clientele. Most of the diners are in dinner jackets and evening dresses, but there is a sprinkling of European refugees who are either not in evening dress or in a very tattered version of it. There are also a few travelling salesmen in cheap suits, and a group of businessmen entertaining some young girls on another table.

In a corner of the room on a small, shabby dais a string quartet of elderly musicians are playing light music.

The adjoining dining room is roped off, with a large notice saying NO ENTRY, DANGEROUS CEILING. *In consequence, a few guests are being served at tables in the passage.* **Callum** *surveys the room.*

CALLUM
Blimey! Not exactly buzzing in here, is it?!

EXT. BOMBSITE/CONNINGTON HOTEL. EVENING

We cut to the back exterior of the hotel. The sun is setting, the light falling fast.

We see there are now people scavenging right inside the crater on the bombsite. Kids are still playing along the rim, running along the flimsy walkways.

INT. DINING ROOM. EVENING

We cut back inside the dining room, the lights are on now, but only a few of them, electricity is being saved.

Callum, Ringwood, Lotte *and* **Dieter** *are sitting together in the main dining room.* **Lotte** *is still wearing her overcoat. The food has arrived, a small unappetising piece of pork, some boiled potatoes and a plate of very soggy cabbage.*

Ringwood *is eating heartily, but* **Dieter** *and* **Lotte** *are refusing to touch their food.*

Across the dining room, we catch our first sight of **Harold**, *a distinguished-looking middle-aged man in evening dress. He is eating alone, but he exudes an air of stylish independence. He is struck by the sight of the small girl in her overcoat and what is going on at* **Callum**'s *table.*

We cut back to **Callum**, *staring at* **Lotte** *not eating.*

There is a sense of a real battle of wills over the food.

CALLUM
Mr Ringwood here is clearly enjoying it . . . so don't you want to see if it tastes better than it looks?

Lotte *shakes her head.* **Dieter** *addresses* **Callum** *with steely quietness:*

DIETER
You must understand the shock of suddenly being seized in one's home, and brought here – does not make one hungry. You know what happened . . . ?

We are on **Lotte**'s *eyes.*

The door bursts open . . .

We are still on **Lotte**'s *eyes. There is a sudden cut.*

FLASHBACK: INT. GERMAN APARTMENT. NIGHT

A door flies open in a German apartment block, uniformed figures in silhouette rampaging through the apartment, seizing **Dieter** *and* **Lotte**, *who are sleeping in their beds. Torches are flashing in their eyes blinding them. The bedclothes being pulled off the beds. We hear* **Dieter**'s *voice-over.*

DIETER
(*voice-over*)
People screaming at us . . . guns pointed at our faces . . . the British were 'picking up', as they put it, anybody they thought might be useful. Not just scientists . . . absolutely anybody.

INT./EXT. GERMAN APARTMENT BLOCK STAIRCASE/
STREET. NIGHT

We see an old couple in their seventies being escorted down a large stone staircase carrying a bundle of their belongings.

Then we see them being put into a truck waiting in a night street which has a cross-section of other people in it.

> **DIETER**
> (*voice-over*)
> Even an old couple who had worked for a drinks company . . . and you thought they might have the secret formula for the spicy alcoholic drink that's very popular!

INT. CONNINGTON DINING ROOM. EVENING

We cut back to **Dieter** *who is staring straight at* **Callum**.

> **CALLUM**
> (*responding calmly*)
> I'm sure that was a mistake . . . the old couple and the spicy drink.

> **DIETER**
> No, you are seizing anybody who can give you an advantage –

> **CALLUM**
> Over the Americans and Russians, yes. (*A more emollient smile.*) Well at the moment that's necessary . . . in the present circumstances.

> **DIETER**
> (*indicating the other guests, including an old couple with battered faces*)
> Maybe there are others here you've collected . . .?

> **RINGWOOD**
> No, no, you're our special guests!

> **DIETER**
> (*looks down at the soggy meat and vegetables*)
> And then there's this food . . .

CALLUM
It's fairly disgusting isn't it?!

RINGWOOD
It's really not at all bad!

Dieter *pushes his fork into the green sludge of cabbage on his plate.*

DIETER
This cabbage is most strange . . . (*He indicates* **Lotte**.) She loved how her mother used to cook cabbage, with garlic and onions and butter. And when she died . . . when my wife died . . . our cook always cooked the cabbage like that.

He looks straight at **Callum**.

So you realise my daughter and I will not be eating.

Callum *meets* **Dieter**'s *look.*

Callum *looks down at the cabbage, and then suddenly summons the* **Maître d'**.

CALLUM
Excuse me . . .

The **Maître d'** *is a thin man with a long severe face.*

MAÎTRE D'
Yes?

CALLUM
We would like some more cabbage please.

The **Maître d'** *nods and is about to move off.*

But this time cooked with onions and garlic and butter.

MAÎTRE D'
We can't do that, sir, not cabbage with onions.

CALLUM
You cannot do cabbage with onions?

Faces are turning towards them.

You have an orchestra – if one can call them that – which allows you to charge more than the permitted five shillings per head, so is it too much to ask for this cabbage? This different cabbage?

MAÎTRE D'
It is, sir, yes.

CALLUM
And what if I ask you to bring a plate of onions – just a plate of onions, on the side . . . and then we could mush them into the cabbage . . . would that be possible?

The whole dining room is now watching.

MAÎTRE D'
That would not be possible, no, sir.

CALLUM
(*staring straight at the* **Maître d'**)
A plate of onions, not possible . . . (*A dangerous smile.*) Are you sure about that?

MAÎTRE D'
I am sure about this, yes, sir.

Callum *suddenly gets up.*

He crosses the dining room with everybody watching.

We see a shot of **Dieter** *but his face gives nothing away.*

INT. HOTEL KITCHEN. EVENING

We cut to **Callum** *moving purposefully into the hotel kitchens. A large old-fashioned room, but very clean.*

It is presided over by a working-class man in his forties, the head chef, **Leonard**, *who has a confident air about him. He is surrounded by two old sous chefs, and three young chefs. They all turn in surprise as* **Callum** *enters.*

LEONARD

What are you doing in here? Whoever you are, you cannot come in here.

Callum *stops.*

CALLUM

Would it be possible to cook a portion of cabbage with garlic, butter and onions?

There is a stunned silence.

LEONARD

You mean Austrian cabbage?

CALLUM

If that's what you call it . . . yes.

Leonard *is staring at him.*

It would be extremely helpful to me, at this particular moment, if you could cook a plateful of Austrian cabbage.

Callum *stares at* **Leonard**.

LEONARD
(suddenly)

I can do that.

Now get the hell out of my kitchen!

Callum *smiles and leaves.* **Leonard** *calls after him:*

I have only one clove of garlic . . . And it won't be quick!

INT. DINING ROOM. NIGHT

We cut back to the dining room, the last light has gone from the windows, it is now night. Everybody is straining to see as a silver trolley is being pushed by one of the young chefs into the dining room, with **Leonard** *walking behind it.*

On the trolley is a plate covered by a silver cloche.

The trolley reaches **Callum**'s *table.* **Leonard** *takes off the cloche to reveal a glistening portion of brown, buttery Austrian cabbage.*

LEONARD
Who is this for?

Callum *indicates* **Lotte**.

RINGWOOD
What extraordinary-looking cabbage!

LEONARD
A lot of butter rations went into that, I will need to know whose room –

CALLUM
Put everything on my room!

Dieter *watches his daughter receive the plate of cabbage. His manner is polite but distant.* **Lotte** *nods a thank you at* **Leonard** *but totally ignores* **Callum**.

She starts to eat.

We cut across the dining room to **Harold** *watching the scene. He summons a waiter.*

HAROLD
That smells absolutely delightful. What do I have to do to get some too?

INT. HOTEL. MAIN GROUND FLOOR PASSAGE. EVENING

We cut to **Dieter** *and* **Lotte** *walking together along the central ground-floor passage after the meal.* **Lotte** *has taken her overcoat off now.* **Callum** *and* **Ringwood** *are following behind. There's a dull thudding sound coming from the basement.*

Ringwood *is watching* **Lotte** *and* **Dieter** *in front of them.*

RINGWOOD
I think that might be round one to us, don't you think?

Callum *watches* **Dieter** *and* **Lotte** *talking softly to each other.*

CALLUM
Not sure about that . . .

Callum *pauses, listening to the thudding noise from the basement. It sounds like somebody is drumming below them. He decides to investigate. He turns to* **Ringwood**.

CALLUM
You can put them to bed, Ringwood . . . and make sure there's somebody outside their door at all times.

INT. STAIRS/BASEMENT PASSAGE. NIGHT

Callum *is following the sound of the drumming down some stairs and into the basement. He moves along a dark passage which has some very faded decor, like it was once a subterranean bar area. The drumming is getting louder and louder. He pauses for a second at the door of the basement ballroom.*

INT. BASEMENT BALLROOM. NIGHT

Callum *enters a long room with a low ceiling. The room is quite dark. At the far end there is a small stage on which a lone drummer is drumming.*

*He is a white lad of eighteen (***Richie***). For a moment* **Callum** *thinks he's alone in the room with the drummer and then a voice calls from behind him:*

EVA
Can we help you?

He turns to see a black American woman, **Eva**, *who is in her forties. She is sitting at a round table watching the drummer, smoking, and with a drink in front of her. She has a powerful aura about her, like someone who is used to being listened to. But she has a sharp, witty manner.*

CALLUM
No, I just heard a noise . . . or rather, some drumming.

EVA
You're right, it may be just a noise . . . (*She indicates* **Richie**.) The kid is showing us what he can do. He wants to see if he can get on stage with Joe here . . .

We see an elderly black man, **Joe**, *sitting in the corner watching the kid.*

EVA
You coming to the opening?

CALLUM
The opening?

EVA
Well they've sure done a great job of advertising, if people in the hotel don't even know about it!

Joe *smiles drily at this.*

EVA
Now I know we can look forward to it being really heaving down here on Thursday, standing room only!

CALLUM
I'm sorry, I've only just arrived . . .

So this was the basement bar was it?

EVA
It was the basement 'ballroom' . . . Been shut since the middle of the war . . .

Eva *watches* **Richie** *drum for a moment, then turns to* **Callum.**

We've been hired for the grand opening . . . Don't feel the need to come, please. (*She laughs.*) We'll manage without you! (*She drinks.*) Not even heard about it in the hotel!

CALLUM
I'll definitely be coming, I can assure you.

EVA
You will, will you? (*Looking at him.*) It's a funny place this hotel isn't it?! I heard the army was using it . . . Is that you?

Callum, *who has been watching the drumming, turns.*

Don't worry, I won't tell anybody.

The old man joins on the stage. He begins to drum with the lad, the two of them side by side. We see **Callum** *watching this, fascinated.*

Eva *notices the look in his eyes.*

EVA

Do you want to join them up there?

CALLUM

No, no . . . I play a little piano, but not the drums!

EVA

So, are you any good?

CALLUM

(*pauses for a second, smiles*)

Not at the moment . . . bit out of practice.

EVA

Do you want us to be the judge of that?

CALLUM

(*grins*)

Definitely not!

We stay on the old man and the boy drumming together.

INT. HOTEL. MAIN GROUND-FLOOR PASSAGE. NIGHT

We cut to **Callum** *walking along the ground-floor passage. There is the sound of a piano tinkling from the lounge. We can still hear the muffled thud of the drumming from the basement. Many strange faces pass him, haunted European faces, two very old English ladies who look like they must live in the hotel, a young woman on her own walking very slowly.* **Callum** *turns to watch her go and sees that* **Harold** *is standing at the far end of the passage.*

Harold *calls out to him, he has a charming, authoritative manner.*

HAROLD

That cabbage smelt delicious, if you don't mind me saying so.

CALLUM

It was delicious, I had a taste.

HAROLD

I'm very jealous . . . I failed to get any. Next time, I must try storming the kitchen myself.

CALLUM

I recommend it, yes. It works.

HAROLD

Then I may definitely try it . . . if I ever come back here . . . (*He smiles at* **Callum**.) which is quite possible.

There is a momentary pause. **Callum** *is on his guard. He instinctively feels* **Harold** *might know something about what he is doing in the hotel.*

HAROLD
(*indicates the sound of the drumming*)

Do you hear that drumming?

CALLUM

I do.

HAROLD

Funny isn't it . . . that going on in the basement. It used to be quite a lively spot before the war down there . . . the basement ballroom.

CALLUM

If you'll excuse me, sir . . .

HAROLD

Of course, forgive me. I merely wanted to congratulate you on your cabbage, and your triumph over the maître d'.

Callum *moves off down the passage.* **Harold** *watches him go.*

INT. SECRET FLOOR. NIGHT

We cut to **Callum** *entering the attic room on the secret floor.* **Ringwood** *is there, with just two women now listening in on their headphones.*

CALLUM

Are they safely tucked up in bed now?

RINGWOOD

They are sir. And we have two people in the passage outside their door all night.

CALLUM

And what about here? Is there someone up here all night listening in?

One of the women, **Ruth**, *turns.*

RUTH

That would be me.

CALLUM

Right . . . (*He grins.*) must be rather strange alone up here at four in the morning. (*To* **Ringwood**.) So if you give me the file you have on him, I'll take it.

Ringwood *reaches for the file.*

And while you're at it, give me some more files too, somebody better have a look at them before we get rid of them – and it'll keep me occupied tonight!

RINGWOOD

Tonight sir? It is rather late . . .

CALLUM

Yes. But I don't always need to sleep.

The phone is ringing.

RINGWOOD

Why is somebody calling now?

RUTH

(*has answered it, turns to* **Callum**)
It's for you sir. They're putting through a call that was made to your bedroom, a Mr Alex Lombard.

CALLUM

Who knew how to find me? I thought this place was meant to be secret, it seems the whole hotel knows!

RINGWOOD

It's just reception, they need to know.

Callum *takes the call. We hear* **Alex**, *an upper-class voice:*

ALEX

(*voice-over*)

Cal, there you are?! What on earth are you doing cancelling dinner with us tomorrow? I thought you were on leave?!

CALLUM

That's just been changed unfortunately. It's only for a few days, Alex, I have to do something.

ALEX

(*voice-over*)

But it can't wait for a few days . . . I so want you to meet her.

CALLUM

Alex, we haven't seen each other for years — it can wait a few more days, surely?! I'm dying to meet her too of course, but —

ALEX

(*voice-over, very firmly*)

No, it definitely can't wait. We'll meet for elevenses tomorrow, that's what we should do — I'm sure you can get away for that?! At Fuller's, in Oxford Street, at 11.30.

*As **Alex** has been saying this, **Callum** has noticed **Ruth** in the corner. She has her headphones back on, and is looking very disconcerted about what she is hearing.*

*We move in on her and then cut back to **Callum**.*

ALEX

(*voice-over*)

Cal? Did you hear me? Fuller's in Oxford Street for elevenses . . .

CALLUM

I'll be there . . . (*Watching **Ruth**.*) I've got to go now, Alex.

*He puts down the phone and immediately moves over to **Ruth**.*

What is it?

RUTH

I think you'd better hear this sir.

She gives him the headphones. He listens. We can hear **Lotte***'s voice, yelling furiously, shouting and screaming, and* **Dieter** *reasoning with her.*

Lotte*'s yelling is an alarming sound, it could be a tantrum, or something more serious.* **Callum** *turns to* **Ringwood** *as he listens.*

CALLUM

The child's screaming . . .

We hear **Lotte** *getting even louder.*

She's yelling she wants to go home.

RINGWOOD

Do we go down there, sir?

CALLUM

No, we do nothing.

Lotte *screaming.*

This could be just for our benefit . . .

We stay on **Callum***.*

It's not the real thing yet.

INT. SECOND-FLOOR PASSAGE. NIGHT

We see the second-floor passage, dimly lit at night. There are pairs of shoes and room-service trays outside some of the bedroom doors. **Julia** *is moving along the passage. She knocks at one of the doors. A man in his fifties answers it. As the door closes, we hear his voice saying, 'I thought maybe you weren't coming.'*

INT. CALLUM'S BEDROOM. NIGHT

We cut to **Callum** *lying fully dressed on the bed in his spartan room. He is reading* **Dieter***'s file, which has a red folder. The other files, which have green folders, are also lying on the bed. We can hear the sound of the night city, a clock striking the quarter, distant trains shunting. Through this sound comes the unmistakable noise of people making love in the room next door.*

Callum *smiles to himself as he hears it. He puts down* **Dieter***'s file and picks up one of the others.*

The sound of sex is getting louder and louder from the next door room.

EXT. CONNINGTON HOTEL. NIGHT

We cut to a night exterior of the hotel, seen across the bombsite. Most of the lights are off, just the passage lights shining.

INT. CALLUM'S ROOM. NIGHT

We cut to back to **Callum***'s bedroom. It is dark now in the room but* **Callum** *is still lying fully dressed on the bed. He has stopped reading, he is smoking.*

A high shot of him unable to sleep, staring upwards.

We hear a sudden clatter from the passage, as if somebody has tripped over something.

INT. SECOND FLOOR PASSAGE NIGHT

We see **Callum** *looking out into the passage.* **Julia** *has tripped over a room-service tray outside one of the doors. She turns to see* **Callum** *watching her.*

JULIA

Sorry . . . !

CALLUM

That's okay.

JULIA

It doesn't look like I woke you though.

CALLUM

No, you didn't.

JULIA

Can't sleep?

CALLUM

No, no, I've been working . . . (*He pauses for a second.*)

JULIA

You were about to say – and that makes two of us!

CALLUM

No, no, no!

JULIA
(*amused, imitating him*)
No, no, no! Of course not . . . didn't cross your mind?!

CALLUM

I wasn't going to say that.

JULIA

Well, thank you. (*She begins to move off.*) Have a good night working won't you . . .

INT. MAIN GROUND-FLOOR PASSAGE. MORNING

We cut to the main ground-floor passage that leads to the dining room. Strong morning light coming through the one big window that is not shuttered. **Callum** *is approaching holding three green files.* **Dieter** *and* **Lotte** *are sitting very still on two high-back chairs; behind them the dining room is being closed.* **Ringwood** *is in the middle of the passage, looking concerned. He moves to meet* **Callum**.

RINGWOOD

I'm afraid, sir, I can't get them into breakfast, I've been trying for well over an hour! (*Quietly.*) They seem absolutely to be on hunger strike again, sir.

CALLUM
(*lightly*)
Remember, don't call me sir.

He reaches **Lotte** *and* **Dieter**. **Lotte** *seems calm, but will not look at him.*

Good morning, you two. Don't fancy the breakfast here, I see?!

DIETER

We wish to return to our rooms.

CALLUM

In a minute, of course. (*He smiles.*) But I think I know where I can find something you will eat.

EXT. BACK ENTRANCE OF CONNINGTON/BOMBSITE. MORNING

We cut to **Callum** *leading* **Dieter**, **Lotte** *and* **Ringwood** *out of the back entrance of the Connington and on to the bombsite. The air is thick with dust.* **Callum** *deposits the three green files into the hotel dustbins on the edge of the bombsite. At the very moment he is doing this, he notices a young woman, who is standing smoking by the low wall at the back entrance of the hotel. It is* **Kathy**; *she has been watching him throw away the files.*

We cut to **Callum** *leading* **Dieter** *and* **Lotte** *and* **Ringwood** *along the flimsy walkways that cross the bombsite. We see the large crater to the left of them. They are heading through a cloud of dust to the buildings on the other side.*

INT. SMALL GROCER'S SHOP. MORNING

We cut inside the dark interior of a small grocer's shop. The windows are filthy, streaked with dirt. The shop has a pitiful amount of goods on display. The effect of rationing is very evident. There is a red-faced man behind the counter. **Callum** *address him, as* **Dieter**, **Lotte** *and* **Ringwood** *watch.*

CALLUM

This is a little bit of a guess, but I believe you may have some toffee apples for sale . . .?

The red-faced man looks very disconcerted. **Callum** *ruffles a pound note.*

We will pay a very good price for them.

We cut inside a dark, inner room in the shop. **Callum**, **Ringwood** *and* **Lotte** *are staring fascinated and longingly into a vat of hot toffee that the man is stirring. He dips a green apple into it.*

Dieter *is watching from the shadows.* **Callum** *grins.*

CALLUM

The only hot toffee for miles around, and it's on our doorstep! (*He turns to* **Dieter**.) Isn't that a bit of luck?!

Lotte *stares at her father, extremely eager to be allowed to have one.*

DIETER

You can have a toffee apple, just this once.

He turns to **Callum**, *his tone polite but steely.*

You seem to think the way to get me working for you is through my daughter's stomach . . .

Callum *smiles. He suddenly notices, through the filthy yellow glass of the window, that* **Kathy** *has followed them across the bombsite and is leaning against a wall, staring at them.* **Callum** *turns, gives* **Ringwood** *the money.*

CALLUM

You can take care of it from here, Ringwood. (*Indicates* **Dieter**.) And try to get him eating one too! I'll be back in an hour and a half without fail . . . keep them entertained till then.

EXT. THE EDGE OF THE BOMBSITE. MORNING

We cut to **Callum** *emerging through the dust outside the shop and setting off down the street. He has to pass* **Kathy**. *He indicates the shop over his shoulder.*

CALLUM

I should go in there . . . it's well worth a visit.

KATHY

Thanks for the advice.

CALLUM

Or maybe that's why you're here?

KATHY

Not exactly . . . I came to visit the hotel, but then I saw you . . . (*She looks straight at him.*) Are you from T-Force?

CALLUM
(*meeting her look*)

And who are you?

KATHY

Sorry, I'm Kathy Griffiths, from the War Crimes Unit. (*Her tone is pleasant, not confrontational.*) You haven't answered my question . . . We know T-Force is using the hotel to entertain people of interest . . . So I just thought you might be from T-Force?

Callum *just watching her.*

And if you're not, of course, I've just given you a rather interesting piece of information.

CALLUM

And if I am?

KATHY

Then I would ask you – (*She smiles.*) very politely, if you can be of any help to me getting into your records – somehow. I've been to Enfield of course, several times –

CALLUM

But they've been very slow.

KATHY

Exactly . . .

CALLUM

Miss Griffiths, I'm sorry . . . I have an appointment, in a few minutes, which I really have to keep.

KATHY

Oh yes, same old story, you definitely are from T-Force . . . !

CALLUM

No, I really do have an urgent appointment. (*He smiles.*) My oldest friend is home from Washington, and he's brought back a new wife with him. He wants me to meet her. So you see, I have to go, can't miss that . . . (*He smiles.*) And he's very posh so I mustn't be late!

KATHY

I'll give you this – I haven't heard that excuse from Brigadier Wainwright.

CALLUM

But come back to the hotel at four o'clock tomorrow and we'll have a meeting.

KATHY
(startled)

A meeting?

CALLUM
(moving off)

Yes, a meeting . . .

EXT. STREET. FULLER'S COFFEE SHOP. DAY

A shot through glass of **Callum** *approaching Fuller's coffee shop. We cut to his point of view of the interior of the shop, the muted pastel colours, the middle-class women in hats drinking tea.*

INT. FULLER'S COFFEE SHOP. DAY

We cut to **Callum** *entering the shop. He is very late. He scours the customers, nearly all of whom are female. Then suddenly a man's voice calls:*

ALEX

We're here! We're over here!

We see **Alex** *and* **Rachel** *sitting in a little alcove. Both of them rise on seeing him.*

Alex *is the same age as* **Callum** *but is upper middle class and has rather an intellectual appearance. He is dressed in a dark suit.*

He moves towards **Callum** *to greet him, but* **Callum** *is also looking at* **Rachel**. *She has an extraordinary poise about her, a natural style that contrasts with all the people in the coffee shop. She is dressed in fashionable, very expensive clothes, but she has an immediate warmth that pulls you towards her. She has an American accent.*

Callum *and* **Alex** *embrace as they meet, the reunion of two friends. This spontaneous gesture startles some of the older women in the café.*

> ALEX
>
> Cal! There you are, how good to see you!
>
> CALLUM
>
> Yes. (*Grins.*) Back at last, Alex – thought you were never coming home! I'm terribly late, I know, I'm sorry –
>
> ALEX
>
> And this is Rachel . . . !
>
> CALLUM
>
> Delighted to meet you.
>
> RACHEL
>
> And so am I, to meet you. (*She smiles warmly.*) I've been really impatient for this moment . . .
>
> CALLUM
> (*surprised*)
>
> Have you?!
>
> ALEX
>
> I keep on mentioning my friend Cal . . . !
>
> CALLUM
>
> Well I'm really sorry I'm so late.
>
> RACHEL
>
> But we were too, so that's perfect, isn't it. (*She sees* **Callum** *hesitate.*) Isn't it?
>
> CALLUM
>
> Well, most unfortunately, I can't stay, I just came to tell you –
>
> RACHEL
>
> You came to say you can't stay?!
>
> CALLUM
>
> Yes. I just have something rather important to attend to, which I can't get out of –

ALEX

You haven't changed, Cal! (*He smiles.*) How many years is it . . .? What with the war and everything, most people look different, but not you, Cal. (*To* **Rachel**.) He hasn't changed at all!

CALLUM

I promise you I have.

This is embarrassing – that I have to say hello and goodbye like this, but I got delayed coming here, and I have to be back at a certain time –

RACHEL

You're spending so long making excuses, you might as well sit down with us while you make them, Cal. (*She smiles charmingly as she sits at the table.*) Come on and tell us why you can't stay . . . and besides, I promised myself an English ice cream.

ALEX

I've told her that's not a good idea at all!

RACHEL

Yes . . . (*She laughs.*) Alex says, even before the war, it was the worst ice cream in the world! Come on, you've got to stay and watch me taste one . . . and see what happens!

Time cut:

We see **Callum**, **Rachel** *and* **Alex** *all staring down at the ice cream in front of them. A blob of discoloured vanilla each.*

RACHEL

It is a very strange colour . . .

ALEX

We may well be endangering our health . . . (*He prods at the blob of ice cream and laughs.*) No good can come of this at all!

RACHEL

Cal is eating his!

CALLUM

I'll eat anything.

ALEX

You know we used to make marvellous ice cream in the eighteenth century, here in England . . . no we did!

RACHEL

You were there then darling, were you?!

ALEX

Parmesan cheese ice cream . . . No, it's true . . . Parmesan cheese ice cream was a particular speciality. (*He beams.*) Truly delicious . . . somewhere we lost the knack of how to do it!

RACHEL

Parmesan cheese ice cream?! I can't believe that. Can you believe that, Cal?

Callum *watching them together, their sparkling closeness, their ease with each other.*

CALLUM

I don't believe that, no.

RACHEL

So, Cal, what is the really serious work you're doing that means you can't stay . . .? (*She smiles warmly.*) Even though you have in fact stayed quite a few minutes now . . .

CALLUM

Yes, I have to go, you're right!

RACHEL

Oh no, I didn't mean that . . . please, just stay a moment longer, tell me about your work.

CALLUM

Well, yesterday I was given an unexpected assignment –

RACHEL

'An assignment', how exciting! Is it secret? Or can you tell us?

CALLUM

It's not particularly secret.

ALEX

It's got to be a bit hush-hush — Cal is in military intelligence — but he doesn't always have to wear uniform. He rounds up people who could be of help to us . . .

RACHEL

So you *are* in the Secret Service.

CALLUM

No, no, we look down on them of course! And I'm not going to be doing it much longer. I'm about to get out. Can't wait in fact . . .

ALEX

I'm not surprised . . . ! (*To* **Rachel**.) Cal had an extraordinary war, while I was sitting comfortably in Washington, he saw a lot of action and he did intelligence, evaluating vital bits of things . . . he is both boffin and soldier!

RACHEL

You're a war hero are you?!

CALLUM

I certainly am not.

ALEX

He hasn't told me exactly what he did . . . He wrote to me a lot, but never about that . . . (*He grins.*) I plan to get it out of him . . . !

RACHEL

People don't like to talk about what they did, do they?

CALLUM
(*lightly*)

This is true.

RACHEL

So what about this secret assignment that isn't really secret?

CALLUM
Oh, I'm just looking after a German scientist who might be of great use to us – trying to make him happier . . .

RACHEL
And have you made him happier?

CALLUM
Not quite yet . . . funnily enough, it's all about food at the moment! –

RACHEL
But of course, food is the most important thing of all, bar nothing! The greatest pleasure by miles . . . (*She smiles across the table.*)

ALEX
Not sure that applies at the Connington Hotel though! Spooky old place . . . it's difficult to get good food anywhere in town at the moment, but at the Connington . . .?!

CALLUM
Ah, but I'm working on that . . . It's a pretty strange place though, you're right, you really don't know who you're going to meet there . . .

ALEX
And it's not exactly humming, is it?! You don't get a great floor show there, for instance.

CALLUM
Well, as it happens, they've got the 'grand' re-opening of their basement ballroom tomorrow night – but nobody seems to know about it.

RACHEL
Then we must come!

Alex *looks startled at the suggestion.*

No, we must.

ALEX
Really darling . . .? I think we have an engagement tomorrow night –

RACHEL
Then we'll change it.

CALLUM
I hardly think it'll be worth it . . .

RACHEL
Well it sounds very intriguing to me . . . and we can see how you've got on with your assignment, Cal – if you've triumphed yet.

INT. DINING ROOM. CONNINGTON. AFTERNOON

We cut to a harpist playing in the main dining room of the Connington, people are having afternoon tea. The harpist is looking extremely tense.

We cut across the dining room and see the cause of the tension. **Dieter** *is sitting with* **Lotte** *at a corner table, watched over by* **Ringwood**. **Lotte** *is rocking backwards and forwards in her chair, and making a deeply unsettling loud whining noise, as if she were a much smaller child.*

We see a shot of **Callum** *approaching down the main passage.* **Ringwood** *springs up, hurries across the dining room and intercepts* **Callum** *in the doorway.*

RINGWOOD
Where have you been, sir . . .?

CALLUM
I got unexpectedly delayed. You've been able to manage haven't you, Ringwood?

RINGWOOD
No sir, I didn't know what to do –

CALLUM
Didn't know what to do about what?

*Then **Callum** sees into the dining room, **Lotte** rocking in her chair and crying out,* 'Nach Hause gehen ... Ich möchte nach Hause gehen' ['*Go home ... I want to go home*'].

*The harpist is playing louder and louder to try to compete with **Lotte**.*

> RINGWOOD
> I brought her down here because she was making such a noise in her room.

> CALLUM
> And you thought a little harp music might stop her?

> RINGWOOD
> All I could think of ...

Callum *moves over to **Dieter** and **Lotte**. As he reaches the table, he suddenly notices **Harold** on the far side of the dining room, who is having tea with a young woman of about twenty, and watching **Dieter** and **Lotte** closely.*

*At this moment, everybody in the dining room is looking across at **Lotte**. The faces of the older guests registering disgust.* **Callum** *sits opposite* **Lotte**.

> DIETER
> I have tried to make her sit still ... but she is a very unhappy child, who wants to go home.

> CALLUM
> So you let her behave like a toddler instead?

> DIETER
> And how would you behave if you were her? (*Straight at* **Callum**.) Would you be sitting quietly, as if everything was normal?

Lotte *and* **Callum**'s *eyes meet. We see from* **Lotte**'s *point of view all the people staring.*

> CALLUM
> Yes, you've got them all looking at you, Lotte!

Callum *leans close to* **Lotte**. *Then he points at* **Harold**, *who is watching them.*

CALLUM

You see that man there?

Lotte *doesn't look at* **Harold**.

He is watching us, isn't he? Maybe, just as I am here to keep an eye on you, he is here to keep an eye on me . . .? What do you think?

Now **Lotte** *can't stop herself looking at* **Harold**.

That would be interesting, wouldn't it? If that was what he was doing?!

Callum *suddenly gets up and walks over to* **Harold**.

Lotte *is now completely quiet and watching the scene.*

CALLUM

Hello again . . .

HAROLD

I just don't seem to be able to keep away, do I . . .?

His manner is unfazed, he indicates the young woman, who is pale and rather serious looking.

This is my ward Lucy.

CALLUM

Hello, I'm Callum Ferguson.

LUCY

How do you do.

CALLUM
(*turning back to* **Harold**)
I just thought we should be properly introduced . . .

HAROLD

Absolutely . . . How very rude of me. I'm Harold Lindsay-Jones . . . (*To* **Lucy**.) we met over some cabbage last night . . .

He looks across at the harpist, then to **Callum**.

I told you this was the place for music, didn't I?!

He indicates **Lotte**, *who is beginning to rock again.*

She is quite right, your friend, the little girl, this music should not be endured in silence!

CALLUM
(*watching* **Harold** *closely*)
She has quietened down a bit now I hope, apologies for the disturbance.

HAROLD
Yes, yesterday she looked like an angel, in that coat that was too big for her . . . (*He watches* **Lotte** *rocking.*) One night in this hotel, and look what happens!

INT. WAR CRIMES INVESTIGATION UNIT OFFICE. EVENING

We cut to the War Crimes Unit office. The light is just going down outside and the lamps are on in the dark panelled room. It is a much smaller outfit than T-Force. At the far end of the room is a large desk, at which **Kathy's** *boss,* **Miss Clarkson**, *is working.* **Kathy** *is sitting amongst four other women and one man, who are all working at separate desks. A clock is ticking loudly.* **Miss Clarkson** *looks up.*

MISS CLARKSON
It's very late, you don't all have to stay past 7.30, you realise.

There is a general murmur that nobody wants to leave.

Very well . . . (*She looks across at* **Kathy**.) Miss Griffiths, can you come up here?

Kathy *approaches her.* **Miss Clarkson** *lowers her voice.*

You do realise we are losing two more of them next week . . . (*She indicates the women working.*)

KATHY
Two people are going?! I thought it was only one –

MISS CLARKSON

No, two . . . they want us to move into a smaller office as well, but I am resisting that. It's a particularly horrible room . . . (*She speaks even more confidentially.*) I just wanted you to know, we probably don't have a lot of time before they start winding us down . . .

KATHY

Yes, Miss Clarkson, I know time's short.

MISS CLARKSON

Have you had any luck with T-Force or BIOS, or any of them, in fact?

KATHY

No, not in Enfield . . . not yet.

MISS CLARKSON

They're under their own pressure to come up with results there – to get all those scientists working for them. They don't consider us a priority.

KATHY

I know . . . but I do have a lead at the Connington.

MISS CLARKSON

What sort of lead?

KATHY

There's somebody new there, from T-Force.

MISS CLARKSON

It would be interesting to know, once and for all, how much information they've got stored there!

KATHY

Yes . . .

We are close on her, she smiles.

I fully expect to find that out.

INT. BASEMENT BALLROOM. NIGHT

We cut to the darkness of the basement ballroom, just two pools of light at either end of the room. At one end, on the little stage, **Joe** *is drumming hard. And at the other end,* **Richie** *is drumming. They are both in unison, but there is also a competitive edge.*

INT. THE ATTIC ROOM. SECRET FLOOR. NIGHT

We cut to a close-up of **Ruth** *in the attic room, looking really alarmed. We cut wide and we can see that* **Callum, Ringwood, Ruth** *and the transcribers are listening to the sound of* **Lotte** *screaming.*

This time the sound is coming out of a Tannoy in the corner of a room.

Callum *is sitting very still,* **Ringwood** *is pacing agitated.* **Lotte**'s *cries are now genuinely disturbing.*

RINGWOOD

I think sir . . .

CALLUM

Shhh!

RINGWOOD

We can't just let this go on without doing something . . . surely, sir?

Lotte's *screams continue, we move in on the Tannoy.*

RUTH

This is awful, sir, listening to this –

CALLUM

Listening to it? – It certainly is.

RINGWOOD

Maybe we should call a doctor, get him to give her something . . .

We stay on **Callum***. He suddenly gets up.*

CALLUM

No doctors, we don't need a doctor. (*He begins to move out of the room.*) I know what to do . . . (*At door.*) I think.

INT. THIRD-FLOOR PASSAGE. NIGHT

We see **Callum** *approach* **Dieter***'s room. The two watchers, a man and a woman, at either end of the third-floor passage, are looking pale and very disturbed by* **Lotte***'s screams.* **Callum** *nods at them and knocks on the door.* **Dieter** *opens it immediately. He indicates the watchers in the passage:*

DIETER
So these wardens told you what was happening, did they?

CALLUM
They did . . . (*He enters the room.*)

INT. DIETER'S ROOM. INTERCUT WITH ATTIC ROOM. NIGHT

Callum *immediately moves across* **Dieter***'s room and goes into* **Lotte***'s room. She is kneeling on her bed in her nightdress, squashed against the bedstead, screaming.*

DIETER
This cannot go on, my daughter cannot stay here. As you can see, she has to go back to Germany . . . that is the only thing that can be done.

Callum *looks at* **Lotte** *screaming, her defiant look. She yells at him in English:*

LOTTE
Let me go home. Please, please let me go home!

Callum *starts prowling the two rooms. There is a bottle of wine that has been left for* **Dieter** *to open.* **Callum** *picks it up and flicks it between his hands, the movement is edgy, dangerous.* **Lotte** *does not stop.*

DIETER
What are you going to do about it?!

CALLUM
Not sure yet . . . I just know I'm not having a great success, giving you the time of your life here.

He puts the wine bottle down. He moves very purposefully into **Lotte***'s room.*

He throws everything off her bedside table on to the floor. He throws the table on the floor. He kneels by her bed. **Lotte** *is startled, frightened.*

CALLUM

I'm going to show you something now Lotte, which maybe you didn't know was here.

He tears the bug off the wall that was hidden behind the bedside table.

That's one less listening device here.

We cut to the attic room: a loud crackling and hissing from the loudspeaker. **Ringwood** *and* **Ruth** *stare at the loudspeaker in surprise. They can still hear them, but more muffled.*

We cut back to **Dieter**'s *room.* **Callum** *turns to* **Lotte**.

CALLUM

Come on, we're going to find every one! Are you going to help . . .? I'm going to dig out every one!

In a series of fast cuts we see **Callum** *totally stripping out the room. He upturns chairs, pulls up a section of carpet, strips* **Dieter**'s *bed, leaps up on a chair to examine the main light fitting. A series of listening devices are revealed; he rips out each one.*

CALLUM

Here's another one!

At first **Dieter** *is watching this devastation of the room with deep suspicion, but as each device is found, he gets more drawn in. And* **Lotte** *climbs out of her bed and watches fascinated, as* **Callum** *rips up part of the carpet.*

We cut back to **Dieter**'s *room.* **Callum** *is now tackling the big wardrobe that dominates the room. He calls over to* **Dieter** *and* **Lotte**:

CALLUM

Come on, there's bound to be a big one behind here!

And **Dieter** *and* **Lotte** *find themselves moving over and helping with the wardrobe. For a moment,* **Callum** *can't see the bug, and then he spots it high up. He reaches up and tears it off the wall. He turns to* **Lotte** *and smiles.*

He is covered in dust and sweat. He holds out the bug in his hand.

As I thought, a nice big one!

He gives it to **Lotte**.

I think we've got 'em all?!

INT. ATTIC ROOM. NIGHT

We cut to the attic room: a loud crackling and hissing from the loudspeaker. **Ringwood** *and* **Ruth** *stare at the loudspeaker in surprise. They can still hear them, but more muffled.*

We cut back to the attic room; as each bug is torn out, **Callum**'*s voice is getting fainter and fainter.*

We cut back to the attic room; just the crackling, hissing sound over the Tannoy. **Ringwood** *and* **Ruth** *stare at one another.*

RINGWOOD
Now what do we do?

INT. DIETER'S ROOM/INTERCUT WITH ATTIC ROOM.
NIGHT

We cut back to **Dieter**'*s room. It is much later now, very dark, only one bedside light is on. Both* **Callum** *and* **Dieter** *are drinking the red wine.* **Dieter** *is sitting on the bed and* **Callum** *across the room on the floor, against the wall.*

Lotte *is fast asleep, the one-eyed donkey next to her on the bed.*

There's the sound of distant trains shunting. **Dieter** *looks across at* **Callum**; *for the first time, his manner is more expansive as he drinks.*

DIETER
I expect you think the sound of one city is much like another . . .

Callum *looks across at him.*

What you don't realise . . . even for me, being here, after all that has happened, is terrifying. The noise of a strange city at night – you don't know what's coming for you. The sounds from this hotel too . . . it gives one nightmares.

He looks across at **Callum**.

I will not work with you. I will not work with the British government . . .

We cut up to the attic room. We see the room is empty now, except for **Ruth**. *She is sitting at the corner table with her headphones on. As we move closer, we realise she can still hear what they are saying. There is one bug left.*

We cut back to **Dieter**'s *room:*

DIETER
You must realise how much I mean this?

He looks across at **Callum**, *his tone strong.*

Or, I should say, I hope you realise, how very much I mean it.

CALLUM
I do, I think . . . I was going to leave all this until at least we'd had some chance to get to know each other . . . (*He drinks, looks at* **Dieter**.) But you have to realise – I will do anything to make you cooperate.

You may think this is just another job for me . . . but I have my own personal reasons for being here.

DIETER
Because of the war, obviously?

CALLUM
No . . . not in the way you think anyway . . . (*He looks at* **Dieter**.) I am an engineer, like yourself. I worked for some brilliant people before the war . . . things happened . . . all sorts of things happened . . . They would really surprise you . . . wonderful work was wasted . . . golden opportunities missed, which would have made us so much more powerful. We should never have been so badly equipped when the war broke out . . . (*He drinks.*) And it's not going to happen again.

We cut to **Ruth** *listening to* **Callum**'s *voice: 'When you're ready to talk to me . . . I will tell you everything, about what happened, what I saw, the enormous mistakes that were made.'*

We cut back to **Callum** *sitting drinking on the floor.*

CALLUM
So you see, there's nothing I won't do to make this work.

Suddenly his arm shoots out and he reaches along the wall.

Including . . . !

He tears another bug off the wall, which was hidden in the skirting.

He looks across at **Dieter**

Now, we really are alone.

INT. SECOND-FLOOR PASSAGE. EARLY MORNING

We cut to a subjective shot moving along the second-floor passage in the hotel. It is dawn. We see an elderly European-looking woman walking slowly towards us in her dressing gown. A middle-aged man, also in his dressing gown, moves briskly past her in the passage without acknowledging her.

We then see **Julia** *in the distance, standing by the window at the end of the passage, staring out. She has her back to us. She is in her nightdress and dressing gown.*

We then cut to **Callum** *moving along the passage towards her. He is fully dressed, clearly not been to bed.* **Julia** *senses his presence, turns:*

JULIA
So what's it been today? Can't sleep, or have you been having fun?

CALLUM
It's been a little bit of work.

JULIA
Working again?!

Julia *stares out of the window at the bombsite.* **Callum** *stands next to her.*

We see below them people have already begun to scavenge in the dawn light. The old man and his son are right at the bottom of the crater.

> JULIA
>
> So you've done away with the need to sleep, have you?
>
> CALLUM
>
> Maybe for the moment . . . (*He smiles.*)
>
> JULIA
>
> No sleep at all?! (*She laughs.*) It's a bit exhausting, even just standing next to you!

She is staring down at the scavengers.

> You would've thought there wouldn't be anything left for them to find . . .

*We are on **Callum**, close. He is staring down into the crater on the bombsite. There is the sound of some building works beginning across the city. A machine thumping out regularly.*

*We move in on **Callum**'s eyes. We cut back to the crater, the dust rising as the figures crawl across its scavenging. **Julia**'s voice is getting fainter.*

> JULIA
>
> Maybe as they dig away at all the rubble, they find more layers with new stuff in it . . .

*We are on **Callum**'s eyes. The sound of the building works turns into the crackle of machine-gun fire. We see, from a great height, men in uniform, lying on their backs, their bodies making strange distorted shapes, as they writhe in death throes.*

*We are back on **Callum**'s eyes.*

INT. ATTIC ROOM. MORNING

*We cut to **Ringwood**'s face coming round the door of the attic room. He is surprised **Callum** is already at his desk, coffee is brewing. **Ruth** is typing in the corner.*

> RINGWOOD
>
> Here already, sir?

CALLUM

I am . . . but I'm about to leave you in charge again. I have one other appointment to keep, I won't be long. They shouldn't be any trouble today . . . Here are some clothes coupons – get Lotte a new dress!

RINGWOOD

Right, sir . . .

He switches on the Tannoy, it hisses and crackles.

What on earth was last night about, sir?

CALLUM

Trying to get a result, that's what.

INT. MAIN PASSAGE/LOBBY. MORNING

Callum *is moving along the ground-floor passage purposefully. He decides to cross the lobby and leave by the main entrance. Just as he does so, a voice calls him:*

SALTER

Where are you going?

Callum *turns to see the large, fleshy* **Salter** *standing behind him.*

CALLUM

What did you say?

SALTER

I said, 'Where are you going?'

CALLUM

Do we know each other?

SALTER

We do . . . or at least, I know you. (*He looms closer.*) Even though I'm quite sure we've never met. Brigadier Wainwright wants to know how you're getting on?

CALLUM

If he does, I will let him know personally. Now if you'll excuse me, I have an urgent appointment –

SALTER
Going to see a woman are you? (*His eyes very beady.*) Is that why you're leaving the hotel?

Callum *is totally unfazed. He treats* **Salter** *with light contempt.*

CALLUM
As it happens, I'm going to see my brother.

SALTER
Your brother? And that's urgent, is it?

CALLUM
Yes! (*He smiles.*) And I can't be late, he tends to get a little wound up if I am.

SALTER
You know it's not anybody at T-Force you have to worry about . . . (*He moves closer.*) It's me.

Callum *just smiles at this. He is watching the two old women moving together in the lobby.*

I didn't want you put on this – even for a few days, because you think you can make up the rules, don't you . . .?! And now you're not even listening to me . . .

CALLUM
Not that closely, no.

SALTER
So you want me to make you listen, do you?

CALLUM
That sounds interesting . . . (*Staring straight back at him.*) How would you do that?

SALTER
(*his face very close, his eyes narrow*)
You don't want to lose them, I promise you, you really don't want to find you've lost them.

INT. PUB/SUBURBAN STREET. DAY

We cut to the interior of a pub in the suburbs. We can see through the window a street where some of the houses are boarded up and others have been wrecked by bombing. The dark interior of the pub is almost empty except for the barmaid, two old men and **Victor**, *who is in his late twenties. He has a vibrant, restless manner, seemingly an excess of energy. His tall figure can be intimidating, but there's a warmth in his voice. As we cut into the scene, he is laying out a line of pennies very carefully along the counter and addressing the barmaid:*

VICTOR

Masses of money, you see, masses! Don't know what you've been worried about, good for two more rounds at least. And my brother's coming any moment, he will top me up! (*He grins to the barmaid.*) I will be overflowing . . .

As **Victor** *counts his pennies, he glances towards the window, where he sees a group of young men, awkward, bulky individuals in the street.*

Victor *moves up to the window. He sees the group of young men are leafleting the street. He becomes immediately extremely energised:*

VICTOR

Can you believe that? Look at the lumbering bastards – the Blackshirts, they're crawling back already . . .

Victor *suddenly moves to the door and starts yelling into the street:*

Get out of here, you fuckers . . .

The men throw looks at him but go on leafleting.

Cockroaches . . . ! In fact you're worse than vermin . . .

He stands in the door with his pint of beer and merrily abuses them.

You're far worse than vermin!

The young men look in his direction and then move on down the street.

EXT. SUBURBAN STREET. DAY

We cut to **Callum** *approaching the street. He can hear* **Victor**'s *voice shouting. But when he comes round the corner, there is nobody to be seen, and*

Victor *is in the doorway of the pub, abusing an empty street full of bombed houses.*

As **Callum** *appears,* **Victor** *calls out to him:*

> VICTOR
>
> They're lucky, very lucky, that I'm not in the mood for action! And my brother showed up in the nick of time too!

> CALLUM
>
> What are you doing? What's all this noise?! I'm only a few minutes late!

> VICTOR
>
> And I'm lighting up the street already!

Callum *reaches* **Victor**. *They greet each other affectionately.*

> You bastard, I thought you weren't coming!

> CALLUM
>
> Well I hope you're not going to make me wish I hadn't.

> VICTOR
>
> Of course not!

Callum *moves to enter the pub.*

> Where are you going?

> CALLUM
>
> What do you mean? I'm going to get a drink!

> VICTOR
>
> I don't want you getting too comfortable in here – because we're going shopping . . .

> CALLUM
>
> Shopping? Around here?

> VICTOR
>
> Of course, I need some new shoes . . . quality shoes. Where better to get them?!

EXT. SUBURBAN PARK. DAY

Victor *is leading* **Callum** *at a furious pace, along a path in a scraggy-looking suburban park. One or two people are moving ahead of them on the path.*

> VICTOR
>
> You're in for a treat today, I promise.

> CALLUM
>
> Am I? Where are we going, Victor?

> VICTOR
>
> Ah, the best store in the world. You'll be tempted by everything.

> CALLUM
>
> (*watching his brother's frenzied walk*)
> And have you been to the doctor, Victor?

> VICTOR
>
> I have indeed . . . He said I was in 'splendid condition' . . . that I'd made a remarkable recovery from my troubles – he said I was an example to others, and was now a model citizen . . .

> CALLUM
>
> And he gave you something for your headaches did he?

> VICTOR
>
> My headaches are gone . . . (*He taps his head.*) gloriously empty up here . . . ! No pain, no worries . . . (*He smiles.*) No thoughts of any kind!

> CALLUM
>
> But you need the medicine in case they come back, the headaches, you know how strong they can be –

> VICTOR
>
> They won't come back . . . (*He grins.*) If I do enough shopping, they won't come back!

EXT. BASE OF RAILWAY VIADUCT. DAY

We cut to **Victor** *and* **Callum** *emerging round the corner of the park, and finding themselves at the base of a railway viaduct. In the arches of the viaduct stalls have been set up and people are selling black-market goods. A surreal jumble of articles: tins of soup, sanitary towels, clothing coupons, sweets, handbags, electric fires. There is quite a bustle of local residents taking advantage of the stalls.* **Victor** *beams at* **Callum.**

VICTOR
You see, everything you could have ever wanted! It's all here!

CALLUM
But at black market prices, Victor.

VICTOR
A small detail – especially as you are paying.

We move along the stalls with **Victor**. *He starts bartering with the various stallholders, a vivid collection of contrasting people. Most are working class but some are ex-military: a red-faced major, selling sherry and whisky, and one or two middle-aged women selling jam and eggs.* **Victor** *seizes on one particular stall full of tins.*

VICTOR
Look at this – this is peroxide! There's nothing more useful – (*Knowing grin.*) or guaranteed to get results, than this! I will have five please.

He turns and loads up **Callum** *with everything he buys.*

Some marmalade! We really need some of that, three jars please!

CALLUM
Marmalade! Yes, let's get some (*He stares at a jar.*) The nearest anybody will get to fresh oranges for years probably.

We see shots of nylons, a whole stall of handkerchiefs and another of cutlery.

VICTOR
All this cutlery! (*He picks up a fistful.*) It's all been stolen from London Transport canteens . . . I need a few more knives,

definitely! (*He whispers to* **Callum**.) I love some of the people here – they probably never thought they'd be doing this ever!

We see a shot of guns being sold in the open, next to the shoes **Victor** *has been looking for. He surveys the guns with a glint in his eyes.*

VICTOR
Guns or shoes? What do you think? Probably need shoes just a little more . . . Tough choice though!

He chooses the most expensive shoes, having checked the size.

Told you this was the place for shoes! Why don't you get some? Good shoes are the answer to everything!

But **Callum** *spies a stall full of dolls, some of them damaged, some of them in good condition. He decides to choose one for* **Lotte**. *He is in the process of selecting one, when* **Victor** *spots somebody lurking in the trees. He immediately moves off to investigate. For a second* **Callum** *doesn't notice this, as he is buying the doll. When he turns around,* **Victor** *is plunging through the edge of the wood by the viaduct, in pursuit of the men he has seen. He is shouting:*

VICTOR
Ah, the vermin are back . . . I'm certainly not going to let them go shopping!

Callum *turns, his arms full of the goods they have bought. He sees* **Victor** *running through the thick undergrowth in the wood, screaming at the men.* **Callum** *follows him into the wood. He catches glimpses of* **Victor**, *and then about four men moving through the trees. Two of the men run away but the two others turn on* **Victor**.

Victor *suddenly hurls himself at one of the men, wrestling him to the ground and hitting him really hard. The other man runs off.*

VICTOR
Fucking Blackshirts! Blackshirts want to go shopping do they?!

He is fighting furiously with the man, both of them smashing each other in the face. There is blood all over **Victor**'s *clothes and face.* **Callum** *can see the* *fight, half obscured by the trees. He throws down all the goods he has been carrying so he can get to* **Victor** *faster.*

The fight is savage. The two men scrabbling at each other's faces on the ground. Then the man manages to break away from **Victor** *and hurtles off through the wood.* **Callum** *reaches the spot just in time to see* **Victor** *emerge victorious.*

Victor *turns and beams at* **Callum***, wiping the blood off his face.*

VICTOR
They won't come shopping again in a hurry!

Victor *moves down to the stream that runs along the edge of the wood to wash his face.* **Callum** *moves back to retrieve the goods that he had dropped in the wood. Suddenly he hears* **Victor** *call. He moves to join him, holding all the goods, branches snapping in his face.*

When he reaches the stream, he sees one of the other men, a big heavy young man, has attacked **Victor** *just as he was washing himself. This time the man has a knife and has hit* **Victor** *to the ground.* **Callum** *reaches them just in time, he rips the man off* **Victor***, smashes the knife out of his hand. The man fights back, hitting* **Callum** *very hard in the face. But* **Callum** *is suddenly possessed with ferocious energy, coming to the aid of his brother. He hits the man back really powerfully. The man tries to get away across the stream, but* **Callum** *catches him, twists his arm behind him and then pushes his head under the water.*

He holds the man under the water for a considerable moment. He then pulls his head up, letting him splutter for a moment, and then pushes his head down again. This time he just holds him there under water.

Victor *shouts from the bank:*

VICTOR
Cal, don't kill him – you don't need to kill him!

But **Callum** *is holding the man under the water.* **Victor** *calls again, suddenly passionate:*

Don't want to kill him, Cal!

At the last moment **Callum** *pulls the young man, spluttering and retching,* *up out of the water and on to the bank. The man crawls away into the undergrowth. Both* **Victor** *and* **Callum**'s *shirts are covered in blood. The bank and the stream are scattered with the belongings that they have bought.* **Victor** *and* **Callum** *sit together on the bank. For a moment they don't say anything.*

VICTOR

Thought I'd better stop you! (*He grins.*) I'd have loved to have seen you kill him . . . but in the end, it might've spoilt our day a bit!

CALLUM

This is true . . .

We see **Callum** *gradually coming out of his furious adrenaline burst.*

But if somebody's going to kill you, Victor, it's not going to be a Blackshirt . . .

VICTOR
(*suddenly*)

The shopping! We've lost all the shopping! (*He leaps into the stream.*) Got to get some of it back at least . . . (*He finds the jar of marmalade and holds it up triumphantly.*) And here are the shoes, that's fantastic!

He sits on the bank, starts taking his shoes and socks off to try on the sodden shoes.

Got to see if they still fit!

EXT. BACK ENTRANCE CONNINGTON/BOMBSITE. AFTERNOON

We see **Callum** *approaching the back entrance of the Connington, along the rim of the bombsite. One of the watchers from the third floor is pacing outside. When he catches sight of* **Callum**, *he looks worried.*

INT. THE CONNINGTON, PASSAGES/KITCHEN. AFTERNOON

We see **Callum** *enter the dark ground-floor passage at a rapid pace.*

Ringwood *is sitting waiting for him, he springs up as soon as he sees* **Callum**, *an alarmed look on his face.*

> CALLUM
> What's happened? (*Looking at his alarmed expression.*) They haven't gone missing have they?!

> RINGWOOD
> No sir, they're being happily looked after.

> CALLUM
> So what's the matter then?

Ringwood *indicates his clothes,* **Callum** *looks down at his blood-stained shirt.*

> Oh that's nothing . . . I've just been fishing!

> RINGWOOD
> And there's a lady waiting for you upstairs, sir, and I think she may be from the War Crimes –

> CALLUM
> I know.

He is setting off down the passages. **Ringwood** *keeps pace.*

> Don't worry about it . . .

We cut to them moving along one of the back passages, passing the door of the kitchen. **Callum** *pauses for a second to glance in. He sees the head chef,* **Leonard**, *and the sous chefs preparing the food for the opening, corn on the cob and small rissoles/burgers. He is being watched by* **Lotte** *and* **Dieter**, *who is reading a book in the corner. Another of their minders is also in the kitchen.*

Lotte *is moving with* **Leonard** *as he cooks.*

> RINGWOOD
> They seem to like it in there, sir . . . (*He watches the food being prepared with a puzzled expression.*) I think it's going to be an American kind of meal, for the grand re-opening.

INT. SECOND-FLOOR PASSAGE. AFTERNOON

We cut to a shot of **Kathy** *standing waiting at the end of the second-floor passage. Her head turns sharply as she hears* **Callum** *approach.*

KATHY

There you are. I thought you weren't going to turn up.

CALLUM

I may be from T-Force, but I always keep appointments.

KATHY

They told me to wait up here, that this is where your office is?

CALLUM

And so it is.

He unlocks the door of the small office. As he doing so, **Kathy** *is staring at his blood-spattered shirt.*

KATHY

How did you get like that?

CALLUM

Oh that? I've just been on a little trip to the suburbs, I had to do some shopping . . . (*He adds with a smile.*) And ran into some Blackshirts . . .

Kathy *looks startled. The door of the small office opens.*

So here's the office! And our files . . . as you see, there's not a great deal here –

KATHY

This is your office? (*She gives him a searching look.*)

CALLUM

At the moment, we're looking after a German aeronautical engineer, and his daughter – that's all we're doing here. You don't need a big office for that! (*He looks straight at her.*) I'll see if I can get permission to show you his file – but I doubt he's one of the people you're interested in.

KATHY

I'm always interested in seeing files . . . (*She is watching him closely.*) Surprised you haven't got a lot more. You're sure you haven't got any other rooms in the hotel you've forgotten about?

CALLUM

Well, this is where I'm sleeping, right here.

He starts to unlock the door across the passage.

You can search my bedroom if you like, but I don't have any more files . . .

KATHY

I don't think I need to search your bedroom, no. (*She smiles.*) But I doubt that's where you'd keep a lot of files . . .

CALLUM

Ah. (*He is standing in the open doorway of his bedroom.*) They delivered my dinner jacket, good! I need it for the grand re-opening of the basement ballroom tonight. I really hope they get an audience! (*He smiles.*) I ought to start getting ready, if you'll excuse me . . .

KATHY

That's it? That was our meeting, was it?

Callum *turns.*

I know everybody at T-Force thinks the War Crimes Unit belongs in Germany with the leaders who are going on trial there, and that's the end of the story. But there are in fact a lot of other people it is right to be concerned about . . . people who aren't famous who are guilty of war crimes, and they need to be found . . . (*Staring straight at* **Callum**.). Isn't that true?

CALLUM

Of course. (*His tone serious.*) I'll tell you what I'll do, Miss Griffiths – if you give me all the names you are interested in, I will personally make sure they are checked at Enfield.

KATHY

Will you? (*She sounds sceptical.*)

CALLUM

What's that meant to mean?

KATHY

It means I don't know how seriously to take that – a lot of people on T-Force think we're on different sides.

CALLUM

Do they?

KATHY

(*sharply, impatient with his innocent tone*)

Yes – you're bringing over Germans who you think are vital for our national security, and one or two of them may be the same people I'm trying to catch. So of course, there are officers in T-Force who think we're on different sides.

CALLUM

But you don't know what I think . . .

Kathy *stares at him for a moment.*

KATHY

So that's a promise is it then? You checking the names?

CALLUM

Yes. (*He smiles at her.*) It is a firm undertaking.

KATHY

Right. (*She stares at him.*) In that case, I'll hold you to it.

INT. BASEMENT BALLROOM. NIGHT

We cut to the musicians warming up on their instruments in the basement ballroom. They are spread across the room. **Joe** *is on the drums,* **Richie** *is watching from the side. The room has been decorated with candles and a few flowers.*

The door suddenly bursts open, and **Eva** *appears in a striking red dress.*

Behind her are two large crates on a trolley. The crates are each covered with a cloth, so you can't see what is in them.

EVA

So boys . . . look at this! A present from a fan on a US airbase here – and you'll never guess what!

She pulls the cloth off to reveal two crates of fresh oranges.

Now that's what I call a gift!

INT. ALEX AND RACHEL'S HOUSE. EVENING

*The hall of **Alex** and **Rachel**'s house, a period town house with a Georgian staircase. **Alex** is waiting, ready to go out, in his coat and hat. **Rachel** is just about to put on her fur coat; a maid is waiting with it. **Rachel** is in a magnificent evening dress, made of expensive material. She glances at herself in the mirror – a humorous, self-aware look.*

RACHEL

I'm not sure this is right – but then how does one dress for a really spooky place?!

ALEX

You look wonderful, my dear, and that's all that matters . . . (*Softly, touching her shoulder, looking at both of them in the mirror.*) I'm so proud of you.

INT. BASEMENT BALLROOM. EVENING

*We cut to **Joe** drumming hard on the stage, the other musicians still improvising by themselves, but beginning to take their positions on the stage. A pulsating rhythm starts to form between them and is building on the soundtrack. It continues under the next scenes.*

INT. KITCHEN. EVENING

*We see **Leonard** carefully preparing the corn on the cob and the little rissoles that are being passed off as burgers. The music is pulsing louder on the soundtrack.*

INT. PASSAGE/GOLD DRAWING ROOM. INTERCUT WITH
BASEMENT BALLROOM. NIGHT

We cut to **Callum** *in his dinner jacket walking down the main passage. He sees a door open that has not been open before, and which leads into a gold drawing room. It has large mirrors along the walls, and gilt decorations all around, in imitation of an eighteenth-century salon. But the walls are now filthy, and the decorative patterns faded under layers of dirt. A notice says,* DO NOT ENTER, DANGEROUS CEILING. *In the corner of the room is a grand piano. We see* **Callum** *staring at it with a glint in his eyes. He cannot stop himself moving into the room. He sits at the piano.*

We cut down to the basement. **Richie** *has joined* **Joe** *on stage and is drumming next to him. They are beginning to play the intro to the first number.*

We cut back to **Callum**, *who is playing the piano. The sound of the drumming fades away, and we just hear* **Callum** *playing. His concentration is total as he plays.*

A voice suddenly says:

HAROLD

You play very well.

Callum *looks up.* **Harold** *is standing in the doorway in evening dress.* **Callum** *smiles, a little embarrassed at having been caught playing.*

CALLUM

I just wanted to see if it was in tune.

HAROLD

And it is. Nobody can have played it for years. What was the piece?

CALLUM
(hesitates)

I forget what it's called . . . I picked it up somewhere, heard somebody playing it once –

HAROLD

So you wrote it, did you?

Harold *looks straight at him.*

> CALLUM
>
> No, no, absolutely not! I don't write music. It was a friend, an acquaintance, it was his piece –
>
> HAROLD
>
> A friend? I see . . .

Harold *glances over the faded decorations in the room.*

> They spent a great deal of money on this room before the war . . . When this hotel was briefly fashionable . . . there were always a lot of extremely beautiful women in this room.

He stares for a second in the mirror, as if imagining this, and then looks directly at **Callum***:*

> And they had no idea what was coming – what was about to hit them. It's amazing how unprepared we were . . . Still surprises me, how that was possible?!
>
> CALLUM
>
> Yes.
>
> HAROLD
>
> Is that 'yes', you agree, or are you just saying 'yes'?
>
> CALLUM
>
> Yes . . . I agree with you.

He meets **Harold**'s *look, trying to work out what he wants.*

> Few people could disagree with that, could they?
>
> HAROLD
>
> Oh, you're very wrong about that! (*He smiles.*) Some people want to protect themselves from blame in the face of everything . . . (*He looks at him.*) You're from T-Force, aren't you? (*He smiles.*) Come on . . . I think you can tell me that, can't you?!

Lucy *appears in the doorway in a plain evening gown.*

You are saved by my ward! (*Affectionately.*) Doesn't she look good?! (*To* **Lucy**.) Say hello to the pianist, or maybe even the composer . . .

Lucy *nods hello to* **Callum**.

HAROLD

We're going to the basement after dinner. Not going to risk the food down there. I have a feeling that's what everybody is doing, because the chef has decided on an American feel, and is serving corn on the cob – quite forgetting we only feed that to cattle in this country . . . ! Even in the war we didn't eat it!

He moves off with **Lucy**.

Some habits take a lot of breaking . . .

INT. BASEMENT BALLROOM. NIGHT

We cut to the basement ballroom. **Eva** *is at the piano. The instrumental intro is finished and* **Eva** *starts to sing, a vibrant up-tempo number.*

She looks charismatic, powerful at the piano as she sings.

We cut wide in the ballroom and see there is almost nobody there. One very thin-faced man is sitting on his own eating the rissoles/burgers and the corn on the cob.

Waiters and waitresses are standing along the walls staring at all the empty tables.

We cut back to **Eva**; *there's a fierce glint in her eyes.*

INT. MAIN DINING ROOM. NIGHT

We cut to the main dining room where the guests, all in full evening dress, are eating little pieces of meat and watery cabbage. They can hear the music pulsating towards them from the ballroom downstairs.

We see **Dieter** *and* **Lotte** *approaching the dining room, escorted by* **Ringwood**. **Lotte** *is wearing her bulky new dress, which does not fit at all.*

Callum *is waiting for them at the table. He compliments* **Lotte** *on her new dress.*

CALLUM

Mr Ringwood has done you proud!

Lotte *looks extremely serious as she sits, poised, trying to look grown-up.*
Dieter *is in a suit and tie.* **Ringwood** *does not sit with them.*

INT. BASEMENT BALLROOM. NIGHT

We cut back to the basement ballroom. **Eva** *is finishing the number. There are only two more people now in the room. The atmosphere is funereal, a tiny spattering of applause.*

Eva *is looking defiant. She turns to* **Joe**.

EVA

How long do we have to wait before they start crawling down here . . .?!

She leans back, decides not to resume playing immediately.

Give me one of those oranges, boys . . . I'm certainly not going to kill myself for this lot!

One of the oranges is taken out of the crate and brought to her. She notices the three members of the audience are riveted, staring at the orange, stunned.

Eva *grins and calls out to them.*

EVA

You want a piece of this, do you?!

INT. MAIN DINING ROOM/INTERCUT WITH BASEMENT BALLROOM. NIGHT

We cut back to the main dining room, just as we hear the music restart – a strong, propulsive instrumental number, drifting up from the basement.

Alex *and* **Rachel** *are entering the dining room. She looks stunning in her evening gown, and everybody cannot stop looking at her.* **Alex** *and* **Rachel** *greet* **Callum**. **Rachel** *surveys the room . . .*

RACHEL

My . . . ! This is not spooky at all! (*She laughs.*) Just a little bit quiet, maybe. And you must be the German family.

She greets **Dieter** *and* **Lotte**. **Dieter** *stands up formally, shakes her hand and sits.*

RACHEL
How delightful to meet you both . . . (*She looks at* **Lotte**.) Is that a new dress? (**Lotte** *nods*.) Were the boys in charge of getting that?!

Lotte *is just staring at her, entranced by* **Rachel**'s *beautiful dress.*

Well, whatever happens, I think we need to go shopping again, don't you?!

Lotte *nods.*

I'll help you get a real dress . . . I'm sure there's somewhere in town we can find one!

We cut back to the band playing powerfully in the basement ballroom, the music getting faster, and then there is a trumpet solo. **Eva** *has left the stage.*

We cut back to the dining room, with the trumpet ringing towards the dinner guests, loud and clear from the basement.

Eva *suddenly appears at the entrance of the main dining room, and begins to confidently cross it, slowly. Behind her,* **Richie** *is carrying a pile of oranges on a silver tray.*

The diners are mesmerised by the sight. Even **Harold** *is impressed.*

Eva *casually makes out she is just there to ask the waiters for a sharp knife. She can see all the diners staring. She deliberately prolongs the moment, as she invites the waiter to choose an orange. Then she turns to face the dining room. She addresses the diners:*

EVA
Come on downstairs, and you can have one each! Oh yes, it's hard to believe, I know, but you can! (*She grins.*) You just don't know what's going on down there, do you?!

The diners stare at her, almost in amazement.

RACHEL
How marvellous!

*She is riveted by **Eva**'s boldness, deeply impressed.*

Who could resist that?!

MONTAGE. BASEMENT BALLROOM/HOTEL PASSAGE/DINING ROOM/DIETER'S BEDROOM

We cut to an explosion of drumming, as a montage begins.

*First we see **Eva** resume her position at the piano in the basement ballroom. She and the band start a new number.*

Then we cut to the first people standing up in the main dining room and choosing to go down to the basement.

Then we cut back to the basement ballroom, and see diners beginning to spill into it. They are each given an orange as they enter.

They look very surprised that the offer turns out to be true.

*We then cut to the main passage, where **Alex**, **Rachel** and **Callum** are moving off to go down to the basement. **Ringwood** is escorting **Dieter** and **Lotte**. **Callum** notices **Dieter** is intrigued by the sound coming from the band. He calls to him:*

CALLUM
You must come too . . . you must come with us!

DIETER
I will put Lotte to bed . . . and then I will see . . .

We cut back to the basement ballroom. It is now getting completely packed.

Some people are eating the oranges, and some are just holding them tight. They are staring at the musicians. The diners' faces are pale, rather haunted, as if startled by the energy and joy in the music.

Harold *is sitting at a corner table with* **Lucy**, *watching the scene with an amused smile. He has an orange too.*

HAROLD
All of us being fed by an American band! Nobody could've dreamt that would happen to us . . . !

We cut to **Lotte**'s *bedroom,* **Dieter** *putting her to bed and kissing her goodnight, speaking to her softly in German. He switches off the bedside lamp. He leaves* **Lotte** *holding her one-eyed donkey tight, seemingly going to sleep.*

We cut back to the music, and **Eva** *singing.*

We see **Callum** *in the doorway, watching the musicians, thrilled by the sound.*

And then we see him watching **Alex** *and* **Rachel** *dancing together, a beautiful couple in the middle of the dance floor.*

Rachel *looking so radiant,* **Alex** *so delighted with his bride.*

We cut back to **Callum**, *watching them closely.*

Suddenly **Callum** *realises* **Dieter** *is standing next to him in the doorway.*

Dieter *is staring rapt at* **Eva** *on stage. For a moment, it is almost as if he is unaware of anything else. Then he looks at* **Callum**:

DIETER
This is forbidden music for me . . . we were never allowed to listen to this music. (*He watches* **Eva**.) It was always completely forbidden . . .

Dieter *cannot take his eyes of the stage.*

INT. LOTTE'S BEDROOM/PASSAGES

We cut back to **Lotte** *in bed; her eyes are wide open.*

She can hear the music pulsing up towards her. She suddenly gets out of bed and crosses her father's bedroom. She is just in her white nightdress and barefoot.

We cut to the passage and see the bedroom door opening just a crack. We see **Lotte**'s *face staring through the crack, out into the passage. We cut to her point of view, through the crack of the door. She can see the watchers, a man and a woman, talking together at the end of the passage. The man is flirting with the woman. For a moment,* **Lotte** *just watches them. Then the man leans forward and lights the woman's cigarette.*

Lotte *seizes her chance and rushes in the opposite direction, down the night passage.*

Then we cut to her descending down the main staircase, following the music. She dodges across the main lobby passage without being seen by any of the hotel staff, and she races towards the back stairs, following the music all the time. She arrives at the bottom of the back staircase and moves along the basement passage, towards where she can see the door of the ballroom, and the lights and the music, really loud.

INT. BASEMENT BALLROOM. NIGHT

We then cut inside the ballroom. **Dieter** *is staring, riveted by the band. He has moved a little closer. He is just completely concentrating on the music.*

Callum *has also left the doorway and found himself a better vantage point.*

He notices **Dieter**'s *rapt fascination with the music.*

Then **Callum** *watches* **Rachel** *dancing with* **Alex**, *her warmth and confidence.*

We move in on **Callum**.

We cut to **Lotte** *getting to the doorway of the ballroom.*

We see her point of view of the room, glimpses of the band, of her father, of **Rachel** *dancing.*

We see it all from **Lotte**'s *height, through gaps between people standing at the back. She keeps shifting a few inches this way, a few inches that, to try to get a better view. She dares to move just a tiny bit closer.*

We then cut to **Harold**. *For a moment he thinks he catches a glimpse of* **Lotte** *in her nightdress in the doorway, and then his view is obscured by dancing couples.*

We cut back to **Lotte**. *She has seen* **Harold** *looking at her, and she vanishes back down the passage.*

When **Harold** *gets a clear view again, there is no little girl watching.*

He turns to **Lucy**.

HAROLD

I thought I saw . . . (*He smiles.*) no, I can't have . . . ! I must be seeing things . . . the shock of eating my first orange for so long!

INT. PASSAGES AND STAIRCASE. NIGHT

We cut back to **Lotte** *running furiously fast back along the basement passages and up the back staircase.*

She emerges into the main passage, and starts to run along it.

Suddenly she runs straight into the stomach of somebody. She looks up.

She finds herself staring into the round face of **Mr Emmanuel**, *the man who took her toy in the opening sequence.*

MR EMMANUEL

Oh it's you! My little one . . . how nice to meet you again.

Lotte *looks very startled to see him.*

MR EMMANUEL

Are you lost?

LOTTE

No, I'm not lost . . . not very much.

MR EMMANUEL

Just a little lost? So, let me . . .

He takes her hand.

MR EMMANUEL

Let me take you back to your room . . .

They walk down the passage, hand in hand, away from us, as the music pounds.

They disappear around the corner.

CREDITS

Part Two

CREDIT SEQUENCE

EXT. BOMBSITE/CONNINGTON. NIGHT.

We are tracking across the bombsite, towards the Connington Hotel in the distance. We can hear the sound of **Eva**'s *band, the music pulsating out of the basement of the hotel.*

The shot reaches the back door of the Connington. It snakes its way around the entrance, and into the main ground-floor passage. And now we are tracking fast along the basement passage, towards the light and the music.

END OF CREDIT SEQUENCE

INT. BASEMENT BALLROOM. NIGHT

We cut into the basement ballroom. **Eva** *is sitting at the piano singing with the band; the lad* **Richie** *is drumming next to the old drummer,* **Joe**. *We see the faces of the diners, and the audience standing at the back, pale-looking people, tired and drawn, but for a moment, transported by the music.*

We see **Rachel** *and* **Alex** *dancing together; they seem such a glamorous couple on the dance floor. We see the audience are watching them dance.*

Dieter *has had several drinks. He is watching* **Eva** *singing and the band playing; his eyes shining, a look of absolute fascination on his face.*

Callum *is watching* **Rachel** *and* **Alex** *dance; we move in on* **Callum**'s *face.*

Joe *and* **Richie** *have a sudden drumming section together. We cut to* **Harold** *sitting with his ward,* **Lucy**. **Harold** *is taking in the whole scene with an amused expression, all the orange peel everywhere, but his look ends on* **Callum**.

Eva *sings the last verse of the song. There is loud applause.* **Rachel** *and* **Alex** *clapping from the dance floor.*

The musicians begin to move off the stage.

RACHEL
Don't stop now! We must have an encore, surely?!

Don't go, give us another number!

Eva *looks at* **Rachel**, *in the middle of the dance floor in her magnificent dress.*

EVA

You want another number, do you? Well, honey, you may have nothing to do tomorrow, but I do, so goodnight everyone.

We see **Rachel**'s *face, startled by* **Eva**'s *bluntness.*

INT. SECOND FLOOR PASSAGE. NIGHT

We cut to **Mr Emmanuel** *leading* **Lotte** *along the second-floor passage, where there are no people keeping watch. He offers her a little paper bag,* **Lotte** *hesitates.*

MR EMMANUEL

No sweets from strangers . . .? But we're not strangers, are we, little one – and maybe these are the last sweets anywhere in the city.

Lotte *takes one, so does* **Mr Emmanuel**.

These are from Belgium. (*He moves on with* **Lotte**.) Only two left now.

INT./EXT. LOBBY AND FRONT ENTRANCE CONNINGTON. NIGHT

We cut to **Rachel**, **Alex** *and* **Callum** *moving across the lobby and out into the night, where* **Alex**'s *chauffeur-driven car is waiting. Other guests are leaving, some of them in more humble cars.*

ALEX

So the basement ballroom is well and truly re-opened!

RACHEL

Yes, it was marvellous, even if she was a little fierce, that singer . . . (*She laughs.*) Rather terrifying in fact!

CALLUM
She is quite frightening, yes.

ALEX
But it was the perfect way to spend our first night out together, Cal –

RACHEL
The first of many, I hope. (*She turns to look at him with a smile.*) Don't feel the need to see us right to the car . . . You have to keep watch on the German family don't you?

CALLUM
Oh that's okay, they're being well looked after.

INT./EXT. SECOND-FLOOR PASSAGE/FRONT ENTRANCE. NIGHT

We cut up to the second-floor passage. **Mr Emmanuel** *and* **Lotte** *are standing side by side at the window staring down at the front entrance of the hotel, at* **Rachel** *and* **Alex**'*s car. They can see the whole scene but are in the shadows so they cannot be spotted.*

EXT. FRONT ENTRANCE CONNINGTON. NIGHT

We cut back to **Alex**'*s car;* **Rachel** *is just getting onto the back seat. She talks to* **Callum** *through the open door.*

CALLUM
This is a beautiful old car . . .

ALEX
Yes, it's ancient, but it works!

RACHEL
And the seats smell truly fantastic! (*She beckons* **Callum**.) See what you think?!

Callum *leans in and smells the leather.*

CALLUM
Yes, they do!

RACHEL
I must take that little girl shopping by the way –

CALLUM
You really don't need to bother.

RACHEL
Oh yes I do, she can't wear that dress every evening! And you never know, it might make all the difference . . . (*She smiles.*) Or do you think it's worked with the German? He really loved that music – maybe you've triumphed already?

CALLUM
Well, I'm about to find out.

ALEX
Goodnight my old friend and thank you for this evening. (*He laughs.*) Just you watch, you're not going to be able to get rid of us from now on!

The car drives off. As **Callum** *turns,* **Harold** *and* **Lucy** *are coming down the front steps to get in a taxi.*

HAROLD
So, Mr Ferguson, the hotel came back to life, didn't it!

CALLUM
It did.

HAROLD
Do you think it is for one night only?

CALLUM
I have no idea, who knows?

HAROLD
You're quite right, who knows. It doesn't need to be just tonight, of course . . . (*Warmly.*) Lucy enjoyed it, didn't you?

LUCY
Yes, it was quite exciting. I wasn't expecting that.

HAROLD

Ah, that's a compliment indeed! My ward is a very serious person. (*Affectionately.*) You don't mind me saying that do you, my dear?

Well, we must let Mr Ferguson get back to his duties . . . (*A searching look.*) Whatever they might be . . .

For a moment **Callum** *watches* **Harold** *and* **Lucy** *move towards their taxi.*

INT. SECOND FLOOR PASSAGE. NIGHT

We cut to **Mr Emmanuel** *and* **Lotte** *staring down. As soon as he sees* **Callum** *move,* **Mr Emmanuel** *draws away from the window.*

MR EMMANUEL

We have to get you back to your bedroom without you being seen. (*Glancing down at* **Lotte**.) Because if we are seen, you may get into trouble, and so, my little one, might I . . . Do you want me to help you?

Lotte *hesitates for a second, then nods.*

INT. MAIN GROUND FLOOR PASSAGE. NIGHT

We cut to **Dieter** *being escorted along the main ground-floor passage by* **Ringwood**. **Dieter** *glances over his shoulder; he sees at the other end of the passage some of the musicians, including* **Richie** *and* **Joe**. *He immediately starts moving towards them.*

DIETER

Excuse me just a moment . . .

He reaches the musicians and starts engaging them in conversation.

INT. THIRD-FLOOR PASSAGE NIGHT

We cut to **Lotte** *and* **Mr Emmanuel** *reaching the door of the third-floor passage.* **Mr Emmanuel** *opens it a crack. The watchers are at the other end, chatting together and smoking, but they keep looking up, giving them a clear view of the passage.*

MR EMMANUEL
I can't think of any other way but this . . . If it works, we may be able to see each other again . . . (*He looks down at her, his smooth round face.*) I must tell you my little tale – we all have little tales to tell, haven't we?! I will visit you . . .

Mr Emmanuel *suddenly erupts into the passage, calling out loudly to the watchers:*

Excuse me! Excuse me! I need your help to find myself to my room – these numbers don't go in the right order! My room is on this floor, but the numbers go in the wrong order . . . I will show you . . . (*He is gesticulating.*) This way, I will show you! Please, they jump from 331 to 340!

As the watchers look in the direction he is gesticulating, **Lotte** *runs furiously down the passage and into her room.*

INT. GROUND-FLOOR MAIN PASSAGE. NIGHT

We cut back to **Dieter**, *deep in conversation with the musicians. He is in an expansive mood, having had some drinks, and is laughing and joking with them. For a brief moment, we see an entirely different side to him, a humorous, relaxed man.* **Ringwood** *is watching from a distance.* **Dieter** *thanks the musicians, and moves towards* **Ringwood**.

DIETER
Forgive me, I had a lot of questions to ask them!

INT. THIRD-FLOOR PASSAGE/DIETER'S BEDROOM. NIGHT

We cut to **Ringwood** *escorting* **Dieter** *to his bedroom door.* **Dieter** *opens the door and looks across, to where* **Lotte** *is lying in bed, her bedside light on, her eyes closed.* **Dieter** *is about to go in when he sees* **Callum** *is standing on the other side of the passage, smoking.*

CALLUM
Just came to say good night. I'm glad you seem to have had such a good evening – you stayed for all of it and more.

DIETER

Yes, it was a good evening, perhaps even tremendous! But it makes no difference to anything.

CALLUM

Of course, one night, how could it?!

DIETER

It doesn't matter how many nights!

He is near **Callum***; his voice full of drink, but intense.*

I have one desire – to go home, and every time I see you, that is what I will tell you.

We see a shot of **Lotte***, watching from her bed.*

I will not cooperate with the plans you have for me – whatever happens, whatever you do.

CALLUM

Well that's pretty clear . . . (*Smiles.*) Of course, if we were to discuss your work, you and I, and you showed me some of it, then maybe I'll be able to get you home . . .

DIETER

Since I have not brought any work with me, that is not going to be possible, is it?

Their eyes meet.

EXT. BOMBSITE. EARLY MORNING

We see a group of hotel staff arriving for work in the early morning, a line of young women, chambermaids and waitresses. They have to pick their way along the perilous paths that zigzag across the bombsite.

The camera picks out one of these girls who looks much younger than the rest, no more than a child, **Anna***. There is trepidation in her eyes, but also determination.*

INT. HOTEL KITCHENS. EARLY MORNING

*We cut to those girls, who are waitresses, all lined up in the hotel kitchens. They are now in their black and white uniforms. We see **Leonard**, the head chef, who rules the kitchen, staring at **Anna**. The **Maître' d** is standing next to him, inspecting the waitresses.*

LEONARD

I haven't seen you before, who are you?

ANNA

Anna, sir . . . Anna White, sir.

LEONARD

You're very young, Anna White.

ANNA

I'm not really sir.

MAÎTRE D'

What does that mean, not really? How old are you?

ANNA

I'm seventeen, sir.

LEONARD

And that is a real seventeen is it, not just a number you've made up?

ANNA

That's a truthful seventeen sir, I wouldn't lie about my age.

LEONARD

But you would lie about something else would you?

ANNA

No sir.

LEONARD

I can never tell nowadays how old people are, sometimes they look twenty-two – but are really fourteen.

ANNA

I saw Mr Halstead, sir, here last week, sir, he gave me the job.

MAÎTRE D'

Clearly, otherwise you wouldn't be here! Well we'd better start you off in the basement ballroom – they won't notice your mistakes nearly so much down there.

INT. THE SECRET FLOOR. ATTIC ROOM. MORNING

Ringwood's *head comes round the door of the attic room.* **Callum** *is sitting at the table, at the far end, looking at people's files.* **Ruth** *is typing in the corner.*

RINGWOOD

You're here already, sir! However early I am, you manage to beat me.

CALLUM

That's because I've got an important assignment for you, Ringwood.

RINGWOOD

That's good sir. (*Correcting himself.*) Sorry, I will try to stop that – calling you sir.

CALLUM

I want you to keep them at breakfast for as long as possible this morning, I'm going to search his room.

RINGWOOD

But you've done his room sir?! You tore up the carpet! –

CALLUM

But I didn't go through their things – I know he's brought some work with him, he must have. I know I would have done.

INT. MAIN DINING ROOM. MORNING

Dieter, **Lotte** *and* **Ringwood** *approach the door of the main dining room. There is a scattering of residents having breakfast, a real mixture of people. European faces, old English ladies, travelling salesmen.* **Dieter** *surveys the room.*

DIETER
How many of these are you spying on, Mr Ringwood? (*Turns.*) Listening to their conversations in their bedrooms?

RINGWOOD
It's only you, Mr Koehler, you're very special to us. And we're not spying on you, not any more! Now . . . (*Moving them into the room.*) A chance to have a real English breakfast. We've collected all of our rations book together, so you can have an egg each, and a slice of bacon!

INT. THIRD-FLOOR PASSAGE/DIETER'S ROOM. MORNING

We cut to **Callum** *unlocking* **Dieter***'s bedroom door. Just as he has got the door open,* **Julia** *walks along the passage.*

JULIA
That's not your room, is it?

CALLUM
No, it isn't! And this isn't your floor is it?

JULIA
Ah, but you don't know that. You don't know which is my real floor, where my room is . . .

CALLUM
I don't, this is true.

JULIA
And you haven't tried very hard to find out, have you?

Callum *smiles at this.*

Well don't let me keep you, whatever you're doing . . . You probably don't have a lot of time to do it. (*She moves off.*)

We cut to **Callum** *entering* **Dieter***'s room, which has been tidied since he tore out all the bugs.*

INT. MAIN DINING ROOM. MORNING

A waiter is standing by **Dieter** *and* **Lotte***'s table, ready to take their order.*

DIETER
We will just have some toast.

RINGWOOD
Just toast . . . no!

Dieter *looks surprised.*

You must have the eggs, we've arranged it.

DIETER
We will have the toast and nothing else, please.

INT. DIETER'S ROOM. MORNING

In a series of sharp cuts we see **Callum** *searching the room. He opens drawers, he searches the wardrobe, he puts* **Dieter***'s suitcase on the bed and looks inside. It is empty. He feels the lining. He thinks he detects a bulge in the lining. He takes out a knife and slices right through the lining, opening it. A tin rolls out. He opens the tin, it contains barley sugars. He tastes one – it is a barley sugar.*

He goes into **Lotte***'s room.*

INT. MAIN DINING ROOM. MORNING

Dieter *and* **Lotte** *have both eaten their toast.* **Dieter** *sips his coffee.*

DIETER
I don't know how you manage to make coffee taste like this?

RINGWOOD
Yes, quite. (*Smiles.*) That's one thing the war hasn't changed!

DIETER
We have now finished, thank you.

RINGWOOD
No, please . . .

Dieter*'s eyes flash,* **Lotte** *and* **Dieter** *exchange looks.*

Isn't there anything else you want?

Dieter *gets up from the table.*

INT. LOTTE'S ROOM. MORNING

We cut to **Callum** *searching* **Lotte**'s *bed. He picks up the stuffed donkey. He is about to slice it open with the knife, but then thinks better of it, and feels it thoroughly.*

We see quick cuts of him looking under **Lotte**'s *bed, amongst the two pairs of shoes and one pair of slippers. We then see him go through the drawers of her cupboard, scattering her clothes.*

In the bottom drawer, squashed right in the corner, amongst the underwear, there is a man's sock. Inside the sock are three very small black notebooks, about two inches across. **Callum** *tips out all the underwear, searching for more. At that very moment, the door starts to open. He looks up; a maid is standing watching him.*

Callum *meets her alarmed look.*

> CALLUM
> Sorry, nearly finished in here!

The maid leaves in a hurry. **Callum** *looks down at the tiny notebooks; they are full of diagrams and writing, very neat, minuscule handwriting.*

INT. THIRD-FLOOR PASSAGE. MORNING

We cut to **Dieter** *walking very briskly back towards his bedroom with* **Lotte**. **Ringwood** *is right behind them; he suddenly stops:*

> RINGWOOD
> My God!

Dieter *turns.* **Ringwood** *is by the window.*

> The light is amazing isn't it?! So bright with all the buildings missing, the views you suddenly see now . . . !

Dieter *ignores this and moves on.*

INT. DIETER AND LOTTE'S ROOMS. MORNING

Dieter, Lotte *and* **Ringwood** *enter* **Dieter**'s *bedroom. They are greeted by the mess* **Callum** *has created. They look across into* **Lotte**'s *room, and see* **Callum** *calmly sitting on the bed, holding the three little black notebooks.*

DIETER
What are you doing?!

CALLUM
What does it look like? Given you won't talk to me about your work, I had to take the obvious course . . .

DIETER
Which was crawling about in my daughter's cupboard was it? . . . So nothing is private here.

CALLUM
Not quite yet, no. (*He smiles.*) But hopefully soon . . . I'd love to know why you hid the barley sugars, though?

DIETER
They were for her. (*Indicating* **Lotte**.) And of course I knew your Customs would take them.

CALLUM
Here you are. (*Handing the barley sugars to* **Lotte**.) Don't lose them!

Callum *then holds up the tiny black notebooks.*

But I'm going to keep these for a day or two.

DIETER
You won't understand them.

CALLUM
We'll see . . . I'm an engineer remember . . . In fact I worked on jet engines before the war, so let's see if I can surprise you!

DIETER
(*disbelieving*)
You're going to surprise me with your response to my work?

CALLUM
I am.

DIETER
(*looks intrigued despite himself*)
What is really interesting is not written down, of course . . . (*He taps his head.*) It is in here.

CALLUM
Naturally . . . (*Smiles.*) And that's what I'm going to unlock.

Callum *moves over to the door with the black notebooks.*

DIETER
You really think doing this will make the situation any better?

CALLUM
Well, it can hardly make it much worse – since I've made no progress at all so far!

EXT./INT. HAROLD'S HOUSE. WALLED GARDEN. DAY

We cut to a shot of chickens scrabbling and clucking. We then cut to **Harold**, *who is staring out of the window in his narrow town house, down into his walled garden, where he has some chickens in a coop. The coop occupies most of the garden.*

Lucy *is standing next to him.*

HAROLD
Mrs Gorton is off today, so if we want any eggs this morning my dear, we will have to obtain them ourselves! (*He turns.*) I have been known to do this successfully on my own – but only once or twice! I usually manage to let at least one chicken escape –

LUCY
We'll manage . . .

We cut to **Harold** *and* **Lucy** *moving among the chickens, trying to close the door of the coop without letting any get out. The chickens scatter.*

HAROLD
They do peck, it's what people never tell you. They do give quite a peck!

LUCY

(*brandishing an egg*)

I've got one!

HAROLD

Magnificent, well done . . . Now the war is over, there are only two things that matter – first and foremost, stopping people stealing my eggs!

LUCY

And what is the other one?

HAROLD

Ah my dear . . . (*We are close on* **Harold** *as he stands surrounded by chickens.*) that's not quite so easy to explain . . . but soon I will tell you.

INT. LOBBY. CONNINGTON. DAY

We cut to the lobby of the Connington. A voice is calling 'telephone call for Mr Ferguson, telephone call for Mr Ferguson'; we see a bell-boy weaving among the guests. **Callum** *is just entering the lobby, carrying the small black notebooks. He picks up the phone in the booth the bell-boy indicates.*

CALLUM

Yes?

VICTOR

(*voice-over*)

It's me. I need your help Cal.

CALLUM

Victor? What's wrong?

INT. VICTOR'S LODGINGS/INTERCUT WITH LOBBY, CONNINGTON. DAY

We cut to **Victor** *sitting on the floor of the hall of a suburban house, next to a little table. There is coloured glass above the front door, throwing light across his face.*

VICTOR
I find I'm on the floor. I can't move . . . I just can't move.

CALLUM
Come on Victor, what are you doing on the floor?!

VICTOR
Mrs Tooley will find me any moment and start yelling, and I don't know what'll happen then, we'll have a fight –

CALLUM
You've got to get yourself to the hospital, Victor, can you do that? Can you get there?

VICTOR
I can always do that, but they're bloody useless . . .

CALLUM
So you can move?! You're not completely stuck! (*Relief in his voice.*) Get yourself to the hospital and I'll meet you there. I have to see the Brigadier first, but I'll be there by twelve . . .

As he says this, he sees **Kathy** *across the lobby.*

Promise me you'll get yourself there.

VICTOR
I will. But only for you, Cal!

Callum *rings off. He knows* **Kathy** *has seen him. He hesitates, wondering if he can get out any other way. Then he crosses the lobby and walks up to her.*

KATHY
Thought better of trying to get out by the back entrance, did you?

CALLUM
Why would I want to do that? (*Smiles charmingly.*) But believe it or not, Miss Griffiths, I'm in a terrible hurry this morning, even worse than before . . .

KATHY
Naturally. I expect each time we see each other you'll have

even less time, until you're running in the opposite direction. But since I've got you for a moment, I'll be very quick . . .

She hands him a folder.

Here is the list of names we're interested in – Brigadier Wainwright has been sent it many times, so if there's anything you can do to make sure we get a response . . .

CALLUM

Yes. I will see if they have any information on any of these names . . . and it is sent straight to you.

KATHY

How long will it take?

CALLUM

Obviously I'll tell them it's very urgent.

KATHY

You will?

CALLUM

Yes – why do you doubt that?

KATHY

I don't. I just know everything is called 'urgent' at the moment for everybody and of course because we're on different sides, as it were, it's difficult and probably a bit of a nuisance for you –

CALLUM

You keep saying that, about different sides – as far as I'm concerned, it just isn't true.

KATHY

Good. (*Straight at him.*) Then prove it to me.

CALLUM

I have to go.

Kathy *watches through the glass doors.* **Callum** *gets into a jeep outside the front entrance of the hotel, driven by the* **Second Lieutenant***.*

CALLUM
Go, go! As quick you can, Rogers! (*As the jeep roars off.*) But we don't need to kill any children on the way.

We stay on **Kathy** *for a moment.*

EXT. SUBURBAN STREETS/MILITARY HEADQUARTERS

We cut to the **Second Lieutenant** *driving furiously fast along the suburban streets, the residents watching them pass from behind net curtains.*

Then the jeep drives up to the mansion where the military HQ is housed. **Callum** *can see smoke rising from the bonfires, where they are still burning files.*

INT. WAINWRIGHT'S OFFICE. DAY

Brigadier Wainwright *is looking down at the tiny black notebooks.* **Callum** *is sitting opposite him in his office.*

WAINWRIGHT
And that's all you've got?! Notebooks from a doll's house!

CALLUM
They're full of interesting stuff, I've had a quick look – but no, I don't have a happy German for you, ready to work for us for the rest of his life, and give us all his secrets. I've failed completely. He wants to go home.

WAINWRIGHT
The only place he's not going is home.

I will have these doll's books checked out – but we need him cooperating with us.

CALLUM
Well, somebody else may do better than me – they're going to have to aren't they?!

WAINWRIGHT
Nobody else is going to do better. You have to do it . . . He could be of vital strategic importance, just crack his resolve.

CALLUM
The trouble is, I don't know how to do that . . . sir.

WAINWRIGHT
You've got a whole bloody hotel at your disposal, what more do you want?!

CALLUM
Well since you ask, a piano in my room would be nice . . . (*He smiles.*) but then I've only got three days left, it might not be worth it . . .

WAINWRIGHT
I lied. You've got four more days.

CALLUM
I won't be able to do it in four days, I can tell you that now.

WAINWRIGHT
You're going to bloody have to!

CALLUM
What's more, there's a woman from the War Crimes Unit poking around –

WAINWRIGHT
Miss Griffiths, yes I know.

CALLUM
Not that there's anything in his file that will be of interest to her – but she wants to go through those records that are stored in the attic of the hotel.

WAINWRIGHT
You can't let that happen, under any circumstances. Those are our files! There may be important people we're interested in that she turns out to be interested in too – be a total fucking nightmare! She'll want to lock them up for years, we want them working for us!

CALLUM
She gave me a list of names to get checked. (*Producing folder.*) I said I would.

WAINWRIGHT

Give it to me

Callum *hesitates.*

Come on, give me the list!

Callum *does so.*

CALLUM

She's not going to go away, sir.

WAINWRIGHT

Of course she isn't.

Suddenly an idea seems to hit him, his tone changes, his fleshy face close.

Has it occurred to you she could be useful to us, if she's handled right? Especially useful to you at this present moment?

CALLUM

How?

WAINWRIGHT

Oh come on, Ferguson, I've never known you be slow on the uptake before!

I will have these names checked, and depending on what we discover, you'll be able to give her what we find.

He looks straight at **Callum**, *who meets his gaze.*

Because she could be highly useful. And I can see you know exactly what I mean.

Their eyes meet. **Callum** *then looks at the little black notebooks on the desk.*

CALLUM

I better have those doll's books back, sir.

WAINWRIGHT

Why?

CALLUM

I've got to read them properly . . . because the only thing I can think of is to try to use his work to get him to open up . . . I need to make him want to share things with me. I have to show him I have knowledge.

Wainwright *looks sceptical, he hesitates.*

WAINWRIGHT

If you must.

He hands the black notebooks over.

But don't you dare lose them. And don't whatever you do give them back to him. Understand?

CALLUM

Very clearly . . . sir. (*He slips the tiny books into his pocket.*) Now you have to excuse me sir if that's okay . . . I happen to have another emergency going on right at this moment . . . (*He gets up.*)

WAINWRIGHT

So you're going to give it everything aren't you, Ferguson?

CALLUM

Yes, but I'm pretty certain everything isn't going to work.

EXT. HOSPITAL. DAY

Victor *is standing outside the hospital waiting for* **Callum**. *He is watching people bustle past him, smiling at some, scowling at others. He is eating something out of a paper bag. He sees* **Callum** *approach and smiles broadly.*

As **Callum** *reaches* **Victor**, *he sees he is eating raw potatoes out of the paper bag.*

CALLUM

That's ridiculous, what are you doing eating that? It's not all you've got to eat?! Do you need money, is that what you're saying?

VICTOR
I always need money, but these are good for you. Try one?

CALLUM
No thanks, I'm not eating raw potatoes!

VICTOR
I've been waiting ages here for you, so this is in fact my second helping! Better than anything they'll give me in there . . .

CALLUM
Victor!

VICTOR
What's that voice for . . . (*Imitates.*) 'Victor'?!

CALLUM
We need to get you some more medicine, maybe stronger – a new treatment. You need to remain calm in there and tell them the truth.

VICTOR
Calm! There's no point being calm at the moment – where are all these calm people?! I don't meet any, do you?!

INT. HOSPITAL ROOM. DAY

We cut inside a consulting room in the hospital. It has a frosted-glass wall through which we can see silhouetted figures moving. The **Doctor** *is a man in his fifties with a large head and a very circumspect manner. He is staring at* **Victor**'s *file.*

Callum *is sitting next to* **Victor**.

DOCTOR
So you haven't had a job for three months . . . since the incident when you struck your employer?

VICTOR
I did not strike him, I had a disagreement with him that could only be resolved one way. I haven't hit anybody since – not unprovoked, anyway!

The **Doctor** *looks up sharply.*

Of course, there have been times I've been provoked, but that is unavoidable at the moment . . . (*He smiles sweetly.*) As I'm sure you find yourself.

DOCTOR

You say you have these migraines . . . (*He looks down at the file.*) And that causes you not to be able to control your behaviour? And you have in fact presented yourself at this hospital several times recently, saying it's an emergency?

VICTOR

Clearly coming here was a mistake . . . each time.

CALLUM

My brother is very keen to work, to lead a normal life again. But like a lot of people, his experiences during the war have stayed with him and mean –

VICTOR

It's not about the war! You're wrong! You're the one who had the worse experiences –

CALLUM

And the memories cause sudden changes in his mood, and that can lead to some rather chaotic behaviour –

VICTOR

I'm sorry, it's not about the war, it's about now – what's happening now! (*Indicating* **Callum**.) And while we're about it, he's the one who has the nightmares. And now he is the one who has to snatch people off the streets of Germany and then do anything to make them work for us –

CALLUM

Shut up, Victor, stop this!

VICTOR

And they have all these outfits with silly names – MI16, T-Force, BIOS – chasing after him for results . . . ! And none of them know what the other is doing! Talk about chaos, that's real chaos!

CALLUM

You will stop this, Victor, at once. (*To* **Doctor**.) I'm sorry about this –

VICTOR

Quite right. He wants me to remain calm. But also tell the truth . . . (*He leans towards the* **Doctor**.) And in case you were wondering, we can, of course, afford to pay for any new treatment – although when this National Health Service starts, you won't need to keep thinking about that!

CALLUM

Victor.

DOCTOR

What I will do – (*Checking file.*) Mr Ferguson, is to refer you to a specialist as soon as possible. Though in the meantime, I suggest you find something to occupy your mind. A lot of returning servicemen who have difficulties find that something that occupies their mind each day is –

VICTOR

I'm glad I don't occupy your mind. (*He smiles sweetly at the* **Doctor**.) I wouldn't want to be inside there, inside that dome!

EXT. HOSPITAL. DAY

We cut to **Callum** *and* **Victor** *on the steps of the hospital.* **Callum** *is furious.*

CALLUM

What was that?! What on earth was that about?! What's the point, if you're rude to everybody all the time, nobody is going to help you?!

VICTOR

That doctor had no interest in helping me.

CALLUM

You don't know that.

VICTOR

No interest at all.

CALLUM

But believe it or not, I do, and I'm going to see you get well, I will Victor . . . but you've got to stop behaving like this, because you know you can, you know you can control it –

VICTOR

Can I?

CALLUM

Some of it, yes! A lot more than you are! And what was all that stuff about me? Why did you suddenly start that?

VICTOR

I was only trying to tell the truth!

CALLUM

The truth? About me! You don't know anything about that Victor –

VICTOR

Don't I? (*Grins.*) We'll see about that . . . (*Suddenly.*) Getting nowhere with your German are you? In a bit of a panic?

CALLUM

There's no panic! (*He smiles despite himself at* **Victor**'s *insight.*) There's absolutely no panic. I always have a plan.

INT. BASEMENT BALLROOM. DAY

We cut to **Richie** *rehearsing on the drums, a powerful explosion of drumming. He is getting more confident. His drumming runs under the next scene.*

INT. THIRD-FLOOR PASSAGE, CONNIGTON. DAY

Ringwood *and* **Callum** *approaching down the passage. They are both in different clothes than the previous hotel scene; we have the sense of a time cut, a day or two later.* **Ringwood**'s *tone is exasperated.*

RINGWOOD

I don't know why we have to do this sir . . . treating them like film stars to try to make them work for us?! (*It suddenly erupts out of him.*) We won the fucking war didn't we?! They were the enemy till last year! Till a few months ago!

Callum *looks sideways at him.*

Excuse me, sorry sir, it just makes my blood boil, it isn't right.

CALLUM

It is. If it works.

INT. DIETER'S BEDROOM DAY

We cut to **Dieter** *looking up sharply. He is reading a book.* **Lotte** *is sitting on her bed, squashed into a corner.* **Callum** *and* **Ringwood** *are standing in the doorway.*

CALLUM

Just came to tell you . . . (*Smiles breezily.*) You will eat all your meals from now on in the basement ballroom – where the music is and the food is much more interesting.

Dieter's *expression is impassive.*

And here are your books back (*He produces the tiny black books.*) With some of my notes . . . you'll be pleased I think, it shows I can appreciate it. (*With feeling.*) It's remarkable your work.

Now **Dieter**'s *eyes flicker with interest. He receives his books back.* **Ringwood** *looks very surprised that they are being returned, real tension on his face.*

DIETER

But I'm not allowed to go out still? Even for a few minutes?

CALLUM

Not yet – but everything you need will be provided here. (*He smiles knowingly.*) And I mean everything . . . (*Turning to* **Lotte**.) And there's a large car waiting for Lotte downstairs to take her shopping.

Lotte *looks excited at this. She glances across at her father, who indicates she can go.*

INT. BASEMENT BALLROOM. DAY

We cut to the basement. **Eva** *is on the piano; she has joined the rehearsal with* **Richie**.

EXT. FRONT ENTRANCE OF CONNINGTON. DAY

Lotte, *escorted by* **Ringwood**, *moves down the steps outside the Connington and towards a large car.* **Rachel** *is on the back seat waiting for her.*

RACHEL

Nice to see you, my dear

Lotte *sits next to her.*

People tell me it's impossible in this town – but let's see if we can have a truly tremendous shop!

INT. BASEMENT BALLROOM. DAY

We cut to **Eva** *on the piano,* **Richie** *on the drums.* **Callum** *is standing in the doorway of the basement ballroom watching them.* **Eva** *stops playing.*

EVA

Who are you?!

CALLUM

What do you mean?

EVA

I don't know who you are Mr Ferguson . . . you seem to have some sort of power in this hotel!

CALLUM

I don't have any power here, no.

EVA

You're lying! (*She grins.*) I'm suddenly told I have a booking here for the next few nights, which I have to agree to! And they pushed money into my face!

CALLUM

Who told you that was anything to do with me?

EVA

Nobody did . . . but for some reason I have a feeling it was you. I don't know who you are really and what you are doing . . . but you have influence, and that always makes me suspicious.

CALLUM

No need to be suspicious.

EVA

I ought to tell you, in the US they think I'm a communist.

CALLUM

And are you a communist?

EVA

That's for you to find out, Mr Ferguson . . . (*She begins to play.*) now get the hell out of here, I'm busy!

Richie *starting drumming again hard.*

INT. SECOND-FLOOR BEDROOM PASSAGE. AFTERNOON

We cut to the second-floor passage, full of late afternoon light. Two delivery men and a hotel porter are wheeling an upright piano along the passage. **Callum** *is standing by his bedroom door watching it approach. The workmen reach him and show him the delivery address with his name on it.* **Callum** *signs for it.*

CALLUM

Never underestimate that old bastard Wainwright, I should know that!

At that very moment a voice rings out from the other end of the passage. He looks up to see **Ringwood** *approaching with* **Lotte**.

RINGWOOD
We came to find you!

Lotte *is dressed in a beautiful little red dress, as if she is dressed for a children's ball. She looks thrilled with her dress.*

CALLUM
You look wonderful!

LOTTE
I have a message for you, Mr Ferguson

She hands him an envelope.

It's from the lady . . . from Mrs Rachel Lombard.

INT. BASEMENT BALLROOM. NIGHT

*It is night now. The basement ballroom is full of cigarette and cigar smoke, and diners eating at the round tables. **Eva** and the band are playing a powerful, soulful number.*

*We see **Lotte** sitting in her splendid dress looking quite excited to be up so late. She notices **Anna** serving at the tables. **Lotte** is drawn to the youngest face in the room. **Anna** comes over and takes her plate away and smiles. A moment of connection.*

ANNA
Lovely dress . . . you're a lucky girl!

Dieter *ignores this moment. He is sitting impassively eating his food next to* **Callum**. *Tonight* **Dieter** *seems oblivious to the music.*

Across the room, **Julia** *is sitting with a middle-aged man. She is looking across at* **Callum**. *He beckons to her. She excuses herself from her table and moves up to* **Callum**, *who introduces her to* **Dieter** *as the music plays.* **Julia** *is wearing a low-cut dress and looks really sexy.* **Dieter** *smiles faintly at her; he shows as much interest in her as if she had come over with the bill. After she's moved off* **Dieter** *leans over to* **Callum**, *his voice quiet.*

DIETER

That was a little obvious don't you think?

CALLUM

(*grins*)

Maybe a little . . .

DIETER

I will return to my room now.

CALLUM

But the music has only just started.

DIETER

Unless I'm forced to stay here I will go back to my room. (*Indicating the minders at the door.*) I see the jailors are waiting for me.

He takes one of the black books from his pockets, his face close.

I read what you said about my work by the way.

CALLUM

Good. I just wanted to share my thoughts, make a few suggestions . . . what do you think?

Dieter *stares straight at him for a second, his voice intense.*

DIETER

That you're not even close.

CALLUM

Close?

DIETER

To being in my league. Not qualified really to say anything about my work . . .

Callum *is truly startled. He tries hard not to show his surprise at this rejection of his expertise, but he doesn't totally succeed.* **Dieter** *takes* **Lotte**'s *hand and leaves; the watchers from the third floor escort him away.*

Lotte *looks back from the doorway and sees* **Callum** *taking* **Rachel**'s *note out of his pocket and re-reading it.*

EXT. ALEX AND RACHEL'S HOUSE. MORNING

We see **Callum** *approaching* **Alex** *and* **Rachel***'s imposing town house. It stands in a period terrace. The house next door is completely boarded up because of bomb damage. A maid opens the door and* **Callum** *is ushered into an elegant hall.*

INT. ALEX AND RACHEL'S HOUSE. HALL AND DRAWING ROOM. MORNING

CALLUM

I believe Mrs Lombard is expecting me.

A voice calls from above him:

RACHEL

Mrs Lombard is up here, come on up, Cal.

Rachel *is standing at the top of the stairs staring down at him.*

Callum *starts going up the stairs.*

RACHEL

I have to confess it still takes me a moment or two to recognise my name, 'Mrs Lombard' . . . Not quite used to it yet. I was Mrs Goetz for a number of years, as you probably know . . .

CALLUM

I didn't know that, no.

RACHEL

I keep forgetting you and Alex haven't really had a chance to catch up yet! Well Mr Goetz is no more, he's been gone three years now . . . (*Momentary pause.*) He died . . .

But that Goetz name seems to really stick to me for some reason . . . (*She smiles charmingly.*) Maybe it's because of all his money . . . !

She suddenly looks straight at him.

I hope you're not going to be shocked now, Cal?

CALLUM
Shocked? By what? It's quite difficult to shock me.

RACHEL
(leading him into the drawing room)
By what this place looks like . . .

All the furniture has been piled up at one end, except for the grand piano.

> As you see, I've pushed everything around – because so much of the furniture is truly hideous . . . but of course one doesn't want to seem extravagant, what with the present shortages. So I'm going to get rid of it bit by bit. I want to create something a little more lovely . . .

She turns to **Callum**, *a warm smile.*

> I wouldn't let most people see my house like this!

CALLUM
I'm flattered. You said in your note you had a favour to ask me?

ALEX
She does!

Alex *suddenly appears at the other end of the room. He greets* **Callum** *warmly.*

> It's a very small favour . . . but I think she's a little bit embarrassed by it, aren't you darling?!

RACHEL
I am . . .

ALEX
(grins)
But I'm not going to help you! *(Moving across the room.)* Look at this piano, Cal, it's the only splendid bit of furniture we've got, and it's totally undamaged, perfectly in tune. You must make Cal show you how good he is, darling . . . you must make him play, he's terrific –

CALLUM

No, no, no, no, I'm not any more, I'm totally out of practice.

RACHEL

Maybe it'll come back . . .

ALEX

He won't have lost it, he was too good, it's the truth! We just have to make him admit it . . . remember, Cal is very good at finding out the truth about everybody else . . .

RACHEL

Is he?! Now I've been warned.

ALEX

We go back a long way, of course.

CALLUM

Yes . . . Alex has always been a great help to me . . . opening doors after Oxford –

RACHEL

That's what close friends are for!

ALEX

Exactly! (*He smiles affectionately.*) But Cal never needed me really . . . He's a scholarship boy, no advantages but nothing stops him! . . . (*He turns in the door.*) And underneath he's not that modest, I promise! (*As he leaves.*) Ask him the favour . . .

Rachel *and* **Callum** *alone.*

RACHEL

First, Cal, you must answer this completely honestly, if you can.

CALLUM

I'll try. (*He smiles.*)

RACHEL

So – would it be absolutely dreadful of me to hold a party?

Callum *laughs.*

Why are you laughing?

CALLUM

I had no idea what you were going to say?! Of course it wouldn't, people still have parties!

RACHEL

Yes, but the whole town is so miserable. I didn't know, having just arrived – if it was the right thing to do.

She is standing by the window with her back to him.

It's a terrible thing to say, but when I was here during the war it was –

CALLUM

You were here? I didn't know you'd been here before.

RACHEL

Oh yes, at the beginning of '41, right in the middle of the Blitz . . .

Callum *joins her by the window.*

My husband was a foreign emissary for the president . . . and the awful thing is – and you will hate me for saying this – but London was really exciting then . . . everybody was so alive, living just for the next day, but so full of ideas and hope too! It was extraordinary, the atmosphere . . . frightening of course but – and this is the terrible part – amazingly pleasurable . . . Do you hate me for saying that?

CALLUM

Of course not. That isn't how I remember it, but then I wasn't in London much –

RACHEL

No, you were doing incredibly important things . . . secret things.

CALLUM

Sometimes, yes.

RACHEL

And now I'm back here and the friends I knew before have vanished . . . I don't know anybody really – so a party seemed a good idea. But because people are depressed and life's hard, I don't want it to seem insensitive . . . vulgar, even?

CALLUM

(*looking at her in her exquisite dress*)

There's no danger of that.

RACHEL

Thank you. We're allowed to flatter each other, just this once, I think . . . (*She looks straight at him.*) As long as we don't make a habit of it.

CALLUM

What's the favour, Mrs Lombard . . .?

RACHEL

Rachel . . . (*She moves.*) I want you to ask that terrifying singer, Eva, whether she will sing at my party?

CALLUM

Ah . . . ! That's not quite such a small favour!

RACHEL

So she scares you too, does she?! I don't think she approved of me, hopefully that's only temporary – maybe it was my dancing?! But she might agree if it comes from you, from a fellow musician?

CALLUM

An amateur musician . . .

RACHEL

Her music will be so good at the party. Will you do it?

CALLUM

Yes. (*He smiles.*) But it may take me a day or two to summon up the courage . . . By the way, I nearly forgot, I must arrange for you to be paid for the little girl's dress.

RACHEL
Don't be silly. (*She smiles.*) Let it be my contribution to your assignment!

INT. VICTOR'S LODGINGS. STAIRCASE/BEDROOM

We hear a record, a Beethoven symphony, pouring out of **Victor**'*s bedroom and filling the whole of the boarding house. His bedroom door is firmly shut.*

Mrs Tooley *is running up the stairs.*

MRS TOOLEY
Mr Ferguson! Mr Ferguson! (*She bangs on the door.*) Turn that down, Mr Ferguson!

Victor *opens the door, the music is deafening.*

VICTOR
Mrs Tooley! I was so hoping you'd drop by.

He makes no immediate attempt to turn down the music. **Mrs Tooley** *stares into the room. It is full of objects and fragments of houses that* **Victor** *has picked up from all over London – stained glass, half a fireplace, ornamental tiles and street railings.*

The objects are haphazard but rather attractive.

MRS TOOLEY
The music is far too loud, turn it off at once! And this room is such a horrible mess . . . and it gets worse every week –

VICTOR
A mess?! (*He turns the music down but not off.*) It's my collection, Mrs Tooley, that I've picked up from all over the place. And I'm adding to it because I have to occupy my mind! Is there anything you particularly fancy? I might part with it, if you ask me nicely.

MRS TOOLEY
Mr Ferguson, I have warned you many times about your room, and your music. I will not have strange behaviour in this house.

VICTOR
I quite agree. There must be no strangeness here, under any circumstances.

His face is very close, **Mrs Tooley** *is suddenly quite frightened.*

We'll both keep a lookout for it, I promise.

INT. DIETER'S ROOM. THIRD-FLOOR PASSAGE. EARLY EVENING

The Beethoven hangs over the cut, as we see **Dieter** *sitting very still in his room, reading a book. The door of his bedroom is open.* **Lotte** *is being taken for a walk by one of her minders, up and down the passage. She has insisted on wearing her red dress.*

Suddenly we see a nervous look come into her eyes.

Mr Emmanuel *is coming down the passage towards them.*

MR EMMANUEL
My little one, out for your walk are you? How good you look!

DIETER
(*calling through the open door*)
They won't let us out, so she walks here . . .

Mr Emmanuel *nods at* **Dieter** *politely and then turns back to* **Lotte**.

MR EMMANUEL
We must have another one of our adventures soon, mustn't we . . .? (*Turns to the minder.*) I mean a story from a storybook, of course, only that! I will read to her.

INT. CALLUM'S BEDROOM. EVENING

We track across **Callum**'s *bedroom. He is sitting at his new upright piano, playing. There is deep concentration on his face; he is completely immersed.*

Then he senses something; he looks up sharply and stops playing.

Salter *is standing very still in the doorway, watching him.*

SALTER

So you are a pianist as well?! You sound a little bit out of practice to me . . .

CALLUM

This is my bedroom.

SALTER

I do realise that.

CALLUM

I don't remember inviting you . . . When I want an audience, I'll let you know.

Callum *has remained at the piano, determined not to let* **Salter** *unsettle him.*

SALTER

Just checking on your progress Mr Ferguson.

CALLUM

When I've made any, I expect somebody'll remember to inform you.

SALTER

They'd better . . . I hear you're just mollycoddling the German?

CALLUM

That's right.

SALTER

You've still got those little black books you've found I hope?

Callum *turns.*

Yes, I do know about them.

CALLUM

Of course I've got them. (*He smiles nonchalantly.*) Never let them out of my sight.

SALTER
(standing over him)
Well it's reassuring to see you so busy anyway, so thoroughly focused on the task.

CALLUM

It may surprise you, but there isn't a moment when I'm not thinking about it. (*Sharp smile.*) And I'm confident I will succeed . . .

SALTER

Still making up the rules as you go along are you?!

CALLUM

And of course, if I don't pull it off . . . (*Looks straight at* **Salter**.) You can have a try yourself, the way you lot like to do things – beating the shit out of him and all that.

SALTER

You don't want to think about not succeeding, I promise you.

CALLUM

Then I won't. (*He gets up.*) And now, if you'll excuse me, there's a lady waiting for me downstairs . . .

He is very close to **Salter** *now.*

Quite an attractive lady, as it happens.

SALTER

Wainwright may be prepared to give you more time. (*His steely blue eyes.*) But I'm not . . .

CALLUM

You have no idea how alarming I find that threat!

INT. BASEMENT BALLROOM. EVENING

A subjective track across the basement ballroom. We move among the tables, and discover **Kathy** *sitting on her own in a corner, having a drink. She looks up as* **Callum** *approaches. It is early evening and the ballroom is not very full, and there is no band playing.* **Kathy** *is wearing an evening dress, but quite a plain one.*

KATHY

Mr Ferguson, good evening.

CALLUM
Miss Griffiths . . . and before I even sit down, I have something to give you – here is the list, with all the names checked . . . where we think some of them might be.

KATHY
That is quick! (*She takes the list.*) Extraordinarily quick, in fact . . . (*She looks across at him.*)

CALLUM
Yes. I told you I would label it 'very urgent'.

Callum *sits as* **Kathy** *glances at the information. She is impressed, despite herself.*

KATHY
This is useful . . . thank you.

Anna *appears with a tray of appetisers, little vol-au-vents on a silver tray.*

ANNA
Would you like to try some of these? They're a new recipe, new this evening!

KATHY
We certainly would!

As **Anna** *serves them both, she smiles sweetly.* **Callum** *is struck by her young face.* **Kathy** *takes a bite of the vol-au-vent.*

These are delicious! (*She looks across at* **Callum**.) You've got yourself nicely settled in here, haven't you?!

CALLUM
Absolutely! I even have a piano in my room.

KATHY
You do?! They must really think you're important then.

CALLUM
Or desperately in need of help. Something to inspire me . . .

KATHY
You'll soon be running the whole of the hotel!

Callum *smiles at this, watching her closely.*

> Talking of which – are you really telling me you don't have any more rooms in this place? Or at least one big room where you are keeping your records?

CALLUM

I am really telling you that.

KATHY

(pauses, giving him a searching look)
I know it must drive you lot to distraction, me suddenly popping up all the time, usually without an appointment, and I hate having to do it that way – but time is so short. And it's not just the trials in Nuremberg that are important, everybody thinks that's all that matters, but that's simply not true! It's all the other people we need to find, that we need to trace, before their trails become invisible. We need to stop them disappearing.

(She drinks.) Sorry . . . I just feel I have to say that.

CALLUM

I do realise, Miss Griffiths, time is very short.

KATHY

Anyway, I'm going to surprise you – I'm going to stop lecturing you tonight . . . be a little less serious, because I can be like that, believe it or not. *(She laughs.)* Although it's been a long time, it may not be very convincing!

CALLUM

Why would you want to do that? Be less serious?

KATHY

To get your attention, naturally, *(She smiles.)* try another approach . . .

CALLUM

Miss Griffiths, you have my attention. *(He leans forward.)* In fact, you have all my attention – and I'm going to prove it to

you. I will have something for you, something else, in the
next twenty-four hours or so, which will mean us working
together . . .

KATHY

Working together? (*Puzzled.*) You and me?

CALLUM

Yes. Now I've got your attention . . . Are you interested?

KATHY

Of course I am.

INT. HOTEL KITCHENS/PASSAGE. NIGHT

*We see **Leonard** preparing some different vol-au-vents and savoury
delicacies, bigger than the ones available in the basement. We then see a
special silver tray being made up with the delicacies on them. A waiter picks
up the tray and we follow it in a series of cuts, out of the kitchen, along the
back passage, into the main passage and towards the drawing rooms.
Callum is coming down the main passage in the opposite direction. He
catches sight of this tray of new delicacies and cannot resist following it,
hoping to get one.*

*The waiter stops at the entrance to the gold drawing room. He ignores the
notice saying* DANGER, NO ENTRY *and moves inside.* **Callum** *follows him.*

INT. GOLD DRAWING ROOM. NIGHT

*At the other end of the gold drawing room **Harold** is sitting in splendid
isolation. The tray of delicacies is for him. He thanks the waiter, then he sees*
Callum *watching him.*

HAROLD

Ah! You discovered me about to make a complete pig of
myself, Mr Ferguson.

CALLUM

So they've opened up this room, have they?

HAROLD

They've opened it at my request, only for me . . . at my own risk. You must have one of these . . . (*Eating the vol-au-vent.*) In fact several, they're delicious!

But **Callum** *stays near the door.*

The food has suddenly exploded at this hotel . . . You must have noticed that?! A few mistakes, of course, like serving corn on the cob, but these are a real surprise. It must have been that Austrian cabbage that started it all!

CALLUM

Maybe. So you're here without your ward tonight, Mr Lindsay-Jones?

HAROLD

Yes, tempted back by the ingenious food. (*He looks up.*) And because I was hoping to see you. After I'd finished these, I was about to look for you . . .

Callum *gives him a steely look, thinking he might have a connection to* **Salter**.

CALLUM

So you've got some kind of message for me have you? About getting results?

HAROLD

I have no message, no. I have something personal to ask you. We don't know each other, Mr Ferguson, I realise . . .

CALLUM

We certainly don't.

HAROLD

But since you haven't denied you're a member of T-Force . . . (*Smiles.*) And are not doing so now, I want you to arrange for me to go to the military camp in Enfield, Altringham Park. Because it is high security, it's impossible to get in there unless you have a contact.

CALLUM

Really? You need a contact? I'd have thought for somebody like you, that would be easy . . .

HAROLD

Somebody like me? You think I'm in some way connected with the Secret Service, Mr Ferguson?! No, no, I'm afraid I haven't got an exciting or mysterious job at all. I'm merely a Foreign Office official a few weeks away from leaving the service.

That's all I want – to visit the camp. You can keep guard on me while I'm there the whole time. Will you arrange it? . . . Tomorrow?

CALLUM
(*startled*)
Tomorrow?! . . . Why do you want to go there?

Harold *looks straight at him.*

HAROLD
It needs to be in the evening. Please do this for me.

EXT. MILITARY CAMP. DUSK

We see a shot through the windscreen of a jeep, approaching the gates of the military camp, which are manned by sentries. It is dusk. In front of the gates a solitary figure is standing, in overcoat, and leaning on an umbrella. It is **Harold.**

Then we see it is **Callum** *driving the jeep, staring at* **Harold** *as he gets closer.* **Callum** *has no idea what to expect, he is intrigued but also amused. He reaches* **Harold** *at the gates.*

HAROLD
Admirably on time, thank you.

CALLUM
So jump in, Mr Lindsay-Jones.

Harold *sits in the jeep.* **Callum** *shows his pass to the sentries and drives through the gates.* **Harold** *is holding his umbrella tight, staring ahead, concentrating intently as they move down the long drive.*

CALLUM
We could have met at the hotel, I could have driven you all the way, Mr Lindsay-Jones.

HAROLD
No, no . . . I needed to make the journey on my own.

Callum *glances at him, seeing his intense mood.*

Military vehicles are passing them in the other direction along the drive.

CALLUM
Where in the camp do you want to go?

HAROLD
Please just drive, for the moment.

They pass the stable block where there is a lot of activity, vehicles moving, men in uniform coming in and out of the buildings. The light is falling fast.

HAROLD
Now, up to the house, please.

We cut to the jeep stopping on the hill, at the bottom of the steps that run up to the huge, ruined facade of the house. There are several signs warning it is dangerous to enter. **Harold** *gets out of the jeep and stares up at the building, which has no roof, no glass in the windows. The pillars of the portico are scarred and blackened by the bomb blast.*

HAROLD
Now we must wait, Mr Ferguson, just a few minutes, if that's allowed, until it is dark. Before we go in.

CALLUM
It has to be completely dark?

HAROLD
If that's not too inconvenient, yes.

Callum *watching* **Harold** *closely.*

CALLUM
Well that could just be a good idea! These ruins are used for combat training now, house-to-house fighting . . . with live

ammunition . . . I'm not sure they do it in the dark – so there might be less chance of us getting shot!

                    HAROLD
              (turns, his tone serious)
You don't have to come with me, you know.

Callum *stares at* **Harold**, *surprised by his tone, the intensity of his mood.* **Harold** *stands a little apart, leaning on his umbrella, gazing up at the building.*

We see a wide shot of the camp, as the light dips into night. Then we cut back to **Callum** *and* **Harold**. *Arc lights have come on high up in the building.*

                    CALLUM
You didn't live here by any chance, Mr Lindsay Jones?

                    HAROLD
No, no, absolutely not! I'm not an aristocrat, Mr Ferguson, far from it . . .

Shall we go in? (*He is moving up the steps.*) You really don't need to come if you don't feel it's safe, but I'm going to go in – unless you stop me, of course.

Harold *sets off up the steps without looking back. And then he enters the house through the pillars of the portico.* **Callum** *follows him.*

We cut to **Harold** *moving through the ruined hall and ballroom of the great charred building. A high shot of the two of them, isolated figures among the ruins.*

Then we cut down to be with them, as **Callum** *looks around, checking that nobody is lurking on the walls staring down, or in the alcoves of the building.*

He then lets out a whooping series of shouts.

                    CALLUM
If we make enough noise, they ought to know we're here, and not use us for target practice!

                    HAROLD
Make as much noise as you like, Mr Ferguson, there's no danger of you waking the building. (*He stares about him.*)

I didn't live here . . . but I did come here a few times, my wife knew the family . . . Sir Henry Markham.

And the last time I was here . . . it was just three weeks before the outbreak of the war . . . there was the most enormous ball, a coming-out party for the daughter of the family, it was the most extraordinary occasion . . .

He is moving among the ruins, staring at all the rooms, which now have no ceilings.

Everything was so lavish, the fountains were all lit up in the garden . . . There were flowers and decorations over all of these walls . . . The king and queen were here, princes, ambassadors, Neville Chamberlain and half the cabinet, Noël Coward and film stars . . . in fact, it took two hours to get along the drive because there were so many cars . . . *(We are close on his eyes.)* And my wife, Isabelle . . .

We move in on **Harold**. *And then we see, from his point of view, glimpses of shadowy figures in ball gowns, a long way away, passing through the ruined rooms. We hear the sound of laughter, music and voices.*

Flashback:

Suddenly a door opens, and for a moment we are standing in a room full of light and decorations and pictures and people.

A figure turns in the distance, his wife, looking directly at him.

We cut back to **Harold** *in the ruined ballroom. We are very close on his face.*

HAROLD

My wife was wearing a particularly fetching dress that night. She died less than a year later in one of the first bombing raids of the Blitz . . . I wasn't with her, I was working late at the Foreign Office . . .

It wasn't here that she died . . . but for some reason, whenever I think of her, I see her as she was that night . . .

We see her, a figure in the distance. And then we see a group of women crossing the ruined room. She joins them and disappears. We cut back to **Harold** *and* **Callum**.

CALLUM

You think of her here during the ball?

HAROLD

Yes . . . (*Suddenly very sharp.*) And they were *all* here that night, Mr Ferguson . . . right where we're standing! Can you imagine it?! (*Suddenly he lets out a little laugh.*) And now look . . . !

We see cigarette packets and fag ends all over the ruined ballroom floor. **Harold** *stoops to pick up an empty packet of Woodbines and then turns, holding it, calling up towards the high ruined walls:*

If there's anybody here watching – then shoot me for being so violently nostalgic . . . ! (*Pointing to the middle of his forehead.*) Shoot me right here for sentimentality!

Silence. His voice echoes round the ruined building. He looks straight at **Callum.**

I'm sorry I made it sound so urgent about coming here . . . I just didn't want to lose contact with you, in case you left the hotel. I know you don't believe me, Mr Ferguson.

CALLUM

About the ball? Of course I do.

HAROLD

No, about the fact that I claim not to be part of the Secret Service.

CALLUM

I don't believe you, no.

HAROLD

Well what I'm about to say will make you believe me even less . . . but I've looked into who you are, Mr Ferguson, I have checked a few things about you.

CALLUM

I thought you had . . .

HAROLD

But only by asking your friend Alex Lombard, because we are both at the Foreign Office.

I know you worked with Mr Frank Whittle before the war on his invention and development of the jet engine – and you saw at first hand the terrible obstacles and indifference that he encountered, and what that led to . . . I know you understand the cost of ministerial incompetence and official deceit . . . Am I right, Mr Ferguson?

CALLUM

You could be.

We move in on **Harold** *as he stands in the middle of the ruins.*

HAROLD

Now it is possible I saw some things myself, in the circles that I move in . . . that could be of interest to you, Mr Ferguson . . . I'm guessing, of course, that you'll be interested?

Callum *watching him.*

But I know some things that few other people do . . . about what really went on . . . how we could have won the war before it had even started, how none of this need have happened . . . ! Stories about some of the highest people in the land, and what they have got away with . . . what they actually did, in secret . . .

I have to piece it all together still . . . find out a little more before I'm certain . . . (*He turns.*) And I might need your help.

CALLUM

Might you Mr Lindsay-Jones?

HAROLD

I might . . . I haven't decided yet if I absolutely need somebody else or not.

But if you are intrigued, or quite interested, or merely just curious . . . you must let me know – because it's possible you might really understand . . .

Harold *watches* **Callum** *closely for his reaction.*

CALLUM

Well I'd be an idiot not to be curious, Mr Lindsay-Jones, but at this moment I have a very full schedule, especially, as it happens, tonight!

We cut wide, **Callum** *staring at* **Harold** *in the middle of the ruined ballroom.*

HAROLD

Always so busy . . . even tonight?!

INT. SECRET FLOOR, CONNINGTON. NIGHT

We cut to the secret attic room. **Ringwood**, **Ruth** *and one other transcriber sitting with headphones, listening in.*

Callum *enters the room. He moves towards* **Ringwood**, *who is concentrating so deeply he hasn't seen him.* **Callum**'s *mood is edgy, tense.*

CALLUM

Who are you listening to?

RINGWOOD

Oh it's you, sir!

CALLUM

I'd like to know who the hell you're listening to?!

RINGWOOD

Oh, it's just one of the other people we're interested in.

CALLUM

I didn't realise you were still listening to other people?

RINGWOOD

Yes, I told you that on the first day, don't you remember, sir? It's just three other rooms, not nearly as important as Mr Koehler. I didn't want to bother you with the details, sir –

CALLUM

I didn't know you could speak German?

RINGWOOD

I can't sir, but they're speaking French . . .

He offers up the headphones.

It's somebody who claims to be Swiss . . .

CALLUM
(*doesn't bother to listen*)
Okay . . . I like to know everything that's going on,
Ringwood, always. But you're right – tonight is not the night.

RINGWOOD
Yes, when's it going to happen, sir? Do you know?

CALLUM
Around three o'clock in the morning . . .

INT. THIRD-FLOOR PASSAGE/DIETER'S ROOM

We cut to **Callum** *knocking on the door of* **Dieter**'s *room.* **Lotte** *opens the door. She starts at him coldly.*

CALLUM
I just came to see how you are? And I'd like a word with your father.

LOTTE
My father will not talk to you.

Lotte *shuts the door in his face.* **Callum** *moves off, anger in his eyes. We see* **Julia** *pass him in the passage.* **Callum** *is so preoccupied, he does not even notice her.* **Julia** *turns to watch him go.*

INT. CALLUM'S BEDROOM. NIGHT

We cut to **Callum** *lying in his bed, fully dressed, his eyes open. The clock by his bed says it is ten past one. We move in on his eyes. Far away there is the sound of voices, of the outdoors, birds singing, and then the unmistakable sound of eggs being fried.*

EXT. FLASHBACK. A WOOD. DAY

We cut to a frying pan full of an English breakfast being cooked. Then we cut wide to see an army cook preparing food for a group of soldiers in camouflage uniforms, manning a position in a wood. The sound of the eggs is getting louder and louder. Suddenly, the soldiers are ambushed, relentless machine-gun fire from the bushes all around them. We see a flash cut of somebody's head being shot away, the blood and other matter splashing across the eggs in the pan.

INT. CALLUM'S BEDROOM. NIGHT

Callum's *eyes spring open, somebody is knocking at the door. He looks urgently at the clock. It is only one twenty-five. The knocking gets louder. He moves to the door and opens it.* **Julia** *is standing in the passage in her nightdress and dressing gown.*

JULIA
Hello . . . (*She smiles.*) It's so extraordinary having to try to get to sleep next door to somebody who never sleeps. (*She looks straight at him.*) I just came to see if I could do anything about that?

INT. CALLUM'S BEDROOM NIGHT

We cut to a wide shot of the bedroom. **Callum** *is sitting on the bed smoking.* **Julia** *is sitting on a chair next to the piano, also smoking.*

CALLUM
So next door's your real room?

JULIA
My 'real' room, yes. What are you waiting for tonight?

CALLUM
How do you know I'm waiting for anything?

JULIA
Because you seem very tense.

CALLUM

It's that obvious, is it?

Julia *gets up and moves over to the bed.*

JULIA

When is it going to happen, whatever it is?

CALLUM

In about an hour and a half.

JULIA

Then we might have time, mightn't we . . .

She takes off her dressing gown and sits on the edge of bed, right next to him.

JULIA

Don't look like that! Lots of people would be pleased! (*She laughs.*) Thrilled in fact . . .

CALLUM

What makes you think I'm not?

JULIA

Oh come on! You should see your face! You're such a snob . . .

She touches him.

You're thinking, 'Am I going to have to pay for this? Is that what she expects?' But you know . . .

She starts to unbutton his shirt.

I'm not really a tart at all, that's what you think I am isn't it?

CALLUM

No. You have far too posh a voice.

JULIA

Oh, so *you* are a snob! Well I didn't used to sound like this as a kid. I had to change my voice to stand any chance of getting on as an actress. I should be really furious that you think I am a tart.

CALLUM
(*lightly*)
So why aren't you furious with me then?

JULIA
I don't know . . . (*She smiles.*) maybe because we're both insomniacs . . .

INT. ATTIC ROOM. NIGHT

We cut up to the attic room, only **Ruth** *is there now. She has her headphones on. We move closer towards her, until we hear the voices she is listening to. Suddenly we realise she is listening to* **Callum** *and* **Julia***. We hear* **Julia***'s voice saying, 'It's not good to be so obsessed with work, not good at all . . . '*

INT. CALLUM'S ROOM. NIGHT

We cut back to **Callum***'s room. Both of them are now naked, sitting facing each other, entwined together on the bed. She is kissing him.*

JULIA
It's not good to be so obsessed with work, not good at all.

You are thinking, 'She's got the room next door, will I ever be able to get rid of her?!'

CALLUM
No . . . (*He smiles.*) you don't know everything I'm thinking, and I'm certainly not thinking that . . .

JULIA
Good.

Julia *gently pushes him down on the bed; they start to make love.*

But I've got to stop you thinking so much.

CALLUM
Yes . . . (*He smiles.*) especially about later tonight . . . me having to take advice from the lunatics . . . That fat man Salter or whatever his name is, and his friends . . . the vermin!

JULIA
(*laughs*)
You start talking about a fat man at a time like this!

She kisses him.

I have got to stop that . . .

She lies on top of him, kissing him.

INT. ATTIC ROOM. NIGHT

*We move in on **Ruth**, as she listens to them making love. Her face is impassive, detached. We see her make a note of the time.*

INT. DIETER/LOTTE'S BEDROOM. NIGHT

*It is pitch black in **Dieter**'s bedroom. Suddenly the door bursts open, the light streams in. We see silhouetted figures of military police in the door, yelling into the room. The light is blinding; they are shining torches into **Dieter**'s face and **Lotte**'s.*

Voices are shouting at them: 'You're coming with us right now, both of you.'

*We see **Lotte** sitting up in bed, caught in the blinding light. **Dieter** tries to argue with them, his tone forceful as he addresses the silhouetted figures.*

We cannot see their faces.

DIETER
We must have time to get dressed. You must allow my daughter to put her clothes on . . .

A voice yells, 'Just put a coat over her!'

EXT./INT. CAR. NIGHT

*We cut inside a large saloon car, military police driving and in the front seat. Next to **Dieter** and **Lotte** on the back seat is a thin man in civilian clothes. **Lotte** is wearing her large overcoat over her nightdress. We see **Lotte**'s point of view: the police, the car driving through the night streets, the thin man next to her, who keeps looking at his watch, her father who is staring ahead defiantly.*

There is sudden noise and light in the dark street, as they pass close to workmen under arc lights, repairing the damaged road. The sound of the machinery is very loud and the arc lights stark and disconcerting. **Lotte** *tries not to look terrified as they move past the road works and into darkness.*

We then cut to the car moving down a very dark narrow street and stopping by a back entrance surrounded by dustbins. **Lotte** *stares out of the window, as the thin man gets out of the car and beckons to them.*

INT. TILED BUILDING. NIGHT

We cut to **Dieter**, **Lotte** *and their escort going through the back entrance and finding themselves in a tiled passage that opens into a large room full of baths. The building has the feel of a deserted municipal bath house that has been partially converted for another purpose. There is a sinister, soiled atmosphere about the interior.*

They move past the baths. **Dieter** *is just staring ahead, his demeanour very dignified, but he is coldly furious. He is wearing his overcoat over his pyjamas. In the passage they pass three men in dark suits who watch them go by. A large woman in civilian clothes beckons to* **Lotte** *to sit on a bench next to her in the passage.*

Dieter *is taken straight through the door in front of them.*

INT. TILED INTERROGATION ROOM. NIGHT

Dieter *finds himself in a very large tiled room with washbasins along the walls. The basins are filthy. There are desks in the room, as if it has been crudely converted into some sort of office, or interrogation room.*

Standing in the left-hand corner of the room is **Callum**. *On the other side is a large man in a brown suit.*

Sitting in front, at the central desk, is **Kathy**.

KATHY
Mr Koehler, please take a seat.

Dieter *sits.*

I'm Kathy Griffiths, from the War Crimes Unit.

DIETER

War Crimes? And you need to see me at three in the morning? Is that what you think is 'civilised'?

KATHY

We are seeing you at this time of night, yes.

Her gaze is strong, unflinching, her manner authoritative.

We want to examine your record to see exactly which were the sites you say you were working at . . . and whether there are any gaps or inconsistencies –

DIETER

I did all this in Germany, when I was interrogated by the people he works for – (*He indicates* **Callum**.) And now it starts again, just because you can think of no other way of dealing with me – and for some extraordinary reason, you feel it necessary to bring my daughter here as well, in the middle of the night?! Is she going to be interrogated as well?!

Kathy *is truly startled.* **Callum** *also looks very surprised by this.*

KATHY

Your daughter? Your daughter is here?!

Dieter *gets up and moves over to the door and opens it. We see the small figure of* **Lotte** *sitting in her overcoat and slippers on the bench, surrounded by the dead baths.*

CALLUM

That is clearly a mistake . . . Lotte should not have been brought with you.

Kathy's *eyes flash; she looks extremely angry for a moment.*

KATHY

I agree with you, Mr Koehler, that is an unforgivable error. I will conduct my own investigation into how that happened, I assure you.

She turns sharply to **Callum** *and the man in the brown suit.*

Can you both leave now, I will continue the rest of this interview on my own.

Callum *hesitates.*

Leave, Mr Ferguson.

Callum *leaves.* **Kathy** *stares at* **Dieter** *for a moment.*

Now we're alone, Mr Koehler . . . despite what's happened, I'm still going to ask you some questions.

She looks down at the files, and then at him.

You say you were working at the beginning of the war, at the Heinkel Headquarters, in Rostock? And then you moved to the Luftwaffe testing facility at Rechlin-Larz?

####### DIETER

Yes.

####### KATHY

So, Mr Koehler – (*She gives him a searching look.*) you're telling me you never worked, at any stage of the war, at the underground works at Mittelbau Nordhausen? Or at Peenemunde? Where slave labour was used.

####### DIETER

You know I didn't. (*Indicates all the papers on the desk.*) You can see that from all the files they've made about me.

INT. PASSAGE. MUNICIPAL BATHS. NIGHT

We cut to the passage where **Lotte** *is sitting with the large woman standing next to her.* **Callum** *is close by.* **Lotte** *is staring at the rusty old tap that is dripping next to her, filthy water going into a stained basin.*

####### CALLUM

You should not be here Lotte . . . I am very sorry. (*He glances over the dead baths.*) I wish I could find something for you to do – but it's not obvious what . . .

INT. INTERROGATION ROOM. NIGHT

We cut back to **Kathy** *and* **Dieter** *alone in the bleak tiled room.*

KATHY

And you never worked at Redl-Zipf? In Austria? Or Raxewerke?

DIETER

No.

KATHY

Or visited them?

DIETER

No. I was always working on jet engines, never on the V1 or V2. I am not a rocket man. Everybody knows that! But that has nothing to do with it, does it? (*He looks at her.*)

If you are determined, you can give anybody the history you want them to have . . . to suit your purpose. You're trying to give me a choice, work for you or we make you a war criminal. I thought you British were above such things.

There is silence, just the sound of dripping water.

We move in on **Kathy***; we sense she is deeply uncomfortable with the situation.*

KATHY

Mr Koehler, that is certainly not what I'm doing.

And as it happens, I believe you . . . about your work. But just as important as that, it is clear you should never have been brought here tonight, least of all with your daughter. For that I apologise.

INT. PASSAGE. MUNICIPAL BATHS. NIGHT

We cut outside to where **Lotte** *and* **Callum** *are waiting. The man in the brown suit is watching them. The door of the interrogation room opens –* **Kathy** *is in the doorway.*

KATHY
Mr Koehler is going home now.

CALLUM
(*startled*)
You've finished already?

KATHY
I most certainly have. I have absolutely no more questions for Mr Koehler, and definitely none for his daughter.

The military police escort **Dieter** *and* **Lotte** *past the dead baths and out of the building.* **Lotte** *turns as she goes, to see* **Callum** *standing alone in the passage.*

INT. INTERROGATION ROOM. NIGHT

We cut to **Callum** *walking into the tiled room.* **Kathy** *is standing right at the other side, leaning against the basins. Her tone is controlled but ferociously direct.*

KATHY
How dare you . . . how dare you use the unit like that?!

A shot of **Callum** *watching her.*

And what's more, you even bring the girl here, in the middle of the night – I can't believe you did that?!

CALLUM
That was clearly a mistake. That should never have happened. I've already said –

KATHY
What on earth did you think you were doing?! Trying something like this! You saw me, and thought why not let her loose on him for a bit – let him realise if he doesn't cooperate he may have war crimes pinned on him?! (*Her voice rising.*) There's nothing in his file, you knew there was nothing there, but you dropped those hints to me, 'Oh, we know more about him than his record shows, he may have a connection with

slave labour and people dying' – You knew all that wasn't true, didn't you?!

CALLUM

I had no evidence of that, no.

KATHY

The whole thing was just a fucking ploy, to scare the wits out of him!

CALLUM

Not completely –

KATHY

'Not completely' – what does that mean?! You should be ashamed of yourself, you really should! Isn't it enough that you've got all these resources and we're just this tinpot little outfit, running around, having to beg for information, having to plead to be shown people's records – isn't that enough?!

CALLUM

That's not how I see you.

KATHY

Yes, it fucking is. Absolutely, it is! You laid on this whole charade . . . you knew I'd probably leap at the chance to question a real-life suspect, didn't you? And of course, like an idiot, that's exactly what I did! And then you make sure it happens in the worst possible place – one of your old torture haunts you used during the war . . . I hate to think what went on here! You're probably still using it, aren't you?!

CALLUM

I've never tortured anybody – I'm not one of those morons from the Cage. I've never had anything to do with those people –

KATHY

Well you did tonight, didn't you?! You were working with them!

CALLUM
(*suddenly loud, he erupts into a passionate rebuttal*)
I was working with them, yes! Extraordinarily reluctantly – because somehow I've got to get that man cooperating with us . . . it is vital for our security. We just *cannot* make the mistakes we made before, not have the latest technology, be caught unprepared . . . I can't let that happen . . .

He looks across at her. The sound of the dripping tap.

I'm sorry for tonight, Miss Griffiths, I am. I know this won't make any difference, but this was not my idea . . . and clearly it was not a good plan.

KATHY
You're bloody right – it doesn't make any difference. You fucking agreed to it didn't you!

CALLUM
I did.

She stares at him. For a moment **Callum** *thinks she might soften, at least be less furious with him.*

KATHY
Anyway, I don't believe you, you've done nothing but lie to me ever since I met you.

She walks out of the room.

We stay on **Callum** *for a moment, a shot of him among the dead basins.*

EXT. STREET. DAWN

We cut to **Callum** *emerging out of the back entrance of the municipal baths. There is an early morning fog. A car is sitting across the street, its yellow headlights shining in the foggy dawn light. There is one person in the car,* **Salter**, *at the wheel, staring at* **Callum** *through the windscreen.* **Callum** *turns and walks in the opposite direction. The car comes up behind him, driving very slowly. It pulls abreast of him.*

SALTER

Want a lift?

CALLUM

No. Thank you.

He doesn't break his stride. **Salter** *keeps alongside.*

SALTER

Went well in there, did it?

Callum *refuses to look at him, keeps walking.*

I have a message for you.

CALLUM

I bet you have.

SALTER

It's not what you're expecting . . . Brigadier Wainwright is going to give you another three weeks – it's not what I'd be doing, of course, but for the moment, he's running the show. And out of the goodness of his heart, he's given you three more weeks.

CALLUM

Tell him I don't need them. I don't need more time.

EXT. VICTOR'S LODGINGS. EARLY MORNING

We cut to **Callum** *ringing the doorbell of* **Victor**'s *lodgings. It is still very early morning. The door opens,* **Mrs Tooley** *is in her dressing gown.*

CALLUM

Mrs Tooley, I'm very early, I know. I do apologise.

MRS TOOLEY

You're as bad as your brother . . .

Nevertheless she lets him in.

What could be so important you have to be here at this time?!

INT. VICTOR'S ROOM. EARLY MORNING

*We cut inside **Victor**'s cluttered room. **Victor** is lying on the floor smoking, **Callum** is sitting on the bed.*

VICTOR

You might have brought me something, you know.

CALLUM

You're quite right, I should have done, next time . . .

VICTOR

But I'm flattered you came here for my advice.

CALLUM

Well, 'advice' might be putting it a bit high!

VICTOR

That you seek sanctuary here anyway, amongst my collection. (*He smokes.*) In Mrs Tooley's house! (*He looks across at **Callum**.*) You always find a way, Cal . . . I'm sure you will.

CALLUM

I'm very angry with myself for being talked into such a ridiculous plan . . . never again.

VICTOR

Of course! Never do what you're told. You know I believe that more than anything!

CALLUM

(*smiling at this*)

So how've you been managing these last couple of days? You feeling okay?

VICTOR

Improving, I think . . . (*Grins.*) looking forward to the specialist and telling him the truth, as I see it . . . ! But there is one problem – Mrs Tooley and I . . . The love affair is over! (*He laughs.*) She's always hated me, but now it's got worse.

I'm so envious of you being at that hotel. So what I want to do is – come and be there too . . . it's the obvious thing! You must be able to get me a job there?

CALLUM

A job at the Connington?! (*Very startled.*) That's not a good idea, Victor.

VICTOR

Please . . . Remember, I need to occupy my mind, where better to do it?!

CALLUM

I can't get you a job there, Victor.

VICTOR

(*we are very close on him*)

Won't take the risk, eh?

INT. THIRD-FLOOR PASSAGE. DAY

We cut to a silver trolley being pushed towards us by a waiter down the third-floor passage. The trolley is laden with breakfast, sausages, bacon, eggs. **Callum** *is walking behind the waiter.* **Callum** *knocks on* **Dieter***'s door.*

Dieter *opens the door in his pyjamas, looking dishevelled with sleep.*

DIETER

And now he wakes me up!

CALLUM

All the ration books we could get hold of have gone into this breakfast.

He sees **Lotte** *in her nightdress, standing behind her father.*

We even have sausages today!

DIETER

It will take more than this breakfast to stop me thinking about last night . . .

CALLUM

I had guessed that, yes. So how about this? You're free to go.

Dieter *stares at him.*

DIETER

What do you mean by that?

CALLUM

You can go.

Dieter *still staring at him.*

Leave the hotel, for a walk in the park, or along the river . . . or maybe a visit to the American or Russian Embassies, to see what they have to offer? Or of course, you could jump on the boat train and go home to Germany . . . There will nobody following you at any time.

He hands **Dieter** *an envelope.*

Here's some money . . .

DIETER

I don't believe you. It's not going to be as you say.

CALLUM

Why don't you put it to the test and see?

EXT. CONNINGTON/BOMBSITE. DAY

We cut to **Dieter** *and* **Lotte** *emerging from the back entrance of the Connington. They are in their travelling clothes.* **Lotte** *is carrying a suitcase. They move across the bombsite towards us,* **Lotte** *looking into the crater where people are scavenging. We cut close to* **Dieter**. *He looks behind him. Nobody is following. We stay close on him.*

INT. SECOND-FLOOR PASSAGE/INTER-CUT WITH BOMBSITE. DAY

We cut to **Callum** *and* **Ringwood**, *watching* **Dieter** *and* **Lotte** *walking away.*

RINGWOOD

I've never known somebody take such a risk about anything, sir!

CALLUM

He'll come back . . .

He is watching their figures getting away.

For the first time he has a real choice . . . He'll work out where his best chance is . . . If he goes home to Germany, he has no job, he has no money – I didn't give him much – he's thinking, 'How will we live?'

RINGWOOD

But he's also thinking, he could go to the Americans or the Russians . . . And the girl's got a suitcase!

CALLUM

He'll want to stay with the devil he knows. I'm betting everything on him wanting to continue his work . . . and thinking he can do that with me – a fellow boffin . . . hopefully I've shown him I'm nearly one!

We see the figures getting further and further away.

I'm the least worst option . . .

RINGWOOD

God, I hope you're right, sir!

We cut down to **Dieter** *and* **Lotte**, *walking towards us. They reach the other side of the bombsite. We then cut back to* **Callum** *and* **Ringwood**, *watching them go.*

RINGWOOD

Can't we put just one tail on him . . .?

CALLUM

No, it's all or nothing, Ringwood. Don't worry, I'll get all the blame . . .

Lotte *and* **Dieter** *disappear from sight.*

RINGWOOD

All hell will break out, sir . . . if they don't come back.

CALLUM

It will.

RINGWOOD

I'm tense already! How are you going to spend the time?!

CALLUM

By doing something even more nerve-racking . . .

INT. BASEMENT BALLROOM. DAY

We cut to **Callum** *approaching* **Eva**, *who is sitting in the empty ballroom doing her accounts.* **Anna** *is cleaning in the background.* **Eva** *looks up sharply.*

CALLUM

Hello Eva, just came to see if I could steal an orange?

EVA

There are only two left. (*She smiles.*) Give me a good reason why one of them should go to you?

CALLUM

I couldn't possibly . . .

EVA

Well they're locked up, where nobody can get them! So you'll have to wait a while, till I've finished this . . .

EXT. STREET NEAR BOMBSITE. DAY

We cut to **Dieter** *and* **Lotte** *moving down a street, people watching them pass from doorways. We see a couple of stalls with black-market goods, people trying to sell a pathetic collection of tins and old clothes. They call out as the two of them pass. We stay on* **Dieter**'s *face. And then they disappear, away from us, round the corner.*

INT. BASEMENT BALLROOM. DAY

We cut back to **Eva** *and* **Callum**. **Eva** *is still working on her papers;* **Callum** *is by the piano, playing a few notes with one hand. We move in close, see his tension.*

INT./EXT. SECOND-FLOOR PASSAGE/BOMBSITE. DAY

*We cut to **Ringwood** pacing on the second-floor passage. He stops and stares out across the bombsite. The light has changed, there is now smoke blowing across from a bonfire. He stares through the smoke towards the other side.*

*There is no sign of **Dieter** and **Lotte**.*

INT. BALLROOM. DAY

*We cut back to the ballroom. The tables have now been laid ready for lunch, waitresses are standing along the walls. **Eva** has finished her papers and is drinking a glass of wine. She is watching **Callum** peel his long-awaited orange.*

There is a sound outside; he turns sharply.

EVA

Never seen somebody so jumpy peeling an orange! What do you really want, Mr Ferguson?

CALLUM

Oh . . .

*He offers some segments of the orange to **Anna**, who smiles in appreciation.*

It's that obvious I've come for something else is it?

EVA

Yes, and since I'm pretty sure you're some sort of spy, maybe it shouldn't be that obvious.

CALLUM

Okay . . . *(He looks at her.)* I've been asked to ask you . . .

EVA

That's not a good beginning.

CALLUM

You're right . . . *(He smiles.)* Remember when you first played here the other day, there was a well-dressed woman who danced a lot? She's married a close friend of mine, and she's just arrived in town . . . She would like you to play at her party?

EVA

She's having a party? Just arrived here, and she's having a party! Of course, what else is there to do?!

CALLUM

She wants to meet people.

EVA

I bet she does.

CALLUM

Why don't you like her?

EVA

She hasn't really spoken to me, so how can I like her? But maybe she's one of those people that treats you like a gramophone . . . a machine in the corner, they want to turn you over and play you, they don't even see you –

CALLUM

She's not like that.

EVA

Ah, Mr Ferguson . . . ! How do you know that? (*She looks straight at him shrewdly.*) You sound very sure.

CALLUM

(*smiles.*)

So will you do it?

EVA

Maybe, if the fee is right . . . (*She laughs.*) Seems you're in charge of everything I do at the moment! Not sure the night will go that well though . . .

CALLUM

Why do you say that?

EVA

Because I'll have to keep my mouth shut . . . and I'm not very good at doing that, as you may have noticed . . . back home I got into trouble. (*She looks at him.*) A lot of trouble . . . I lost bookings because I wouldn't play to certain audiences, segregated audiences – I said you hire somebody else if you want that, and they did!

That's why I'm here . . . in this basement now. *Your* basement, Mr Ferguson.

The door opens, **Callum** *spins round.* **Ruth** *is standing in the doorway.*

CALLUM

Yes?!

RUTH

You're wanted in the lobby, sir –

Without waiting for her to say anything, **Callum** *rushes past her. We stay on his face.*

INT. CONNINGTON. MAIN LOBBY. AFTERNOON

We see **Callum** *entering the lobby, expectation in his eyes. He is startled to see instead* **Rachel**, *waiting for him, exquisitely dressed as usual in a pale-blue coat.*

RACHEL

This the wrong moment, I can see that. I'm sorry –

CALLUM

No, absolutely not, I was just –

RACHEL

It looks like you were expecting somebody else!

CALLUM

No, it's not that, in fact I was literally, right at this moment, in the middle of asking Eva if she would play at your party . . . !

RACHEL

Were you really? Then it was truly bad timing on my part! Unless she said yes, of course?!

CALLUM

I think she said yes . . .

RACHEL

I just wanted your advice . . . I was passing in the car, and thought why not pop in and see if you were here?

CALLUM

Advice about what?

RACHEL

Well it will seem very trivial, especially as you've been kind enough to ask the singer. (*She looks at him.*) And you have your important assignment going on all the time, I know, so forgive me – but I was just ordering the catering for the party, which fast approaches! – And I had this totally mad idea of hiring the chef from here to do it, and then I realised you were about the only person I could ask if that was a ludicrous notion –

CALLUM

Sounds a very bold idea to me!

RACHEL

Bold? Is it?! (*She laughs.*) I'm not sure I want to be bold at my first party here, what if it went terribly wrong?!

CALLUM

Then you can blame me.

RACHEL

I would never blame you.

Suddenly **Callum** *catches sight of* **Ringwood** *out of the corner of his eye, beckoning.*

I see you need to go.

CALLUM

I'm sorry, I just have to check something –

RACHEL

No, no, please, you're always so busy, Cal. (*She laughs.*) That's what I plan to become.

Callum *crosses the lobby rapidly towards* **Ringwood**.

INT. SECOND-FLOOR PASSAGE. AFTERNOON

We see a high shot of the bombsite. **Dieter** *and* **Lotte** *are moving back towards the hotel.* **Callum** *and* **Ringwood** *staring down at them as they approach.*

RINGWOOD
That's amazing sir! You were right!

CALLUM
Maybe . . . (*Staring down as they get close.*) Of course we don't know where they've been, or what he's planning yet. Now we're going to be here for a few weeks, Ringwood – it's what he does next that matters.

INT. MAIN LOBBY. CONNINGTON. DAY

We see **Dieter** *and* **Lotte**, *with her suitcase, walk up to the reception desk.*

DIETER
I would like some paper please.

DESK CLERK
Would that be one or two sheets, sir?

DIETER
(*smiles*)
That is as much paper as you can possibly give me.

INT. DIETER'S BEDROOM. AFTERNOON

A large wad of paper is placed sharply by **Dieter** *on the table in his bedroom. We cut wide to see him positioning himself at the desk and starting to write.* **Lotte** *is standing, still with her suitcase, watching her father getting immersed in his work.*

There's a knock at the door; it is **Callum**. **Dieter** *looks up from his papers and addresses him.*

DIETER
To quote Greta Garbo not quite correctly – I want very much to be alone, right now, for a while. Then we might talk . . .

He returns to his work.

EXT. BOMBSITE, CONNINGTON. MORNING

Kathy *is walking towards us along the rim of the bombsite in morning light. Initially, we see her from a great distance – we sense some days have passed, new shapes have appeared on the bombsite. She is carrying a bag and walking very purposefully. She reaches the back of the Connington and takes a camera out of the back of her bag. A couple of the hotel staff are beating out rugs near the door.* **Kathy** *surveys the building, staring up especially at the top windows.*

She fits a telephoto lens on the camera and starts taking photographs.

INT. ALEX AND RACHEL'S HOUSE. AFTERNOON

We track through the flower decorations that now fill the hall and the stairs of **Rachel** *and* **Alex**'s *house. We have reached the day of the party. We discover two maids carrying more flowers up the stairs and entering the drawing room.* **Rachel** *is standing across the room. As the maids enter she smiles.*

RACHEL

Have we rather overdone it?! . . . Well, if nobody comes, we can really enjoy ourselves!

INT. THIRD-FLOOR PASSAGE. DIETER'S BEDROOM. EVENING

We cut to **Ringwood** *knocking on* **Dieter**'s *bedroom door.* **Lotte** *opens it.* **Dieter** *is sitting at his desk, deep in his papers.*

LOTTE

My father is working –

RINGWOOD

Everything alright, Mr Koehler?

DIETER

Yes, Mr Ringwood. (*Hardly looking up.*) Everything is not too bad.

INT. CALLUM'S BEDROOM. NIGHT

We cut to **Callum** *in his dinner jacket, just doing up his bow tie. He stares* *at himself in the mirror. There is a knock.* **Ringwood** *puts his head around the door.*

RINGWOOD
Everything is under control sir, he's buried in his work.

CALLUM
Good. The more he works, the better.

RINGWOOD
Been like that for days, hasn't it, sir?! You still don't want any watchers in the passage?

CALLUM
Absolutely not. He won't be going anywhere tonight.

INT. WAR CRIMES UNIT. NIGHT

We see **Kathy** *sitting at her desk in the War Crimes Unit office. She is alone with* **Miss Clarkson**, *who is at the other end of the room. Just the loud ticking of a clock.* **Kathy** *is studying the photographs she has taken. She has had them blown up to quite large prints. She is studying the upper storeys of the hotel. The camera tracks across the boarded-up windows, and then we see windows that are not boarded up, right at the top of the hotel. She picks up a magnifying glass. We see the image very close.* **Kathy** *thinks she can just make out figures in the window. She gets up sharply, holding two particular photos.*

EXT. ALEX AND RACHEL'S HOUSE. NIGHT

We see **Callum** *crossing the road towards* **Rachel** *and* **Alex**'s *house.*

People are arriving in cars and taxis. The house is glowing out, dominating the street.

INT. ALEX AND RACHEL'S HOUSE. STAIRS/DRAWING ROOM. NIGHT

We follow **Callum** *into the hall of the house. We see him staring at all the decorations and flowers, the warmth and colour contrasting with the dankness of the Connington. There is the sound of the party coming from the top of the stairs.*

Callum *goes up to the central drawing room.*

There, in the middle of the guests, are **Rachel** *and* **Alex**, *talking, laughing, greeting people. They seem so confident together, so assured.* **Rachel** *is wearing another magnificent dress. She is a striking presence amongst the other women in their pre-war or austerity dresses. Both* **Alex** *and* **Rachel** *wave at* **Callum** *as soon as they see him in the doorway.* **Callum** *notices* **Harold** *sitting in a corner, holding court.*

INT. DARK PANELLED ROOM. NIGHT

We cut to a small panelled room lit by one large lamp hanging over a heavy desk. **Salter** *is sitting at the desk. In front of him is a tape recorder out of which* **Callum**'s *voice is coming. It is the moment he is in bed with* **Julia**.

We hear **Callum** *saying:*

> CALLUM
> (*voice-over*)
> I'm having to take advice from the lunatics . . . that fat man Salter or whatever his name is and his friends . . . the vermin!

We see sitting behind **Salter**, *in the shadows, is the thin man who escorted* **Dieter** *and* **Lotte** *to the deserted bath house. We move in on them.*

INT. ALEX AND RACHEL'S HOUSE, DRAWING ROOM. NIGHT

We cut back to **Callum** *moving among the party guests. There is champagne everywhere, and he is determined to drink a lot. He studies* **Harold** *for a moment as he holds court across the room. And then he watches* **Rachel** *in her beautiful dress, as she hosts her party.*

INT. CONNINGTON. LOBBY. RECEPTION DESK. NIGHT

We cut to **Victor** *entering the main lobby at the Connington. He sweeps past guests in evening dress and marches up to the reception desk. He is looking rather wild, as if he has been drinking. He is wearing an old mackintosh and does not have a tie.*

> VICTOR
> I want to see my brother. Please.

DESK CLERK

Your brother? And who might that be, sir?

VICTOR

Cal . . . Mr Callum Ferguson. I think he's virtually running the hotel at the moment.

DESK CLERK

Mr Ferguson is not currently here.

VICTOR

Is that the truth?

DESK CLERK

That is the truth. (*Startled.*) Why would it not be sir? He had an engagement this evening.

Victor *stares at him.*

VICTOR

Then I will stand right here and wait for him.

DESK CLERK

That may well be pointless, sir –

VICTOR

On the other hand it might not be! It is very important I see him.

INT. RACHEL AND ALEX'S HOUSE. DRAWING ROOM. NIGHT

Eva *and some of her musicians have entered the drawing room at the party. The drum kit has been set up near the piano,* **Richie** *is on the drums tonight. The musicians begin to take up their positions.*

Callum *is watching* **Rachel** *as she hosts her party. She greets* **Eva** *warmly. He then looks across at* **Harold** *holding forth in the corner,* **Lucy** *is standing next to him.*

Alex *suddenly appears by* **Callum**. *He indicates the guests who seem to be almost huddled together.*

ALEX

Not a very happy lot, are they?! Haven't seen some of these people for so long. Hopefully the music will help turn them back into friends . . .

He watches **Rachel**, *adoration in his eyes.*

I'm so glad you made her have the party, she's got so much to offer.

CALLUM

I don't think it was me that made a difference!

ALEX
(*seeing him look at* **Harold**)
I hear you met Harold Lindsay-Jones . . .

CALLUM

I did, yes.

ALEX

He is an interesting man, a little mysterious . . . I told him what you really think, Cal.

Callum *turns sharply.*

That we must never be caught out again . . . we must always be ready for the next war – and we've got to be prepared to do almost anything to make sure we are . . .

Richie *starts to drum,* **Eva** *begins to sing.*

ALEX

You didn't mind me telling him that, did you?

Callum *impassive, watching the music. We stay on* **Eva** *singing for a moment, the guests all at one end of the room, watching awkwardly. The music spills across the cut.*

INT. THIRD-FLOOR PASSAGE DIETER'S BEDROOM. NIGHT

We see **Mr Emmanuel** *walking towards us along the third-floor passage. He is holding a book. He knocks on* **Dieter**'s *door.* **Lotte** *opens it.*

MR EMMANUEL
My little one . . . I have come to see you.

Lotte *looks disconcerted.* **Mr Emmanuel** *calls out to* **Dieter**.

MR EMMANUEL
You don't mind me reading her a story from this storybook?
We know each other.

DIETER
No, no, come in . . . I have to work . . . (*He smiles gently at*
Lotte.) Something to entertain her, that's a good idea. (*He turns back to his papers.*)

INT. WAR CRIMES UNIT. NIGHT

We see **Kathy** *re-entering the War Crimes Unit office. She is carrying more photos. She has had them blown up even larger. She drops them on her desk. We cut to her staring at them, magnifying the image. We track across the detail in the pictures, the upper windows of the hotel. We get closer and closer. We see the grainy shape of a woman wearing headphones, sitting working.* **Kathy** *staring intensely. Then we see the blurred images of* **Callum** *behind the woman with headphones. We are on* **Kathy**'s *eyes, realising she has found the room. We go right inside the photo, as she stares at the interior of the attic room behind* **Callum**, *and the shelves of files.*

INT. ALEX AND RACHEL'S HOUSE. DRAWING ROOM. NIGHT

We cut back to the party. **Eva** *is singing.* **Harold** *beckons* **Callum** *to join him; he is sitting at the other end of the room to the music.* **Richie**'s *drumming is electrifying in the intimate space.*

HAROLD
So the music is your doing, I gather?

CALLUM
Not exactly, I just encouraged her to be here.

HAROLD
And, apart from our hosts, what a drab lot we are! (*He stares at the guests.*)

LUCY
Maybe we have forgotten how to have a party . . .

The song finishes; there is a spattering of applause.

HAROLD
Have you given any thought to what I said to you the other day?

CALLUM
I have. I've found it difficult to get it out of my mind, which I'm sure is what you intended.

HAROLD
Want to hear more?

CALLUM
Of course, Mr Lindsay-Jones – but it's not clear to me what you'd want me to do . . . apart from listen to your stories?

HAROLD
(*smiles*)
Classified stories of course . . . That might be a rather sensible way for us to get to know each other? . . . (*He looks straight at him.*) And to see if we can trust each other?

Eva *is moving away from the piano. She helps herself to a glass of champagne, and then mingles freely among the guests. One of the male guests is watching her behaviour with disapproval, and makes no effort to lower his voice.*

MALE GUEST
You can tell the socialists have really taken over, can't you?!

EVA
(*without missing a beat.*)
And not before time!

The guests all staring at her.

EVA
That went down really well didn't it?! . . . Since this is a party . . . I won't start an argument . . . I promised Mr Ferguson over there I wouldn't.

Shot of **Callum**.

But if there is a doctor in the house, I just might . . . because they hate the idea of this new Health Service that's coming, don't they?! . . . So if you're a doctor, and think like that, I suggest you *hide*. Hide from me anyway . . . !

She stares at the guests.

Anybody owning up?

She stares back at them and smiles.

No? Okay, let's have a party.

Eva *is totally unruffled. She toasts the guests with a smile. They stare back, startled, discomfited by her confidence.* **Harold** *is watching them, their appalled faces.*

HAROLD
Look at them . . . some things never change . . .

INT. CONNINGTON. RECEPTION DESK. NIGHT

Victor *is leaning on a pillar in the lobby, staring unnervingly at the* **Desk Clerk**.

DESK CLERK
Sir, I really don't want you to waste your time.

VICTOR
Thank you. Then I won't. I need to see him so badly, I will go and look for him!

Victor *sets off across the lobby and into the main passage. The* **Desk Clerk** *calls after him, a bellboy tries to catch up with him. But* **Victor** *is too quick for him, and disappears up a side staircase.*

INT. LOTTE'S BEDROOM. NIGHT

We cut to **Mr Emmanuel** *staring down at* **Lotte** *through his little round glasses. He has the storybook on his knee, but it is unopened.*

Lotte *is holding her toy donkey very tight.*

> MR EMMANUEL
>
> So my little one . . . we must have a story in a moment. (*He leans closer.*) We've lost so much, so many things, haven't we? So much that was precious . . . (*His face very close now.*) We understand each other, I think . . .

INT. SECOND-FLOOR PASSAGE. CONNINGTON. NIGHT

We cut to **Victor** *moving along the second-floor passage of the hotel.*

A passerby, a pompous-looking man in a dinner jacket, suddenly calls after him.

> MALE RESIDENT
>
> Excuse me, are you a resident of the hotel?

> VICTOR
>
> (*turns sharply*)
>
> Are you talking to me?

> MALE RESIDENT
>
> I most certainly am.

> VICTOR
>
> Then I will talk to you.

He advances on him.

> MALE RESIDENT
>
> If you are not a guest of the hotel, you have no business being up here –

> VICTOR
>
> No business? (*He smiles.*) Except perhaps to say . . . (*He is very close to the man's face.*) I see a lovely eyeball here . . . during the war, I popped some eyeballs out just like this.

He moves as if to get hold of the man's eyelid. The man swerves away very frightened, and scuttles off down the passage.

INT. LOTTE'S BEDROOM/DIETER'S BEDROOM. NIGHT

Mr Emmanuel's *face is looming over* **Lotte**, *the book still unopened.*

MR EMMANUEL
My little one, what is the matter? We will just have a story –

LOTTE
One moment please . . . I must go to the lavatory.

Lotte *puts on her dressing gown and slippers as* **Mr Emmanuel** *watches her.* **Lotte** *moves into her father's room.* **Dieter** *is working at his desk.*

LOTTE
Papi?

DIETER
(*in German*)
Not just now my dear . . . (*He glances up.*) I hope you're having a good story.

He resumes his work. **Lotte** *stares at her father for a moment.*

INT. THIRD-FLOOR PASSAGE. NIGHT

We cut to **Lotte** *moving along the passage, away from her bedroom. She hears something behind her and turns.* **Victor** *is at the other end.*

He sees down the length of the passage this little girl in a dressing gown.

VICTOR
Somebody who looks intelligent at last!

He moves up to her.

And where are you off to? If it's alright to ask?

LOTTE
Please, not go back . . . I don't want to go back to my room.

VICTOR
So that makes two of us! . . . Well let's see if we can find some late-night chocolate instead! (*He smiles.*) It used to be the answer to everything, but it's so difficult to find now!

They move off together along the passage.

INT. RACHEL AND ALEX'S HOUSE. DINING ROOM. NIGHT

We cut to **Callum** *looking down at the party food, the half-eaten buffet laid out in the dining room, rather unappetising cooked meats. He is alone.* **Eva** *is playing to the guests in the drawing room, just the piano and her voice, a lilting, expressive song.*

Rachel *enters the room.*

RACHEL

I wasn't brave enough!

CALLUM
(*looks up*)

Brave enough about what?

RACHEL

To have the chef from the Connington . . . and now look at this food. (*She laughs.*) Not exactly a joyful spread, is it?! That's what I think he would have provided . . . and they haven't even eaten much!

I should have taken your advice . . . been bold!

CALLUM

Well you were bold enough to have Eva here, weren't you?!

Rachel *smiles at this.*

And there's always next time.

RACHEL

You think there will be a next time?! Not judging by all those long faces next door! Maybe it's because of what I'm wearing . . . but I couldn't have dressed drably for the occasion, could I? Trying to show solidarity by wearing second-hand clothes – that would've seemed so patronising surely?!

CALLUM

Undoubtedly.

There is a momentary pause. She looks stunning in her dress.

Lotte looking for her donkey in the immigration hall

Lotte meets Mr Emmanuel

The immigration hall

Dieter and Lotte at the Connington Hotel

Callum arrives at the Connington for the first time

Callum in charge at the Connington

Callum's first sight of Rachel

Ringwood and Callum discussing how to get Dieter to cooperate

Julia and Callum stare down at the bombsite in the early morning

People scavenging on the bombsite

Victor eating raw potatoes outside the hospital

Kathy in the secret attic office

Callum almost drowning the Blackshirt near the railway viaduct

Harold and Callum together at night in the ruins of the bombed mansion

Eva in the basement ballroom

RACHEL

You don't mind what people think of you, do you?

CALLUM

No, I stopped worrying about that on the first day of the war . . . and haven't started again – not yet.

RACHEL

You're very lucky then, would we could all be like that!

CALLUM

And you're not?

RACHEL

No, I worry what people will think far too much . . . especially, I find, now I'm here.

There's so much I want to do you know, get involved with things that really interest me, help them happen. Things that are far more important than a good party . . .

CALLUM

Of course.

RACHEL

I will tell you about them. We must meet properly. We haven't done that yet.

Callum *looks at her.*

RACHEL

You and me and Alex. That is of course, if you can spare the time, Cal?!

CALLUM

I think I might be able to manage it . . .

He smiles at her. At that moment, a maid appears at the door.

MAID

There's a telephone call for Mr Ferguson.

RACHEL

Oh, Cal, even here?!

MAID

It's very urgent, they say.

EXT. BOMBSITE. NIGHT

Victor *is crossing the bombsite with* **Lotte** *in her dressing gown and slippers.*

VICTOR

We'll find some hot chocolate . . . I have these migraines, you know, headaches, which are so strong. And hot chocolate in the middle of the night is the one thing that sometimes stops them . . .

A wide shot of **Victor** *and* **Lotte** *crossing the bombsite together, moving away.*

INT. THIRD-FLOOR PASSAGE. NIGHT

We cut to **Callum** *and* **Ringwood** *coming round the corner of the third-floor passage.* **Callum***'s manner is very urgent. They see* **Dieter** *standing at the other end, absolutely frantic with worry.* **Mr Emmanuel** *is standing near him. There are also hotel staff there.* **Dieter** *shouts the length of the passage.*

DIETER

My daughter has gone! Lotte has vanished!

CALLUM

She can't have gone far! (*His tone is forceful.*)

DIETER

They say this madman was in the hotel, and he has taken my daughter . . . ! And that man is your brother –

CALLUM

My brother?! He can't have been here!

DIETER

He was here. They say he was acting crazily!

He stares at **Callum**.

Your brother has taken my daughter.

CALLUM

He will not hurt her. He can't hurt her. He would never do that –

DIETER

How do you know? You don't know that?!

We are close on **Callum**. *We see he is worried. His tone very forceful.*

CALLUM

I promise you I will find her. I will find both of them! I'll get her back.

EXT. STREET NEAR BOMBSITE. NIGHT

We cut to **Victor** *and* **Lotte** *moving down a night street past parked cars.* **Victor** *is trying all the doors of the cars.*

VICTOR

We'll take a car! Because it will make our search so much easier . . . so much quicker.

He finds a car he likes. He settles **Lotte** *into the passenger seat. He gets in and starts the car.*

VICTOR

We'll find the only hot chocolate left in England . . . we may have to travel far, many miles . . . but we will discover it. And nobody will stop us . . . or find us . . . And we're going to do it fast!

The car moves off, **Victor** *clenched over the steering wheel. We see a shot of* **Lotte** *and then her point of view of the road ahead.*

We see **Victor** *and* **Lotte** *together, through the windscreen.*

And then we see the car roar off down the street, and away from us, into the night city.

CREDITS

Part Three

Part Three

CREDIT SEQUENCE

ALEX AND RACHEL'S HOUSE. NIGHT

We are in amongst the party which is in full swing in **Rachel** *and* **Alex**'s *house.* **Callum** *enters the drawing room; his manner is urgent. He moves over to* **Rachel** *talking fast; we can only hear the music. Guests' faces turn, sensing something is wrong. We see* **Harold** *watching the scene carefully.*

Callum *leaves the room abruptly and hurtles down the stairs and out of the house.*

We cut back to **Rachel** *standing in her stunning evening dress among her guests and the party decorations. We move in on her face.*

Then we see **Callum** *and* **Ringwood** *walking towards the frantically worried* **Dieter** *in the bedroom passage at the hotel, as he yells at* **Callum** *about* **Victor** *taking* **Lotte**.

Then we cut to the night exterior of the Connington; many lights shine out, as the huge shape of the hotel looms over the bombsite.

END CREDIT SEQUENCE

INT. CONNINGTON – MAIN GROUND-FLOOR PASSAGE. NIGHT

With an abrupt cut we are suddenly among the swirl of agitated people in the main ground-floor passage of the Connington. There are uniformed police, hotel guests, porters, waiters and desk clerks. **Dieter**, **Callum** *and* **Julia** *are all in a huddle with the police.* **Callum** *is talking urgently,* **Dieter** *is looking incredibly tense.*

In a corner **Mr Emmanuel** *is watching them all. There is a hallucinatory, intense feel, a sense of shock at the abduction of a child. Everybody is talking at once.*

Mr Emmanuel *moves across the passage; he is now hovering close to the police.*

> MR EMMANUEL
> Excuse me, I must tell you what I know . . . I was reading her a story and she disappeared. She just vanished! That's what happened . . . Please, I must tell you what I know . . .

Callum *looks at* **Mr Emmanuel**, *he senses something disquieting about him. More guests are filling the passage.* **Callum** *turns to* **Dieter**.

> CALLUM
> We'll do better on our own . . . Come on.

INT./EXT. CALLUM'S ROOM/BACK ENTRANCE OF THE HOTEL. NIGHT

We cut to **Callum** *and* **Dieter** *in* **Callum***'s hotel room.*

Callum *is pacing and smoking.*

> CALLUM
> Okay, so what happened with that little man? What was he doing with Lotte?

> DIETER
> He was reading her a story, I was right in the room next door . . . I could hear him reading to her . . .

> CALLUM
> That's not all he was doing . . .

> DIETER
> I didn't hear anything else, nothing —

> CALLUM
> I think she ran away from him . . .

He hears a noise outside; he glances out of the window. He sees two jeeps with armed military police drawing up at the back entrance.

> Christ, we don't want them having anything to do with this

> DIETER
> Why did somebody call them?

> CALLUM
> (*staring at military police*)
> Because they think you're important, that's why.

EXT. BOMBSITE. NIGHT

We cut outside the hotel. The uniformed police, the hotel staff and military police are moving across the bombsite in a long line, searching with their torches, the lights stabbing out in the darkness.

INT. CALLUM'S HOTEL ROOM. NIGHT

We cut back to **Dieter** *and* **Callum***, both talking fast, interrupting each other.*

DIETER

Come on, come on, you should think where your brother might be . . . where he likes to visit? What are his special places in the city?

CALLUM

There're a lot of those . . . he likes to roam about and –

DIETER

What does he do when he roams about?

CALLUM

He collects things . . . picks things up, off the pavement, off bombsites, anything that catches his eye, street signs . . . whole railings even or –

DIETER

His room? What's he got in his room? Should we go there? –

CALLUM

The police have been there already . . . not a trace of them –

DIETER

No, no of course, but maybe if we look at what he's collected – that might tell us something –

CALLUM

(suddenly turning)

His collection? . . . That's a good idea . . . *(Trying to visualisse his room.)* There are so many things there I just have to –

DIETER
Think what there is on the floor . . . on the bed . . . what really stands out? . . .

We are on **Callum**'s *face. Then we see a subjective shot of* **Victor**'s *room, the collection of objects on every surface, piled on the bed and all over the floor.*

We cut back to **Callum**.

CALLUM
There's a lot of stained glass, big pieces, little pieces, he picks a great deal of that up . . .

DIETER
Then we need a church . . . Where does most of that come from? Does he have a favourite church?

EXT. BOMBSITE. NIGHT

We cut back to the bombsite. More people have joined in the search party. **Julia** *is there, and* **Mr Emmanuel**.

Suddenly there are shouts from across the bombsite and then in the beam of a torch we see a shape curled up at the bottom of the crater. We see alarmed faces. But as more torches are trained on it and we move closer, we see it as an old mattress squashed up.

EXT. RUINED CHURCH. NIGHT

A taxi draws up in the shadow of a ruined bombed church. **Dieter** *and* **Callum** *get out of the taxi rapidly.* **Callum** *calls out to the driver.*

CALLUM
Just wait for us here please.

We see a subjective shot moving through the ruins of the church. There are small pieces of stained glass all over the ground. There are shapes of people in the dark, sleeping rough in the one corner that still has a roof.

Dieter *and* **Callum** *call out to them.*

CALLUM
Have you seen a man with a young girl? With a child?

Does anybody know Victor? . . . He collects things . . . Victor is my brother . . .

One of the men calls over to them. They approach him; he is quite young but looks severely under-nourished.

SLEEPING MAN

I know Victor . . . he's often here . . . Sometimes he sleeps here . . . not seen him tonight though.

CALLUM
(*turning to* **Dieter**)
This is one of his churches . . . but they've not been here.

DIETER

Then we have to do every church we can . . .

EXT. STREET AND DARK BULDING. NIGHT

We cut to a shot through the windscreen of the stolen car as **Victor** *drives.*

Lotte *is sitting next to him in her nightdress and dressing gown. They are approaching a large dark building which stands at the end of a street of warehouses. There is some light spilling from its ground floor. We cut to them getting out of the car.*

VICTOR

So, Lotte, if we manage this right, we really will reach the countryside. But whatever you do don't say anything . . . they'll ask you questions, just nod, they musn't know you're German . . . Do you understand?

Lotte *nods; she looks determined, excited even.*

INT. DRIVERS' CAFÉ. NIGHT

We cut inside the large interior of a drivers' café. The room is full of lorry drivers and taxi drivers; the air is thick with smoke. The drivers turn in surprise to see **Victor** *standing there with a small girl in a dressing gown and nightdress. The room falls silent.*

                        VICTOR
So gentlemen, I need some petrol coupons . . . (*Flourishing his wallet.*) I will pay handsomely for them. Who's going to be the lucky one then?!

The men start calling out to **Lotte**. *We see them through her eyes, tall men, some of them with leering faces, shouting at her through the thick smoke.*

                        MEN
'Women aren't allowed in here, love!' . . . 'Been out for the night dressed like that have you, love?!' . . . 'What's your name dear, have you got one?' . . . 'It's not a good idea to go out like that, love, you never know what might happen!' . . .

Lotte *just nods and stares at them.*

                        VICTOR
Our house just collapsed . . . the whole ceiling came down . . . Bang! Just like that! So we've got to be on our travels . . .

The men stare at them; he stares right back.

Who's going to help us?

INT. CONNINGTON PASSAGES/DINING ROOM. NIGHT

It is three-thirty in the morning; the lights are all low in the passages of the hotel. **Callum** *and* **Dieter** *are pushing their way through the throng of military and uniformed police, hotel staff and guests. They are both covered in dust and dirt from the ruins they have been searching.* **Julia** *is waiting in the passage.*

                        JULIA
Any news? Anything at all?

                        CALLUM
No . . . not yet.

Ringwood *suddenly appears behind them in the passage, calling urgently.*

                        RINGWOOD
Where've you been, sir?!

CALLUM
We've been in church.

DIETER
Many churches . . . but not praying.

CALLUM
(*indicating all the police*)
And they've got nowhere obviously?

RINGWOOD
No, sir.

CALLUM
For Christ's sake . . . (*Staring at the military police.*) You've got to get them out of the hotel, get rid of them!

RINGWOOD
I can't get rid of them, sir. I don't know how to do that . . .

CALLUM
It'll end badly if they're still here . . . it'll end in tears. Keep them away from me at least . . .

Dieter *and* **Callum** *are moving further down the passage. They are startled to see waiting for them, in the mouth of the dining room, are* **Rachel**, **Alex** *and* **Harold**, *standing in their evening dress.*

CALLUM
What on earth are they doing here?

INT. DINING ROOM. NIGHT

It is just a few minutes later. The dining room is very dimly lit; there are hotel guests milling around, some in their dressing gowns. We see the whole sequence through **Harold**'s *point of view. He sees* **Dieter** *and* **Callum** *working in unison, discussing where to look next, talking intensely as they move around the dining room.*

He sees **Julia** *chatting up the military police, trying to distract them and prevent them meddling.*

He sees a moment of connection between **Rachel** *and* **Callum** *that* **Alex** *doesn't seem to notice.* **Rachel**'s *gentle solicitous manner towards* **Callum**.

RACHEL

We came to see if we could help – of course we can't help, I mean you will have thought of absolutely everything . . .

ALEX

But we wanted to be here . . .

CALLUM

You didn't need to do that.

HAROLD

The party was well and truly over . . . we had to come. (*Indicating their clothes.*) You've been scouring the city it looks like.

DIETER

We tried to predict where they were. I thought we were going to find them, I really did . . . it was like we were so close –

CALLUM

Everything will end peacefully . . . (*Indicating military police.*) Just as long as those idiots don't blunder in.

DIETER

Captain Ferguson will stop them doing that.

CALLUM

I'll do my damnedest . . . (*Staring across at them.*) I can't control them everywhere though.

RACHEL

Maybe it would calm us all if we tried to get a cup of tea . . . (*She looks across the dark dining room.*) I wonder if that's possible in the middle of the night . . .

ALEX

Why don't we put it to the test?

EXT. THE COUNTRYSIDE. DAWN

We cut to the stolen car driving fast down a country road. There is thick woodland on one side, a view of hills on the other. **Victor** *is hunched over the wheel.* **Lotte** *is staring at the view, excitement in her eyes.*

VICTOR

This is more like it, Lotte, isn't it? A bit of countryside . . . a bit of clean air!

LOTTE

It's so beautiful . . . (*She looks thrilled.*) The most beautiful thing I've ever seen.

VICTOR

Better than bombsites and wrecked buildings? That's probably all you can remember ever seeing, isn't it, Lotte?!

We stay on **Lotte**'*s face staring out.*

INT. CONNINGTON DINING ROOM/PASSAGE. DAWN

We cut back to the dining room in the Connington, the dawn light spilling through the heavy curtains. **Julia** *is curled up now on two chairs, asleep. Various hotel staff are lying down on chairs in the passage.* **Harold** *glances over the sleeping figures*

HAROLD

It could be the Blitz all over again . . . everybody's staying close in case they are needed.

Anna, *the young waitress, is bringing in the tea on a large silver tray.*

ANNA

Sorry it took so long.

She smiles at **Dieter** *as she sets down the tray.*

They will find your daughter, sir, I'm sure.

DIETER

Thank you. (*Indicates* **Callum**.) He's doing everything he can . . .

Callum *is by the window.* **Rachel** *comes up to him.*

CALLUM
Now it's light we have a better chance. I've managed to get it on the radio, on the first bulletins . . . My brother stands out a mile wherever he goes, and with a little girl in tow . . .

RACHEL
Why is everybody so worried about your brother?

CALLUM
That's simple, they think he's mad. (*He looks at* **Rachel**.) But he won't lay a finger on the girl . . . he would never harm a child.

Harold, *sitting next to* **Alex**, *is watching* **Callum** *across the dining room.*

HAROLD
To feel responsible, even though you're not at all, that must be truly difficult.

EXT. COUNTRYSIDE — PETROL STATION. EARLY MORNING

We cut to a shot through the windscreen as the car approaches a petrol station in the distance. There are three pumps and a shack-like building on a lonely country road.

VICTOR
Alright, we'll have a go here . . . I should have filled up earlier, Lotte, but I didn't want to stop.

He begins to slow the car.

Get on the back seat, Lotte, lie down as if you're asleep, don't move please, and don't say anything whatever happens . . .

Victor *draws up at the petrol station. The* **Attendant** *is a stocky man with a military bearing and a beady look. He nevertheless has a lighted cigarette in the corner of his mouth. He stares at* **Victor**'s *wild appearance as he emerges out of the car.*

We can hear the sound of a radio coming out of the shack.

VICTOR
Fill her up please. (*Waving coupons.*) As much as I can get for these!

The **Attendant** *gives him a hard look. He moves to the car and sees* **Lotte** *sleeping on the back seat. He stares at her closely as he begins to fill up the car.*

VICTOR
You know you shouldn't be smoking while you're doing that?

ATTENDANT
You're telling me what to do, are you?! I don't advise you to do that again. Get your daughter out of the car if you don't like it.

Victor *goes up to the car and gets* **Lotte** *out. The* **Attendant**'s *tone is vicious; there is a contained fury about him.*

ATTENDANT
Worried I'd set her alight were you?! Well there's always a first time! . . . I've only been doing this six weeks . . . you think this is what I want to do with the rest of my life?!

He sees **Lotte** *in her dressing gown standing next to* **Victor**.

ATTENDANT
Had to leave somewhere suddenly did you?

His hard eyes staring at them. **Victor** *can't resist.*

VICTOR
You haven't got some spare chocolate by any chance?!

We cut to a shot in the driving mirror of the receding petrol station as **Victor** *and* **Lotte** *drive away. The* **Attendant** *is staring after them. As soon as they are around the corner and out of sight,* **Victor** *starts driving really fast.*

We see a wide shot of the car speeding through the landscape.

Then suddenly **Victor** *brakes. He stops the car.*

VICTOR

We're in trouble . . . that man's going to report us. Better get out of this car, now!

INT. CONNINGTON DINING ROOM/PASSAGE. EARLY MORNING

Ringwood *is running along the passage towards the dining room calling to* **Callum** *and* **Dieter**.

RINGWOOD

Sir! There's been a sighting of them, sir! At a petrol station in Sussex.

DIETER

They've seen them?!

RINGWOOD

Yes, there's an army base very close, they're sending out a patrol.

CALLUM

No, that is not going to happen! It's not the right move at all. They must use the local police . . . Get me the commanding officer on the phone now! (*To* **Dieter**.) If they go in, they're going to start shooting . . .

He calls out to the military police.

Come here . . . Yes, you. I may need you to talk to them if I can't make them see sense . . . They've got to realise the man's not dangerous . . .

Dieter *watching* **Callum** *take control of the situation.* **Callum** *turns to him.*

CALLUM

I've got to stop them.

EXT. COUNTRY ROAD WHEAT FIELD. MORNING

We cut to **Victor** *and* **Lotte** *running along the rim of a wheat field.*

We cut to two military jeeps pulling up by the abandoned car on the road.

We cut back to **Lotte** *and* **Victor** *beginning to cross the wheat field itself. Suddenly they see two more jeeps pulling up on the other side of the field in front of them. Armed men get out and set up positions along the edge of the field.*

Victor *and* **Lotte** *dodge down amongst the wheat. We see from their point of view the marksmen with their guns trained on the field.*

We then cut to the marksmen and see them scouring the field through their gun-sights.

We cut back to **Victor** *and* **Lotte**.

VICTOR
Lotte, get away from me . . . you're not safe with me . . .

Lotte *staring at him, not wishing to leave him.*

You've got to do it, Lotte, you have to, now. Crawl over there . . . as far as you can . . . Lotte, go . . . quick, GO!

Lotte *begins to crawl through the wheat away from* **Victor**.

We cut back to the marksmen.

We cut back to **Victor**, *alone, crouched amongst the wheat. He begins to take his shirt off. We then cut to him standing up, bare-chested in the field, his arms above his head.*

We cut to the marksmen. We cut back to **Victor**.

VICTOR
Okay, here I am. A nice target? . . . Why don't you have a go?! . . . (*He shouts.*) I don't think you can really miss can you?!

The marksmen suddenly swivel round. There is some movement in the field.

Lotte *stands up with her arms above her head. They stare at this small figure in a nightdress and dressing gown in the middle of a wheat field.*

EXT. CONNINGTON – FRONT ENTRANCE. AFTERNOON

We see a large black saloon, escorted by two military jeeps, drawing up to the main entrance of the Connington. On the steps of the hotel watching them arrive are **Dieter, Callum, Rachel, Alex** *and* **Harold.** *There are several inquisitive guests watching as well. We see the whole sequence through* **Harold***'s eyes. He sees* **Lotte** *leap out of the car and hug her father. He sees the joy on* **Dieter***'s face at the reunion and his gratitude to* **Callum.** **Dieter** *holds* **Lotte** *tight.*

DIETER
All together again. (*He repeats it in German to* **Lotte**.)

Harold *watches* **Rachel** *and* **Alex** *join in the celebration and* **Rachel** *congratulating* **Callum** *in front of the others.*

RACHEL
He got her back.

Then **Harold** *watches* **Callum** *cross over to the saloon car where* **Victor** *is standing surrounded by military police.* **Harold** *sees* **Callum***'s fury but also his deep concern about his brother.* **Callum** *calls out to* **Victor** *as he approaches.*

CALLUM
What the hell do you think you were doing?! What on earth possessed you to do that?

VICTOR
Don't yell at me, please, I've had a big night.

CALLUM
Of course I'm going to yell at you, I can't believe you've been this stupid . . . They're going to lock you up now, and I'm not going to be able to do a single thing about it, nothing! That's a brilliant result isn't it, Victor?!

The military police put **Victor** *back in the saloon car, sitting either side of him on the back seat. The car begins to drive away,* **Victor** *looking back at them through the rear window.* **Lotte** *whispers to her father, then tugs at* **Rachel***'s sleeve.*

LOTTE
He was nice to me . . . what are they going to do to him?

Callum *watches his brother disappear.*

HAROLD

I know you'll find this very surprising but if they don't lock him up, I may be able to help you with your brother.

CALLUM

They will lock him up.

INT. WAR CRIMES UNIT. LATE AFTERNOON

We cut to **Kathy** *pinning up her long-lens photos on a large board in the War Crimes Unit main office. She is alone with* **Miss Clarkson***. The extent of the secret office on the top floor of the Connington begins to take shape in her collage of photos.*

MISS CLARKSON

So they've got a whole floor up there have they?

KATHY

Yes. (*Pointing at details in the photos.*) With a lot of files it looks like. They absolutely deny it exists.

MISS CLARKSON

Well they're hardly going to help us are they?! Official priorities have just got even clearer apparently, they want to get hold of every German that might be useful before it's too late, and it doesn't matter what they've done! All the resources are going into that.

KATHY

But surely that can change? Something can change that?

MISS CLARKSON

(*looks sceptical, turns to photos of secret office*)
You'll never get in there, Kathy.

KATHY

Maybe not, but I can have a hell of a try.

EXT. ARMY CAMP/SUBURBAN STREETS. DAY

Victor *is being led out of a building in the army camp by military police.*

Then we see him being driven through the suburban streets towards the military headquarters.

INT./EXT. WAINWRIGHT'S OFFICE MILITARY HEADQUARTERS. DAY

Callum *enters* **Wainwright'**s *outer office where five female orderlies are typing.* **Wainwright** *is waiting for him in the doorway of his inner office.*

WAINWRIGHT
You've been very lucky, Ferguson. Amazingly lucky!

CALLUM
Lucky! I've been lucky?!

INT./EXT. WAINWRIGHT'S INNER OFFICE MILITARY HEADQUARTERS. DAY

Wainwright *is now standing by the window of his inner office.* **Callum** *is standing on the other side of the desk.*

WAINWRIGHT
The German is very grateful to you, for how you behaved over his daughter. That's why you've been lucky, we're finally making progress. I want you to stay with him now until he delivers.

CALLUM
Until he delivers? That might be months!

WAINWRIGHT
Certainly it might be months.

He watches through the window as **Victor** *arrives in the jeep.*

Supersonic speed is the only thing that matters at the moment – you'll know far more about this than me – breaking the sound barrier, boom! We've got to do that before the Americans or the Russians of course. Your German –

CALLUM
My German?

WAINWRIGHT

Yes, your German can really help us do that can't he?

CALLUM

Probably, yes.

Callum *has joined* **Wainwright** *by the window; both are watching* **Victor** *with his military escort.*

WAINWRIGHT

And your German trusts you now – we need you to build on your new 'friendship' . . . till he's done it for us. Stop him going to the Americans. That's all you have to do. And sort those files out in the hotel of course. Most people would kill for such a job.

CALLUM

I'm not going to do it.

WAINWRIGHT

Oh yes you are. (*Staring straight at him.*) Shall I tell you why? Because your brother has committed a series of criminal offences, abducting a child, stealing a car, he will go to prison unless I stop it happening.

CALLUM

You're blackmailing me?

WAINWRIGHT

In a way, yes.

They are both watching **Victor** *through the window.*

But I don't really need to . . . What are you going to do with your life now if you refuse? This way you have the run of the hotel, lots of free time to do what you want . . . to work out your future . . .

We move in on **Callum***.*

You're doubly, maybe trebly, lucky!

Victor *has got out of the jeep and is gesticulating wildly to the military police.*

CALLUM

Am I? I'm certainly not if I've got MI5 or MI19 or any other bloody outfit on my back monitoring everything I do.

WAINWRIGHT

That's over, that's been stopped. There are none left in the hotel.

CALLUM

None?

WAINWRIGHT

No, all gone, except your outfit! (*His tone softens.*) If you do this, Ferguson, we'll get your brother good treatment in a hospital.

CALLUM

No, absolutely not, I'm not having him locked up in one of your asylums. I will look after my brother.

WAINWRIGHT

It's a deal.

EXT. MILITARY HEADQUARTERS/SUNKEN GARDEN. DAY

A subjective shot approaching **Victor**. **Callum** *crosses the courtyard towards him.* **Victor** *is arguing with his military escort. When he sees* **Callum** *he calls out.*

VICTOR

So what've you arranged with them then?! They're going to strap me down are they, put wires all over my head, give me electric shocks?

CALLUM

Come here, come with me . . .

He leads **Victor** *away from the military police.*

VICTOR

Mind you, you probably get incredible dreams when they fry you like that . . .

They enter a sunken garden down some stone steps next to the courtyard. The military police are right behind them. **Callum** *turns to them.*

CALLUM

I need to talk to my brother in private . . .

He moves **Victor** *further into the garden.*

Don't worry I won't let him run away.

VICTOR

What a beautiful place! (*He stares about the garden.*) The army won't want to give any of these houses back will they?! I wonder where all the aristos have moved to . . .? They'll pop up again soon I expect!

CALLUM
(*his tone very sharp*)

You're not going to go to prison, Victor. They're not going to press charges.

VICTOR

Why not? Are they going to lock me away in a hospital?

CALLUM

No, you can go back to Mrs Tooley.

VICTOR

Can't wait! So you did a deal did you? (*Staring straight at him.*) They want you to go on working with the German . . . Well why not? You've always loved that haven't you! Flight, speed – (*He swoops his arms through the air.*) Building the fastest plane in the world . . . so why shouldn't you do it?!

CALLUM

There's one condition though.

Victor *turns.*

You're not allowed to go anywhere near the little girl or the hotel. If you go back there, you will be locked up.

VICTOR

Says who?

CALLUM

Says me. Will you promise me you won't try to see Lotte again? Or go to the hotel?

VICTOR

But I didn't abduct her, you know that! She was running away from a horrible man –

CALLUM

Yes, but I still want you to promise me, Victor. Do you promise?

VICTOR

Of course.

The military police are watching.

CALLUM

You better bloody mean it!

VICTOR

Or else? You'll put me in the mad house?! I still have to live don't I? – I was really hoping to get a job in the hotel! Just being a porter or something, nobody else will give me a job –

CALLUM

Ah! It's possible I may be able to do something about that . . .

INT. WAR CRIMES OFFICE. EVENING SUNLIGHT

We see a photo of **Callum** *staring out like a mugshot. It is on* **Kathy**'s *desk. She is staring back at it. There are three other women working in the office.*

Miss Clarkson *walks up to* **Kathy**'s *desk.*

MISS CLARKSON

What're you doing?

KATHY
I'm trying to compile a file on him . . . (*She moves the photo closer.*) Know one's enemy . . .

MISS CLARKSON
It must be difficult to get any real facts on him?

KATHY
Yes, it is very difficult. So I'm putting down some guesses as a start . . . some thoughts . . . he is the way in.

INT. HAROLD'S HOUSE THE HALL. DAY

Victor *and* **Callum** *are being let in by the housekeeper,* **Mrs Gorton**. *The hall of* **Harold***'s house is very dark, with one striking abstract painting dominating the space. The sound of chickens from the garden.* **Victor** *lowers his voice to* **Callum**.

VICTOR
This doesn't look very promising . . .

Mrs Gorton *indicates they should follow her.*

INT. HAROLD'S HOUSE THE LIBRARY. DAY

We cut to **Victor** *and* **Callum** *sitting side by side in the library. The room is even darker than the hall and completely stuffed with books right up to the ceiling, and there are piles along the floor in an overflow section.* **Harold** *comes into the darkened library.* **Callum** *stands to greet him.* **Victor** *remains seated.*

HAROLD
There you are! The two brothers. (*He moves forward.*) We haven't been formally introduced, Victor . . . I'm Harold Lindsay-Jones, so pleased to meet you.

VICTOR
Are you?

He smiles and shakes **Harold***'s hand.*

HAROLD
Well seeing you up close, Victor, you don't look mad to me . . . not mad at all. Please, be seated.

They sit. **Harold** *sits across the room.*

CALLUM
So Mr Lindsay-Jones –

HAROLD
Harold, please –

CALLUM
Harold, you were saying you might have something for Victor to do . . . some odd jobs around the house –

VICTOR
I'm not terrific at cleaning . . . I just thought I better make that clear right away –

HAROLD
Cleaning is not what I had in mind, no.

CALLUM
Victor can buckle down when he wants to, he surprises people –

VICTOR
I do surprise people, often, but I'm not sure that's what he's looking for!

HAROLD
(*calmly*)
This library was a passion . . . both for my wife and myself . . . We loved books. Since she died, it hasn't been quite the same. What do you notice, Victor, about this library? What do you see?

Victor *looks around the room fleetingly,* **Callum** *watching him closely.*

VICTOR
What do I see? That the books are not in the right order . . . they are in no order at all in fact! Neither alphabetically – by author or by title . . . or by subject.

*We see **Callum** looking relieved and impressed.*

HAROLD

Exactly, Victor! You spotted it at once. During the Blitz I had all the books moved at great expense to the country. When they returned the removal men just put them back in any order . . . and I didn't have the heart to do anything about it.

I will pay you, Victor, to arrange them alphabetically by author, and when you've done that, to arrange this overflow on some new shelves in the room next door. Can you do that?

VICTOR

I can do that, yes.

HAROLD

That's terrific. This room is full of an unhealthy sense of grief, it's probably time to get rid of it. Shall we say you start next Monday?

CALLUM

How much will you pay him?

HAROLD

Ah of course, the only important question! I will pay you nine pounds a week. Does that sound reasonable?

VICTOR

Yes, sir. (*He smiles.*) As a starting figure.

HAROLD

Good. (*To **Victor**.*) By the way I'm not just doing this out of the kindness of my heart as I'm sure you will have guessed, there's something I may need your brother's help with in due course, something that interests me intensely.

VICTOR

And I'm sure he will give you that help!

*He looks at **Callum**.*

INT. HAROLD'S HOUSE THE HALL. DAY

Harold *is about to show* **Victor** *and* **Callum** *out.*

Lucy *appears on the stairs above them.*

>HAROLD
>
>Ah, this is Lucy, my ward. This is Victor Ferguson.

>LUCY
>
>Hello, Victor.

Victor *looks back at the young woman.*

>HAROLD
>
>Lucy is about to go back to Oxford.

>LUCY
>
>So I won't see much of you, Victor.

>VICTOR
>(*to Harold*)
>Ah! So you won't have to worry about me being alone in the house with her!

>CALLUM
>
>Victor...

>HAROLD
>
>I was not worried about that, no.

>VICTOR
>
>Quite right. In fact, despite appearances to the contrary, it is my brother you really have to worry about.

>CALLUM
>
>I better get him out of here before you withdraw the offer!

>VICTOR
>
>My brother needs looking after too. (*He smiles.*) You ought to believe me...

INT. CONNINGTON DIETER'S ROOM/THIRD-FLOOR PASSAGE.
NIGHT

We see two young girls running down the passage, one of them on roller skates. We cut to **Mr Emmanuel** *watching them from the far end of the passage. He then sees* **Callum** *appearing down the passage, the girls rushing past him.* **Mr Emmanuel** *disappears before* **Callum** *can see him.* **Callum** *knocks on* **Dieter**'s *door.*

We cut to **Callum** *entering* **Dieter**'s *room. He sees* **Dieter** *and* **Lotte** *sitting opposite each other at a table.* **Dieter** *is teaching* **Lotte** *how to play chess.*

CALLUM

Ah, I won't disturb you, especially not in the middle of a chess lesson. I just came to say we're off in the morning, to show you your new office.

DIETER

Good, I'll be very interested to see what they've given me.

CALLUM

You're coming too, Lotte

Lotte *smiles.*

We cut to **Callum** *moving back along the passage, round the corner. Suddenly he senses something and looks behind him. It is* **Mr Emmanuel** *in the shadows.*

CALLUM

Ah, I've been looking for you . . . we need to have a word.

INT. CONNINGTON BACKSTAIRS/LANDING. NIGHT

We cut to **Callum** *and* **Mr Emmanuel** *moving fast down the back stairs,* **Callum** *is holding* **Mr Emmanuel** *by the arm.* **Mr Emmanuel** *is very agitated.*

MR EMMANUEL

Where are we going? What do you want to say to me? I'm very busy tonight . . . I have a meeting to go to . . .

Callum *stops outside the gentlemen's toilet.*

INT. GENTLEMEN'S TOILET/PASSAGE. NIGHT

Callum *is facing* **Mr Emmanuel** *across the white tiles of the lavatory.*

CALLUM
What were you doing to that girl?

MR EMMANUEL
I was just reading her a story . . . that's all it was!

Callum *moves over and hits him in the face. He then hits him in the stomach.*

CALLUM
What were you doing to that girl?

MR EMMANUEL
Nothing! (*There are tears pouring down his face.*) Nothing!

Callum *hits him again several times, blood pouring from his face.*

MR EMMANUEL
Stop this . . . Please, please . . . I can tell you something . . . if you stop . . . something that will interest you . . . about Room 602 .

CALLUM
Tell me some other time . . .

He hits **Mr Emmanuel** *again really hard.* **Mr Emmanuel** *is in the foetal position on the floor.*

Now I'm going to tell you what you're going to do. You're going to book out of this hotel tonight and never ever come back, do you hear me?

Mr Emmanuel *doesn't reply.* **Callum** *picks him up and hits him again.*

CALLUM
Do you hear me now?

Mr Emmanuel, *covered in blood, nods as he kneels on the floor.*

At that moment we hear **Ringwood**'s *voice calling 'Captain Ferguson . . . Captain Ferguson . . . sir' down the passage. We cut outside into the passage.*

Callum *emerges alone. There is blood on his shirt.*

RINGWOOD
Are you alright, sir?

CALLUM
Absolutely.

RINGWOOD
Mr Lombard is waiting for you in the conservatory bar, sir . . . he said you had an appointment.

INT. CONNINGTON CONSERVATORY BAR. NIGHT

We cut to **Callum** *approaching* **Alex** *in the conservatory bar.* **Callum**'s *jacket covers the blood on his shirt, but he nonetheless moves confidently, unembarrassed by his appearance.*

At the far end of the bar, among the potted plants, an elderly pianist is playing.

ALEX
There you are! At last! (*Indicating the pianist.*) I've had to listen to this bloody music for at least half an hour . . . (*He glances at* **Callum**'s *dishevelled appearance.*) Are you alright?

CALLUM
Yes . . . just had one little matter I had to attend to. Sorry to keep you waiting.

Eva *enters the bar with three of her musicians and sits at a table across the room.*

She waves and calls out to **Callum**.

EVA
I hear you *really* are running the hotel now!

Callum *smiles and waves back.* **Eva** *turns to her musicians, talking loudly.*

He is going to be here for a little while now – so maybe we'll get to hear him play the piano. (*Pointing at the elderly pianist.*) He'll be up there next week!

ALEX

So you're staying here for a bit?

CALLUM

Yes, it seems like it, looking after my German.

We cut back to **Eva** *at her table.*

EVA

I can't really work out our friend Mr Ferguson . . . never gives me a straight answer. He's doing something very hush-hush obviously and keeping us here in the hotel as part of it . . . I don't know what the hell that is though – what he's up to?! I ought to go over there and get him to tell us shouldn't I . . . (*She drinks.*) Maybe later . . . !

Callum *watches* **Eva** *laughing with the musicians; he grins across at her.*

ALEX

You know I envy you. (*His tone is warm.*)

CALLUM

You envy me, Alex? That's a mistake I promise you! I'm going to be unemployed in a few weeks.

ALEX

Yes, but for now you're in control of how you spend your day. You decide what you do, don't you?

He leans forward, his tone intense.

I have to work so hard at the moment at the Foreign Office. It is so bloody competitive and the hours are unbelievably long. And I feel I have to stay later than anybody else because I had such a cushy time during the war in Washington . . . I have to be seen to be working the hardest.

He leans closer.

I need to ask you a favour, Callum.

CALLUM

A favour? Of course.

ALEX

Will you have lunch with Rachel?

Callum *looks startled.*

You know all about music and everything . . . I know nothing about the arts and I'm totally tone deaf . . . she needs somebody to talk to about her ideas. Will you do it?

We move in on **Callum**. **Alex**'s *tone is insistent.*

Please.

EXT. SALOON CAR. STREETS NEAR BOMBSITE. DAY

We cut to a close-up of **Lotte**; *she is staring out of a car window. Then we see her point of view of the dust and the streets near the bombsite as the car travels through them.*

People standing in doorways amongst the wrecked landscape. **Lotte** *is sitting next to her father.* **Callum** *is on the front seat, and they are being driven by an RAF driver.*

CALLUM

You're going to get out of the dust, Lotte . . . and this time it's legal . . .

EXT. COUNTRYSIDE/GOVERNMENT RESEARCH FACILITY. DAY

We cut to a wide shot of the car travelling through countryside. And then we see through the windscreen the car approaching a military research facility, a barrier across the road manned by armed RAF personnel.

We see the car drive through the barrier and enter a strange private world, a whole cluster of buildings, like a secret village. Some large impressive buildings and some small cottages with neat gardens. There is a red postbox and the facility has its own pub.

*We see **Dieter** and **Lotte** staring out at the buildings with great interest.*

The car draws up in front of a large, very long building.

Military jeeps are passing them as they get out of the car.

> CALLUM
> Okay, I'm going to show you your rather poky office, Dieter.

INT. THE HANGER RESEARCH FACILITY. DAY

We cut to a huge interior with a glass roof. It is the size of a hangar. It has two levels, with a metal staircase running up to the higher level. It is completely empty except for piles and piles of boxes, some of which are covered with tarpaulins.

Dieter *and* **Lotte** *are staring at the colossal interior.*

> CALLUM
> This is all yours, Dieter. It looks big enough do you think?

> DIETER
> This may just be big enough, yes. (*He grins.*)

> CALLUM
> It was full of hundreds of people during the war –

> RITA
> And now there's only me.

They look up – a black woman in her thirties is coming down the metal staircase.

> CALLUM
> This is Rita . . . She's going to work with you.

Callum *watches* **Dieter**'s *reaction to her closely.*

> DIETER
> I'm very glad to hear it.

He shakes her hand.

CALLUM

Rita and I worked together before the war . . . she knows a lot about jet engines.

RITA

(*to* **Dieter**)

Not as much as you of course . . . ! (*She smiles.*) But I know something.

CALLUM

You see, Lotte, Rita and I worked with this wonderful man who invented the jet engine, Mr Frank Whittle –

DIETER

Well we Germans might dispute that – that you were the first!

CALLUM

And then our government refused to give him the money he needed to develop his invention, Lotte – so we lost our lead! And now your dad is going to help us get it back again, by breaking the sound barrier . . .

RITA

(*to* **Lotte**)

A plane that goes really really fast, supersonic fast . . .

Lotte *smiles excitedly*

We cut to the upper level. There is a row of empty desks. **Callum** *sits at one of them.*

CALLUM

You've got to choose a desk, Dieter. (*He grins.*) Or of course you could have a different one each day . . .

DIETER

No. (*He chooses one and sits.*) I will have this one.

He looks at **Callum**.

Do I get my own car now? So I can drive myself here every day?

CALLUM

You don't get that yet, no. (*He smiles.*) You might drive somewhere we don't want you to.

INT. HAROLD'S HOUSE. THE LIBRARY. LATE AFTERNOON

We cut to **Victor**, *in* **Harold**'s *dark library, pulling books from the shelves. We see, in a series of rapid cuts,* **Victor** *opening the books to look at the illustrations — beautiful colour plates of tropical birds, of imperial military campaigns, of ocean voyages with sea monsters. Out of one of the books an official document drops. It is marked 'Highly Confidential' at the top of the page.*

We cut to **Victor** *sitting on the floor in the middle of the library reading the book on tropical birds using the official document as a bookmark.* **Harold** *appears in the doorway.* **Victor** *holds up the document without getting up.*

HAROLD

Ah thank you for finding that! There may be various little documents from the Foreign Office that I should have given back — some even marked secret . . .

He takes the document, then indicates the many books lying open on the floor.

So, Victor . . . you've begun I see.

VICTOR

I have . . . my progress will vary though. How quick I am will depend how often the books interrupt me.

He resumes studying the tropical birds.

HAROLD

I see. I don't mind you taking some pauses, Victor, but maybe not every few minutes . . .

VICTOR

When I get going you'll be surprised how dramatic the progress will be. (*He looks up at* **Harold**.) You think you've made a mistake don't you?

Harold *looks at* **Victor** *sitting in the middle of the floor.*

HAROLD

I would be lying if I said I was completely confident at this point . . . but then we all have our different methods about how we approach things.

VICTOR

That's very true . . . but nobody has my methods.

He stares straight at **Harold**.

I am definitely going to surprise you.

INT. FULLER'S COFFEE SHOP. EARLY AFTERNOON

Callum *approaches* **Rachel** *across the Fuller's coffee shop where they first met.* **Rachel** *is sitting immaculately dressed in the corner.*

CALLUM

I'm late, I'm sorry.

RACHEL

Don't worry, I was expecting it. I know you're always late.

CALLUM

I'm not always late, you forget I'm still in the army. (*He smiles.*) Sort of anyway . . .

RACHEL

So you mean you're only late for me! (*She laughs.*) I quite understand.

A waitress is approaching across the tea room carrying two very tall fluted glasses.

RACHEL

I took the liberty, I hope you don't mind, I've ordered us some ice cream.

CALLUM

Some ice cream?! That's very bold . . . because last time —

RACHEL

It was disgusting, yes . . . ! (*She smiles.*) But today I have a plan.

WAITRESS
(*reaching the table*)
You asked for it in these tall glasses ma'am, is that right?

RACHEL
I did.

WAITRESS
It's just they're rather large for the ice cream ma'am.

The tall glasses have one very small dollop of grey ice cream in each of them.

RACHEL
Please, that's perfect, thank you.

The waitress, very dubiously, sets the ice cream down.

Callum *watches* **Rachel** *intrigued.*

RACHEL
It's very kind of you to see me, Callum . . . (*She reaches into her bag and produces a silver Thermos.*)

CALLUM
Don't be silly, I was very happy to . . . Alex said you wanted to talk about some of your ideas, how you might get involved in music or the theatre . . .?

He is watching **Rachel** *unscrew the thermos.*

On the funding side . . . (*He stops.*) Sorry, I keep wondering what on earth you're going to do?

RACHEL
Ah, I've come prepared . . . (*She smiles at him.*) This ice cream was a challenge that I was determined to take on.

She tips some fresh strawberries and blackberries out of the thermos on to the ice cream.

RACHEL
Last strawberries of summer! Cooking in public . . . It's obscene isn't it?! (*She laughs.*) I'm probably breaking all the rules . . . Do you want some?

CALLUM

Absolutely!

Faces are turning, women in hats looking disapproving.

RACHEL

And this is my master stroke . . . (*She produces a hip flask.*) A dash of alcohol!

She whispers as she pours it on the ice cream.

Will we get thrown out do you think?

CALLUM

No, they'll be queuing at our table in a minute more like . . .

We see shots of the women's faces, staring at them and muttering.

RACHEL

Well one has to make one's own excitement doesn't one, even out of ice cream . . . !

She smiles across at him.

What does it taste like?

CALLUM

Rather wonderful in fact.

RACHEL

So, Callum . . . (*Her tone changes.*) Here we go! My husband –

CALLUM

Alex.

RACHEL

No, sorry, my last husband! (*Sharp laugh.*) I should have said my late husband . . . that's a brilliant start, sorry!

No, my late husband, was much older than me, and he died very suddenly, and he left me rather a lot of money . . . he adored the arts, and taught me a great deal about how to appreciate them – Well I already loved music of course and ballet, but he introduced me to all sorts of things in a wonderful way really . . . and so now I am here, I thought maybe you could be my guide, a starting point for me, about how I might go about it all . . . Because I don't want to be this wealthy American . . . blundering about, offering people money which they might not even want! They might run a mile . . . thinking I want to interfere!

CALLUM

That again! You're always wondering about how things might seem, what people might think . . .

RACHEL

Well that's not so foolish . . . I want to get this right. Anyway it's not true (*She laughs.*) I've just done some public cooking haven't I?! (*Looking around the tea rooms.*) Probably never be able to come back here!

Callum *cannot stop staring at her, her warmth and charisma.*

CALLUM

There's a problem, I don't know anybody in the arts.

RACHEL

Yes, but I can discuss things with you can't I, as Alex suggested? Rehearse my plans, who it may be a good idea to approach . . .? And you have the time haven't you, Callum?

CALLUM

I might have . . . I have the German to look after, and of course all the files to sort out – I can't really tell you about those, it's confidential . . . (*He grins.*) Our secret office . . .

RACHEL

No, please, don't tell me! (*She looks at him.*) You must keep your secrets. I don't want you suddenly being thrown out of the hotel!

INT. ATTIC OFFICE/INTERCUT WITH WAR CRIMES UNIT. EVENING

The phone is ringing in the attic office on the secret floor. **Ringwood** *answers, a switchboard voice puts the call through.* **Ruth** *is watching the conversation beadily. There are three other people in the office working on the files.*

KATHY

Hello, this is Kathy Griffiths, could I speak to Captain Ferguson please?

RINGWOOD

Ah, Miss Griffiths . . .

KATHY

You remember me do you?

RINGWOOD

Miss Griffiths, of course we remember you.

KATHY

I'm glad to hear it, so can you put me through to Captain Ferguson?

RINGWOOD

You want to speak to Captain Ferguson?

We now see **Callum** *standing in the doorway of the office. He shakes his head.*

I'm afraid he's not here at the moment.

KATHY

He's not? May I ask where you are?

RINGWOOD

I'm in his office.

KATHY

Oh that very small office I was shown?

Ringwood's *eyes flick.*

Well shall I hold then, while you have a hunt for him?

RINGWOOD

No I'm afraid there's no point holding . . .

KATHY

Well can you tell him I need to meet him and maybe he can give me a time –

RINGWOOD
Yes, I will pass on that message.

KATHY
– in the next twenty-four hours. Tell him I have something to give him. (*She rings off.*)

CALLUM
There's no getting rid of her is there.

RINGWOOD
She'd love to get hold of these files wouldn't she if she could?!

INT. CONNINGTON THIRD-FLOOR PASSAGE/DIETER'S ROOM. EVENING

Dieter *is getting out the chess set.* **Lotte** *is standing in the doorway of the room, watching the two girls of her age running up and down the passage. One of the girls is on roller skates again and the other girl is trying to catch her. The girl on the roller skates beckons to* **Lotte**, *encouraging her to join them.* **Lotte** *turns and looks at her father pleadingly for permission.* **Dieter** *watches the girls play for a moment and then nods.*

DIETER
(*in German*)
But you must be back in five minutes.

Lotte *smiles and runs after the girls who are whooping up and down the passage. She joins in enthusiastically and they all three of them hurtle along the corridor and round the corner. They run straight into the stomach of a tall man in a dark suit. He is flanked by two other younger men. The tall man,* **Kleinow**, *stares down at the girls; he has a sharp cold stare and a severe tone. He speaks with a German accent.*

KLEINOW
Careful, children . . . you do not run in the passage. Never run in the passage.

He moves off with the two men and they reach a door further down the passage. One of the men has the room key and he opens the door. **Kleinow** *looks back at the girls.*

KLEINOW

Are you all English?

The two other girls nod. **Lotte** *does not reply.* **Kleinow** *spots this and addresses her in German. He then moves into the room with the two men and the door is shut.*

FIRST GIRL

What did he say?

Lotte *hesitates.*

Come on, what did he say?!

LOTTE

He said . . . do you want some chocolate?

We cut to a close-up of the **First Girl** *knocking sharply on* **Kleinow***'s door.* **Lotte** *and the other girl are behind her. We see the number of the room for the first time, 602.*

The door opens. **Kleinow** *stares at them; he has a formidable frightening appearance.* **Lotte** *is keeping well back in the shadows.*

KLEINOW

Yes?

FIRST GIRL

Do you have some chocolate please, sir?

Lotte *stares at* **Kleinow***'s severe face, then at the two men watching him.*

KLEINOW

Do I have some chocolate? That depends . . .

His hard eyes looking at the girls then he turns into his room. The other men are watching the children. **Kleinow** *turns back.*

It depends on you being good children . . .

He holds up the chocolate.

Are you good children?

He scours their faces. **Lotte** *is keeping well back in the shadows.*

Are you?

The **First Girl** *nods vigorously.*

> Then you may have the chocolate . . . one piece each. (*He smiles.*) And nobody else must know of course or they will all want some . . .

INT. HAROLD'S HOUSE THE LIBRARY. DAY

Victor *is alone in the dark library. The books are now in tall individual piles all over the floor. He is moving between these high columns of books, humming to himself.*

He looks round. **Lucy** *has entered the room.*

LUCY
Hello, Victor . . . I just came to say goodbye, I'm off this morning.

VICTOR
What a pity!

He stares at the young woman.

> We've hardly spoken.

LUCY
Well you never know you might still be here when I get back.

VICTOR
You mean it looks like I will take for ever to do this?!

LUCY
No, no . . . (*She indicates the piles.*) it seems you've made a real difference already . . .

She looks straight at **Victor**; *she senses his vulnerability and warmth.*

> You will look after each other won't you? I know he misses me far more than he says . . .

VICTOR
Of course we'll look after each other. (*He smiles.*) My speciality of course, looking after other people!

LUCY
I'm sure you'll do it very well, Victor . . .

HAROLD
So there you are, Lucy!

They look round – **Harold** *is in the doorway. They don't know if he has heard.*

Well, Victor, I can see you're making a little progress.

VICTOR
Yes, I'm at a crucial stage as it happens.

HAROLD
Good. And to make things even easier . . . (*He is by the window.*) I think it's time we dealt with these shutters don't you? They're kept closed because sunlight is meant to be very bad for some of these valuable books . . .

He pulls open the shutters.

But to hell with that!

Strong light pours into the room.

HAROLD
Time to ignore those rules isn't it?!

LUCY
That's so much nicer.

VICTOR
It's always a good idea ignoring rules . . .

INT. CONNINGTON. THE MAIN LOBBY. MIDDAY

Callum *is sitting in the lobby of the Connington.* **Kathy** *is moving towards him, carrying a folder.* **Callum** *stands to meet her.*

KATHY
Thank you for making time to see me, Captain Ferguson.

CALLUM

Of course . . . but I didn't think you'd want to see me again.

Kathy *doesn't react to this.*

What would you like to drink?

KATHY

I'm not here to have a drink . . .

She sits opposite him.

I've come to show you these.

She produces out of the folder the photos she took of the secret floor. The photos have been blown up into big prints; we see images of **Callum** *through the attic window, standing among the shelves of confidential files.*

CALLUM

Who took these?

KATHY

I did.

CALLUM

I've seen more flattering pictures of myself . . .

KATHY

I always knew you were lying to me about not having another office here. (*Her tone is calm.*) I don't know why you simply didn't own up about it and tell me I couldn't see it – that way you might have got rid of me . . .

CALLUM
(*carefully looking at the photographs*)
I could say I had to lie . . . It's officially secret, it is illegal to tell people about it – but I'm not saying that . . .

KATHY

Really? So what are you saying?

CALLUM

I'm saying . . . (*He looks up from the photographs.*) I will take you up there.

INT. SECRET FLOOR CONNINGTON. LATE MORNING

We cut to **Ringwood** *and* **Ruth** *and the other workers in the attic room looking up from their work, startled to see* **Callum** *escorting* **Kathy** *into the secret office.* **Kathy** *stares about her, she is surprised by the size of the room, the number of people working there.*

KATHY
It's quite an operation you've got here.

CALLUM
It is, yes.

Ringwood *is looking particularly tense at* **Kathy** *being allowed in. We notice* **Ruth** *watching the situation very carefully.*

CALLUM
I'm not going to introduce you to everybody as this is an informal visit. (*He turns.*) Could you all go to lunch? Take a particularly early lunch today?

Nobody moves; they are all watching him.

Blimey, that usually causes a stampede, come on, lunch!

Ringwood *and the others move towards the door; we stay on* **Ruth** *for a moment.*

Time cut:

A close shot of **Callum** *pulling a thick file down from one of the shelves. We cut wide to see he is now completely alone with* **Kathy** *in the attic office.*

CALLUM
I've got some pictures to show you now.

He drops the file down in front of him with a loud thump.

KATHY
Why have you brought me here? Because I know you're not going to let me go through all these files are you?

CALLUM
You're quite right I'm not.

KATHY

So why are you doing it then? I can't see any advantage to you, unless it is to win a bet with someone . . .?

CALLUM

What sort of bet would that be?

KATHY

I'm not even going to try to guess.

Callum *has been spreading a series of photographs, portraits of men, across a desk.*

CALLUM

Come here, have a look at these, rather an ugly collection I admit.

Kathy *examining the photos.*

These five Germans all have vital information, some about the workings of Soviet intelligence, some about the latest developments in armaments, in technology. I can't tell you the details obviously – and this happened before I was here – but they've all been spirited away . . . they're now in safe houses or been given new identities . . . because they have knowledge that is crucial for the defence of this country.

And none of them are on your wanted list.

KATHY

You made sure you chose the right file didn't you? So I didn't see anybody I was after?!

CALLUM

No, I chose the file that would best show you what T-Force and the Secret Service are doing –

Suddenly two female cleaners are in the doorway. They are very startled to see **Callum** *there with a visitor.*

CLEANER

Oh sorry, sir, beg your pardon, we thought we could clean this room now, we saw everybody leaving for lunch, we thought it was a good moment . . .

CALLUM
(*turning to Kathy*)
Let's get out of this place shall we?

EXT. BOMBSITE. LUNCHTIME

We see **Callum** *and* **Kathy** *walking through the thick dust on the edge of the bombsite by the back entrance of the Connington.* **Kathy** *glances behind her.*

CALLUM
What's the matter? Expecting somebody to be following us?

KATHY
Maybe . . . even the cleaners looked shocked to see me in that room.

CALLUM
Yes, they're our special cleaners who have security passes, very few people know about that floor in the hotel . . .

KATHY
You must really like that? The secrecy of it all?

CALLUM
I'm used to it now. (*He smiles.*) And of course nobody gets to see what's in those files . . .

KATHY
So you broke the Official Secrets Act for me? Why exactly?

CALLUM
To get rid of you. You just said if I hadn't lied to you, you would have gone away. (*He looks straight at her.*) So I think there's a good chance of it working, don't you?

KATHY
Or of course it could have exactly the opposite effect . . .

She looks straight back at him. The dust swirls around.

CALLUM

It's lunchtime . . . I think I want something really sweet for lunch, something with a lot of sugar! Since I haven't managed to get rid of you yet, maybe you would like to join me?

KATHY

Something sweet . . . for lunch?! That's crazy, you can't get any sugar anywhere, especially not round here . . .

INT. CONNINGTON PASSSAGE/ROOM 602. LUNCHTIME

A trolley is being pushed by a room-service waiter along the passage. It stops outside room 602. The waiter knocks. **Kleinow** *opens the door.*

We see the other two men sitting in the shadows.

KLEINOW

Ah the food is exactly on time, that's good . . .

He smiles at the two men.

Especially as you're going to start starving me soon . . .

One of the men gets up, wheels the trolley into the room, stopping the waiter entering.

EXT. PARK. AFTERNOON

We cut to **Callum** *and* **Kathy** *sitting on the grass in a London park. They are both eating toffee apples. In front of them is a broad path and a boating pond and people are promenading in the sun. There are nannies pushing prams, children out with their mothers, a man with his son feeding the ducks. Nearly everybody as they pass cannot stop themselves staring at* **Callum** *and* **Kathy** *as they eat their toffee apples.*

KATHY

This is definitely my first toffee apple since before the war! (*Indicating the people staring at them.*) But I'm not sure eating them here was such a brilliant idea . . . we're making people jealous.

CALLUM

Yes . . .

Two boys come very close.

But however many children gawp at us . . . I'm not going to feel guilty.

KATHY
(*suddenly*)
Yes, it's difficult to make you feel guilty, isn't it?

Momentary pause; **Callum** *unruffled.*

CALLUM
I was waiting for you to say something like that.

KATHY
Then you're all prepared aren't you . . . (*Giving him a searching look.*) I'm sorry but showing me that file and buying me a toffee apple is hardly going to change what I think . . .

CALLUM
Which is?

KATHY
That it is extraordinary . . . that only a year ago crimes were being committed, people being murdered on an unimaginable scale in camps and yet somehow it seems that's a side issue for nearly everybody! It's not remotely as serious as beating the Russians or getting ahead of the Americans – those are the only things that count now . . . (*Staring straight at him.*) That's shocking isn't it?

CALLUM
Put like that, it is shocking of course.

KATHY
How else could you put it so it doesn't sound shocking? I don't see how you can do that, Captain Ferguson?

CALLUM
(*firmly*)
Some people might say if we don't make national security our first priority – what happens next could be even more horrific than what happened in those camps . . .

KATHY
Are you one of those people saying that?

CALLUM
Yes, in a way.

KATHY
In a way? (*Sharp.*) what does that mean?

CALLUM
It means I know how dangerous the present situation is, that the Soviet Union is a real threat right at this moment, far more than people realise, and I also know from my own personal experience how terrible it is if we're not ready for that —

KATHY
So nothing else matters?! That will always take precedence? Being ready for the next war?!

CALLUM
Stopping the next war.

Kathy *is staring at him.*

When that danger lessens . . . we can go after all these people.

KATHY
It'll be far too late by then . . . !

We cut across the park in amongst the promenading people. We see faces watching **Kathy** *and* **Callum,** *who are now so intensely wrapped up in their conversation they are oblivious to who is watching them.*

We cut back to **Kathy** *and* **Callum.** **Kathy** *is in mid-sentence looking down at the grass as she speaks, her tone intense.*

KATHY
During the war I worked at SOE headquarters in Baker Street. I saw what happened to many of our agents after they got across the Channel — they were betrayed, brutally tortured and then executed.

My old boss, Vera Atkins, is at this moment criss-crossing
Europe trying to find those responsible and bring them to
justice – that is what has had such an effect on me . . . and
made me so committed to catching people guilty of war
crimes.

Callum *watching her closely.*

And then of course finding out some of these people are right
here under our nose, being looked after by you . . . that's
really hard.

CALLUM

But you don't know that yet, that we've got anybody really
bad . . . ! In fact now there's only one German left in the
hotel, my scientist, nobody else –

KATHY

I'm not sure I believe that, Captain Ferguson.

CALLUM

I wish you'd stop calling me Captain Ferguson . . . Why have
you started that?

KATHY

Well you are one aren't you, even though you aren't in
uniform?! I've been doing some research on you . . .

CALLUM

Have you? (*Startled.*) What have you found out?

KATHY

I've found out two things. That you had a very complicated
war . . . and, of course, that we see things very differently,
you and I . . . (*She looks straight at him.*) Or am I wrong about
that? (*She holds her gaze.*)

CALLUM

Is that some sort of challenge?

He meets **Kathy***'s searching look.*

For me to do something?

KATHY

It's not a challenge to you, no, because having just seen your real office and how big your operation is in the hotel, I've realised you are in fact in no position to help, Mr Ferguson.

CALLUM

I don't follow.

KATHY

Because they won't let you, they'll finish you off if you try to help me.

CALLUM

'Finish me off'? That's an odd thing to say?!

KATHY

They'll destroy you.

CALLUM

Destroy me?! How?

KATHY

Well that will depend on how much you inconvenience them . . . (*Her tone calm.*) If what you did proved a major nuisance you'll be disappeared most probably.

CALLUM

'Disappeared'? (*He grins.*) Nobody's going to lay a finger on me, Kathy, I assure you and especially not at the moment when I've got the German working really well . . . !

KATHY

You're almost certainly being watched right now . . .

She turns and looks across the park.

Let's see if we can spot them?

We see the faces in the park, the nannies, the couples, the solitary figures.

Which one do you think it is?

CALLUM

I can promise you I'm a real problem for them – I'm not easy to intimidate . . . (*He smiles.*) And nobody's watching.

KATHY

I'm glad to know you think you're untouchable, Mr Ferguson. But it doesn't matter if I'm right or not about that does it? Because why would you want to help me anyway? Even a little? You've just said what I'm doing is not urgent —

CALLUM

I didn't say that. I said right at this moment there are other things that have to be done —

KATHY

Thank you for the toffee apple. (*She gets up.*) It was a rare treat . . . so this is going to seem doubly ungrateful, but the only reason I can think of why you might do something for me . . . (*She stops.*)

CALLUM

Is what?

KATHY

Is because you really like taking risk, Mr Ferguson.

Kathy *moves off across the park.* **Callum** *watches her go. He suddenly notices the man feeding the ducks is no longer with his son. He is just standing on his own looking across at* **Callum***. We see other faces in the park. We move in on* **Callum***.*

INT. HAROLD'S HOUSE. DINING ROOM. LUNCHTIME

Victor *and* **Harold** *are eating lunch together, cold meat and mashed potato. They are either end of the dining room table;* **Victor** *is wolfing down his food.*

VICTOR

It is very kind of you, Mr Lindsay-Jones, to suggest we have lunch together . . . thank you so much.

HAROLD

That's quite alright . . . (*Watching him eat.*) You don't have to eat quite so quickly Victor, we are not in a race.

VICTOR
Not in a race, no . . . but I don't want to take too much time away from my work – I want to get the task done.

HAROLD
I know you do.

VICTOR
And today I'm doing very well . . . Sometimes I do get distracted I know . . . not just by the books, but I think about things, things that have happened in the past, and I get angry . . . (*His tone intense.*) Rather angry.

HAROLD
It is quite alright to be angry, Victor.

Victor *looks up from the food, surprised.*

You can be as angry as you like here . . . although preferably not with me.

VICTOR
No, of course not. Do you ever get angry, Mr Lindsay-Jones? I can't really imagine that.

HAROLD
Oh you'd be surprised Victor, there are some things that have happened which have made me angry, really angry . . . and which I think about every day.

VICTOR
Every day? Really?

HAROLD
Yes, sometimes even more. Because the truth has never been told about these particular things. I'm still trying to disentangle it. When it seems right I'll tell you about it. But first I think we have to . . .

VICTOR
(*smiles*)
Disentangle me?

INT. RACHEL AND ALEX'S BEDROOM. EARLY MORNING

A close-up of **Rachel***; her eyes flick open.* **Alex** *is across the room, fully dressed, holding a briefcase and papers.*

ALEX
Sorry, darling, I just realised I left my papers in here. I fell asleep working on them last night . . . so much to do, it's incredible how much! (*Softly.*) I didn't mean to wake you.

RACHEL
Don't be silly, it was time I was awake.

ALEX
No, it isn't, it's much earlier than you think! (*He looks across at her.*) Is everything alright, darling?

RACHEL
Oh yes . . .

Alex *is moving to go.*

By the way, I don't think I told you, it went quite well with Callum . . . at least he seemed to listen to me rattling on . . . I've sort of arranged to meet him again. (*She looks at him.*) I hope that's okay?

ALEX
Of course, darling, have as many meetings as you like. (*As he leaves.*) I knew he'd be helpful.

We stay on **Rachel**.

INT. CONNINGTON KITCHEN AND PASSAGES. DAY

We cut to **Callum** *appearing in the doorway of the hotel kitchen.* **Leonard** *and the other chefs are preparing food.* **Lotte** *is sitting on the side watching.*

CALLUM
Are you alright here, Lotte?

Lotte *nods.*

I won't be gone for long.

LEONARD

Don't worry, Mr Ferguson, we'll take good care of her . . .
She loves learning about cooking doesn't she?!

Callum *leaves. We stay on* **Lotte**. *At the far end of the passage she can see the two girls of her age, both now on roller skates.*

The **First Girl** *meets* **Lotte**'s *gaze with a conspiratorial smile.*

INT. THE GOVERNMENT RESEARCH FACILITY. EARLY AFTERNOON

We cut to a high shot of **Dieter**, **Callum** *and* **Rita** *kneeling on the floor of the hangar, surrounded by technical drawings that fan out around them. They are dwarfed by the large space, but as we crane down towards them, there is a sense of excitement, of three people brainstorming, beginning to work as a team.*

CALLUM

I don't believe it! You're actually saying we don't need a sweptback wing to go supersonic?! –

DIETER

Of course they are the future, there's no question of that, but if –

RITA

They are the future! We can't go backwards, that's not what they want to hear!

DIETER

What I'm saying is, if your priority is to beat the Americans, to do the sound barrier before anybody else, if that is the number one objective, you can do it with a fixed-wing plane.

CALLUM

Rita is right, we can't present them with that! We can't say we went to all this trouble to get him working for us – and now he is recommending we stick with what we've got already!

RITA

The government's just cancelled the latest fixed-wing fighter –

We see cuts of the drawings that surround them: different fighter planes, some with straight wings and then more modern-looking planes with sweptback wings.

DIETER

You are too obsessed with copying what we were doing! What I'm telling you is – if you want to be absolutely certain of being first, you can do it with a fixed-wing plane and the new engine we're going to build here –

CALLUM

We are going to be first and we are going to do it with a sweptback wing –

DIETER

That's an order is it? (*He grins.*)

CALLUM

It's a request . . . (*He smiles.*) Which you can't refuse. (*More serious.*) Can you do it, do you think?

DIETER

Well I like this office quite a lot . . . (*He looks up from the drawings.*) So that's a good start.

INT. CONNINGTON THIRD-FLOOR PASSAGE. AFTERNOON

We cut to the three girls moving along the third-floor passage. **Lotte** *is having a go on the roller skates, stuttering along, but grinning enthusiastically.*

We then cut to the three girls outside room 602. The **First Girl** *knocks. One of the men opens the door.* **Kleinow** *is standing further back in the room in shirt sleeves. For the first time we see there is a nurse in uniform sitting deep in the shadows.*

The **First Girl** *looks at* **Kleinow**.

FIRST GIRL

We just wanted to know, sir . . . if you have any more chocolate?

At that moment **Julia** *is coming down the stairs. She sees the three girls clustered round an unfamiliar door. She instinctively moves towards them.*

JULIA

What are you three up to?

The door of 602 is closed sharply as **Julia** *approaches.*

FIRST GIRL

We had the wrong room number, miss . . . we were just looking for somebody, we got the wrong person . . .

JULIA

Don't you fib to me?! What were you after?

LOTTE

He's got chocolate.

Julia *turns and knocks sharply on the door.* **Kleinow** *answers.* **Julia** *immediately takes in the strange atmosphere, the two men lurking, the nurse in the shadows.*

KLEINOW

Yes?

JULIA

Please do not give these children chocolate. They shouldn't be asking strangers for sweets or for anything else. (*She stares straight at him.*) Thank you.

KLEINOW

Are you their sister? (*His steely gaze.*) Or their mother even?

JULIA

I'm just a resident in the hotel.

She turns and shepherds the girls away.

INT. GOVERNMENT RESEARCH FACILITY. AFTERNOON

We cut to a close-up of **Callum** *suddenly looking up, an urgent expression in his eyes. The three of them are now sitting around the table on the higher level.*

CALLUM

Oh my God I forgot! (*He jumps up.*) I've got to be back in the hotel by three o'clock.

DIETER

Well that's going to be difficult, it's now ten to four.

CALLUM

Ten to four?! It can't be . . . ! (*He starts to move off.*)

DIETER

Is it because of Lotte? Then I will come –

CALLUM

No no, Lotte is fine – she is spending all day in the kitchens . . . but I have an important meeting, I promised . . .

INT. CONNINGTON GROUND FLOOR. LATE AFTERNOON

We cut to **Callum** *moving fast along the ground floor towards the conservatory bar. He can hear a woman's voice in the distance: 'Then they entered a dark passage, they could smell the food, it was the most delicious smell they had ever smelt. They just couldn't stop themselves opening the door . . . '*

A subjective shot leads us round the corner. There we see **Rachel** *sitting reading a story to the three girls who are listening absolutely rapt at her feet.* **Callum** *watches for a second; he is intensely struck by this image of* **Rachel** *reading to the children. The conservatory is deserted except for two waiters who are listening too.*

Rachel *looks up from the book.*

RACHEL

There you are! That is definitely a record, nearly two and a half hours late!

CALLUM

I'm very sorry. (*He moves nearer.*) You've found a way to spend the time I see!

RACHEL

Well we had a little hunt among the books in the hotel and

found this strange story about three hungry witches! We'll finish this another time, girls . . .

The girls look very disappointed.

I promise you we will . . . now go and play in the yard by the kitchens, do not go upstairs!

As the girls move off.

They've been running all over the hotel apparently . . .

*As **Lotte** leaves, she gives **Callum** a note in an envelope. **Rachel** watches this.*

LOTTE

From the other lady.

CALLUM
(*putting the note in his pocket*)
Your dad will be back soon . . . (*Watching the girls go.*) I'm impressed, they do everything you say!

RACHEL

Well today they do . . . (*She looks up at him.*) Now, we're far too late to go to that gallery . . . would it be very wicked if we went to the movies?

INT. CINEMA STALLS. EARLY EVENING

*We cut to **Callum** and **Rachel** entering the darkened cinema. A war film is playing; it is already well under way. They stand on the edge of the stalls which are mainly full of old men and old couples; the air is thick with smoke, people coughing, wheezing, some even spitting their phlegm out. Next to them is a notice saying:*

ENTRY TO ROYAL CIRCLE STRICTLY FORBIDDEN,
DANGEROUS CEILING

CALLUM

Let's go up there . . .

RACHEL

Why? You see a notice and you have to disobey it?!

CALLUM
It'll be nice up there, you'll see! Come on, I'm sure it'll be safe, at least for today . . .

RACHEL
We're going to spend the whole of the movie worrying about the ceiling falling on our heads!

She is laughing as they start to go up the stairs.

CALLUM
It will make it more exciting.

RACHEL
You chose the movie!

INT. CINEMA CIRCLE. EARLY EVENING

We cut to them emerging into the plush royal circle. It is completely deserted.

CALLUM
I told you, the best seats in the house!

RACHEL
Yes, but each time this seat creaks – I'm going to think the ceiling's coming down!

CALLUM
And we're completely alone . . .

RACHEL
Well almost alone –

She indicates the middle-aged usherette with a torch patrolling below them in the stalls. For a moment they watch the movie but **Rachel** *cannot stop herself checking the progress of the fierce-looking usherette through the haze of cigarette smoke.*

CALLUM
She can't see us, don't worry, I promise . . .

At that very moment the usherette thinks she hears something from the circle and shines her torch up towards them. They dodge down and the torch beam moves on.

CALLUM

You see . . . she can't!

RACHEL

You love this don't you?! (*Her tone warm.*)

CALLUM

Love what?

RACHEL

You're just like your brother . . . you have to take on authority! Doesn't matter who it is, you have to try and break the rules?!

CALLUM

Yes, well if the rules are particularly stupid, like now, yes I break them . . . but I'm not nearly as wild as my brother. . . (*Smiles.*) he is doing much better at the moment . . . I speak to him every day, he has a job now with Harold –

RACHEL

Oh that's good! (*She looks at him.*) I really like that, how much you take care of him, look out for him . . .

They are facing each other, while the film is playing out of focus behind them; they are totally concentrating on each other.

Both your parents are dead aren't they?

CALLUM

How do you know that?!

RACHEL

Oh come on, Callum, that's easy – you're so obviously on your own, you and your brother . . . and of course you clearly never ever worry about what they'll think . . . !

The usherette is now on the other side of the stalls. She shines her torch up to the circle, convinced she can hear voices. They dodge down again. **Rachel** *is laughing, indicating the action in the war film, a commando raid, dodging the enemy.*

RACHEL

This is like what they're doing up there!

CALLUM
Except she's more frightening!

The torch beam moves on. They sit up, **Callum** *watching the gun battle.*

RACHEL
It must be strange for you isn't it?!

Callum *watching the machine-gun fire.*

Because you were in the fighting . . . seeing it up there now . . . I expect it was very different?!

We hear the restrained voices from the screen.

CALLUM
A little different . . .

We stay on his eyes. **Rachel** *watching him. The torch beam hits the circle again, now much closer; the usherette is standing in the middle of the aisle directly below them.*

RACHEL
She's going to get us soon!

CALLUM
Let's move . . .

INT. CIRCLE BAR. EARLY EVENING

They move into the circle bar. All the glasses are still there shining in the late evening sun; the whole place is clean and polished. Old movie posters stare from the walls.

CALLUM
Look at this, it's waiting for us! It's all clean! (*He moves towards the bar.*) Somebody's been polishing it even though nobody's allowed in

RACHEL
Did they leave any liquor for us?

Callum *goes behind the bar.*

Can you give me a whisky soda, barman?

CALLUM
Sadly they didn't leave any drink behind . . . but here's a key . . . maybe there's a cupboard full of alcohol somewhere. (*He moves.*) If only we can find it!

Their faces are very close, their lips almost touching.

RACHEL
You know why we're meeting . . .?

CALLUM
Tell me why we're meeting? (*He smiles.*) I'm quite interested . . .

RACHEL
Because Alex is so busy, he really is, he has to work such long hours right now . . . and that's why . . .

Suddenly they are kissing passionately in the empty circle bar.

The old movie posters staring down at them. **Rachel** *and* **Callum** *move along the wall, kissing all the time, their bodies wrapped together.*

We cut to the auditorium, the war movie still playing, the thick smoke, the audience coughing and wheezing.

We cut back to the circle bar. Their kissing is now in powerful close-up, extremely passionate. They are oblivious to everything else.

Suddenly there is a noise. **Rachel** *turns and lets out a stifled scream. Standing in the doorway is the usherette, shining her torch. For a moment she looks deeply frightening, her face in shadow, just her small eyes glistening.*

EXT. TREE-LINED STREET. DUSK

Callum *and* **Rachel** *are moving down a very leafy street, big tall trees, the light just coming on in the houses.*

RACHEL
She was terrifying! Absolutely terrifying!

CALLUM
Yes, like the murderer coming in! Her eyes . . . she looked so excited to catch us!

RACHEL

Did she?! But it was only a kiss after all . . . (*She stops and looks at him.*) And that's all it was, Callum.

CALLUM

Was it? Only a kiss?

RACHEL

That's what I'm calling it and that's what it was. (*Her tone warm but firm.*) It's because you were really late today . . . so everything became chaotic. (*She looks at him.*) You brought chaos . . .

CALLUM

So it's all my fault is it?!

RACHEL

Of course . . . entirely . . . (*Softly.*) Being late is never a good idea, I told you. But it won't happen again . . . any of it . . .

CALLUM

Won't it?

RACHEL

No I'm not going to be terrorised by another usherette that's for sure! Anyway let's talk about more important things . . .

CALLUM

(*surprised*)

What's more important?

RACHEL

Well, Lotte, she needs to be found a school for a start.

Callum *startled by the ease with which she has changed subject.*

CALLUM

Of course . . . the government will arrange that –

RACHEL

She needs to go to a good school . . . And she wants to see your brother again.

CALLUM
No, that's not a sensible idea at all —

RACHEL
I think it is . . . (*Suddenly.*) Harold is having a dinner party on Thursday, maybe we can get him to invite your brother, Lotte and Dieter? And you of course too —

CALLUM
What?! That's doubling the size of his dinner party probably! We can't ask him to do that —

RACHEL
Of course we can. Your brother was nice to Lotte, she wants to see her friend again . . . It will be perfectly alright, Callum.

INT. SECOND-FLOOR PASSAGE/CALLUM'S BEDROOM. NIGHT

Callum *is walking towards his room.* **Julia** *is hovering in her doorway watching him approach.*

JULIA
I've been waiting for you . . . did you get my note?

CALLUM
I did . . . it was a bit cryptic wasn't it, 'I've got to talk to you about what's happening on the third floor'?!

Callum *moves into his bedroom, goes straight over to the piano in the corner, starts playing a few fragments.* **Julia** *stands in the doorway.*

JULIA
Are there other people from the Secret Service operating in this hotel?

CALLUM
No, no one, except my team —

JULIA
I think whoever told you that was lying. You should have a look at room 602.

Callum *looks up sharply, recognising the room number.*

INT. CONNINGTON THIRD-FLOOR PASSAGE/ROOM 602. NIGHT

We cut to **Callum** *and* **Julia** *heading towards room 602.*

JULIA
So what are we going to do?

CALLUM
You're going to go in there on your own.

JULIA
Me?! I am? Why me?! You're the one in Intelligence –

CALLUM
But you're the actress.

Julia *rolls her eyes.*

And you've met him already – you've got a better chance of finding out something . . .

Callum *pauses in the shadows.*

JULIA
But I also *live* here in case you've forgotten, I've managed to get a very good rate for my room – maybe with a little help from one of my gentleman friends . . . but I *have* managed it, and I've got a roof over my head, Callum, and I intend to keep it!

CALLUM
Nobody gets thrown out of this hotel, Julia, unless I agree to it.

JULIA
At the moment that's true, but it may not last . . .

CALLUM
Don't worry, you can do it, Julia. I'll be right here . . . (*He smiles.*) I know you'll do it well.

Julia *goes and knocks on 602. One of the young men opens the door.* **Julia** *is startled to see* **Kleinow** *is now propped up in bed in the shadows; the nurse is right by him.*

JULIA
(*addressing* **Kleinow**)

Hello again . . . I just wanted to apologise for sounding so bossy this afternoon, you know with the children . . .

KLEINOW

No, what you said was perfectly right . . .

His voice is weak. He beckons her to enter; the door is shut behind her.

JULIA

Yes, but I didn't mean to sound so rude. I'm staying just on the floor below . . . (*She smiles sweetly.*) And I know how horrid it is if you feel you have to avoid people in a hotel . . .

We cut into the passage. **Callum** *is watching 602. Suddenly a voice calls out.*

SALTER

Hello, Mr Ferguson . . .

Callum *sees* **Salter** *watching him from the end of the passage.*

I wondered when you'd be along here! (*Indicating 602.*) Sent somebody into the room to nose around for you have you?

CALLUM

Maybe . . . Who've you got in there?

SALTER

Quite a catch in fact, Horst Kleinow . . . he's a senior German counter-intelligence officer. He did all sorts of unpleasant things to our agents when he interrogated them, and God knows what else besides . . . helped kill a lot of Jews too, but he has astonishing information on the Russians . . .

CALLUM

Astonishing is it?

SALTER
Astonishingly valuable, yes. (*His beady eyes watching.*)

CALLUM
And that little man Mr Emmanuel, what about him?

SALTER
Ah that tiny man! He's just a contact for us, a go-between to help us get Kleinow here . . . (*His eyes glint.*)

We cut back to **Julia**. *She is standing in the middle of the room.* **Kleinow**, *the two other men and the nurse are all staring at her.*

JULIA
. . . so you see because of what happened when I was little, that bad experience, I always keep an eye out for young children . . . and of course with so many children running wild at the moment over the bombsites and everything . . .

She stops. **Kleinow** *is giving her a searching look; she can't tell if he believes her.*

KLEINOW
Children should not run wild, no.

JULIA
So we agree! . . . Are you staying here long, Mr – ?

KLEINOW
Schmidt . . . Hans Schmidt. No, I will be leaving in a few days. (*He stares at her.*) And what about you?

JULIA
I'm an actress, Mr Schmidt . . . my career is still in its early stages I have to confess, but I'm quite determined. (She smiles.) Which is a good thing don't you agree?

KLEINOW
Oh yes.

JULIA
(*staring straight at him*)
Maybe we should discuss each other's futures before you leave, Mr Schmidt . . . What do you think?

We cut back into the passage.

CALLUM
So what are your plans for the invaluable Mr Kleinow?

SALTER
We're going to disappear him.

CALLUM
'Disappear' him?

SALTER
Absolutely, we're going to fake his death. He's going to get pneumonia over the next few days right here in the hotel . . . so lots of witnesses can see him deteriorate. Then off he goes to 'hospital' to die. (*He grins.*) One of the old tricks, still very reliable though! The Americans are doing a lot of this too with their Nazis right now, it seems the season for it . . .

CALLUM
Why are you telling me this?

SALTER
Because you asked me and I wanted to see what you'd say. (*Pointedly.*) I'm beginning to know you, Ferguson, more than you think . . . (*Watching for* **Callum***'s reaction.*)

CALLUM
(*stares right back at him*)
Are you . . .? Well we both have our job to do don't we?

Julia *is coming out of room 602.*

SALTER
Had a nice chat in there?

CALLUM
(*quickly*)
This is Mr Salter, a colleague of mine, in a way —

JULIA
(*immediately sensing* **Salter** *is trouble*)
Yes, he was a most charming gentleman!

SALTER

Of course he is.

INT. ALEX AND RACHEL'S HOUSE. DRAWING ROOM. NIGHT

Rachel *is sitting at the piano in the main reception room, playing. There is just one lamp on.* **Alex** *enters the room, he is in his overcoat.*

ALEX

Still up, dear!

RACHEL

Yes . . . I wanted to see you. (*She turns.*) If I don't stay up I hardly ever see you! (*She smiles.*) You're still in your coat . . .

ALEX

Yes, I just ran straight up the stairs when I heard the noise.

RACHEL

It is a 'noise'. (*Indicating piano.*) Yes, you're right!

ALEX

It's a lovely surprise that you're still up, darling.

He leans over and kisses her.

You look so beautiful.

INT. CONNINGTON THIRD-FLOOR PASSAGE. DAY

Kleinow *is coming out of his room escorted by two nurses in uniform. He is in a dressing gown and slippers. Then we see him being helped down the stairs by the nurses, his body hunched, wracked by coughing. Guests pass him on the stairs staring at him. Then we see him being escorted along the second-floor passage; he is seemingly moving with great difficulty.* **Callum** *is in the doorway watching him approach.*

CALLUM

Are you alright, Mr Schmidt?

KLEINOW

It's my lungs.

He looks at **Callum**, *surprised he knows his name.*

The air is filthy in this city . . . quite filthy . . .

He moves past **Callum**, *who watches his receding figure.* **Kleinow** *suddenly looks back at him, a shrewd piercing stare. Their eyes meet. We move in on* **Callum**.

INT. WAR CRIMES UNIT/CALLUM'S HOTEL ROOM. DAY

We cut to the War Crimes Unit office. **Kathy** *is working at her desk. Her phone rings.*

CALLUM

Miss Griffiths, it's Callum Ferguson.

KATHY

Yes, Mr Ferguson?

CALLUM

Horst Kleinow? Is he on your list?

KATHY

He most certainly is.

CALLUM

Well he's staying here in this hotel, I've just found out –

KATHY

You've 'just' found out? That's convenient! –

CALLUM

I have just found out.

INT. CONNINGTON BATHROOM. DAY

We cut to **Kleinow** *in the bathroom; he is bare-chested, coughing violently. The nurses are tending to him, washing his arms gently. The door of the bathroom is open; more nurses come in and out, offering passing guests a glimpse of* **Kleinow**.

INT. WAR CRIMES UNIT/CALLUM'S BEDROOM. DAY

CALLUM
(*on phone to* **Kathy**)
I can't use anybody here obviously . . . but since he's on the official wanted list, you can get a warrant for his arrest using the local police. They'll take him into custody. Can you do that?

KATHY
I will do that, yes.

CALLUM
But you don't have long, forty-eight hours at the most . . .

KATHY
I understand (*Crisply.*) Thank you, Mr Ferguson.

We stay on **Kathy** *for a moment. A look of determination and excitement in her eyes.*

INT. CONNINGTON BASEMENT BALLROOM. EARLY EVENING

Eva *is alone on stage in the basement ballroom, playing the piano and singing softly. The tables are being prepared for the evening meal.* **Anna** *is there.* **Eva** *looks up, sees* **Callum** *in the doorway watching her.*

EVA
Ah, Mr Ferguson, we haven't seen you for a while.

CALLUM
I know, I've missed being here.

EVA
I'm just rehearsing something. Anna makes a good audience.

ANNA
I *hope* I'm a good audience . . .

EVA
She's quite musical, aren't you, Anna!

Anna *smiles shyly.*

> You on the other hand, Mr Ferguson, are not a good audience, you always seem to come here when there's something on your mind.

CALLUM

Do I? (*He grins.*) It's that obvious again is it?!

EVA

It certainly is. I keep telling you, if you're some sort of spy you must be a really lousy one. Just can't hide it!

Callum *looks at her, she smiles.*

> You think that's amazing don't you. I can see that! I can tell you – there's nothing amazing about it . . .

CALLUM

I believe you.

EVA

Anna . . . Callum here's a musician, but he won't show us how good he is . . . Why do you think that is?

ANNA

Maybe because it's easier to play in private . . .?

EVA

And of course it is, you're right – but one day he's got to be brave enough. (*Looking straight at* **Callum**.) So what's going on right at this moment? Worried about making the wrong decision?

Callum *turns sharply.*

> I hit the mark there!

We stay on **Callum**.

EXT. BOMBSITE. MORNING

Children are running across the bombsite in the morning light, including the two girls from the hotel. One of them is on roller skates, moving fast through the dust.

INT. CONNINGTON ROOM 602. MORNING

We cut inside **Kleinow**'s *room. He is now lying seemingly semi-unconscious, an oxygen mask held over his face by one of the nurses. He smiles through the mask.*

Salter *is sitting smoking in the shadows.*

SALTER
Thank God we're still allowed to do this . . . (*He smiles wistfully at the nurses.*) They'll come a time when it won't be so easy . . . One day they'll change the rules.

INT. HAROLD'S HOUSE. DINING ROOM. AFTERNOON

We cut to **Harold** *staring down at the dining-room table which has been laid with proper silver and flowers.* **Mrs Gorton**, *the housekeeper, is standing next to him.*

HAROLD
How exciting, Mrs Gorton, our first dinner party for quite a while . . . and rather larger than we were initially planning!

Mrs Gorton *smiles.*

I have to admit I'm strangely nervous . . . being the host once more . . . isn't that funny?

INT. CALLUM'S ROOM/SECOND-FLOOR PASSAGE. LATE AFTERNOON

We cut to **Callum** *in his room, hearing a noise. He opens the door in time to see a hospital stretcher being wheeled along the corridor by two male hospital porters; two nurses are in attendance as well. The men start carrying the stretcher up the stairs.* **Callum** *moves sharply after them.*

INT. THIRD-FLOOR PASSAGE/ROOM 602. LATE AFTERNOON

We cut to **Callum** *moving urgently down the third-floor passage, the stretcher is just entering room 602.* **Ringwood** *suddenly appears behind him.*

####### RINGWOOD

Ah, there you are, sir! I need to consult you about the files, sir, which sections we're going to throw out first –

####### CALLUM

Not now, Ringwood!

Callum *can see into room 602 as the stretcher is wheeled in. He sees* **Kleinow** *breathing with difficulty under the oxygen mask, the nurses all standing around the bed. The door has been left open so passersby can see in.* **Callum** *turns sharply.*

I've got to make an urgent phone call!

EXT. CONNINGTON BACK ENTRANCE. EARLY EVENING

Three police cars are approaching the back entrance of the hotel. **Kathy** *is standing impatiently, watching them approach. Suddenly* **Callum** *is by her side.*

####### CALLUM

There you are! I didn't know you'd arrived.

The cars draw up and uniformed policemen spill out.

INT. CONNINGTON THIRD-FLOOR PASSAGE. EARLY EVENING

We cut to the police and **Callum** *and* **Kathy** *approaching room 602.*

There is also a member of the hotel staff with a large bunch of keys. The police knock on the door, wait for a moment. They indicate to the hotel manager to open it. The door swings open to reveal an entirely empty room. It is spotless; the bed has fresh sheets and there is no sign of the oxygen cylinders. **Callum** *moves into the room.*

####### CALLUM

I don't know how they did that?! I was keeping watch all the time. (*To* **Kathy**.) You took too long.

####### KATHY

I took too long?! You let them get away from under your nose. Why on earth didn't you stay right outside this door?!

CALLUM
I did, they couldn't have done this in two minutes –

KATHY
(*turns to police*)
Sorry, gentlemen, for wasting your time.

EXT. CONNINGTON BACK ENTRANCE. EVENING

We cut to the police cars driving off, kids from the bombsite running alongside the cars. **Kathy** *and* **Callum** *watching them go.*

KATHY
Well that went well didn't it?!

CALLUM
They can't have got far. (*He turns sharply.*) Maybe they left something in that room we missed –

INT. CONNINGTON THIRD-FLOOR PASSAGE/BATHROOM. EVENING

We cut to **Callum** *moving really fast along the third-floor passage,* **Kathy** *right behind him. Suddenly, on an impulse,* **Callum** *turns and doubles back. He goes up to a door marked 'Ladies Bathroom'. Without warning he bangs through the door to find a young woman just changing out of her nurse's uniform. She looks totally startled and very nervous.*

CALLUM
I thought there might be one left.

He advances on the woman, his manner controlled, cold, rather frightening. **Kathy** *is watching from the doorway.*

Where did they go?

NURSE
To the hospital . . . they went to the hospital – the man was very ill.

CALLUM
I'm not going to hurt you.

His tone seems to contradict this; the woman stares at him very frightened.

> But you are going to tell me . . . just nod, understand? Did they go to the airport at Croydon?

The woman is just staring at him.

> To Southampton . . .? Come on! To Harwich?

Now her eyes flick, a tiny nod.

INT. CONNINGTON STAIRCASE. EVENING

We cut to **Callum** *and* **Kathy** *moving fast down the staircase.*

CALLUM
We need a car . . . we need a car . . .

Suddenly on the landing below them is **Dieter** *and* **Lotte**, *all dressed up on their way out.* **Dieter** *is in a dinner jacket,* **Lotte** *in her red party dress.*

DIETER
Callum, you're not ready?! You're not dressed!

CALLUM
Oh God the dinner party! (*He moves up to them.*) I hadn't forgotten, Lotte . . . tell them I will be joining later.

He is moving past them with **Kathy**.

> Tell Victor, I will definitely be there soon.

EXT./INT. HAROLD'S HOUSE. EVENING

Victor *is on the doorstep of* **Harold***'s house being let in by* **Mrs Gorton**. *He has made an effort with his clothes, a white shirt and a bow tie, but a battered old jacket.*

He is carrying a crumpled bag.

VICTOR
I'm very early, I'm the first probably aren't I?

HAROLD

Ah, Victor... (*Approaching across hall.*) You are a little early, but I always like people who are early.

VICTOR

I brought some food...

He produces tins out of the bag.

Just a few tins I had, of spam and sardines.

HAROLD

In case we run out of hot food? How sensible!

VICTOR

I ought to say... (*He holds the tins.*) I haven't eaten with more than one person in a long time. My brother tends to get a little nervous about me meeting new people. (*He smiles.*) I hope I remember how it's done.

EXT. SALOON CAR. ROAD. NIGHT

Headlights of a large truck coming straight towards us, blowing its horn really loudly.

Then we see **Callum** *driving fast,* **Kathy** *watching him from the passenger seat. Through the windscreen we see they are stuck behind another large truck.*

Callum *is trying to overtake, more headlights coming straight at him.*

KATHY

I want Horst Kleinow, of course, but...

CALLUM

But you don't want to be killed in the process.

He is hunched over the wheel.

I understand.

He tries to overtake again, two cars coming straight at him. He has to go back.

KATHY

I hope you understand . . . Why are they taking him to Harwich? If they really are?

CALLUM

Because he's going back to Germany I expect, so he can go through all the intelligence they've got on the Russians. But they needed to stage his death in England – so many people 'disappear' in Germany it's difficult to be officially dead and be believed . . .

We see a shot of parked trucks in a lay-by, their headlights shining, drivers drinking tea, watching **Callum** *trying to overtake.*

KATHY

Why did you change your mind? Why are you suddenly helping me get Kleinow?

CALLUM

Because I didn't like the way he looked at me.

KATHY

Are you going to tell me the real reason?!

CALLUM

No, that is the real reason.

He overtakes the truck, driving really fast.

I didn't like the blatant way they were going about it! I can believe totally in what we're doing, getting the best German minds working for us, and I can also believe that one or two really nasty people deserve to answer for what they've done. I don't see any contradiction . . .

KATHY

Others might. Some of your colleagues for a start . . .

CALLUM

There is no contradiction.

He is driving really fast. **Kathy** *has to hold on tight.*

                    KATHY
You think they're just going to let you do this and get away
with it?

Callum *does not react.*

That nothing is going to happen afterwards?

                    CALLUM
I believe I can get away with it, yes.

We see the night road stretching ahead in the headlights.

Do you want this man or not?

INT. HAROLD'S HOUSE DINING ROOM. NIGHT

Harold *is presiding over the dinner party,* **Rachel** *and* **Alex**, **Lotte** *and*
Dieter, *two late-middle-aged couples, men from the Foreign Office with
their wives.* **Victor** *is sitting up very straight; he has his pile of tins right
next to him on the table.*

Lotte *is watching him closely, sensing* **Victor**'*s anxiety. We keep cutting to
him. The main course has just arrived.*

                    HAROLD
Two slices of beef for everyone . . . the very height of luxury
I hope! I've used weeks of meat rationing for this!

                    RACHEL
Fabulous, what a treat.

                    ALEX
Splendid . . . and unlike everywhere else, it's not overcooked!

                    HAROLD
Yes, the British way, let's make it taste as close to old leather
as we possibly can –

                    VICTOR
                   (*suddenly*)
There may not be enough meat to go round . . . because
some of us were added to the guest list.

HAROLD
No, no, there's plenty, Victor, don't worry.

VICTOR
I have these tins here as you can see. If we need some more.

Lotte *is watching him, concerned. The Foreign Office men are staring; they can't disguise their unease.*

VICTOR
Feel free to ask when you fancy some. (*Taps tins.*)

RACHEL
We will!

VICTOR
Yes. (*Staring at the Foreign Office men.*) No need to be shy.

EXT. SALOON CAR APPROACHING THE DOCKS. NIGHT

Through the windscreen we see arc lights staring down on the approach to the docks. Two large trucks are ahead of them, military jeeps passing them in the other direction.

KATHY
May I ask a very stupid question?

CALLUM
Of course.

KATHY
How are you going to get them to hand Horst Kleinow over?

CALLUM
That won't be difficult . . . provided we can find him.

KATHY
It won't? They're just going to say 'Take him, by all means! He's all yours'?! That's what's going to happen?!

CALLUM
They'll be keeping him in a room somewhere out of the way, waiting for the moment to embark . . . they'll almost certainly

be only two or three guards, everybody else will have buggered off because all the hard work's been done. Nobody's expecting us to show up! I just walk in and say I need to have an urgent word with him – in private. (*He smiles.*) You don't believe me?

KATHY

No.

Callum *suddenly swerves the car away from the trucks they are following, and through an entrance which says:* STRICTLY NO ADMITTANCE FOR UNAUTHORISED PERSONNEL

INT. HAROLD'S HOUSE. THE DINNER PARTY. NIGHT

We cut back to the dinner party. Everybody is eating, except **Victor** *who has cut his meat into tiny pieces. He looks very ill at ease.* **Lotte** *smiles reassuringly at him.*

ALEX

Victor, I hear you've been sorting out Harold's library?

VICTOR

Yes, I think I've been knocking it into some sort of shape.

HAROLD

Victor has brought a sudden energy into this house, it's highly contagious –

RACHEL

Which is a very good thing isn't it?

HAROLD

Absolutely. I think we were all so full of energy during the war, and then we tried to turn it off like a tap, but of course that doesn't work, the adrenaline's still there, ticking away all the time. It's best to do something about it.

DIETER

Like what for example?

HAROLD

Like getting younger for a start.

Rachel *laughs.*

> No, I'm serious, I think we settle for being old far too quickly. I dressed like my father as soon as I could, I looked ridiculous in a bowler at eighteen! You go out in the streets now and young women are dressing like their mothers again, as if nothing had happened. We should all plan to get younger and not pretend that energy has gone away.

VICTOR

> Of course one has to have done something in the war to have that energy.

He stares around the table, pointing at **Dieter**.

> He built jet planes, I was in the army . . . (*Looking at* **Alex**.) What did you do?

ALEX

(startled, flustered)

> I was in Washington, stationed at our embassy.

VICTOR

> And what about you two?

He looks at the other men.

> In the Foreign Office as well no doubt?!

HAROLD

> As was I, Victor. I'm sure we all worked hard.

VICTOR

> I've said the wrong thing, haven't I?

RACHEL

> No, nobody's offended, it is absolutely fine.

VICTOR

> I've said the wrong thing because nobody's allowed to talk about who did what – what some of us really saw . . . really did! It's such bad form!

Lotte *is looking very concerned for him.*

And I'm sorry I look like this. I must have mislaid my dinner jacket, mustn't I?!

We move in on him.

And I realise these tins maybe look a bit ridiculous . . . You see I've not done this kind of thing recently . . . and seeing your faces so clearly – (*Pointing at the middle-aged men.*) Especially your faces . . . has been difficult.

He gets up.

It was a big mistake me coming here. I'm so very sorry . . .

He leaves the room. **Rachel** *immediately gets up and follows him. There is silence.*

HAROLD
Victor has his own approach to everything. It takes a bit of getting used to. I'm sure he didn't mean to be rude.

We stay on **Lotte**'s *face staring after him.*

EXT. APPROACH TO MILITARY AREA. DOCKS. NIGHT

We cut to **Kathy** *and* **Callum** *driving through the military areas of the docks and approaching a checkpoint in the distance. There is a queue of military vehicles ahead of them tailing back from the checkpoint.*

CALLUM
God I hope he's okay.

KATHY
What is it? What's the matter?

CALLUM
I'm just thinking about my brother Victor, I hope he's alright at the dinner party.

KATHY
Why wouldn't he be alright?

CALLUM

My brother's not very well. I have to keep an eye on him . . . always.

He slows the car as they approach the queue of military vehicles.

It's just a meal, he must be alright. Well I'm here now . . .

INT. HAROLD'S HOUSE THE PASSAGE OUTSIDE DINING ROOM. NIGHT

Rachel *and* **Victor** *are together outside the dining room. There are tears pouring down* **Victor***'s face, but he is moving backwards and forwards, pacing.*

RACHEL

Victor, it's alright . . .

She tries to touch his arm but he moves away from her.

Don't be upset.

VICTOR

I'm not upset.

RACHEL

You're crying.

VICTOR

But I'm not upset in that way . . . not the way you think . . .

RACHEL

You don't know what I think. (*Softly.*) Nobody cares about whether you're wearing a dinner jacket, Victor . . . they really don't! (*She holds his arm.*) And the tins were a good idea, they were, I promise . . . after all there were more guests . . .

VICTOR

I find it so difficult . . .

He is suddenly sobbing in her arms.

. . . I find even the easiest things so difficult . . . I just can't get them right . . . however hard I try . . . I can feel it happening, when I'm with people, I start to do things I shouldn't, then I can't stop it, I'm not able to stop myself, and I hate that, I hate not being able to . . .

RACHEL

I know.

Holding him tight, her tone warm, firm, as he cries.

Callum will be here soon . . . it was my idea for all of us to meet – and I want to be able to say to him, Victor's been in sparkling form.

VICTOR

Well that's going to be difficult isn't it?! (*Holding her tight.*) To say that.

RACHEL

He cares about you so much, Victor.

VICTOR

How do you know?

He suddenly looks straight at her.

When did he tell you that?

RACHEL

I know.

She meets his gaze.

VICTOR

If you're right . . . why isn't he here?

EXT. DOCKS. NIGHT

Callum *is driving fast against the traffic, military jeeps nearly hitting them, the drivers yelling at them as they pass.*

We cut to a shot through the windscreen of **Callum** *driving through pedestrians, people moving towards the embarkation hall carrying their luggage. He sends them scattering as he drives, blaring the horn.*

He suddenly slows the car as they approach a swelling queue of people pushing their way through the narrow entrance of the Immigration Hall.

Callum *and* **Kathy** *jump out of the car, abandoning it in the middle of the concourse, and begin to force their way through the queue.*

INT. IMMIGRATION HALL. NIGHT

We cut to **Callum** *and* **Kathy** *pushing their way through the tide of people inside the Immigration Hall. Some are weighed down with luggage, others just have bundles of belongings. There are screaming children, nervous faces all around. Most of the people are waiting to be allowed into the country; there is a separate queue for people about to embark on the ship.*

Suddenly **Callum** *catches a glimpse of* **Kleinow** *moving away from them across the hall. It is a fleeting image. A second later he is gone, obscured by people queuing.*

CALLUM
I think I've seen him . . . ! (*He stares around.*) Where the hell is he now?!

Callum *and* **Kathy** *fight their way through the throng. They catch one other incredibly brief glimpse of* **Kleinow**, *near the stairs at the far end of the hall. We cut to them reaching the stairs, people are pushing past them, going in the opposite direction. Announcements are booming over the Tannoy.*

Callum *and* **Kathy** *emerge on the first floor where there is a row of desks stretching down the whole length of the huge hall. People are sitting at each desk being processed. There is another queue at the top of the stairs, passengers waiting to be summoned to a desk.*

Between the queue and where the desks start there is a bench. Sitting on the bench is **Kleinow**; *he is just having a cigar lit by one of his entourage. He is surrounded by six minders. Sitting at the end of the bench is* **Salter**; *he is also smoking a cigar.*

Callum *and* **Kathy** *stare at the group from their position in the queue.*

Kleinow *is laughing and joking with* **Salter**.

KATHY

You said it would be simple.

A close-up of **Callum**.

CALLUM

I was wrong.

We move in on **Callum**; *we see real determination in his eyes. We cut back to* **Kleinow** *as he holds forth to his minders. The image slows for a moment,* **Kleinow**'s *face animated by laughter, the cigar smoke drifting.*

CREDITS

Part Four

CREDIT SEQUENCE

INT. THE PORT. IMMIGRATION HALL. NIGHT

A high shot of the main ground-floor area of the Immigration Hall: the swirling people, some standing ready to be called to board the ship, others jostling in the far longer queue, waiting to be processed by Immigration.

We cut to the first floor with its line of desks stretching into the distance. At each desk passengers are being interrogated by an immigration official. There are Tannoy announcements jabbing out in the background. We see **Kleinow** *and* **Salter** *sitting on a bench enjoying their cigars, and sipping from a hip flask they are passing between them.* **Kleinow**'s *minders are standing just behind the bench.*

We cut to **Kathy** *watching him, standing next to* **Callum**, *among the passengers huddled at the top of the stairs waiting to be called.*

We cut close to **Callum**. *We move in on his eyes.*

END OF CREDIT SEQUENCE

INT. IMMIGRATION HALL. GROUND FLOOR/FIRST FLOOR. NIGHT

There is the sudden sound of a loud bell ringing incessantly. With an abrupt cut we are back in the Immigration Hall as people pick up their luggage and move to the embarkation doors.

We cut to the first floor. The bells are ringing out loudly there too.

Kleinow *and* **Salter** *get up from the bench in a relaxed almost insolently confident way; they begin to move.* **Kathy** *and* **Callum** *merge into the crowd of people waiting at the top of the stairs.* **Kleinow** *and his entourage pass very close to them.* **Kleinow** *and his minders are moving down the stairs soon to disappear amongst the large crowd in the main hall.*

Kathy *and* **Callum** *are powerless to stop them.*

Suddenly **Callum** *notices in the distance a small man with glasses, his appearance vaguely similar to* **Mr Emmanuel**.

We move in on **Callum**. *He turns sharply to* **Kathy**.

CALLUM

We might just try something . . .

KATHY

Anything is better than standing here watching them go . . .

Kleinow *has almost disappeared into the crowd with his entourage.*

We cut downstairs. We are with **Kleinow** *moving with his entourage and* **Salter**. *The minders are creating a path through the throng of people.*

Suddenly **Kleinow** *feels a touch on his arm.*

He turns to see **Kathy** *standing next to him.*

KATHY

Herr Kleinow . . .?

Kleinow *stares at her.*

I have an urgent message for you – Mr Emmanuel is here . . .

She indicates a door back the way they came.

He must speak with you . . .

Kleinow *trying to work out if he has ever seen her before.*

KLEINOW

Mr Emmanuel? He is here?

Kathy *indicates a doorway behind them.* **Kleinow** *hesitates. We see* **Salter** *and the minders moving through the crowd. For a moment they have not noticed* **Kleinow** *is not following.* **Kathy**'s *tone is very urgent.*

KATHY

They're not taking you where you think you're going . . .

INT. IMMIGRATION HALL. MAIN AREA/LANDING AND STAIRCASE. NIGHT

We cut to **Kathy** *standing in a doorway off the main hall, beckoning to* **Kleinow**. *He moves towards her and steps on to the landing.*

He is startled to be confronted by **Callum**.

KLEINOW

Of course it is you.

CALLUM

We need you to come to London.

KLEINOW

I'm sure you do . . . (*His eyes meets* **Callum***'s.*)

CALLUM

We can do this reasonably . . . (*There is a real threat of violence in his eyes.*) Or we can do this another way . . .

KLEINOW

Or we don't do it at all. (*He turns to go back.*) You must excuse me . . .

Callum *in an instant has a gun against* **Kleinow***'s temple.* **Kathy** *is startled by his casual violence. There is no door to close on the landing, people are swirling past in the background, just feet away.*

CALLUM

Get down on your knees.

Kleinow *kneels on the landing. A child stares at him through the doorway, his mother's startled face seeing what he is looking at.* **Callum** *addresses them casually, as if it is an everyday occurrence.*

Don't worry, we're the police . . .

There are more people, European faces glancing on to the landing, faces used to seeing violence, moving past. We see **Kleinow***'s face in profile in semi-darkness, with the light of the main hall behind him.*

Now do we understand each other?

Kleinow *hesitates, then nods very slightly.*

We're just going to stay here for a moment till I believe you . . .

A close-up of **Kathy** *watching, wanting to get them off the landing.*

We cut back to the main hall. **Salter** *and the minders are gathered by the embarkation doors, staring around them.*

Then they begin to push back against the crowd, looking for **Kleinow**.

EXT. THE CONCOURSE. THE DOCKS. NIGHT

We cut to **Callum** *escorting* **Kleinow** *across the night concourse, he has him by the arm, and* **Kleinow** *can feel the gun pressing into his back.* **Kathy** *is moving just ahead of them towards the car. People are pushing past them in both directions moving with their luggage. They reach the car.*

CALLUM

Kathy, you're going to drive.

He throws her the key, **Kathy** *sits in the front of the car and begins to switch on the engine.* **Callum** *forces* **Kleinow** *on to the backseat of the car and sits next to him. The car drives off.*

EXT./INT. THE CAR. THE DOCKS. NIGHT

We cut to the receding shot through the back window of the car as it moves away from the main building and weaves its way through the pedestrians with their suitcases.

We then cut to a two shot of **Kleinow** *and* **Callum** *sitting next to each other on the back seat of the car.* **Kleinow** *looks over his shoulder out of the back window.* **Callum** *follows his look.*

CALLUM

Amazing isn't it?! No sign of them! . . . never overestimate their efficiency, it's a big mistake.

We cut to a shot over **Kathy**'s *shoulder as she drives. We see the car moving through the passengers with their suitcases but they are walking in the road and slowing their progress.*

We cut back to the receding shot through the back window. Some headlights of a car following in the distance. **Kleinow** *turns to* **Callum**.

KLEINOW

You're not going to get five miles.

Callum *gives him a dangerous smile.*

CALLUM
Oh we're stopping well before then.

We then see a wide shot of the car moving through the passengers on the concourse driven by **Kathy**. *Over this shot we hear* **Callum**'s *voice.*

Come on, Kathy, let's get out of here!

INT. THE HALL. HAROLD'S HOUSE. NIGHT

Harold *is by his front door, the Foreign Office men and their wives are just leaving the dinner party.* **Victor** *is watching them go from the doorway of the drawing room, behind him* **Dieter** *and* **Lotte**, **Rachel** *and* **Alex** *are sitting drinking coffee.* **Victor** *suddenly calls out to the couples.*

VICTOR
Sorry you all have to leave . . . we'll meet again no doubt!

The couples glance uneasily in his direction. **Victor**'s *tone is amiable.*

I hope you're not running away because I asked you what you did in the war?

The couples start to leave hastily.

I'm sure, in your own way, you did your bit . . .

HAROLD
(*turning towards* **Victor**)
Are you feeling a little better, Victor?

VICTOR
I am. (*Suddenly.*) Where on earth do you think Callum is?

INT. ROADSIDE CAFÉ. NIGHT

Lights glowing out of the blackness. A roadside café and car park, a large glass window; lorries and cars drawing up. We are inside. **Kleinow** *and* **Callum** *are sitting opposite each other, as headlights approach the window out of the night. Some families and small children, having come off a ship, are in the café. Some of the children are charging around, playing. There is a jukebox in the corner. A waitress comes up to the table with a tray of tea.*

Kleinow *is watching the children.*

> KLEINOW
> It's so busy at this time of night, I'm surprised.

> CALLUM
> But no sign of your friends.

> KLEINOW
> Not yet . . .

He is taking a little parcel of sugar cubes out of his pocket, which he puts carefully on the table.

> You think they've driven straight past and all the way to London without me . . .? And not turned back?

More headlights approaching the window.

> We'll see . . .

Kathy *comes up to the table and stands in front of* **Kleinow**.

> CALLUM
> Are they coming?

> KATHY
> They are. (*She addresses* **Kleinow**.) The police, who came to the hotel, are now coming here to collect you. They have a warrant for your arrest.

> KLEINOW
> Do you want some sugar in your tea?

> KATHY
> They will take you before a magistrate in the morning . . . you'll be remanded in custody. Arrangements will then be made to take you back to Germany. And after a few days that is exactly where you will go.

> CALLUM
> And when you are there you will stand trial.

KLEINOW

That is not going to happen, we all know that don't we . . .

He takes some chocolate out of his pocket and breaks a bit off.

Please, I don't want this all to myself . . . this is the chocolate the children liked so much. (*He offers* **Kathy**.) Please . . .

KATHY

No, thank you.

KLEINOW

What do you call yourself? A war crimes division?

KATHY

Something like that. (*Her stare is unflinching.*)

KLEINOW

It's not easy is it? The victors being the only ones deciding what is a crime . . . Not the best system maybe . . .?

He looks across at the people in the café.

We are on the same side now. That is what the Americans have realised more than anybody else, the information we can now share with each other . . .

He watches a young woman put money in the jukebox.

And help keep all these people safe.

And your government has realised that too now.

The music from the jukebox starts.

What happened has . . .

KATHY

Has gone? Is that what you think?

KLEINOW

What happened makes cooperation difficult of course . . . but things change so quickly. (*He smiles.*) They always do when the fighting stops.

People you'd never ever think you'd sit down with, you find you're seeing so much of . . . (*He looks across at the jukebox.*) I never thought I'd enjoy this American music . . . but now I do.

INT./EXT. HAROLD'S HOUSE. THE LIBRARY/GARDEN. NIGHT

The camera is moving in a subjective track through the library window and out into **Harold**'s *garden.* **Victor** *is whooping around playing with* **Lotte** *in the chicken coop.* **Rachel** *and* **Alex**, **Harold** *and* **Dieter** *are sitting on the steps leading into the garden. They are all a little drunk.* **Dieter** *watching* **Lotte**'s *delighted face as she plays.*

DIETER
She shouldn't be up so late but why not?! Her last days of freedom before I find her a proper school . . . (*He smiles.*) Except they're making me work so hard I have no time to look . . .

RACHEL
Maybe we can all help look for one? I have the time! It must be a good school.

Dieter *raises his glass to her.*

She is so pleased to see her friend again isn't she?!

VICTOR
The thing about chickens, Lotte, is . . .

We cut amongst the chickens. **Lotte** *is sitting in the middle of the coop.*

They are much braver than you think! They kill snakes in the wild and mice and lizards . . . One must never underestimate the humble chicken!

Lotte's *delighted smile.*

HAROLD
Victor knows far more about things than you would ever suspect.

RACHEL
Just like his brother . . .

ALEX

Yes, Callum is a most remarkable fellow isn't he?! With his music . . . and all his technical knowledge, about machines and engines and nuts and bolts! And then all his hush-hush work too . . . (*He drinks.*) I would call him a truly remarkable chap . . .

RACHEL

You're right . . .

We move in on **Rachel** *until we are close.*

He is . . . a truly remarkable chap.

HAROLD

But something extraordinary must have happened tonight . . .?

RACHEL

For him not to be here.

We stay on **Rachel** *for a second.*

INT. ROADSIDE CAFÉ. NIGHT

Callum, *at the café table, looks up sharply. The café is almost totally deserted now. There is a glint in* **Callum**'s *eye. He sees that the headlights of two police cars are approaching fast across the car park. The cars pull up close to the windows.*

Kleinow *watches the uniformed police get out of the cars.*

KLEINOW

Your police have come after all.

CALLUM
(*to* **Kathy**)

You go with him . . . ride in the car with him.

KATHY

Yes. (*Staring straight at* **Kleinow**.)

I think that's a very good idea.

Faces turn, waitresses staring, as the police enter the café.

EXT. CAFÉ CAR PARK/INT. POLICE CAR. NIGHT

We cut to the police escorting **Kleinow** *towards the police cars.* **Callum** *is standing in the doorway of the café watching them go.* **Kathy** *suddenly moves back to him.*

KATHY

I hope nothing happens to you because of this . . .

CALLUM

Don't worry about me, please . . . never worry about me, ever.

We cut to the police cars moving off. A shot through the side window of **Callum** *watching them go.* **Kathy** *is sitting with* **Kleinow** *and a uniformed policeman on the back seat.* **Kleinow** *watches* **Callum** *in the doorway of the café, a receding shot.*

KLEINOW

I hope his superiors are understanding . . . and what they do to him is not too severe.

We cut to a close-up of **Kathy**. *And then* **Kleinow** *turns to her. We cut back to* **Kathy**, *deep in thought. We stay on her face.*

INT. CONNINGTON. THE LOBBY. EARLY MORNING

Callum *is approaching across the lobby in early morning light. He is very watchful in case* **Salter** *or any of his colleagues are waiting for him. A hotel porter suddenly appears out of the shadows, and* **Callum** *turns sharply. Then a voice calls.*

JULIA

Hello, stranger . . .

Callum *turns again and sees* **Julia** *across the lobby.*

You're very jumpy!

Julia *is sitting on the edge of the lobby, all dressed up in her best coat and hat. She is holding a folder on her knees.*

CALLUM

I am jumpy, yes. (*He moves towards her.*) You look terrific!

JULIA

Thank you. (*She taps the folder.*) I'm going for an audition, for a film . . . It's only a tiny part, but rather a showy one all the same! I'm hours early, but I prefer to get there and then walk up and down outside. Auditions are torture of course. (*She smiles.*) Pray for me won't you?!

CALLUM

I will.

He glances round the lobby and then back to her.

I'm going to have a hell of a day too . . . ! I'm about to be summoned to headquarters.

JULIA

Ah . . . (*She lowers her voice.*) So what have you been up to? What have you done, Callum?

CALLUM

Best you don't know.

JULIA

Been doing something about that spooky German man have you? (*She gets up.*) Well whatever it is, just be smart won't you, what you do next. (*She kisses him on the cheek.*) And take reinforcements if you can . . . I would if I could!

EXT. SUBURBAN STREETS. MILITARY JEEP. DAY

We cut to **Callum** *driving a jeep fast along suburban streets. Sitting next to him and hanging on tight is* **Dieter**.

DIETER

There is no point in me coming to this meeting if you kill us both.

CALLUM

It's one way out though!

He grins as he drives really fast.

DIETER
You really think I can be of help?

CALLUM
Yes, a big help . . . just so long as you agree with everything I say.

INT. MILITARY HEADQUARTERS. WAINWRIGHT'S OFFICE. DAY

Callum *is sitting facing* **Wainwright** *who is behind his desk.* **Dieter** *is sitting slightly behind* **Callum**. **Wainwright** *is staring at both of them.*

WAINWRIGHT
So, Ferguson, let us be clear – you've conspired in the removal of a senior German counter-intelligence officer who was about to reveal vital information about the Russians . . . and you have handed him over to the War Crimes Unit . . . and he is now sitting in a police cell in Covent Garden where he is absolutely no use to anybody.

Is that what you've done?

CALLUM
That's right, yes, sir.

Silence. **Wainwright** *staring at him.*

I was told all other operations in the hotel had been discontinued apart from mine. That was clearly a lie.

Wainwright's *face impassive.*

My one and only objective is to achieve the work that Dieter here is doing, and we're making tremendous progress . . .

DIETER
Tremendous progress yes, every day it goes better. We're getting really very close . . .

CALLUM

I could not afford to let Salter and his lot rampage around the hotel and endanger that work – they had to be stopped. Miss Griffiths had obtained a warrant for Herr Kleinow's arrest. I helped her secure that arrest.

There is silence. **Wainwright** *staring at them both.*

WAINWRIGHT

That is the best you can do?

CALLUM

That is the best, yes, sir. (*He looks straight back at him.*)

WAINWRIGHT
(*suddenly standing up*)

Come on, come with me.

They both get up. To **Callum***:*

Just you!

EXT. THE SUNKEN GARDEN. THE MILITARY BASE. DAY

We cut to **Wainwright** *and* **Callum** *standing in the sunken garden. Armed military personnel are watching at the garden entrance, staring down at* **Callum***.*

WAINWRIGHT

Lovely garden isn't it, I don't know why we should ever give it back . . . (*Turns to* **Callum***, steely.*) I couldn't say it in front of him, but those bloody bastards from MI16 should never have still been in the hotel, so fuck 'em! Absolutely fuck 'em! You were right . . .

Callum *realises something else is coming.*

Just so long as our German friend delivers, you'll be okay. It is me you have to worry about, Ferguson, always remember that.

CALLUM

I do remember that, sir.

WAINWRIGHT

I will handle the bastards for you . . . (*His tone suddenly intense.*) Of course it can never ever happen again, understand?

Callum *nods.*

And for God's sake get rid of those bloody files in the hotel right away! We don't need them any more, chuck 'em all out. They are just a magnet for Miss Griffiths and her lot.

CALLUM

I will do that sir.

WAINWRIGHT

And I have another task for you too.

CALLUM

Ah, is this the punishment then, sir?

WAINWRIGHT

It could easily be, yes. Plastics and perfume!

Callum *looks startled.*

We're going to be using the hotel for a little longer Ferguson, we're still collecting Germans who can be of use to us, and not just scientists, but people who can give us a commercial advantage too.

We've got hold of this widow, Frau Bellinghausen – the family fortune was in perfume, the rival to Eau de Cologne, just as successful! She says she has the secret formula, she alone. You've got to get it out of her . . . or find out if she's just playing us along to make us fund a new life for her . . .

CALLUM

Right . . . I can do that. And the plastics?

WAINWRIGHT

That might come later, Ferguson . . . the plastics. (*Begins to move off, then he turns.*) I ought to warn you, she's absolutely terrifying . . .

EXT. MAIN HOUSE. MILITARY BASE. DAY

Callum *is moving towards* **Dieter** *who is standing next to the jeep outside the main house on the military base.* **Callum** *grins as he reaches him.*

CALLUM

We got away with it!

DIETER

You mean you got away with it!

We cut to the jeep roaring off, **Dieter** *and* **Callum** *together.*

INT. CONNINGTON SECOND-FLOOR PASSAGE/MELBURY SUITE. AFTERNOON

Callum *approaches the Melbury Suite. He knocks on the door. A voice calls 'Enter!'* **Callum** *enters the large but rather shabby suite. Sitting in the centre of the room is a middle-aged woman. Two large trunks stand either side of her, both still firmly strapped shut. One smaller travelling case is sitting close to her on the table.*

Frau Bellinghausen *is dressed immaculately; the clothes are old-fashioned but beautifully chosen. She speaks with a perfect English accent, no trace of German.*

Her tone is formidable, very intelligent, but not completely hostile.

FRAU BELLINGHAUSEN

So you're the one they've sent to deal with me?

CALLUM

I'm the lucky man, yes.

She doesn't smile.

Sent to welcome you . . .

FRAU BELLINGHAUSEN

You're not part of the management of this hotel?

CALLUM

I'm not, no.

FRAU BELLINGHAUSEN
So you're a Secret Service man then, a policeman?

CALLUM
Not a policeman exactly no, I'm part of T-Force, I –

FRAU BELLINGHAUSEN
I will call you a policeman until you prove to me you are not . . . (*She stares straight at him.*)

CALLUM
You speak beautiful English, Frau Bellinghausen, if I may say so.

FRAU BELLINGHAUSEN
That is because I am English. You have come rather badly prepared if you don't know that . . . I married Herr Bellinghausen when I was nineteen –

She stops, then suddenly smiles briefly.

But I will leave you to find out the rest for yourself.

CALLUM
Of course, Frau Bellinghausen . . . or shall I call you Mrs Bellinghausen?

FRAU BELLINGHAUSEN
No, Frau Bellinghausen will do . . . for the moment anyway.

CALLUM
You don't seem to have unpacked yet, Frau Bellinghausen?

FRAU BELLINGHAUSEN
That is for two reasons – first I don't like this suite, though I'm told it is by far the best in the hotel –

CALLUM
It is the best in the hotel, yes.

FRAU BELLINGHAUSEN
And secondly I always have somebody to help me unpack.

CALLUM

I can do that.

FRAU BELLINGHAUSEN

You certainly cannot. I'm not having a policeman going through my clothes! I need a woman to do it.

CALLUM

I can arrange that.

FRAU BELLINGHAUSEN

And she mustn't be a policewoman.

CALLUM

She won't be.

FRAU BELLINGHAUSEN

I had a wonderful maid for years and years, she was called Magdalena, we were very close. She had an adorable smile, she was always smiling.

CALLUM

I think I can find somebody who smiles to help you with your unpacking. I am fairly confident about that, Frau Bellinghausen.

FRAU BELLINGHAUSEN

Yes, you seem a very confident person all round. We will see if that is justified.

CALLUM

Naturally. (*He smiles.*) I know you'll need proof.

FRAU BELLINGHAUSEN

So you want me to take your word for it that this is the best suite in the hotel?

CALLUM

Yes, I do, because it is.

FRAU BELLINGHAUSEN

My first time back in the England for many many years and this is the suite they give me, with damp patches on the walls!

CALLUM
I can get you some pictures to cover those, if you'd like?

FRAU BELLINGHAUSEN
They'll still be there won't they . . . I'll know they are there.

CALLUM
Yes. (*He smiles.*) But they'll be completely invisible.

He moves in the room, glancing towards the little travelling case next to her.

So, Frau Bellinghausen, I just wondered if I could ask you a few questions, about certain things? So I can –

FRAU BELLINGHAUSEN
You certainly may not. You'll be producing a little policeman's notebook next. (*She looks straight at him.*) You were doing quite well until you said that.

INT. HAROLD'S HOUSE. HALL AND LIBRARY. DAY

Victor *is calling from inside the library to* **Harold** *who is waiting in the hall.*

VICTOR
Any second! You can come in any second . . . !

HAROLD
I want you to be completely ready, Victor, so don't worry, I can wait a few more seconds . . .

VICTOR
Right! This is it! (*In the doorway.*) Come and see!

Harold *enters the library. It is now completely rearranged, it is full of flowers and the books are all arranged alphabetically. There are several pieces of* **Victor**'s *trademark fragments of stained glass propped up, catching the sunlight, giving a magical effect.*

HAROLD
It is beautiful, Victor, absolutely beautiful.

VICTOR
I bought the flowers myself, and added one or two things as you can see . . . (*Beams.*) It's a huge improvement isn't it?!

HAROLD
That is exactly what it is, well done, Victor, well done indeed.

VICTOR
So have you been thinking what my next challenge will be? I'm raring to go . . .

HAROLD
Well there are still the overflow shelves to be arranged –

VICTOR
Yes, it's just I was hoping, maybe this is a bit stupid of me, but I was hoping for something more difficult?

HAROLD
Well the new shelves should take you at least another three weeks shouldn't they? And then we'll see . . . There is of course the matter I need to discuss with your brother –

VICTOR
Of course there is. The hush-hush matter?

HAROLD
Yes . . . (*He moves around the library.*) We must have a meal, Victor, to celebrate all your work here.

VICTOR
Thank you. Perhaps I can be of help with the hush-hush matter?

HAROLD
I'm not sure you can, Victor.

VICTOR
I can't? (*His face falls.*) Just remember, once I put my mind to it there are few things I can't do!

HAROLD
And this is probably one of them.

EXT. FRONT ENTRANCE OF THE CONNINGTON/INT. CAR.
MORNING

*We cut to **Rachel**'s large car, driven by a chauffeur, arriving at the front of the hotel. **Lotte** is standing on the steps waiting with one of her minders. She smiles as soon as she sees the car approaching. She is dressed in a dark-blue coat and a sombre dress. We cut inside the car. **Lotte** is sitting next to **Rachel** on the back seat as they move off.*

RACHEL

You are perfectly dressed, Lotte, for looking at schools!

LOTTE

This is my dress for church. I thought I must look serious so a school will take me.

RACHEL

Of course they'll take you, Lotte, I'll make sure of that! But we need to find one you'll like.

EXT. STREET/INT. CAR. MORNING

*We cut to the car moving through the dusty streets next to the hotel. **Rachel** and **Lotte** are both staring at the people on the pavement. They see hunched joyless figures, moving in front of dark damaged buildings.*

RACHEL

God, everybody looks so grey don't they . . . So miserable having to wear all those old clothes because of rationing . . .

Lotte *watching the people too.*

It must be so difficult to look forward to anything in these clothes . . . (*A glint in her eye.*) Somebody ought to do something about it . . .

INT. BASEMENT CORRIDOR/KLEINOW'S POLICE CELL. DAY

Kathy *is being escorted by uniformed policemen along a corridor of cells. The door of **Kleinow**'s cell is then unlocked. He is sitting on his bunk bed reading a book.*

KLEINOW

Ah, Miss Griffiths, you've come to say goodbye?

KATHY

I've come to tell you, you're about to be moved to Reading jail. And then you'll be travelling to Germany, to stand trial at Nuremberg.

KLEINOW

Of course that is the plan . . .

KATHY

It is what's going to happen.

KLEINOW

We will see who is right. (*He smiles calmly.*) They have managed to find me a book, and surprisingly it's a good book, *Treasure Island* . . . somehow I've never read it before. It's excellent for my English.

KATHY

I also came to tell you. (*Her tone is implacable.*) I want you to realise I will be keeping track of you constantly. I will make sure I check where you are every day of the week until you reach trial. I will make contact with each of your jailors – through them I will be watching you.

Kleinow *looks at her, almost amused, disbelieving.*

And by the way, your chances of 'disappearing' have just got rather less. (*She holds up the evening paper.*) Because now, you really are quite famous.

The headline of the paper screams: 'The man who tortured our agents to stand trial.'

EXT. POLICE STATION. DAY

Callum *and* **Victor** *are moving along the street towards the police station. A Black Maria is parked outside and there is a big cluster of press reporters and photographers.* **Callum** *pushes his way through the throng and up the* *steps of the police station.* **Victor** *is following him; he greets the reporters with a cheery smile.*

INT. GROUND FLOOR POLICE STATION/EXT. STREET. DAY

Inside the police station there are more reporters and photographers. They are penned in a tight group just inside the reception area. **Callum** *and* **Victor** *push their way through the crowd.* **Callum** *shows his ID to get access beyond the barrier.* **Kathy** *is standing the other side of the barrier. She smiles at* **Callum**.

> KATHY
> Just in time! They're about to bring him up.
>
> CALLUM
> Good. So, Kathy, this is my brother . . . Victor, this is Kathy Griffiths.
>
> VICTOR
> Hello, I'm the notorious brother.
>
> KATHY
> Very pleased to meet you.
>
> VICTOR
> I wouldn't have missed this for anything! And he wanted to show me what he's been up to, why he missed the dinner party the other night!

Suddenly there is a flurry of activity, as the uniformed police begin to escort **Kleinow** *down the passage towards the waiting reporters. Already flashbulbs are going off, but as* **Callum** *watches he is galvanised.*

> CALLUM
> It's too fast, they're bringing him too fast!

Callum *moves down the passage towards the escort, and has a few words with the policeman at the front. They immediately slow their pace, so* **Kleinow** *is exposed to the photographers for longer, rather than being hustled immediately into the Black Maria. Now the bank of photographers have their real chance; the flashbulbs explode. The image slows for a moment* *as we see* **Kleinow** *stunned by all the press activity. His confident demeanour is vanishing; he tries to hide his face. He seems to be shrinking in front of all the cameras and the reporters yelling questions at him.*

In the middle of it all **Callum** *is in front of the police, making sure they take the best route for the photographers.* **Victor**, *next to* **Kathy**, *is watching his brother.*

VICTOR
He likes to be the showman doesn't he?!

KATHY
Yes, but he's right, we need these photographs to go round the world.

Kleinow *is being moved into the Black Maria.* **Callum** *is encouraging the police to open the door slowly, so* **Kleinow** *is paraded in front of the other photographers in the street. There is also a crowd of onlookers, many of them yelling abuse at him. The Black Maria then drives away among a barrage of flashbulbs going off.*

Callum, *in a highly energised state, comes up to* **Kathy** *and* **Victor** *who are watching from the steps. The reporters and photographers are swirling all around in the street, making it difficult to talk, as the crowd breaks up.*

KATHY
They got the photographs of him alright!

CALLUM
They did . . . The police were very obliging.

VICTOR
He was shrivelling wasn't he?! Herr Kleinow! Not as much I'd like but definitely shrivelling . . . he didn't enjoy that!

KATHY
I haven't had a chance to thank you, Mr Ferguson.

CALLUM
(correcting her)
Callum . . . very pleased to be of help. Unfortunately I won't be able to do it again, not for quite a while anyway.

KATHY

No, of course not.

CALLUM

Otherwise they'll throw me in jail too! So I have to say goodbye . . . Good luck with everything, Kathy.

At that moment he is jostled by reporters as they leave, pushing him down the street. He calls.

I have to get back to work now, perfume and plastics and jet engines . . . !

He disappears down the street. **Victor** *is still standing next to* **Kathy**.

VICTOR

You can't stop now.

KATHY

I'm not stopping.

VICTOR

That's good to hear. I've finished my present job, well almost – so I'm looking for another prospect . . .

KATHY

Are you?

VICTOR

You don't know what to say to that do you?!

KATHY

Not immediately, no.

VICTOR

Well I'll be on the lookout for you all the same, just in case I spot anything useful for you . . . ! (*He begins to move off.*) And remember, underneath I'm much better behaved than my brother.

INT. WAR CRIMES UNIT. PASSAGE/MAIN ROOM. AFTERNOON

We cut to **Kathy** *coming towards us along the dank shabby passage of the War Crimes Unit offices. She pushes open the door of the central room, and* *then stops in the doorway, startled. The staff are all standing, applauding her, including* **Miss Clarkson**. **Kathy** *laughing, watching the applause, her eyes glistening.*

INT. CONNINGTON. BASEMENT BALLROOM. EARLY EVENING

Richie, *the young drummer, is on stage in the basement ballroom, drumming hard, rehearsing with the other musicians. A fast insistent number that pulses under the following scenes.* **Eva** *is sitting watching, peeling an orange.*

INT. ATTIC ROOM. EARLY EVENING

Callum *is standing in the middle of the secret office. It is the same day; he is still wearing the clothes he wore in the police station.* **Ruth**, **Ringwood** *and the other workers are all facing him. We can hear the music pounding from the basement.*

CALLUM

Right, we're going to deal with these bloody files. My latest instructions are these – it's quite simple, they are all going. Ninety-nine per cent of them to be chucked out, one per cent of them to be kept in another location. That one per cent are files relevant to our current work . . . So every file we have needs to be checked, in case it's been wrongly labelled. But this must be done fast. As a reminder – for those with a short memory –

He pins a piece of paper on the notice board.

These are our current concerns . . . Everything to be chucked goes on this side of the room . . . those that are going to be kept go here – that ought to be a tiny pile. Is that clear?

RUTH

That couldn't be clearer, sir. As you say, it's very simple.

CALLUM

Good, Ruth . . . And the great news is we're finally free of the bastards from MI19, none left in the hotel!

A red light is flashing above one of the desks.

So let's make a start shall we! (*Suddenly sees the red light.*) What's that?

RINGWOOD
That's Frau Bellinghausen, sir.

CALLUM
She has her own red light does she?!

RINGWOOD
Yes, sir, whenever she dials reception it automatically flashes here. It's red so we can never miss it.

INT. SECOND-FLOOR PASSAGE/MELBURY SUITE. EARLY EVENING

The sound of the music pounding from the bowels of the hotel.

Callum *knocks at the door of the Melbury Suite.*

FRAU BELLINGHAUSEN
Come!

Callum *enters. The suite has now a few pictures on the walls, English landscapes over the damp patches. The trunks are unpacked and have been pushed into a corner of the room. The little travelling case is slightly open, showing its contents of glass bottles.*

CALLUM
You rang, Frau Bellinghausen?

FRAU BELLINGHAUSEN
I did. So does this mean every time I ring reception, whatever it is I want – even if it's a boiled egg – they're always going to send me the policeman?

CALLUM
It probably means that, yes.

FRAU BELLINGHAUSEN
That may be exhausting, for both of us. So – I would like this music stopped please. If one can call it music.

CALLUM

The music?

FRAU BELLINGHAUSEN

Yes. I would like it stopped immediately please. This is not a nightclub, they have no need to make such a noise. I don't think it's an unreasonable request.

CALLUM

I will see how much longer they will be . . . and if they can do it more quietly.

FRAU BELLINGHAUSEN

No, it must be stopped. (*Staring straight at him.*) If I'm going to stay here.

Callum *smiles, refusing to give in.*

CALLUM

Ah yes, I see you've done a little unpacking . . .

He moves towards the travelling case.

And they put up the pictures as I asked them to . . .

FRAU BELLINGHAUSEN

Yes, it's a trifle more pleasant . . .

Callum *looking at the special bottles of scent in the travelling case; he picks one up.*

Yes, you can touch those if you like . . . it is so much better than Eau de Cologne, and of course it was first too. Eau de Cologne started in 1709, my husband's family started theirs in 1653! And of course Eau de Cologne is quite an ordinary scent in comparison, they even gave it to U-boat crews to stop them smelling so much . . . You didn't know that I'm sure.

CALLUM

I didn't know that, no.

FRAU BELLINGHAUSEN
So the big question is, do I have the formula in my head or written down somewhere? The secret formula . . . so it can be manufactured by the English, and make lots of money for you? (*She gives him a shrewd look.*) That is the big question isn't it, which you need to find the answer to?

CALLUM
That is the big question undoubtedly . . . but for the moment I just want to ask –

FRAU BELLINGHAUSEN
No, no asking, about anything. Not yet, no. Just stop the music.

INT. BASEMENT BALLROOM. EARLY EVENING

We cut to the band rehearsing, the music pounding, really loud, echoing up the hotel.

INT. THIRD-FLOOR PASSAGE/DIETER'S ROOM. EARLY EVENING

*We cut to **Rachel** with **Lotte** in the third-floor passage outside **Dieter**'s room. **Dieter** is just opening the door, welcoming them back. We can see in the depth of the room that **Anna**, the waitress, has a food trolley and has laid the table for supper.*

DIETER
Ah there you are . . . (*Indicating the food.*) Just in time!

RACHEL
And I think we might have found a school . . .

Lotte *moves into the room and whispers to her father.*

DIETER
She says you chose a very good school for her!

RACHEL
Well I hope it wasn't my choice, we did look at four . . .

DIETER

I am so very grateful. Won't you come in? There's lots of food . . .

Anna *smiles welcomingly.*

They are making sure they feed us properly.

RACHEL

No thank you, I can't, I'm late already. I need to get home.

We see the door close. We stay on **Rachel** *for a moment. Suddenly she turns in the passage and sets off away from the exit. We stay on her face as she walks purposefully.*

INT. MELBURY SUITE/THIRD-FLOOR PASSAGE. EARLY EVENING

We cut to **Frau Bellinghausen** *alone in her suite. The music is still thudding down in the basement. She picks up the phone.*

We cut to **Callum** *moving along the third-floor passage with a large bunch of keys in his hand. He approaches room 602 where* **Kleinow** *was staying. He is about to unlock the door when he looks up.* **Rachel** *is at the other end of the passage.*

CALLUM

There you are!

RACHEL

You said that like you were expecting me?!

CALLUM

I was hoping . . . I was hoping I'd see you again. (*He smiles.*) And this happens to be the perfect time!

RACHEL

How come it's so perfect?!

She laughs as she reaches him.

CALLUM

Because I've just been dealing with this very grand perfume

heiress that I've been assigned to for some extraordinary reason . . . and she wants me to stop the music downstairs. (*He smiles straight at* **Rachel**.) And I need a very good excuse not to do anything . . . I don't want her running the hotel!

RACHEL
Instead you're doing it . . . ! (*She indicates the bunch of keys.*)

INT. THE 602 SUITE. EARLY EVENING

Rachel *and* **Callum** *move into* **Kleinow**'s *suite, now completely empty except for the bed and two chairs.*

CALLUM
I just need to work something out . . . how they disappeared. (*He stares about the room.*) They had this Nazi counter-intelligence officer here . . . and I was watching the door in the passage, and they vanished. They managed to get him out of the hotel without me seeing.

He unlocks the connecting door; we see the room next door is empty, and its connecting door is open leading to another empty room.

RACHEL
They had all these rooms . . . that's how they did it!

CALLUM
They did . . . (*He smiles.*) Quite simple really . . . ! Took him down the fire escape from the room down there . . .

RACHEL
Spirited him away under your nose!

CALLUM
Ah yes, but we managed to grab him back . . . He is going to Germany now to stand trial. And I got away with the whole thing.

RACHEL
Good for you, Callum . . . (*Warmly, close.*) No wonder you look so pleased with yourself!

Their lips are very close.

Oh I've missed you so much, Cal . . . so wanted to . . .

She kisses him.

You see I've surprised you . . . (*She laughs.*) I won't be able to do that again, probably . . . surprise you.

CALLUM

You haven't surprised me . . . because I think about you all the time. Every morning I wake up thinking of you –

RACHEL

Please . . . ! (*She laughs.*) Don't spoil it . . . no need to overdo it, Callum. (*She kisses him.*) That can't possibly be true.

INT. ATTIC ROOM. EARLY EVENING

We cut to the attic room. The files are being processed rapidly; **Ruth** *is supervising the work. We see fast cuts of files being dropped onto the reject shelves.*

The red light is flashing again.

RINGWOOD

I thought he was dealing with it! (*He picks up the phone.*)

INT. SUITE 602. EARLY EVENING

We cut back to the empty 602 suite. **Rachel** *and* **Callum** *are kissing passionately. They are against the bedroom wall.*

Rachel *suddenly breaks away. Her tone is direct, but she is smiling as she speaks.*

RACHEL

We can't do this, can we?

CALLUM

You mean because a Nazi slept here? We can't use the bed? There are all the other rooms remember – it was only the Secret Service in there, not quite so bad!

RACHEL
Well that's another reason of course, the Nazi bedroom, that is a fairly strange feeling . . . but maybe, rather more importantly, because Alex is your best friend.

CALLUM
And Alex is your husband (*He kisses her.*)

RACHEL
That is also true . . . (*She kisses him.*)

CALLUM
He is the one who pushed us together, remember. I don't know why – but he did.

RACHEL
He suggested we do this did he?! I don't think so, Callum! This is not what he meant . . . (*She moves to kiss him.*) I'm pretty sure about that! (*She kisses him passionately.*)

INT. BASEMENT BALLROOM. EARLY EVENING

Ringwood *appears in the doorway of the ballroom as the band are playing. Seeing his harassed figure standing there, they stop for a moment.* **Eva**, *who is eating the last piece of her orange, stares at him.*

RINGWOOD
Please, you have to stop playing . . . it's very important you stop please, for the moment.

EVA
You want us to stop rehearsing? The Army thinks they can run everything don't they . . . except you're not even really the proper Army are you?!

I'm sorry we are in charge of what we do down here . . . and we're certainly not stopping for you.

The band starts playing again, loudly.

INT. SUITE 602. EARLY EVENING

We cut to **Callum** *and* **Rachel** *sitting on the bed kissing passionately.*

Rachel's *legs are wrapped round* **Callum**.

Callum *is bare-chested, unbuttoning* **Rachel**'s *blouse.*

RACHEL
Don't rush . . . I need to get used to this Nazi bed . . .

CALLUM
I'm not going to rush . . . (*He takes her blouse off.*)

RACHEL
I've been thinking about clothes a lot recently . . .

She stands up and steps out of her skirt. She is now in her slip.

CALLUM
Just as they're coming off, you start talking about clothes?!

RACHEL
Yes, why not?

She sits back on the bed, and wraps her legs round him again.

I met a clothes designer I want to help . . . she runs a little shop . . .

She gives **Callum** *small kisses.*

Her clothes are lovely . . . and very sexy . . .

She kisses him again.

And affordable for everyone. Since you've been no use at all in introducing me to people . . .

She kisses him again.

I thought I might –

CALLUM
It sounds terrific . . .

He pushes her backward on to the bed. They entwine together. She starts to push his trousers and pants down, and he begins to pull her slip off when they hear **Ringwood**'s *voice yelling in the passage, 'Sir, sir, Captain Ferguson?!'*

For a moment they try to ignore him but he is getting closer.

CALLUM

That voice! I knew that would happen – must be about the bloody perfume woman!

RACHEL

You should have stopped the music, then she would have been happy.

CALLUM

If I had known I was going to meet you . . . I would have certainly let her win that one. (*He kisses her.*) I've got to go . . .

INT. PASSAGE OUTSIDE SUITE 602. EARLY EVENING

Callum *emerges fully dressed out of 602, rattling the large bunch of keys. He sees* **Ringwood** *at the end of the passage and smiles at him, offering no explanation of what he has been doing.*

RINGWOOD

There you are, sir!

CALLUM

So it appears we have no choice . . . we better stop the music!

We cut back into the room, **Rachel** *is buttoning up her blouse, sitting on the edge of the bed. We stay close on her for a moment, a look of longing in her eyes.*

INT. MAIN ROOM. WAR CRIMES UNIT. NIGHT

Kathy *and* **Miss Clarkson** *are sitting alone in the War Crimes Unit office, sharing a bottle of wine. They are both pretty drunk.*

MISS CLARKSON

We should really enjoy this moment, Kathy, because they are going to be moving us out of this office in a month . . . and there'll only be four of us left.

KATHY

Only four of us?! They can't!

MISS CLARKSON

I told you . . . we're so deeply unimportant to them . . . to everybody! And that's before our little victory, your victory —

KATHY

Our little victory.

MISS CLARKSON

They will of course take revenge for what we did . . . We'll never get any more information from them . . . And who knows if Herr Kleinow will ever stand trial . . . ?

KATHY

He'll stand trial! He will definitely stand trial I tell you — if I have to personally drag him into the dock and hold him there. (*Her eyes shining.*) And what's more I'm going to get another one as well!

INT. HAROLD'S HOUSE. THE LIBRARY. DAY

Harold *is standing staring out of the library window at the chickens in his garden. His manner is preoccupied.* **Mrs Gorton** *is tidying in the background.*

HAROLD

That boy Victor is right, one tends to take chickens for granted doesn't one? They are a lot more complicated than they seem. (*Suddenly.*) Don't move that, Mrs Gorton, please!

Mrs Gorton *has moved a shallow box of papers on the desk.*

Even moving it a little is not a good idea . . . It's the extremely secret box. (*He smiles.*) That's why it is out in the open, so it arouses no suspicion . . .

He looks down into the box. We see a key is lying on the top of the papers.

INT. GOVERNMENT RESEARCH FACILITY. THE HANGAR. DAY

A high shot of fifty people pouring into the vast space of the hangar. Desks and work areas have been spread out across the ground floor. **Dieter** *and* **Rita** *are on the higher level staring down at the people arriving. There is a new familiar tone between them.*

> DIETER
>
> I asked for staff —
>
> RITA
>
> And they send you more than you need!
>
> DIETER
>
> I'm certainly not going to tell them that . . .
>
> RITA
>
> No, never ever tell them that! We can use them all easily. It's terrific isn't it, it really feels as if —
>
> DIETER
>
> That we're going to catch up! Catch up the Americans, then overtake them, beat them! Make up all the ground that was lost —
>
> RITA
>
> That we Brits lost you mean! After having invented the bloody thing in the first place!

She watches the workers below.

> They don't know it yet . . .
>
> DIETER
>
> No, they don't. But they're going to help build the fastest jet engine, and what is more they're going to do it really quickly . . .

INT. GENTLEMEN'S CLUB. NIGHT

We cut to **Victor** *sitting waiting in the hall of* **Harold**'s *club, a grand Victorian interior.* **Victor** *is dressed in a dinner jacket with a red bow tie — it is the first time we have seen him in a dinner jacket.*

*We cut to **Callum** appearing at the entrance to the club, seeing his brother across the expanse of the marble hall. **Callum** moves towards him; he is wearing a dark suit.*

CALLUM

My God you look smart! Much smarter than me!

VICTOR

Well I felt I had to, to make up for the dinner party. I've hired it for the night, it fits perfectly doesn't it?!

CALLUM

It does. (*He sits next to him.*)

VICTOR

This is exciting isn't it?!

He sees ancient faces eyeing him suspiciously.

My first time ever in a gentlemen's club . . .

CALLUM

So you're okay? (*Affectionately.*) I mean generally? Feeling happier Victor?

VICTOR

Absolutely! You must come and see my beautiful library . . .

CALLUM

I will.

VICTOR

I'll need a new challenge of course very soon . . . (*Sharp smile.*) Maybe tonight'll provide one?!

INT. GENTLEMEN'S CLUB. DINING ROOM. NIGHT

*We cut to the large shadowy dining room of the club. The heavy chandeliers have been switched off to save electricity; there is a sepulchral atmosphere. All the diners are men, pale faces, old before their time. They are wearing dinner jackets and are eating in pairs or alone. They keep glancing at **Victor**'s eccentric demeanour as he eats. We cut to **Harold**'s table. He is sitting with*

Callum *and* **Victor**, *eating some very overcooked roast beef and watery cabbage.* **Harold** *is trying to cut his meat.*

> HAROLD
>
> It's like eating roast rhino isn't it?! We may have a socialist government now, doing things differently, but nothing it seems will stop the meat being cooked like this . . . !

> VICTOR
>
> It's what they're used to.

He looks at the faces glancing at him.

> They don't want it to change.

> HAROLD
>
> I am planning one day to really shock this place and get them to prepare your legendary cabbage with onions, Callum . . .

> CALLUM
>
> Ah, I'm glad it's become legendary! (*He lifts his glass.*)

> VICTOR
>
> He's very pleased with himself at the moment as you can see –

> CALLUM
>
> Am I? (*Startled by this.*)

> VICTOR
>
> He is working the German very hard with the jet engines and all that . . . and he also managed to get a particularly nasty man locked up the other week, Herr Kleinow. (*Looking at* **Callum**.) He changed sides for a day.

> HAROLD
>
> Oh yes, I saw that in the papers, that was you was it? Congratulations!

> CALLUM
>
> It was partly me . . . (*Sharply to* **Victor**.) It wasn't a matter of changing sides for a day! It's not about sides!

Just as he says this, both **Victor** *and* **Callum** *notice more faces staring at them disapprovingly.*

VICTOR

It may because of what you were just saying about the meat. (*He stares back at the men.*) Or maybe it's because of me – whatever it is, I think they can detect danger . . .

HAROLD

From this whole table I expect . . .

Callum *and* **Victor** *look at* **Harold** *surprised.*

This is both a celebratory meal and a time to tell the truth . . .

CALLUM

That sounds ominous.

HAROLD

It's been delightful getting to know you both of course, I hope it's obvious I enjoy your company a lot. (*He smiles.*) But there's always been a reason for it as you know . . .

Both **Victor** *and* **Callum** *are watching him carefully.*

I'm very aware you don't know really anything about me . . . You probably think he's a touch peculiar, a bit of a man of mystery? Living alone with his ward in a big house? Is he just a retired Foreign Office official? (*He pauses for a second.*) And in fact I am just a retired Foreign Office official . . . (*He looks at* **Callum**.) But one who has embarked on a quest.

VICTOR

What is the quest?

Harold *smiles.*

Why do you need Callum's help?

HAROLD

First you need to believe me. I have to show you I'm a reliable witness. I have a little party trick to help me illustrate that.

He produces a crumpled folded piece of paper from his wallet. He holds it up without unfolding it.

HAROLD
This is a film review written by Winston Churchill.

Both brothers look bewildered.

HAROLD
I was a regular visitor to Downing Street and Chequers during the war because I was thought to be a bit of an expert on how 'foreigners' think . . . especially the Americans.

So imagine this scene . . . (*He leans forward.*) We are all sitting in the middle of the night, there was always a film show at Chequers late at night during the war, and we're all sitting watching Mr Orson Welles' *Citizen Kane* . . . and Churchill starts talking and yelling back at the screen . . . and I say to him, 'The Americans think very highly of this film' . . . and he turns to me, eyes blazing, takes my pen and says, 'I'll tell you what I think of it . . .'

Harold *unfolds the piece of paper and holds it up. It reads in big black ink letters:* 'RUBBISH, RUBBISH, BLOODY RUBBISH, *signed Winston Churchill.*'

Callum *stares at it fascinated. He reaches for the paper. We are close on his eyes.*

Flashback:

There is a quick cut: a dark room, a row of heads in front of us; thick cigar smoke clouds the air, a beam of light from a projector glowing through it. It is as if we are in among the audience, straining to see the screen. We cut back to **Callum** *looking fascinated, at the paper.* **Victor** *notices this.*

HAROLD
Why do you think I told you that?

CALLUM
Because it's rather odd maybe, unexpected? Churchill yelling at *Citizen Kane* in the middle of the war?

HAROLD
No, I want to show you I was quite close to the centre of things . . .

He now carefully produces the key, the same one as in the library.

This will do it too . . . Churchill may have been no film critic, but he was wonderful to work with –

VICTOR
(sharply)
What does that key open?

HAROLD
Of course you know Winston Churchill so nearly didn't become Prime Minister. My boss, the Foreign Secretary, Halifax, who wanted to do a peace deal with the Nazis, was everybody's choice, the press barons, most of Parliament . . . (*He turns the key in his fingers.*) The Royal Family . . .

This key was given to Halifax by the Queen so he could let himself into the Buckingham Palace garden whenever he wanted, use the summer house there whenever he chose . . . his own private key!

And so of course they could meet in secret, him and the Queen, discuss whatever they wanted, about him becoming Prime Minister no doubt . . .

We are close on **Callum***; he is staring at the key.*

Flashback:

We see a door in a wall open, a secret sunlit garden beyond with a summer house in the distance.

We cut back to **Callum***. He takes the key.*

HAROLD
That's how close he came to running the country . . . (*He smiles.*) And us losing the war.

CALLUM
Does it still open the door? (*He takes the key.*) Does it still work?

Victor *again sees how drawn in* **Callum** *is becoming. A look of concern on* **Victor**'*s face, he takes the key.*

                           VICTOR
We must pop along to Buckingham Palace and try it out
tonight.

                           HAROLD
No, it doesn't work any more, they've changed the lock. Halifax
gave it to me when he left for America, a little memento. (*He
takes the key back.*) I often look at it . . . to remind myself what
could have happened . . .

                           VICTOR
Blimey!

He has suddenly noticed the table next door are staring blatantly at them.

They're all looking now . . . not even pretending not to listen!

Victor *stares back at them. The two men nearest them, who have finished eating, get up and leave.*

He turns back to **Harold**, *his tone sceptical.*

It's a good party trick, I have to say . . . the key especially –

                           HAROLD
Thank you for getting rid of them, Victor . . .

There are now no diners close, **Harold** *nevertheless lowers his voice.*

The chance of being overheard is now gone, so I can tell you
something I've never told anybody, nobody outside the
Foreign Office anyway . . .

Close-up of **Callum**.

In the summer of '38, a very neatly dressed German
diplomat came to visit the Foreign Office . . . he had to wait
in the passage for quite a while . . . Herr Theodor Kordt . . .
He came with the most dramatic possible message, this was
before the war remember . . .

We are on **Callum** *again, we are close on his eyes.*

Flashback:

We see a figure with an umbrella sitting patiently at the far end of a long passage.

We cut back to **Callum** *and then to* **Harold**.

HAROLD
He is carrying a message on behalf of the German military, senior figures in the German military, that they would launch a military coup against Hitler, they would overthrow Hitler but they just wanted one guarantee from us – they needed us to say publicly we would go to war with Germany if Hitler invaded Czechoslovakia. Just for us to say it, that's all they needed to justify their action to the German public, and then they would act . . .

CALLUM
So the whole war could have been avoided?! Is that what you're saying?!

HAROLD
I don't know . . . I don't know yet. When Herr Kordt left that passage – which is where I saw him, he went into a very important meeting.

Flashback:

Herr Kordt going through a large door and disappearing into darkness.

HAROLD
There are files in the Foreign Office that tell exactly what happened next – how we missed such an incredible opportunity . . . who was responsible. I need to see those files, because I feel this may be a story I want to tell the public . . .

VICTOR
So why on earth do you need Callum's help?

HAROLD
Because believe it or not it's a lot easier for someone like him to get access than anybody else. Of course the files are top secret, nobody wants the facts to come out – but what T-Force

and MI19 are doing at the moment is such a high priority, they can ask for anything . . .

A close-up of **Callum**.

It was of course no coincidence that I was always hanging around the Connington, I wanted to meet somebody from T-Force . . . (*To* **Callum**.) Because that somebody can write a letter to say they are dealing with such and such a German, he can be fictitious if necessary, and the German claims definite inside knowledge of this story – and you want to check the facts, to establish his reliability, whether he can be trusted . . .

VICTOR
They won't fall for that!

CALLUM
They might . . .

HAROLD
The only problem is of course, if I ever did reveal it to the public, and the leak was traced back to you –

CALLUM
Then I could go to jail!

HAROLD
And I'm certainly not asking you to take that risk . . . ! (*He smiles.*) Why on earth would you want to do that?

VICTOR
So what are you asking him to do?

HAROLD
To do nothing . . . for the moment. I just wanted to tell you the story.

CALLUM
I like stories of missed opportunities, as you know . . . especially crucial ones.

HAROLD

That is why I thought you might be interested.

CALLUM

If there was a way of it never being traced back to me –

VICTOR

Which isn't possible of course.

CALLUM
(grins)
Then I might be interested . . .

EXT. THE CONNINGTON. BOMBSITE. NIGHT

We see the Connington across the bombsite glowing out at night, dominating the landscape. The surrounding buildings have far fewer lights on. Music is pouring out of the basement ballroom. **Callum** *and* **Victor** *are walking together on the edge of the bombsite, a distance from the hotel.*

VICTOR

Funny old bird isn't he, Harold? Do we trust him? *(Looking straight at* **Callum**.*)* Not sure really . . .

CALLUM

Yes, I could feel you getting worried in there. *(Grins.)* Suddenly getting protective! Don't worry, I'm not going to do something really stupid, just because he's given you a job for a few weeks.

VICTOR

Yes, I was hoping it would be for longer too . . .

CALLUM

We'll find you something else –

VICTOR

I feel I could do something more now, Cal, anyway, a lot more . . .

CALLUM

I promise I'll find you another job. *(He stops walking.)* So I think . . . this is where we –

VICTOR

We say goodbye?! (*Startled.*) Are you serious? So I'm not allowed to get any closer to your precious hotel am I?!

CALLUM

No, I told you, Victor, it's not a good idea for you to be round the hotel, okay?

VICTOR

It's not okay . . . not remotely okay.

He seems to be about to get really angry, but then he turns more calmly.

But if this is how it has to be . . . at the moment anyway . . .

Both stare at the hotel with its lights on and the music pouring out.

You love it don't you, having the run of the place?! (*His tone serious.*) You seem to be enjoying it too much, Cal . . . that might not be good –

CALLUM

I'm not enjoying it too much I assure you! We're having to sort all the files in the office at the moment because we're about to throw most of them out. It's pure drudgery –

VICTOR

Can I help then? I'm brilliant at pure drudgery! You know I'd be good at it –

CALLUM

No, Victor, you can't, it's all classified.

VICTOR

Ah, those official secrets, of course. (*He moves.*) I can keep a secret . . . ! (*Suddenly.*) Are you sure you should be throwing all this stuff away then?

Their eyes meet.

CALLUM

Goodnight, Victor.

Callum *moves off towards the back of the hotel. We stay on* **Victor**.

INT. CONNINGTON HOTEL LOBBY/CONSERVATORY

Callum *is crossing the hotel, which is almost deserted. The* **Desk Clerk** *watching him, bell boys scurrying around. Suddenly a voice yells 'Callum, Callum!' He turns to see* **Julia** *standing with a glass of champagne in her hand in the bar area on the mezzanine level. She is in an evening dress and there is a young man in a dinner jacket standing next to her also with a glass of champagne. There are a few late-night drinkers in the shadows behind her.*

JULIA
You'll never guess what's happened, Callum?!

CALLUM
(*smiles up at her*)
What?

JULIA
I've got the part! I didn't hear for days and days and I thought it had gone . . . but I've got the part, Callum!!

INT. CONNINGTON THIRD-FLOOR PASSAGE. MORNING

Morning light. **Lotte** *and* **Anna** *are coming towards us down the third-floor passage on roller skates.* **Anna** *is in her waitress uniform, but she is laughing and kidding around with* **Lotte**.

They pass a chambermaid in the passage who looks at **Anna** *disapprovingly.*

INT. MELBURY SUITE. MORNING

We cut to **Frau Bellinghausen** *sitting in her suite, exquisitely dressed. She has a breakfast tray in front of her and is sipping coffee. There is a knock at the door.*

FRAU BELLINGHAUSEN
Enter!

Callum *enters the suite looking a little bleary eyed.*

CALLUM
You wanted to see me?

FRAU BELLINGHAUSEN
I did, you're late.

CALLUM
It is Sunday . . .

FRAU BELLINGHAUSEN
You're still late. If you are the only one dealing with me, apart from the maids of course – then you have to be on time.

CALLUM
I will do my best . . . (*He smiles.*) From now on.

FRAU BELLINGHAUSEN
Good, after all, policemen are always on time. Now, I asked the other day for the music to be stopped, and you ignored me, and did nothing about it.

CALLUM
That is not the case. I did have it stopped, it just took a little longer than you –

FRAU BELLINGHAUSEN
Please . . . (*She stares straight at him.*) it is important that we understand each other, so I will say this very simply. Don't lie to me.

CALLUM
I wasn't.

FRAU BELLINGHAUSEN
I have something you want . . . and you are, I think, trying to find out if I really do have it, at this moment, here . . . If we're going to get anywhere together – you have to be absolutely truthful to me. Always.

CALLUM
Right . . . (*Looking straight back at her.*) Does it apply to you too?

FRAU BELLINGHAUSEN
That remains to be seen.

INT. ALEX AND RACHEL'S HOUSE. RECEPTION ROOM.
AFTERNOON

*We are with **Alex** moving along the passage in his house towards the reception room. He can hear **Rachel**'s voice. He enters the room. She is on the phone.*

ALEX

Ah, darling . . . I didn't know you were on the telephone . . .
I'll leave you alone . . . (*He smiles.*) If it's private?

RACHEL

No, I'm just saying goodbye . . . (*Into the phone.*) Yes, no I
will . . . I'll do my best . . . he's here now, I'll tell him . . .
Goodbye. (*She rings off and turns.*) That was Callum.

ALEX

Oh yes? (*His manner seems relaxed, not suspicious.*)

RACHEL

I said I would ask you . . . he wants to know if we'd like to
come to something . . . it's a most unusual invitation – an
actress he knows has a small part in a movie, and they are
filming the scene at night by a lake . . . and we could all go
and watch. He's arranging a picnic.

ALEX

A picnic at night?

RACHEL

A picnic at night, yes.

ALEX

That will be rather cold won't it? And there'll be a lot of
standing around I suspect . . . and people shouting –

RACHEL

Please come. (*She smiles at him.*) It would be so nice if you
came too.

INT. ATTIC OFFICE. CONNINGTON. DAY

We cut to the secret attic office. There is a swirl of activity as the rejected files are being thrown into large rubbish bags and tied up ready to be shipped. There are still a lot more files to process and **Ruth** *is supervising the work.*

Callum *is watching from across the room, as he ties up one of the bags himself.*

CALLUM

Good, good, the quicker we finish this, the more days we get off!

EXT. LONDON STREET. EARLY EVENING

Kathy *is just coming out of the front entrance of the War Crimes Unit offices, a rather grubby battered building. We move with her walking along the street; we are close on her face. Suddenly a hand touches her shoulder; she spins round truly startled.*

Victor *is standing there.*

KATHY

Oh my God, it's you! You gave me such a shock!

VICTOR

Sorry . . . I just had to see you.

KATHY

I'm surprised you found me, not many people know where our offices are.

VICTOR

I'm quite good at finding things out.

KATHY

So why do you need to see me, Victor?

VICTOR

Ah . . . did you mean it when you said you weren't stopping?

KATHY

Of course I meant it.

VICTOR

Then I think I might have something for you . . . (*Sharp smile.*) Don't look so surprised . . . !

KATHY

What is it?

VICTOR

My brother is throwing out all those files in his office . . .
I thought you might want them. I thought we could go along and grab them.

KATHY

Well that's a tempting idea, Victor . . . but we're hardly going to be able to walk in and 'grab' them are we?! There'll be people around . . .

VICTOR

I'm not sure about that . . . what if we time it right? Exactly. What if they're all out celebrating and the stuff is nicely bundled up ready to go . . .?

We stay on **Kathy**.

INT. RESEARCH FACILITY. THE HANGAR/MRS TOOLEY'S HOUSE. DAY

Dieter, **Callum** *and* **Rita** *are staring down from the upper levels at the desks in the hangar; paper spread everywhere, people working intently.*

CALLUM

Amazing! It's like a painting of people working hard isn't it? It's so quiet!

RITA

Well they are working hard, they're not posing for you I assure you. They are putting in very long hours.

DIETER

We all are . . . ! And what is more I'm still not allowed to drive myself here . . . (*Smiles, pointing at a man in the corner.*) I have my driver watching me always . . . You have your spies, Callum.

CALLUM

Of course I have my spies . . . I know everything you do!

Rita *exchanges a look with* **Dieter**.

RITA

Not everything I hope . . .

The phone rings. **Rita** *picks it up.*

It's for you.

Callum *takes the phone. We intercut with* **Victor** *in* **Mrs Tooley**'s *house.*

VICTOR

It's me.

He is sitting on the floor in the hall.

CALLUM

Everything alright, Victor?

VICTOR

It might be, yes . . . I just wondered when we could next see each other? How is this week looking? (*Close on his eyes.*) Is there any night you can't do?

CALLUM

It's not too bad . . . just not Wednesday night, that's our night of wild celebrations.

EXT. THE FOREST. FILM SET. NIGHT

We cut to film lights swinging into position on the top of tall towers. They are lighting up a forest and a lake, silver light falling on the water. We cut to **Lotte** *staring across to the other side of the lake where dark figures are just appearing in a ghostly fashion through the trees. Her eyes are wide, she is fascinated but a little scared.*

We cut to the whole group. We see **Harold** *leaning on a shooting stick,* **Callum, Rachel** *and* **Alex, Dieter, Anna** *and* **Lotte** *all standing near the camera and the technicians. The film crew are preparing to shoot the action across the lake; prop men are scurrying among the trees spreading smoke.* **Harold** *is watching* **Rachel** *and* **Callum** *closely,* **Alex** *is* *looking cold,* **Lotte** *and* **Anna** *are sharing the whole experience together. Suddenly a voice shouts 'Action' and the dark figures on the other side of the lake emerge into the light and reveal themselves to be men in heavy armour, their faces covered by visors. A man in dark armour, but on a white horse, is moving among them, followed by his two henchmen on brown horses.*

Through the smoke we then see a beautiful woman, the princess, on a horse, followed by her maid of honour riding just behind her. They are both being escorted by armed men. We see the maid of honour is being played by **Julia**.

The effect is mysterious and frightening; the men look very threatening.

Rachel *leans down and whispers to* **Lotte**.

RACHEL
These are bad men . . . but they won't hurt the princess.

CALLUM
Don't worry, they will lose . . . (*He smiles to* **Lotte**.) The bad people always lose.

DIETER
I think they must have captured the princess and will demand a ransom from the king . . . but he will send his men to rescue her.

RACHEL
Is that your friend? (*To* **Callum**, *watching* **Julia** *on her horse*.) She looks wonderful . . .

HAROLD
Is this Robin Hood? I don't think it can be . . . maybe it's sort of a cousin of Robin Hood, a copy?

A voice is shouting at them 'Stop talking, silence!' **Harold** *begins to whisper as he stares at the dark knight.*

And why is the villain – he must be the villain – why is he on a white horse?

CALLUM
So you can see it in the dark I expect . . (*He grins.*) I'd like a white horse . . .

Callum *is watching the dark knight with interest.* **Rachel** *is watching the princess. She looks at* **Callum** *staring at the knight.*

> RACHEL
> We're all rooting for different people are we . . .?!

> CALLUM
> I love this . . . (*He whispers.*) I love the movies.

INT. CONNINGTON. THE LOBBY. NIGHT

We cut to **Kathy** *entering the main lobby of the hotel looking for* **Victor**.

She sees no sign of him, just elderly couples ready to go out for the night. She spots **Ruth** *in an evening dress with a worker from the attic office moving across the lobby towards the exit. They pass very close but do not see her. Suddenly a voice calls out to* **Kathy**; *she turns to see* **Victor** *standing deep in the shadows. He smiles delightedly at her. She moves up to him. He is looking very energised, excited.*

> VICTOR
> All ready then?!

> KATHY
> Well I'm here . . .

> VICTOR
> Don't look so doubtful! Come on!

He begins to move off, then dodges round a pillar.

> Just got to make sure he doesn't see me . . .

He indicates the sharp-faced **Desk Clerk**.

> He is the only one who knows me around here . . . Okay, let's go and get 'em!

> KATHY
> I know where to go.

She leads him to the back stairs.

> Callum took me there.

INT. CONNINGTON BACK STAIRS/ATTIC OFFICE. NIGHT

We cut to them moving fast up the back stairs. **Kathy** *pauses for a second, glancing back to see if anybody is following them.* **Victor** *is plunging ahead, she now has to catch him up and show him the last bit of the route to the attic office. They reach the office door with its notice* ENTRY STRICTLY FORBIDDEN.

KATHY

Aren't we going to knock?

VICTOR

Knock? No, there'll be nobody there!

He pushes the door open and storms into the office. It is completely empty: not only is there nobody left working there, the shelves are totally bare; the files have gone.

VICTOR

We are late – just too late! They've moved them already . . . ! (*He lets out an exuberant shout.*) That is so annoying!!

KATHY

Well we tried! And you were right, Victor, there was nobody here . . . (*She looks almost relieved that they didn't have to confront anybody.*) It was a bit too much to hope for, wasn't it, that the files'd just be sitting here, unguarded?!

VICTOR

No, no, I'm not giving up . . . (*He turns to her.*) We're not giving up – timing is everything isn't it?! Maybe I haven't got my timing that wrong? (*He looks at her, his eyes blazing.*) Let's see?!

EXT. CONNINGTON BACK ENTRANCE. NIGHT

We cut to outside the back entrance of the hotel.

Victor *is lifting the lid off every dustbin, very fast.*

VICTOR

Empty! Empty! Empty!

He turns triumphantly, holding up a couple of dustbin lids.

I thought so – all the rubbish has just been collected! We're going to go after it, Kathy . . . We're going to catch it!

KATHY
Catch it! How?! Do you know where it's gone?

VICTOR
No . . . but I'm going to guess!

EXT. FOREST FILM SET. NIGHT

We cut to a close-up of **Lotte**, *eyes full of wonder, as the horses with their riders come out of the forest, straight towards her. The group are now right there in the clearing, in amongst the men in armour, as the unit have moved into the forest to shoot closer coverage. The dark knight is leading the princess and* **Julia** *and they are bearing down on the camera and the group.* **Lotte** *stares at the black visor of the dark knight as he towers above her. A voice shouts 'Cut' and the dark knight pulls his visor up and stares straight back at* **Lotte**, *and then chuckles heartily and winks at her as somebody hands him a cigarette.*

A voice yells 'That's supper everybody!' and there is an explosion of activity as technicians and men in armour race through the trees towards a tent where there are steaming bowls of food, trays of sausages, eggs and bacon.

Julia *is helped down from her horse and* **Lotte** *and* **Anna** *head straight for her.*

Dieter, **Rachel**, **Callum** *and* **Alex** *are following a step behind.*

Callum *calls out to* **Julia**.

CALLUM
You look simply magical!

JULIA
Well you haven't heard me speak yet . . . (*She laughs.*) That's not quite so magical I promise you! But don't I look good on a horse?!

ALEX
Indeed . . . and to have to do it so many times, can't they get it right the first time?

Anna *and* **Lotte** *are fascinated by the horses, their ornate bridals and saddles and by* **Julia***'s costume.* **Dieter** *has managed to get hold of a prop sword and he lifts it so it catches the light.* **Lotte** *is laughing delightedly, a moment of joy between father and daughter.* **Julia** *is watching* **Rachel***; she whispers to* **Callum***.*

JULIA
Now I know why I never see you any more.

We cut to **Harold** *taking in the whole scene as he stands under a tree. Great trays of food are being brought over to the people minding the horses. He is by the continuity table where there is a typewriter. The film lights blazing down out of the surrounding darkness give the scene a hallucinatory quality.* **Callum** *comes up to* **Harold***.*

CALLUM
All this food! I didn't need to bring a picnic at all!

HAROLD
And everything has butter with it . . . and not just the tiny pats of butter that we have to put up with, but loads – it's utterly astonishing.

CALLUM
You know Harold, I can't stop thinking about what you told me the other day, I just can't get it out of my head . . .

HAROLD
That is what I was hoping.

CALLUM
I should try to map out a letter shouldn't I . . . as you suggested? Of course not to send to anyone at the moment, but just to see how it might go . . .

He sits down at the typewriter at the continuity table.

HAROLD
Not to send, no.

Callum *puts paper in typewriter.* **Harold** *amused at his boldness.*

What are you doing?

CALLUM
How would it begin? (*He starts to type.*) 'I've recently been interviewing "Herr important German" and he keeps claiming to me that he had knowledge of a high-level plot against Hitler, a military coup proposed before the war started, that was put to the Foreign Office and –

Callum *suddenly sees the very severe-looking continuity woman heading straight for her desk. He stands up rapidly and removes the piece of paper.*

I'm so sorry . . . I was just trying to keep warm. (*He grins.*) I didn't look at anything I promise! (*He turns to* **Harold**.) Perhaps you should draft a possible letter, Harold, for me to look at, just as a start, maybe that's the best plan?

HAROLD
Of course, if you want me to . . . But it must not be sent yet, Callum.

Rachel *is calling; she is moving towards them.*

RACHEL
What are you two doing? You look far too serious! Don't you think it's so terrific being here?! Seeing all these huge men in armour fighting to get to their sausages and eggs. I want to really tuck in too I can tell you! –

ALEX
And you must do that, darling . . .

He suddenly appears out of the shadows from behind the film lights.

But I've got to go . . .

RACHEL
Go?! (*She is very startled.*) You can't go now, darling – everybody's having supper . . . and then there's going to be a sword fight!

ALEX

I know, but I've got to go. You stay by all means. I've got to go to the Carlton Club . . . there was a meeting there earlier this evening, an unofficial meeting there anyway, and I just have to drop by and catch up –

RACHEL

Well, I'll travel back into town with you, darling, if you have to work this evening –

ALEX

No, no, you must stay if you want.

Harold, **Callum** *and the continuity woman all watching the scene.*

I don't want to spoil the outing, absolutely not! I'm sure Mr Lindsay-Jones or Callum will see you home –

HAROLD

Of course.

ALEX

There we are! I understand it's exciting for you . . . all this strange filming at night, you've never seen it before, you must stay, darling, if you want . . .

RACHEL

You can't get out of it, Alex? You really have to go to this meeting?

ALEX

I do, darling . . . (*He kisses her and moves off across the clearing.*) I have to go.

EXT. TAXI/WASTE DISPOSAL DEPOT. NIGHT

We cut to a shot through a taxi windscreen of **Victor** *and* **Kathy** *approaching the waste disposal depot, a large brick building on the river, with a line of rubbish trucks queuing in front of it, waiting to disgorge their waste.* **Victor** *yells at the taxi driver.*

VICTOR
Stop please! Stop here and wait, you've got to wait . . . we shouldn't be long. This is it, Kathy!

KATHY
How do you know this is the right place?

VICTOR
I don't. (*He leaps out of the taxi.*) It's the nearest one . . . we've got to be lucky! We must be!

Victor *runs along the side of the rubbish trucks, followed by* **Kathy**.

Victor *is shouting at all the drivers.*

VICTOR
Are you from the Connington? Who's picked up from the Connington Hotel? Who's got the Connington's rubbish?!

The drivers are looking blankly at this crazy figure or yelling at him to get out of the way. **Victor** *leaps into the back of one of the trucks and starts rummaging through the rubbish on the off-chance. Men are shouting at him and gesticulating. He jumps down from the truck, now absolutely filthy, and continues to move up the line of trucks yelling questions at the drivers.*

He then heads straight to the main building with **Kathy** *trying to keep up.*

INT. WASTE DISPOSAL DEPOT. NIGHT

Victor *and* **Kathy** *enter the main building and are greeted by the sight of three enormous vats full of waste.* **Victor** *is moving along the side of the vats, scouring the detritus of the city, the piles of rubbish and rotting vegetables. He calls out to* **Kathy**.

VICTOR
Are you just going to stand and watch?!

KATHY
I'm certainly not going to just watch!

She jumps on to the side of the vat. Men are yelling at her from the gantry above, to get the hell out of there. Heavy machinery is moving along the side of the huge space, making a menacing sound; it is moving towards them.

Kathy *suddenly thinks she sees something.*

There! What about there?!

Victor *is following where she is pointing and he jumps into the centre of the vat and starts scrabbling into the garbage, to get at the bag. He holds it up; it is full of files from the office. The bag has split open and some of the files have fallen deeper into the vat.* **Victor** *digs furiously into the rubbish, unearthing more bags, and* **Kathy** *jumps into the vat next to him and scrabbles to rescue the files too. The men are descending from the gantry above, shouting at them to get out and that it's not safe.*

                    VICTOR
Don't worry it's official business! . . . (*He yells back at the men.*)
It's all officiall business! Things that never shoud've been
thrown out!

They are hurling the bags out of the vat and on to the ground. **Victor** *suddenly jumps out of the vat and starts running across the building yelling back at* **Kathy**.

                    VICTOR
Transport! I've got to arrange more transport!

Kathy *is alone, as the men approach her, yelling at her, and the heavy machinery is moving towards her.* **Kathy** *stares back at them defiantly.*

                    KATHY
Don't worry . . . I've got what I came for!

We cut to **Kathy** *dragging some of the rubbish bags, bulging with the files, out on to the concourse at the front of the building.*

They join a clump of bags she has already got out.

She suddenly sees a line of four taxis riding in convoy to join the original one that is still waiting. **Victor** *is leaning out the window of the first taxi in the convoy.*

                    VICTOR
I thought I'd take no chances! We've got to have room for
everything we've found! (*He leaps out of the taxi.*) Where are we
taking them by the way?

KATHY

To my flat . . . it's the only place we can be sure to get in to.

She stares behind her. The group of men are standing watching her from the entrance.

Suddenly one of them shouts out at **Kathy** *and* **Victor**.

WASTE DISPOSAL MAN

Thrown something away you shouldn't, have you?

They stare back at him not certain how to respond.

Mate of mine did that once. Threw a ring away he'd bought his girl. She went off with a bloke in the flat above. And he wanted it back. So he came here. Took him all night but he found it. Underneath a five-day-old cauliflower.

For a moment **Victor** *and* **Kathy** *stare back at him and the other men, and then seeing they are making no attempt to stop them,* **Victor** *and* **Kathy** *get into the first taxi and the convoy of taxis drives away.*

EXT. THE FOREST FILM SET. NIGHT

We cut to **Rachel** *and* **Callum** *together, having moved to the edge of the film set. In the distance is the tent with all the extras in armour, eating.* **Callum** *and* **Rachel** *are both eating ravenously too, bacon and sausages.* **Callum** *stares towards the tent.*

CALLUM

They've just brought some puddings too with fresh cream! . . . They have so much food it's extraordinary.

RACHEL

They have everything here you could possibly want!

CALLUM

That's true . . .

Callum *glances towards the film set in the forest clearing.* **Dieter**, **Lotte** *and* **Anna** *are playing together in front of the waiting camera.* **Lotte** *is wearing a helmet with visor and is chasing them.* **Anna** *puts on a helmet too and starts chasing her back.*

I've never told anybody ever . . . but this is what I want to do.

RACHEL

I'm honoured to be the only one who knows. (*Her face close, her tone warm.*) But what exactly is it you want to do, be an extra in a movie?

CALLUM

I want to write music for the movies . . . I would love to be able to do that —

RACHEL

Ah your music! . . . You know I've never heard you play.

CALLUM

No you haven't . . . (*Smiles, very close to her.*) There's a piano at the hotel of course . . . We could go there now?

We cut to the extras in their armour pouring back through the trees into the clearing. **Lotte** *and* **Anna** *come up to* **Harold** *with their visors down, and then pull them up in unison.*

HAROLD

They'll be giving you a part in a minute! (*He looks around.*) Have you seen Callum and Rachel anywhere?

ANNA

Oh they went . . . I saw them go.

We stay on **Harold**.

INT. CONNINGTON SECOND-FLOOR PASSAGE. NIGHT

We cut to **Callum** *and* **Rachel** *in the passage outside his hotel room. He is unlocking the door with his large bunch of keys.*

RACHEL

So you've still got all those keys?!

CALLUM

Yes. It's good isn't it!

The door opens on the bedroom with its piano and quite large bed.

Rachel *hesitates in the doorway.* **Callum** *turns.*

We could always skip the music?

> RACHEL
> Certainly not. (*Softly.*) You don't get out of it that easily . . .

EXT. LONDON SUBURBAN STREET. NIGHT

We cut to the line of five taxis drawing up in a suburban street. **Victor** *jumps out of the first taxi,* **Kathy** *out of the second.* **Victor** *starts pulling the bags out on to the pavement with manic energy. He addresses the taxi drivers.*

> VICTOR
> We'll do this as quick as we can, gentlemen! . . . Come on, Kathy, the faster we do this the less chance there is of us getting noticed –

> KATHY
> You don't think anybody's going to notice this?! We're invisible are we, Victor . . .?!

She is heaving bags out on to the pavement. She sees a face in a window watching. She looks back along the night street to see if anybody has followed them.

INT. CALLUM'S HOTEL ROOM. NIGHT

Callum *is sitting at the piano playing his own composition.* **Rachel** *is sitting at the end of the bed, behind him, watching him play.*

We move in close on her face and then cut back to **Callum**.

> CALLUM
> You're very quiet . . . are you still there?!

He glances over his shoulder as he plays.

> RACHEL
> Yes I'm here . . . I'm listening.

> CALLUM
> Surprised how romantic it is?

RACHEL

A little . . .

CALLUM

You expected a march did you? (*He gets up.*) Something warlike . . . the marines coming over the hill?

RACHEL

I didn't know what to expect . . . (*Softly.*) I liked it.

They are kissing passionately now. She starts to unbutton his shirt. They begin to pull each other's clothes off. Suddenly she stops; there is a sound outside in the passage.

RACHEL

What's that?

CALLUM

Oh that's nothing . . . just a man collecting the shoes! He always makes a racket . . .

We cut out into the passage. A hotel porter is pushing a huge trolley, collecting the men's shoes left outside each door for a polish.

We cut inside the bedroom. They are falling onto the bed together, **Rachel** *laughing.*

RACHEL

He's not going to insist on coming in here is he?! 'Excuse me, sir, don't mind me, sir, please carry on, I'm just here to shine your shoes, sir!'

CALLUM

Don't worry . . . (*Kissing her.*) One thing everybody knows – never ever disturb me in my room . . .

We cut back outside into the passage, the big trolley of shoes trundling along.

The little man pauses for a moment to stare back along the passage.

We cut back to **Callum** *and* **Rachel** *naked in the bed, making love. We move in on* **Rachel**'s *face.*

INT. KATHY'S FLAT. FRONT ROOM. NIGHT

The last bag drops down in the middle of the small front room of **Kathy**'*s ground-floor flat.* **Victor** *and* **Kathy** *stare at the very large pile of filthy bags that now dominate the room. Both of them are exhausted.*

KATHY

I can't believe we've done this . . . (*She suddenly cries out, pointing at one of the bags.*) There are beetles crawling out of that one, look!

VICTOR

Don't worry . . . I will go through them. I don't mind getting filthy.

KATHY

You will go through them? You don't know what you're looking for, Victor!

VICTOR

I've got a bit of an idea. I can make a start anyway. You go to bed . . . (*He looks at her anxiously.*) You don't mind me staying here do you? I'd rather do that if I can . . . Don't really want to be alone now. I'll work all night you'll see . . . and you don't have to worry about anything – with women I'm always a perfect gentleman . . .

KATHY

I'm sure you are, Victor.

She looks at this strange figure kneeling in the middle of the room. She hesitates, then decides.

Of course you can stay tonight . . . Use the sofa.

We are close on her face. She stares at the bags.

They're going to come after these, aren't they?

VICTOR

Maybe not . . . maybe they won't realise they've gone. (*He grins.*) Anyway I've got a plan for that too . . . !

INT. CALLUM'S HOTEL BEDROOM. NIGHT

We cut to **Callum**'s *hotel bedroom, which is quite dark.* **Callum** *is in bed watching* **Rachel** *who is by the window in her slip. She touches the window pane, then runs her hand along the window sill, then moves and touches the side of the cupboard.*

RACHEL

You know the movie . . . with Greta Garbo, *Queen Christina* . . . When she's in this room with her lover, it was a much grander room than this of course, and she starts touching everything, a spinning wheel, the four-poster bed, she touches things very very slowly . . . (*She stretches the word out.*) Sen-sually, and speaks even slower . . . (*Mimics Garbo's accent.*) 'I am . . . memorising . . . this room!'

CALLUM

So that's what you're doing? Memorising this room?

RACHEL

No, hardly. (*She smiles.*) You'd be crazy to remember this one, because there's nothing of you here, Callum . . . No books . . . no pictures, no photos of your family, not even Victor –

CALLUM

Of course not. This isn't my home.

RACHEL

But you haven't got a home, have you? (*Suddenly her tone serious.*) Oh, Callum. I don't want to fall in love with you . . . I have to do everything I can not to . . . not to love you . . .

CALLUM

Why?

RACHEL

Why?! (*She laughs.*) Says he complacently lying there . . . (*She imitates.*) 'Why ever not?!' . . . Because this can't possibly last.

CALLUM

You don't know that.

RACHEL
Of course I do, . . . of course it can only be temporary,
Probably shorter even than that really . . . for so many reasons.

She moves, starts touching the cupboard near the bed.

I don't want to fall in love with you . . . (*She pauses, quiet.*) But right at this moment I'm not at all sure how to stop it . . . (*Suddenly her tone changes.*) This is strange . . .

She pulls an object out from behind the small cupboard.

What on earth is this?

Close-up of **Callum**. *He is totally stunned. It is a listening device in his own room. We move in on him. Then he suddenly adopts a loud casual tone.*

CALLUM
That's nothing . . . just something from work . . .

He holds his finger up to his lips, indicating to **Rachel** *what it is.*

A special notebook . . . they can't clean this room very well, it should have been put back in its drawer . . .

He starts putting his clothes on.

RACHEL
This isn't?! . . . (*She can't stop herself expressing her astonishment.*) They haven't been listening –

Callum *puts his hand softly over her mouth just as she says this. He whispers.*

CALLUM
You better go. Get out of this room . . . I'm going to surprise them. (*Whispers in her ear.*) Don't worry . . .

An intense close-up of **Rachel**'s *eyes. He gives her a long kiss on her lips.*

INT. CONNINGTON PASSAGE. BACK STAIRS NIGHT

We see **Callum** *hurtling along the passage; his shirt is only half done-up and he is barefoot. He charges up the back stairs. A subjective shot as he heads* *straight towards the door of the secret office. He doesn't stop. He bangs straight through the door.*

INT. ATTIC OFFICE. NIGHT

Callum *enters the secret office. A heavy, metal tape recorder with large spools is recording. Sitting completely alone in the office, in evening dress, with headphones on, is* **Ruth**. *She looks astonished to see* **Callum**.

CALLUM
Was it worth coming back for?

Ruth *stops the tape recorder. She takes off her headphones.*

Worth cutting your evening short for that?

RUTH
I was asked to.

CALLUM
Of course you were asked to . . . (*He stands over her, a dangerous smile.*) Play it for me . . .

Ruth *suddenly very nervous of him.*

Go on.

Ruth *hesitates, moves to start the tape recorder. He suddenly reaches out and stops her.*

No, play the whole thing right from the beginning, right from me playing the piano . . .

Ruth *begins to rewind the tape.* **Callum** *watching.*

How useful these German tape machines have proved haven't they?! We really must make our own.

INT. CONNINGTON. LOBBY. NIGHT

We cut to **Rachel** *moving across the hotel lobby towards the street. Her face is pale.*

INT. ATTIC OFFICE. NIGHT

We cut back to **Callum** *sitting opposite* **Ruth**, *the tape machine next to them. There is the sound of* **Callum** *and* **Rachel**'s *love-making.* **Ruth** *is looking down but her manner is now very controlled.* **Callum**'s *gaze is unflinching. The sound of* **Rachel** *and him reaching orgasm comes out of the tape loud and clear. After a moment* **Callum** *casually leans over and stops it.*

CALLUM

Not bad is it? Better than I expected . . . Makes for quite lively listening . . . What do you think?

Ruth *avoids looking at him.*

RUTH

I have to say . . . sir, that I'm surprised . . . very surprised –

CALLUM

That I didn't search my own room for bugs? So am I, Ruth, a basic mistake wasn't it?! Surprisingly naive, I agree! (*Leans forward, a very sharp smile.*) Now I know why Salter hasn't come to find me – he didn't need to, he was still here, listening to everything . . . He is somewhere in the hotel isn't he?!

RUTH

Not tonight . . .

Callum's *look is unnerving her. She is suddenly frightened of him.*

I promise you he isn't here tonight.

CALLUM

Tell your boss, . . . (*His face very close to her.*) I will meet him in the lobby at eight o'clock tomorrow morning. Go and tell him now.

INT. RACHEL AND ALEX'S HOUSE. HALL/BEDROOM. NIGHT

We cut to **Rachel** *approaching the bedroom; light is spilling from under the door. Surprised, she enters gently.* **Alex** *is sitting up in bed, surrounded by papers.*

ALEX

There you are, darling . . .

RACHEL

You're still awake . . . it's nearly three o'clock, Alex.

ALEX

I know, I thought I'd wade through these while I waited. So you stayed for all the filming did you?

RACHEL

Not all of it, no . . . I think they go on till dawn.

ALEX

Till dawn? What else did you see, were they filming anything different?

RACHEL

No, just the men in armour running around . . . I didn't see the sword fight –

ALEX

That's a pity. Did Mr Lindsay-Jones or Callum bring you home?

Rachel *tries not to hesitate.*

RACHEL

No, Callum's still there I think . . . he loves everything to do with the movies. No I took a taxi.

Alex *looks up sharply.*

Shocking isn't it, all the way from Buckinghamshire?! The film people arranged it for me . . .

ALEX

That was kind of them. They seemed rather rude to me.

RACHEL

Yes it was kind of them . . . It was exciting seeing all those people working together like that, concentrating on the same thing . . . It's made me even more determined to do something myself. (*She looks at him.*) Don't laugh at this, but

I'm thinking I might arrange a fashion show for that designer I've met, to show off her clothes –

ALEX

Why not, darling? (*Looking at her.*) I'm not going to laugh at that.

We stay on **Rachel**.

INT. ATTIC OFFICE. EARLY MORNING

We cut to the sun coming through the windows of the attic office. **Callum***'s eyes flick open; he has fallen asleep next to the tape recorder. The red light is flashing on the other side of the room. We move in on* **Callum**.

INT. THE MELBURY SUITE. EARLY MORNING

We cut to **Callum** *entering the suite.*

For the first time **Frau Bellinghausen** *is standing. She is by the window with her back to him. She turns.*

FRAU BELLINGHAUSEN

You look dreadful. Have you not been to sleep?

CALLUM

Not much, last night, no, Frau Bellinghausen.

FRAU BELLINGHAUSEN

You've come to see me unshaven? Looking a total mess. What has happened to you, Mr Policeman?

CALLUM

Nothing I can't handle, maybe you should start calling me Callum?

FRAU BELLINGHAUSEN

I hardly think we're at that stage are we?

CALLUM

Or Captain Ferguson?

FRAU BELLINGHAUSEN

If you were in uniform that might be a little easier . . .

CALLUM
So – what can I do for you? (*His tone sharp.*)

FRAU BELLINGHAUSEN
Ah . . . It won't have escaped your notice that I'm here on my own – and I have not been out of this suite. That is of course my own choice. But maybe you could provide somebody for me to have tea with . . .? Somebody of interest who will come here and be entertaining, for a short while?

CALLUM
You want company, Frau Bellinghausen? Somebody to amuse you?

FRAU BELLINGHAUSEN
For a couple of hours only, and that easily could be too long.

CALLUM
We can always arrange for you to go out, wherever you want. A trip to the theatre and a meal –

FRAU BELLINGHAUSEN
Of course you can. And when I have decided if you and I are going to do business, if we are, then it is possible I might visit somewhere. At the moment I do not want to leave this suite. I have very good reasons for that, extremely important reasons, but I have no wish to explain myself to you or to anyone. Now, can you provide a person for me to have tea with, somebody I'd approve of?

CALLUM
Somebody you'd approve of – that is definitely a challenge, Frau Bellinghausen! (*He moves.*) I have to go – it's quite urgent, I have a little battle to fight downstairs . . .

FRAU BELLINGHAUSEN
Do you? Are you going to win this battle?

INT. LOBBY. CONNINGTON. EARLY MORNING

Salter *appears at the entrance of the lobby. He moves confidently to where* **Callum** *is sitting in one corner, his tone expansive.*

SALTER

Ferguson, we haven't seen each other for a while have we?! (*He sits.*) Tea, how very civilised, but only for one?

CALLUM

Yes, because this isn't going to take long.

SALTER

We need to forgive each other, you and I.

CALLUM

Do we?

SALTER

You took my German –

CALLUM

I did.

SALTER

And I shouldn't still be in the hotel. (*He leans forward.*) I heartily recommend that we really do forgive each other . . .

CALLUM

Or else what?

SALTER

Or else?! Did I say or else? How could I possibly do anything?! I have no means of hurting you, no means at all. You have control of everything here . . . even the food! Because the jet-engine man is coming up trumps and he really likes you doesn't he?!

CALLUM

Show me your room.

SALTER

Ah my room! I'd be delighted. (*He smiles.*) I'm surprised you didn't guess I've had a room here all along . . . (*He gets up.*) It has a lovely smell.

INT. THE KITCHENS/BASEMENT. ROOM

We see **Salter** *leading* **Callum** *through the kitchens past* **Leonard** *and the other chefs, and down into a dark subterranean area full of pipes.* **Salter** *opens the door to reveal a large room among the boilers, full of shelves and tables covered in paperwork and spools and spools of recordings.* **Ruth** *is standing there.*

SALTER

Here we are . . . We get all the smell from the kitchens down here, some better than others of course!

Callum *is moving straight to the tapes.*

Ah yes, that's how we kept track of things, just needed to have a listen in to you, so we knew you were safe . . . it was just Ruth and me, nobody else.

Callum *picks up one of the large spools of tape with its sharp metal case and chucks it dangerously, like a heavy frisbee, across the length of the room towards a bin.*

CALLUM

You've got exactly one minute to get out of this hotel, both of you, and never ever come back.

He picks up another spool of tape. **Salter**'s *tone suddenly becomes serious.*

SALTER

Don't throw me out, Ferguson . . . we can destroy all the tapes of course but don't throw me out.

Ruth *watching from the shadows.*

I can help you.

CALLUM

Help me?

SALTER

Yes, you will need my help very soon. (*Moves closer.*) We both know things are changing, becoming a lot more vicious . . . it won't be our little deceptions any more, yours and mine, our home-made plans – but something far more brutal. And you will need me.

RUTH

You ought to listen to him, sir.

CALLUM

You've got twenty seconds.

He aims the heavy spool.

Salter *and* **Ruth** *begin to move off.*

I'll be right behind you.

We move among the pipes, **Salter** *and* **Ruth** *close together, ahead of us.* **Callum** *emerges into the outer kitchens and sees them disappear across the room through a mist of steam.* **Ruth** *stops for a moment; she is silhouetted in the steam at the other end of the kitchen.*

She stares straight at **Callum** *and then suddenly she is gone.*

CREDITS

Part Five

CREDIT SEQUENCE

EXT. BOMBSITE/CONNINGTON HOTEL. DAY

We see dust blowing across the empty bombsite. Just one small girl stands in the door of a shattered house.

Then we cut inside the Connington Hotel, the main reception area. Part of the ceiling has collapsed and dust has coated everything – the floor, the furnishings, the lights. Hotel staff are working frantically to clear it up watched by a few guests, some of them still in their dressing gowns. We see the startled faces of these guests, staring up at the gaping wound that has appeared in the hotel ceiling.

END OF CREDIT SEQUENCE

INT. KATHY'S FLAT. EVENNG

We cut to **Kathy** *letting herself into her flat. She stops suddenly in the doorway of the front room, startled to see* **Victor** *is still there. He is sitting on the floor surrounded by a mass of files, some open, some discarded, some stacked up in a tall tower on the sofa.*

KATHY

Victor . . . you're still here?!

VICTOR

Yes . . . I'm sorry, I just got so involved, I got lost in these . . .

He looks up, still kneeling among the files.

And all sorts of thoughts have been tumbling about, you know in my head . . . my own experiences . . .

KATHY

Of course. (*She is struck by his sudden vulnerability.*)

VICTOR

I don't know why – because this is all about the Germans. But sometimes – (*He pauses.*) things come rushing back . . .

KATHY

Yes, they must, I understand. (*Quietly.*) I do realise you went through a great deal in the war and –

VICTOR

No, no, we don't need to talk about it – and not now certainly! (*Tone lightens.*) I'm okay, I promise.

He jumps up and moves abruptly to the window, making the tower of files wobble alarmingly.

Just checking . . . !

We see a shot through the window of parked cars. One of them has a man in the driver seat glancing towards the house. **Victor** *studies him for a moment.*

Can't really tell?! (*He moves from the window.*) I know I've made a terrible mess here, but the good news is your room wasn't at all tidy in the first place! I hope you don't mind me saying that?

KATHY

No, it's probably true, I spend so little time here.

VICTOR

But then you should see my room, it is truly chaotic!

He picks up some of the files and puts one under his jersey.

With your permission, I'm going to take some of the files home, quite a lot in fact, because they'll never ever find them in my room!

INT. GENTLEMEN'S CLUB. NIGHT

We cut to **Harold** *sitting alone at a table having dinner at his club. He is writing in a notebook between mouthfuls. A silver dish of steaming brown cabbage is being carried towards him. Many of the old club members are staring at the strange cabbage as if it is completely alien.* **Harold** *smiles back at them.*

HAROLD

Cabbage with onions, gentlemen . . . you haven't lived until you've tasted this!

Victor surrendering to the military police

Callum's invitation to Kathy to have lunch in the park

Callum and Rachel in the forbidden seats at the cinema

Callum intercepts Kleinow as he is about to leave for Germany

Frau Bellinghausen demands a better hotel suite

The hallucinatory night at the film set

Rachel and Callum at the cricket match wondering if Alex knows about them

Alex in the middle of his great innings

Victor steals the blue Rolls-Royce

The jet engine in the tunnel: Dieter and Rita begin to realise something is wrong

Kathy confronts Mentz in the ruined church

Eva inspects the décor for the wedding reception:
'It's like having a wedding at the Pentagon!'

Dieter and Anna's wedding with Callum as the best man

Anna and Lotte build a snowman on the last day of the Connington

Harold sees Lucy and is unable to continue his speech at the farewell dinner

EXT. THE GOVERNMENT RESEARCH FACILITY. DAY

A military jeep is coming towards us fast along the main village street of the research facility, passing the pub. **Dieter** *is driving the jeep with* **Rita** *next to him and* **Callum** *in the back seat. Other jeeps pass them in the other direction.*

CALLUM

It's so busy here now . . .

RITA

It's all due to us of course! (*She smiles exuberantly.*)

DIETER

And now we have a surprise for you, Callum.

The jeep turns off the street towards some strange metal doors.

INT. TUNNEL. DAY

We cut to **Dieter**, **Rita** *and* **Callum** *entering a long tunnel. It stretches out in front of them disappearing into darkness. Near the entrance there is some old army equipment and bits of rubble. They move deeper into the tunnel.* **Rita** *is shining a torch.*

RITA

We're opening all of this up again, they shut it as soon as the war ended –

DIETER

Typically English, they use a tunnel built for the Napoleonic wars to test the latest equipment for this war!

CALLUM

Yes . . . (*Grins.*) Well they had to be safe from all those bloody rockets you were showering down on us!

Dieter *laughs.*

I love this place . . .

RITA

It goes on for three miles!

DIETER
Or even longer, we haven't found the end yet . . . I can get away from all my colleagues here – (*Pointedly to* **Callum**.) And from anybody sent to watch me . . .

RITA
We both escape here!

Callum *notices the carefree manner between them; their energy is infectious.*

We're going to test the engine right here!

DIETER
Yes and after the test has gone well, we're going to get all the senior people here –

CALLUM
The top brass coming here! That's a marvellous idea, stuff them all into this tunnel!

RITA
And then we'll blast them with the power of the engine –

DIETER
Which is so small it will look the size of an egg in this tunnel – but its power will amaze them.

CALLUM
Book me the best seat in the house – I've got to see this!

MONTAGE: EXT./INT. HOTEL DINING ROOM/LONDON STREET/ MRS TOOLEY'S HOUSE AND GARDEN/KATHY'S FLAT

Music starts pulsating, running under the following images of the montage.

We see the faces of young models, pale and nervous, all shapes and sizes, gathered in a room next to the hotel dining room. **Rachel** *stares at the awkward gawky faces of the group. The fashion designer, a short sharp-faced woman, is standing next to her.*

RACHEL
So, to get you ready for the big day, we're going to try a few things . . .

We see **Victor** *in his bedroom, in* **Mrs Tooley**'s *house, among his stained glass, the files spread around the room. He is reading them obsessively. We move in on him.*

We see **Kathy** *coming out of the entrance of the War Crimes Unit building, and walking briskly along the street. She sees a couple of parked cars ahead of her; one of them has its engine running. She can't stop herself staring at the man in the driving seat.*

We see **Rachel** *and the designer working with the models, trying different looks, different sorts of make-up. The space is now full of mirrors propped up across the room and rails of clothes. We see the pale faces of the models just beginning to transform.*

We see **Victor** *digging vigorously at the bottom of* **Mrs Tooley**'s *garden; he is partially hidden by a tree. He starts to bury some of the files near the compost heap. He glances up –* **Mrs Tooley** *is watching from her window.* **Victor** *calls out:*

VICTOR
Just doing some weeding, Mrs Tooley!

Night:
We see **Kathy** *kneeling, like* **Victor**, *in the middle of her front room, surrounded by the files he had left behind. The camera moves round her as she turns the pages. The wind is loud, rattling the window. She looks up, sees it is beginning to snow.*

Afternoon:
We see the models now looking far more glamorous; their make-up is bold. A series of shots of their faces looking more confident but still quite tense. **Callum** *is standing in the doorway watching* **Rachel** *move among the models, her concentration and determination. She catches his eye and smiles. He whispers to her.*

CALLUM
About the other night . . . everything's been taken care of.

Anna *and* **Lotte** *appear behind him staring at the models with fascination.*

RACHEL
Come on you two . . . why shouldn't you be part of it?!

Evening:
*We see **Mrs Tooley** staring through a crack in the door into **Victor**'s room with its incredible collection of objects. He is now striding up and down studying a file as he paces.*

INT. HAROLD'S HOUSE. NIGHT

Harold *is sitting at a desk in his library,* **Victor**'s *coloured glass is still propped up round the room.* **Lucy** *appears in the doorway.* **Harold** *smiles delightedly.*

HAROLD
So it worked — I managed to coax you back!

LUCY
I didn't need much coaxing, a fashion show — I wasn't going to miss that! I've never ever been to one. (*She laughs.*) I didn't even know they still had them! (*She kisses his cheek.*) It's so wonderful to be home . . .

HAROLD
And it's wonderful to see you, my dear.

LUCY
What are you working on? (*Glances at papers.*) Or is it secret?

HAROLD
It is secret, but I haven't written it yet! It is to help me find something out, but I don't want to get anybody into trouble . . . that's never a good idea, especially if you like them.

LUCY
I can't imagine you getting anybody into trouble your whole life . . .

EXT./INT. CONNINGTON DINING ROOM. DAY

It is snowing; we see it falling in the central yard of the hotel. And then we cut to the main dining room now laid out for the fashion show. A catwalk is stretching down the middle with chairs on either side. We can see snow falling through the window; it is bitterly cold. The band are stumbling on to the stage which has been built next to the catwalk at the far end. They are all wearing their overcoats and scarves and hats.

Eva *is muffled up as if she is on board a ship.*

EVA

It's fucking freezing, they can't hold the show now surely?!

We cut next door into the anteroom. The models are all made-up and they are slipping on the first dresses. They are all shivering; some are blue with cold.

RACHEL

Now attention everybody, I realise how cold you all are, today of all days the heating has decided to break down, but we're going to fix it I promise you – we're not going to let some bloody boiler defeat us!

We cut back to the dining room. The audience are now taking their seats. A mixture of some of London's glitterati, looking very patronising and affronted by the cold, some residents of the hotel, old European faces and some people we recognise – the Foreign Office couple from the dinner party and some faces form Harold's club. The audience are all wearing their coats and scarves. The band begins to play, a quiet number.

EVA

My fingers may freeze to the piano but we'll do our best!

We cut back into the anteroom, a close-up of **Lotte**. *She is wearing a little make-up and a stunning young girl's dress.* **Anna** *and* **Julia** *are both made-up and look startling. The clothes are all vibrant, vivid colours.*

We cut back into the dining room; it is now packed. **Harold** *is near the back, with* **Lucy**. *We see* **Alex**, *studying his programme.* **Callum** *appears behind* **Harold**.

HAROLD

Ah there you are . . . I've brought this for you. (*He gives him an envelope.*) It's a version of the letter we talked about. See what you think. Don't send it.

CALLUM

Of course not, thank you. (*He puts it in his pocket. Suddenly he grins.*) Oh, Harold, you are not so interested in fashion you can't spare a moment? I want to introduce you to somebody –

HAROLD
No that's fine, this is more for Lucy than for me . . . (*Looking at club members.*) And I helped get some of the audience!

CALLUM
It's the perfume lady – the one who has a secret . . .

INT. MELBURY SUITE. DAY

We cut to **Harold** *and* **Callum** *entering the Melbury Suite.*

Frau Bellinghausen *is wearing her grandest dress and is drinking lemon tea.*

CALLUM
Here we are, Frau Bellinghausen, I've found a tea companion for you.

FRAU BELLINGHAUSEN
Have you indeed? Somebody who doesn't mind missing the show?

HAROLD
I had much rather be here . . . (*Smiles.*) Harold Lindsay-Jones.

CALLUM
There is some music as you can hear – (*Grins.*) but it will not last long.

FRAU BELLINGHAUSEN
What are you smiling about?

CALLUM
Just you running the hotel now!

FRAU BELLINGHAUSEN
I thought we were both doing that.

INT. VICTOR'S ROOM. DAY

The snow is falling outside the window. We move in on **Victor**. *He is lying on his back on the floor reading a file. He suddenly sits bolt upright, staring at the page.*

INT. MELBURY SUITE. DAY

We cut back to **Harold** *and* **Frau Bellinghausen**.

FRAU BELLINGHAUSEN
You're a friend of Captain Ferguson?

HAROLD
I am. They are two brothers, both exceptional people in a way, very different . . . I am fond of both of them. Callum must be a very exciting person to do business with?

FRAU BELLINGHAUSEN
Am I doing business with him?

HAROLD
I believe you are about to, yes . . . (*Smiles charmingly.*)

FRAU BELLINGHAUSEN
I hope you're not too clever, Mr Lindsay-Jones, for me to have tea with.

INT. ANTEROOM/DINING ROOM/BASMENT. DAY

We cut back to **Lotte** *staring through a crack in the door at the packed audience in the dining room; the catwalk stretches like a huge runway in front of her.* **Rachel** *is addressing all the models who are still freezing.* **Callum** *is in the doorway.*

RACHEL
Now remember, these are clothes most of them won't have seen before . . . clothes made out of material that nearly anybody can get hold of but used in a different way . . . so don't expect them to leap up and start cheering – not at once anyway!

CALLUM

This is crazy, it is *so* cold. I am going to get the heating working *myself*!

We cut back to the audience: some of the old ladies have wrapped themselves tight in their fur coats, like they are in a blizzard.

We cut to **Callum** *moving through the kitchens fast, and down the stone steps. He is carrying a mallet. There are various hotel staff gathered round the pipes and boilers in* **Salter***'s old basement office.* **Callum** *pushes through them and starts pummelling the main metal valve which is stuck. It is a ferocious assault, each blow gets stronger.*

We cut to the first models parading down the catwalk. There is a powerful contrast between the skimpily clad girls and the audience in their heavy coats.

We cut to **Callum** *smashing down on the valve, his eyes blazing; he is determined to get it working for* **Rachel**. *We move closer. The blows get even stronger; one huge blow and the valve moves.* **Callum** *turns and grins; sweat is pouring down his face.*

We cut to **Rachel** *touching a radiator as she watches the models from the side of the catwalk. She feels the first sign of warmth. She smiles; her eyes shine with relief.*

EVA

(*calling out to the audience*)

Great clothes aren't they! . . . A bit of excitement, a bit of fun . . . we all need that! Been miserable for too long haven't we?! . . . Come on everybody!

The music is building, a dynamic fast tempo. The clothes and models are vibrant, very alive compared to the staid audience. **Anna** *and* **Lotte** *walk on to the stage both looking stunning. We move in on* **Dieter**, *who is smiling delightedly seeing his daughter so poised and confident, and* **Anna**, *who suddenly looks a sophisticated woman.*

We see **Alex** *watching* **Rachel**, *her complete focus on the show. The audience, almost despite themselves, are getting energised by the clothes, the models, the colours.*

INT. MELBURY SUITE. DAY

We cut back to **Harold** *and* **Frau Bellinghausen** *together.* **Harold** *is sitting opposite her now, drinking tea. They can hear the music.*

> FRAU BELLINGHAUSEN
> So they really are having a fashion show down there? How strange that seems at the moment.

> HAROLD
> I know . . . but a bit of colour, a bit of fun, how much people need that . . . (*He looks at her.*) It must break your heart what has happened to this city . . . seeing it again after such a time?

> FRAU BELLINGHAUSEN
> I can't bear to look at it . . . the devastation, the horrible wrecked buildings . . .

> HAROLD
> We both I'm sure remember how it was before the first war –

> FRAU BELLINGHAUSEN
> Oh yes, how beautiful it was, nobody ever believes me when I say London was truly beautiful.

> HAROLD
> In autumn especially . . .

> FRAU BELLINGHAUSEN
> Yes, so incredibly lovely in autumn – and now I don't recognise any of it from this window . . .

Suddenly there are tears in her eyes.

> You're right, it does break my heart. How did it all happen? How did everybody let it happen? (*Tears running down her cheeks.*) It's impossible to understand isn't it . . .

INT. DINING ROOM. DAY

We cut to all the models in the show's finale. The music rises to a climax. **Julia** *is at the front of them looking very glamorous.* **Callum** *is applauding* *loudly,* **Alex** *is smiling.* **Dieter** *stands up and others follow, giving the models a standing ovation.*

INT. KATHY'S FLAT. DAY

Kathy *suddenly looks up from her desk where she is studying a file. It is as if she senses something. She moves to the window. The snow is falling. She sees a parked car, near the house, with its windscreen wipers moving, a man's face staring back at her. She watches him closely through the falling snow. We move in on the car. Suddenly a face appears at the window, right up against the glass; she leaps back with shock. It is* **Victor**, *waving urgently. We cut to* **Kathy**, *in the hall, letting him in. He is covered in snow. He is holding a file that is also covered in snow. He waves it at her.*

                    VICTOR
You've got to see this.

INT. ANTEROOM/DINING ROOM. DAY

We cut back to the room next to the dining room. The models are all celebrating excitedly with **Rachel** *and the designer.* **Callum**, **Alex** *and* **Dieter** *are in the doorway and then join them. Champagne is being opened, and everybody is talking at once.*

INT. KATHY'S ROOM. DAY

We cut back to **Kathy** *who is reading the file. We move in on her face, her eyes wide.*

                    VICTOR
I have to tell Callum now.

                    KATHY
Not right away, Victor . . . That isn't the best thing to do, not before we've –

                    VICTOR
No, I've got to tell him! (*He grabs the file.*)

INT. HOTEL COURTYARD/ANTEROOM. DAY

We cut to the models and **Julia** *celebrating in the snow. One of them starts a snowball fight,* **Dieter**, **Lotte** *and* **Anna** *join in exuberantly.* **Rachel**, **Callum** *and* **Alex** *are standing in a doorway drinking champagne. We cut to* **Victor** *storming along the passage towards the courtyard.* **Kathy** *runs to keep up.*

Callum *looks up, sees* **Victor** *bearing down on him.*

CALLUM
Victor you're not allowed . . . you shouldn't be here.

VICTOR
You've been lied to . . .

His tone intense, he shoves the file into **Callum**'s *hands.*

KATHY
I couldn't stop him doing this.

We cut to **Dieter**, **Anna** *and* **Lotte** *having their snowball fight oblivious.*

We cut back to **Callum** *with the file but he is hardly looking at it.*

VICTOR
Look, look, read it!! . . . Your German worked with V2 rockets. (*He points at* **Dieter**.) He worked with slave labour . . . He was in charge . . . Many people died, people were executed! He has lied to you all the time about everything.

CALLUM
I don't believe you. (*He waves the file.*) I don't care what this says I don't believe you.

VICTOR
You don't want to believe it!

CALLUM
You always do this, Victor . . . you try to cause chaos wherever you go – you just can't stop yourself can you?!

He stares across at **Dieter** *and* **Lotte**.

You're not going to this time. I'm not going to let you do that.

We stay on **Dieter** *and the joyful figures in the snow. The image slows.*

Time cut:

We are high above the snow-covered courtyard of the hotel staring down. **Dieter**, **Anna**, **Lotte** *and some of the models who have been fashioning the clothes in the ballroom are still having their snowball fight. We crane down towards this joyous, exuberant scene. As we get closer we can see* **Victor** *pacing, agitated, on the edge of the courtyard. His arms are waving, he is muttering to himself.*

We cut down to the passage next to the courtyard. **Kathy** *is watching* **Victor** *through a window as he paces, oblivious of the snowfight happening all around him.*

INT. ATTIC ROOM. AFTERNOON

We cut to **Callum** *sitting alone in the attic office. The file* **Victor** *brought is lying open on the table in front of him. He is reading it intently. We track towards him until we are close on his eyes.*

INT. CONSERVATORY BAR. LATE AFTERNOON

We cut to **Dieter** *drinking in the conservatory bar, looking animated, happy. Snow is still falling outside.* **Dieter** *is surrounded by* **Lotte**, **Anna**, **Rachel** *and* **Alex** *and the models. Everybody is talking at once; the mood is euphoric.* **Harold** *is sitting with* **Lucy** *watching the whole scene. He sees the sharp contrast between the older guests, looking grumpy and disorientated, and the energy and sexuality of the models still wearing their bright clothes from the fashion show.*

Two schoolboys are peering into the bar; they are dressed like miniature grown-ups, their parents behind them. **Rachel** *comes up to* **Harold** *with* **Lotte.**

RACHEL
She looks so good in these clothes doesn't she?!

Lotte *beams.*

HAROLD

Yes. (*To* **Rachel**.) You've caused quite a stir! (*Indicating the schoolboys and their parents.*) Maybe they'll stop dressing their children as little copies of themselves now?

RACHEL
(*drinking, laughing*)
Well it's not going to happen overnight . . . but who knows?!

We see a shot of **Dieter** *pouring champagne.*

EXT. HOTEL COURTYARD. LATE AFTERNOON

The light is just closing in. **Victor** *is still pacing the courtyard obsessively.* **Kathy** *is now standing on the edge of the courtyard smoking.* **Ringwood** *is approaching.*

RINGWOOD
I have a message from your brother. He says – go home.

VICTOR
I'm not going home.

KATHY
Come with me, Victor . . . we'll go somewhere quiet. I promise you we'll find out what Callum plans to do about what's in the files . . .

She move and whispers to **Ringwood**.

I'll make sure he leaves the hotel.

RINGWOOD
(*to* **Kathy**)
Captain Ferguson wants to know how you got hold of the file?

Victor *suddenly looms up behind them.*

VICTOR
We pulled it out of the rubbish, we stuck our hands right into the shit and grabbed them – and not just one, we got 'em all . . . !

KATHY
(*to* **Ringwood**)

Don't worry . . . they are perfectly safe. They are all in my flat.

Victor's *eyes flash.*

INT. CONSERVATORY BAR. EVENING

Julia *and* **Eva** *appear in the doorway of the conservatory bar, both rather drunk.*

JULIA

Come on everybody! There is a surprise waiting for you downstairs . . . !

EVA

I don't know what I feel about this surprise, but you better come and see . . .

We see **Ringwood** *approach* **Dieter**.

INT. ATTIC OFFICE. LATE AFTERNOON

The file is lying open in front of **Dieter**. *He is sitting at a desk in the attic office directly opposite* **Callum**, *who is staring straight at him.* **Ringwood** *is standing behind* **Callum**. *Next to* **Dieter** *is the bulky metal tape recorder recording their conversation.* **Callum**'s *tone is quiet and direct.*

CALLUM

You were in Peenemuende. You were at Nordhausen.

DIETER
(*his manner calm, open*)

I was, yes.

CALLUM

You worked on the V2 rocket programme at the Mittelwerk plant. You lied to me.

DIETER

I didn't tell the truth, no.

I could say of course that I didn't lie to you, because you've never asked me about what I did in the war, it was Miss Griffiths who interrogated me, remember, from the War Crimes Unit, in the middle of the night, with Lotte there.

If I had told the truth then, I knew there was a good chance of being arrested. Of being separated from my daughter, maybe even not seeing her again. So of course I denied it.

Silence. The tape going round.

CALLUM

And?

DIETER

And that is it . . . (*He indicates the file.*) The statement from a witness here is not true . . . not true about me anyway. But I know that will not be believed.

INT. BASEMENT BALLROOM. NIGHT

We cut to the bar revellers moving along the subterranean passage towards the basement ballroom. **Julia** *is by the door at the far end, beckoning them on. We see the action through* **Lotte**'s *eyes. The door is pushed open and in front of them, standing all alone in the empty ballroom, is a jukebox tied up with a large red bow. They all stare at it.*

JULIA

Who knows where it came from . . .?! But what a present!

EVA

It's going to put me out of a job . . .

She approaches the machine across the ballroom and addresses it directly.

I'm not going to be able to compete with you honey, am I?!

INT. ATTIC ROOM. NIGHT

We cut back to **Callum**. *He is watching* **Dieter** *closely, who is smoking. Clouds of smoke now fill the office.* **Ringwood** *is still standing in the corner.*

RINGWOOD
You were aware of the conditions of the workforce? The slave labour from Buchenwald concentration camp? The executions of those accused of sabotage, the beatings, the hangings? People starving to death?

DIETER
Of course some of these things went on . . . The conditions were appalling. I am not going to sit here and deny that, but I was never involved in ordering executions . . . or ever witnessed any, or knew anyone who was carrying them out. And that is the truth.

Callum *watching him impassively.*

RINGWOOD
Why were you named in this statement then from a witness? That you ordered some executions?

DIETER
I was very well known in Germany by then, famous as the jet plane man, just like Wernher Von Braun was the rocket man, everybody working on that site knew about us. People assumed everything that happened was done in our name . . . was what we wanted. But I say again that was not true in my case. I know you won't believe me. I was in fact at Nordhausen for only three months, I was working in an office at the edge of the site . . . I did not order anybody to be killed. (*Intensely.*) I absolutely did not.

RINGWOOD
But you knew all these things were happening . . .? And you did nothing to try to stop them?

DIETER
Again I don't deny these things happened, of course I don't. It was a terrible place . . . we were trying to win the war when we knew we were probably losing it . . .

Maybe it doesn't make any difference really if I was directly responsible or not, maybe that is the truth of the matter . . . because I was there . . . and it was an awful place.

Silence. **Callum** *watching* **Dieter**. *The red light is flashing on the wall.*

DIETER

I think somebody wants you.

CALLUM
(*to Ringwood*)

You go and deal with it.

Ringwood *gives* **Dieter** *a searching look then leaves.*

DIETER

I realise you don't believe me . . .

CALLUM

It doesn't matter what I believe. (*His tone gives nothing away.*) The government will protect you from any danger of prosecution . . .

DIETER

So you don't believe me?

Their eyes meet.

CALLUM
(*totally impassive*)

Did I say that?

He leans over and stops the tape recorder.

Go and be with your daughter.

INT. MELBURY SUITE. EVENING

Music pounding from below. **Frau Bellinghausen** *is staring at* **Ringwood**.

FRAU BELLINGHAUSEN

So where is my normal policeman?

RINGWOOD
Captain Ferguson is extraordinarily busy at the moment.

FRAU BELLINGHAUSEN
Extraordinarily busy? I've not known him be that before. So my business will have to wait?

RINGWOOD
Just right at this moment it has to wait.

FRAU BELLINGHAUSEN
You can tell him I want to make progress now. (*She smiles.*) That might encourage him to find the time for me.

RINGWOOD
I will tell him that, yes. (*He moves to go.*)

FRAU BELLINGHAUSEN
And this music is a very annoying development.

Ringwood *turns.*

The band stops playing, and then a machine takes over – a machine that can go on and on . . . and never get tired.

RINGWOOD
A machine, Frau Bellinghausen?

FRAU BELLINGHAUSEN
Yes . . . you look surprised I can tell the difference. A jukebox, isn't that what it's called? (*She smiles.*) Appearances can be deceptive, maybe I'm not quite as old-fashioned as you thought.

INT. THE BASEMENT BALLROOM. EVENING

We cut to the jukebox. And then we cut wide, **Julia** *with her young man,* **Rachel** *and* **Alex**, **Lucy**, **Lotte** *and* **Anna**, *the models,* **Eva** *with one of her musicians, and various other guests are all dancing to its music.* **Lotte** *is stretching out her hands to encourage* **Dieter** *to dance, he is standing drinking and smiling at her.*

We see the scene through **Harold**'s *point of view; he watches* **Callum** *appear in the doorway.* **Harold** *notices* **Callum**'s *look of deep preoccupation. He moves through the dancers to join him.*

We cut to **Callum**'s *point of view, all the characters dancing,* **Rachel** *looking radiant and happy. Even* **Alex** *is in an exuberant, carefree mood.* **Callum** *watches* **Dieter** *put down his drink and start dancing with* **Lotte**. *There is an hallucinatory feeling to the scene, of energy and infectious enjoyment. We stay on* **Callum**'s *face.* **Harold** *has now joined him.* **Julia** *suddenly calls over to* **Callum**.

JULIA
You can't just stand there, you've got to dance!

EVA
(*calling over to him*)
See how unnecessary my music is?! Just look at this!

Callum *is staring at* **Dieter** *and* **Lotte**. **Rachel** *and* **Alex** *move towards him.*

RACHEL
You really must dance, Callum, you can't be the only one not dancing . . .

HAROLD
What have you started, Rachel? This place might suddenly become fashionable again?!

ALEX
Yes, that's exactly what I've been saying to her – that this is only the start! She should put on more things here, music and poetry, and bits of new plays even –

RACHEL
Poetry and plays?! Alex! People can't dance to that . . .

She takes **Callum**'s *hand.*

Come on, Callum . . .

CALLUM
One moment . . . okay?

Rachel, *startled by his preoccupation, lets go of his hand and moves off to dance.*

HAROLD

What's the matter, Callum? It's not the letter I hope, the one I've asked you to write? Is that what's worrying you? We need to talk about that . . . we need a plan.

CALLUM
(*moving in on his eyes*)
That's exactly what I need.

He looks across at **Dieter** *and* **Lotte**.

EXT. FRONT OF THE HOTEL. NIGHT

We see **Callum** *jumping into a military jeep parked outside the hotel. He has a briefcase with him. We can still hear the music from the jukebox pouring out of the basement. He drives off rapidly into the night.*

INT. KATHY'S FLAT. HALL AND SITTING ROOM. NIGHT

Kathy *lets herself into her flat with* **Victor** *right behind her. They move into her small front room with the files piled high.* **Victor** *moves towards the piles.*

VICTOR

I wish you hadn't told them they were here – why on earth did you do that?

KATHY

I had to. We stole them, Victor . . .

VICTOR

We didn't steal them! We rescued them!

KATHY

It's their property though! If any good is going to come of this, I have to cooperate with them.

VICTOR

Callum's not going to waste any time, he's going to come after them tonight.

KATHY
Not tonight. He knows he doesn't need to do that.

EXT. MILITARY HEADQUARTERS. NIGHT

We see **Callum** *drive fast down the drive and up to the military headquarters.*

INT. WAINWRIGHT'S OUTER OFFICE. NIGHT

We see **Callum** *moving through* **Wainwright**'s *outer office. Various of his staff are preparing for a Christmas party; the last decorations are being hung, trays of glasses are being laid out.* **Wainwright** *is inspecting bottles of wine as they are being pulled out of a crate by one of his staff. He sees* **Callum** *and booms across the office.*

WAINWRIGHT
Come to wish me happy Christmas, Ferguson?!

CALLUM
Quite the opposite, sir.

He pulls **Dieter**'s *file out of the briefcase.*

INT. KATHY'S FLAT. NIGHT

We cut to **Kathy** *lighting a fire in the small grate in her living room.*

Victor *is sitting, hunched in a chair, still with his coat on.*

KATHY
You see, you were wrong. He's not coming tonight.

VICTOR
I'm never wrong about my brother.

INT. WAINWRIGHT'S INNER OFFICE. NIGHT

Wainwright *is at his desk staring at* **Dieter**'s *file.* **Callum** *is standing watching him. The door is open and we can see the party preparations continuing through it.*

WAINWRIGHT
I had no idea about any of this . . . any accusations against him. (*He turns a page of the file.*) Otherwise I would have told you. (*He looks up.*) Naturally.

CALLUM
I know you would . . . sir. (*His tone is dry, sceptical.*)

WAINWRIGHT
Of course this makes no difference to his work for us . . . he has to finish it. Do you want to stop now? It would be a complete bloody nuisance if you did?! (*He stares, his cold eyes.*) Is that why you've come to spoil my Christmas party? To tell me that?

CALLUM
(*momentary pause*)
No, I'm not saying that. Not yet.

He sits in front of **Wainwright**.

But we have to move him right now as a matter of urgency, we can't take the risk of him bolting to the Americans because he thinks we don't believe him –

WAINWRIGHT
Do you believe him?

CALLUM
Maybe . . . I'm not sure. We'll see.

He looks straight at **Wainwright**.

He can live at the research facility – we can keep him under constant surveillance easier there. He'll have to take his daughter with him – she'll need to be driven into London to school every morning, and back of course. We should do this tomorrow – I don't think he's going to bolt tonight . . .

WAINWRIGHT
This is Ferguson's plan is it?

CALLUM

Yes. And there is more –

WAINWRIGHT

More?!

CALLUM

We need to run a check in Germany on what he really did during the war.

WAINWRIGHT

Why?

CALLUM

Because we should have the facts shouldn't we, sir? Something might happen, it's important we know.

WAINWRIGHT

It will take time.

CALLUM

Naturally . . . but we should do it. And we have two further problems . . .

Wainwright *looks up.*

My brother and Miss Griffiths –

WAINWRIGHT

Miss Griffiths? Oh for fuck's sake she's not still around is she?! We never ever seem able to get rid of her.

CALLUM

I have a plan for that too. For both of them in fact.

EXT./INT. KATHY'S FLAT. NIGHT

We see through the window of **Kathy**'s *front room. Three army trucks full of soldiers and two jeeps with military police are driving up the street of little terraced houses.*

We cut outside to see the soldiers spilling out of the trucks.

And then we see them bursting through the door of the hall of **Kathy**'s *flat.*

Suddenly the small space is crammed with soldiers. They smash through the door of the front room and surround **Kathy** *and* **Victor**.

KATHY

What on earth is this?!

The soldiers start seizing the files and removing them from the flat.

VICTOR

I told you!

KATHY

Who sent you here?

VICTOR

Callum did of course . . .

Victor *makes a grab for some of the files and holds on to them ferociously.*

Don't take them yet! Not till my brother gets here . . .

I'm telling you, DON'T TAKE THEM!

KATHY

Stop it, Victor, that's not going to help.

The soldiers wrestle **Victor** *to the ground and hold him with his arms pinned back.*

KATHY

You don't need to do that for Christ's sake.

VICTOR

I'm going to get shot am I for fishing things out of the rubbish?!

Kathy *is staring at the armed soldiers; some of them are now searching her bedroom.*

INT. BASEMENT BALLROOM. NIGHT

We cut to **Dieter**, **Lotte**, **Anna** *and* **Eva** *standing by the jukebox, the yellow light from the machine glowing on their faces.* **Rachel** *is sitting on the* *edge of the stage smoking; the ballroom is now almost empty.* **Lotte**'s *finger is hovering round the buttons on the jukebox about to make a selection.*

EVA

One day . . . there'll be one of mine on here!

Lotte *presses the button and watches fascinated as the record moves into position.*

EXT./INT. KATHY'S FLAT. NIGHT

We cut to **Victor**'s *face contorted, red, as two burly soldiers hold him really tight so he can't struggle. The room is now empty of files.*

KATHY

You can let him go now can't you? Or are you going to stay like that all night?!

Victor's *head suddenly turns towards the window.* **Kathy** *moves to look out.*

Callum *is driving up the street in his jeep. We cut to him entering the flat.*

He stares at **Victor** *being held by the soldiers and then at* **Kathy**.

VICTOR

I always knew sooner or later I'd get arrested again – but I didn't think it'd be by my brother.

CALLUM

Let him go . . .

The soldiers release him.

You've made things very difficult, Victor. I want to see you at the hotel at three o'clock tomorrow afternoon – without fail.

VICTOR

That's an order is it? I'm not sure you can give me orders can you?

CALLUM

Be there . . . (*He turns to* **Kathy**.) Miss Griffiths, you have no more of our files in this house have you? Or anywhere else for that matter?

                                KATHY
    I have not, no.

Callum *turns.*

    And I have to say sending all these men to get them is totally
    ridiculous!

Callum *just looks at her and then begins to move off.*

                                VICTOR
    And what's going to happen to them now?!

                                KATHY
    Captain Ferguson . . .

Callum *turns.*

    I think it would be a good idea if we met to discuss what's
    happened –

                                CALLUM
    That won't be necessary. But you will be hearing from me.
    (*He looks at her for a moment.*) I have a surprise for you.

He moves through the front door into the night. We stay on **Kathy**.

EXT. GOVERNMENT RESEARCH FACILITY. DAY

We cut to a shot, through the windscreen, of a car approaching the main gates of the government research facility. We then cut to the back seat and see **Lotte** *sitting in isolated splendour, surrounded by hat boxes and a travelling case.*

We cut wide to see a large black saloon in convoy with a military jeep entering the secret village. **Ringwood** *is driving the jeep.*

The convoy drives down the main street of the village towards a reception party: **Dieter**, **Rita** *and* **Callum**. *As soon as the car reaches them,* **Lotte** *jumps out holding the hat box and travelling case, and runs towards her father.*

                                RITA
    You have so much luggage, Lotte! (*Laughing, to* **Dieter**.) It's
    like a little princess arriving!

DIETER
(*embracing* **Lotte**)
She has been allowed to keep all the clothes from the fashion show.

Callum *is standing slightly apart, watching the scene closely. He turns to* **Dieter**.

CALLUM
Show Lotte where you're going to test the engine.

INT. THE TUNNEL. DAY

We cut inside the tunnel. We are on **Lotte**'s *face, her eyes wide, as she sees the length of the tunnel.* **Rita**, **Dieter** *and* **Lotte** *are walking together several paces ahead.*

Callum *is watching the closeness of the body language between* **Rita** *and* **Dieter**.

RITA
This is where it's going to happen, Lotte . . . we test the engine . . . and then we break the sound barrier!

DIETER
(*looking back at* **Callum**)
If we're allowed to get that far?!

CALLUM
We will get that far . . .

Ringwood *watching* **Dieter** *closely.* **Callum** *suddenly focuses on* **Ringwood**.

CALLUM
By the way, did you know my bedroom in the hotel was bugged?

RINGWOOD
(*taken aback*)
No, sir! I did not.

CALLUM
So you never listened to me having sex, Ringwood?

RINGWOOD
(*truly startled*)

No, sir!

CALLUM

Not even once?

Ringwood *is speechless.* **Callum** *smiles.*

Don't worry . . . I believe you.

INT. ALEX AND RACHEL'S HOUSE. EARLY AFTERNOON

We cut straight to a close-up of **Rachel***; she is sitting reading in the living room.*

Her head turns sharply – **Alex***'s voice is calling her.*

Alex *appears at the end of the living room still in his hat and coat, his face flushed.*

RACHEL

Darling!

ALEX
I ran! Out of the office, into a taxi, up the stairs! Suddenly I had an hour or so to spare, I saw a chance to see you in daylight for once . . .

RACHEL

That's a lovely surprise.

ALEX

Madness isn't it . . . that I have so little time at the moment?!

RACHEL

It is mad, yes.

ALEX

And I just wanted to make sure you were okay, you were happy?

RACHEL

That I was happy?

ALEX

Yes. (*He leans over and kisses her gently.*)

RACHEL

Of course I'm happy.

ALEX

Are you? (*He looks at her for a moment.*) Good. I was so proud of you at the fashion show and everything . . . you must do more.

INT. MAIN GROUND FLOOR PASSAGE. CONNINGTON. LATE AFTERNOON

Callum *is approaching* **Victor** *who is sitting at the far end watched over by a chubby young man from the attic office.* **Callum***'s eyes are hard as he gets closer.*

CALLUM

You went behind my back. You stole the files.

VICTOR

They weren't yours any more. You threw them away.

CALLUM

I was ordered to do that.

VICTOR

You don't usually do everything you're ordered to.

Their eyes meet. **Callum** *turns.*

CALLUM

Come with me.

VICTOR

Going to put me in chains?

CALLUM

In a way.

INT. PASSAGE/STOREROOM. LATE AFTERNOON

We cut to **Callum** *and* **Victor** *approaching a door past the kitchens. One of the hotel staff is with them holding a bunch of keys; the chubby man is a pace behind. The door is opened to reveal a long low storeroom, full of dust and hundreds of different items: shoes, suitcases, umbrellas, old lamps, chipped cutlery, battered soft toys.*

A little daylight filters in from an incredibly filthy window.

CALLUM

The hotel's lost property! (*Moving into the room.*) Things left behind or things damaged during the war . . . nobody's had a chance to sort it. (*Turns to* **Victor**.) That's what you're going to do.

VICTOR

Am I?

CALLUM

Yes. (*Moving among the objects.*) Everything's muddled up . . . Start by putting together anything that belongs together . . . what you're good at, Victor. (*Straight at him.*) You wanted a job here after all . . . you're going to get paid.

VICTOR

Do I have a choice?

CALLUM

You have no choice, no . . . I've got to somehow stop them locking you up. This way I can keep an eye on you.

VICTOR

When do I start?

CALLUM

Now. (*He moves.*) I have an appointment . . . I'll be back.

INT. THIRD-FLOOR PASSAGE/KLEINOW'S SUITE. LATE AFTERNOON

Rachel *is standing by the door to* **Kleinow**'s *suite.* **Callum** *is approaching.*

RACHEL

Am I in the right place?

CALLUM

You're in the perfect place.

RACHEL

By the Nazi's suite! (*She laughs.*) How more romantic could you get?!

CALLUM

Ah . . . (*Unlocking the door.*) I have a surprise.

He pushes the door open. The suite is transformed: it has pictures, a beautiful embroidered bedspread and some flowers.

RACHEL

Goodness . . . that is an improvement, yes! (*She moves into the room.*) Did you get your staff to do this?

CALLUM

No, believe it or not, I did it myself. (*Smiles.*) Well sort of anyway . . . Our own private withdrawing room.

At that very second **Ringwood** *appears in the doorway. Both of them turn sharply.*

RINGWOOD

Sir . . . I'm so sorry . . .

CALLUM

Yes, Ringwood?

RINGWOOD

It's her again . . .

CALLUM

Of course, it is always her . . . (*To* **Rachel**.) I won't be a moment . . . (*To* **Ringwood**.) Mrs Lombard is looking at some of the suites here – she has some friends coming over from America very shortly.

Rachel *has to stop herself laughing at his brazen lie.*

Please, take all the time you want . . .

INT. MELBURY SUITE. LATE AFTERNOON

Frau Bellinghausen *is looking at* **Callum.** *Her tone is lightly reproachful.*

FRAU BELLINGHAUSEN
You have been extremely neglectful, Mr Ferguson.

CALLUM
I have. I apologise.

FRAU BELLINGHAUSEN
You're not going to make an excuse?

CALLUM
No. I have a very good excuse, but I won't trouble you with it.

FRAU BELLINGHAUSEN
(*lightly*)
That's a good decision . . . You did arrange a very satisfactory tea companion for me I have to admit, Mr Lindsay-Jones . . . (*She smiles.*) So I forgive you. Now – the moment has come I think when we have to explore whether you and I can really do business. We can't put it off any more.

CALLUM
You're absolutely right, we must do that. But not today.

FRAU BELLINGHAUSEN
You're too busy again?!

CALLUM
Today, yes . . . I am.

FRAU BELLINGHAUSEN
Well we will have many days of negotiation, so I was not intending to start today. But I suggest you get less busy again very quickly.

CALLUM
I will. I promise.

He has been eyeing the scent bottles displayed on the table next to her.

I couldn't borrow two of these could I?

FRAU BELLINGHAUSEN

You can't 'borrow' something like that. (*Their eyes meet.*) You may have two of those, but only two.

INT. KLEINOW'S SUITE. LATE AFTERNOON

We cut to a close-up of **Rachel** *sniffing the bottle of perfume as she sits on the edge of the bed.* **Callum** *is watching her.*

RACHEL

That is a very lovely smell, yes.

CALLUM

Good.

RACHEL

Thank you . . . (*She smiles.*) The only problem is he saw us here, your Mr Ringwood . . . now the whole hotel will know about us, and our private withdrawing room.

CALLUM

No, nobody knows . . . (*He grins.*) Everybody here believes what I tell them. (*He kisses her.*)

RACHEL

That is not true . . . (*Lightly.*) I don't for a start.

CALLUM

For a few weeks at least we can have everything we want.

RACHEL

Can we? Alex came rushing back from work at lunchtime today – the first time he's ever done that . . .

CALLUM

I don't think he knows though . . . You think he does?

RACHEL

I'm not sure . . . The funny thing is he keeps encouraging me to do more here . . .

Callum *kisses her, pushing her gently back on the bed.*

CALLUM

And you must.

RACHEL

I bet . . . (*Kissing him.*) we'll get interrupted.

CALLUM

No, never again. I promise.

INT. ATTIC ROOM. LATE AFTERNOON

We cut to **Ringwood** *in the attic office. There is a series of photographs of* **Frau Bellinghausen** *spread out in front of him and he is studying them. A photo of her as she is now, of her as a young woman with her husband, of the perfume factory in Mainz and then the shattered bombed streets around the works.*

INT. KLEINOW'S SUITE. LATE AFTERNOON

We cut back to **Kleinow**'s *suite.* **Callum** *and* **Rachel** *are making love in the bed. We move in on* **Rachel**'s *face. She whispers to* **Callum**.

RACHEL

Nobody listening this time?

CALLUM

Absolutely not.

INT. STOREROOM. EVENING

The light is just closing in. **Victor** *is moving across the storeroom. He opens the door just a crack. Outside in the passage there are two minders keeping watch: the chubby man and a thin-faced man. The chubby man immediately spots* **Victor** *and stares straight at him. We stay on the chubby man's face.*

INT. STOREROOM. NIGHT

It is night now; the storeroom in darkness. The door opens, throwing a shaft a light from the passage. **Callum** *is standing in the doorway. He can see no sign of* **Victor**.

A look of extreme annoyance in his eyes. He moves a step into the room.

CALLUM

Victor . . . Victor?! (*He switches on a light.*)

VICTOR

Don't panic . . . I'm still here.

Victor *emerges from behind some of the objects.*

CALLUM

You haven't made much of a start . . . You can go home now.

VICTOR

You're really going to keep me caged in here every day?

CALLUM

You're not caged . . . but you won't be able to go anywhere in the hotel without a minder, no. And they'll see you out of the hotel each night.

VICTOR

(*sharply*)

What if I don't turn up one morning?

CALLUM

You will, because you know this is a good idea.

This way everything can work, Victor . . . including me finding out about Dieter . . . I'll keep you informed.

VICTOR

You bet you will! (*Momentary pause; his manner softens.*) I could be so useful going through those files for you Callum, I wish you'd let me, I might spot something else . . .

CALLUM

No, Victor, I can't do that. (*He turns to leave.*)

VICTOR

Are you going to help that funny chap Harold find his secret file by the way?

CALLUM
I am, as it happens. I've worked out how to do it.

VICTOR
Tell me?

CALLUM
I'm going to use Dieter's name, it's obvious, it gives me access to everything. I'm not going to waste time writing some stupid letter, I'm going straight to the Foreign Office –

VICTOR
No . . . no!

CALLUM
Yes, I'm going to say Dieter told me he came to England before the war to discuss cooperating on a commercial jet liner. Because of the political ramifications there was a meeting at the Foreign Office about it –

VICTOR
No, no, don't do it, Callum!

CALLUM
And of course it happened the same week as the meeting Harold is interested in, but I can't be sure of the exact day – so I just say I need to see all the files for that week!

VICTOR
No, no, it's madness, they will trace it straight back to you!

CALLUM
They will not . . . A man came from T-Force asking about aeroplanes, they couldn't be less interested in that . . . !

VICTOR
You think you can get away with absolutely anything at the moment don't you?

CALLUM
Do I? . . . I think I can get Dieter to finish his work certainly, and I can help Harold expose the bastards that missed such a golden chance . . . and get the formula out of the perfume

lady . . . and of course I can keep you out of jail too. (*Lightly.*)
I think I can do all of that yes, without a doubt.

INT. WAR CRIMES UNIT. NIGHT

We cut to photos of **Kleinow** *looking straight at the camera dressed in prison clothes.*

Kathy *and* **Miss Clarkson** *are staring down at the images.*

KATHY

My contact over there says he's refusing to speak to anyone at all. But at least he's still in prison – and not looking that happy about it!

MISS CLARKSON

Yes, but unless we can get some witnesses to give evidence at his trial he may well get off. And of course most of the witnesses are dead –

KATHY

(*fury in her eyes*)
That would be terrible . . . if he got off.

INT. HAROLD'S HOUSE. THE LIBRARY. DAY

Harold *is in the library of his house, sniffing the other scent bottle* **Callum** *got from* **Frau Bellinghausen**. **Callum** *is watching him.*

HAROLD

Is this a present, Callum?

CALLUM

In a way, yes.

HAROLD

A feminine scent . . . a little unusual perhaps as a gift but very kind!

CALLUM

(*looking around*)
I like Victor's library . . . especially the stained glass! He has definitely a gift for organisation, amongst other things . . .

HAROLD

Your brother is a talent . . . if only he could find a way of using it that makes him happy.

CALLUM

I know . . . (*His tone changes.*) I'm going to propose a deal, Harold.

HAROLD

A deal? That sounds intriguing.

CALLUM

I will get your top secret file for you.

HAROLD

How? With the letter I suggested? We still need a way of protecting you in that case –

CALLUM

Don't worry, I think I know how to do it.

HAROLD

But you will discuss it with me first?

CALLUM

(*momentary pause*)

Of course. And in exchange for me getting it, I need you to spend time with the perfume lady.

HAROLD

Ah . . . I wasn't expecting that!

CALLUM

Distract her . . . keep her occupied. And if by any chance you can get the formula out of her for this bloody scent – that would save me an awful lot of work.

HAROLD

It's a deal. (*He smiles.*) I love saying that.

INT./EXT. WAR CRIMES UNIT. DAY

We cut to **Kathy** *working in the War Crimes Unit office.* **Miss Clarkson** *is at her desk.* **Kathy**'s *head turns sharply – there is the sound of large vehicles coming down the street. They move to the window.*

Two military trucks are drawing up outside the office. They are escorted by a jeep with military police. Soldiers jump out of the trucks. A look of real apprehension on **Miss Clarkson** *and* **Kathy**'s *faces.*

We cut to the soldiers spilling into the office. They are hauling large sacks out of which the files that were rescued from the rubbish vats are spilling. A sack is put in front of **Kathy** *with a note: 'I thought you should have these', signed* **Callum**.

KATHY

This is certainly a surprise . . .

Simultaneously a soldier is handing **Miss Clarkson** *an envelope.*

MISS CLARKSON

Good Lord, Captain Ferguson has arranged for us to stay in this office for a few more months! Why has he done that?

INT. FOREIGN OFFICE. LOBBY. DAY

Callum *approaches the reception desk in a hall of the Foreign Office. His manner is calm, subtly confident. A middle-aged man in glasses watches him approach.*

CALLUM

I sent a telegram. Captain Ferguson, T-force. I believe I'm expected . . .

The man looks down his list.

I've requested to see some files from a particular week in 1938.

The man finds his name and picks up the phone. **Callum** *smiles.*

It's a rather urgent matter . . . for those of us who love aeroplanes.

INT. MELBURY SUITE. DAY

Harold *is sitting drinking coffee with* **Frau Bellinghausen**. *She is watching him closely. There are some biscuits and slices of cake.*

> HAROLD
>
> Cake?
>
> FRAU BELLINGHAUSEN
>
> Not at this time of the morning, no.
>
> HAROLD
>
> Can I ask . . .?

He stops, her eyes are beady, watching him.

> What it was like for a young woman arriving in Germany? Was it very different to what you were used to?
>
> FRAU BELLINGHAUSEN
>
> Ah . . . at first there seemed little difference at all! I spent an awful lot of time meeting aristocrats in their castles or big houses . . . (*She laughs.*) Just like I'd done as a child. My husband was very well-connected, despite the fact that he actually made something.
>
> HAROLD
>
> And did you often visit your husband's factory, where he made the perfume? Did you have to attend Christmas parties for the workers and that sort of thing?
>
> FRAU BELLINGHAUSEN
>
> No, I didn't do that, but I did get to sample every new fragrance first . . . which for a young woman was of course quite heavenly. (*She smiles.*) For a time I thought what more could you possibly want?!

She looks straight at **Harold**.

> I'm glad you came back to see me, Mr Lindsay-Jones.
>
> HAROLD
>
> I'm delighted to be here.

FRAU BELLINGHAUSEN

For a moment I thought the policeman had sent you . . .
(*Their eyes meet.*) I don't know how I could have thought that?

INT. ROOM IN FOREIGN OFFICE. DAY

We cut to **Callum** *sitting at a desk in a large room in the Foreign Office. There are bound files in front of him. Each individually marked as a day of one week in August 1938, Monday to Friday. He is alone in the room except for one* **Stern-Faced Woman** *sitting on a chair against the wall. She is watching his every move.*

Callum *is flicking fast through the page of the files, hunting for the vital meeting.*

We see headings, in sharp cuts, each marked STRICTLY CONFIDENTIAL.

'Rubber footwear from the colonies threatens British manufacturing' . . . 'Plans for the visit of the King of Romania' . . . 'Discussion to impose quotas on Indian carpet importers', etc. *The subjects flash past. We move in on* **Callum**. *He looks up.*

*The s***Stern-Faced Woman** *never takes her eyes off him.*

INT. WAR CRIMES UNIT. DAY

We cut to some of the battered files spread out on the table in the War Crimes Unit office. They are filthy and **Miss Clarkson** *is startled to see a beetle crawling out of one of them. She looks at* **Kathy**.

MISS CLARKSON

We will have to keep jam jars on our desks at all times clearly
. . . So why do you think we've been sent these now?

KATHY

To keep us occupied I guess . . . to get us off their backs.

MISS CLARKSON

Exactly . . . I'm sure they will have sifted them for anything that could get in the way of their work.

KATHY

Yes . . . maybe they've taken out everything of interest . . . but you never know.

INT. ROOM IN FOREIGN OFFICE. DAY

*We cut to **Callum** now on the final file, Friday. The headings flash past including* HIGHLY CONFIDENTIAL: *'Repercussions of Royal visit to Paris' . . . etc.*

And suddenly there it is – 'TOP SECRET: *Herr Theodor Kordt conveys a message from senior members of the German military'.*

*We are very close on **Callum**'s eyes. Key phrases jump out in sharp cuts: 'Herr Kordt stressed the seriousness of their intent' . . . 'A planned coup d'état against Adolf Hitler'.*

Callum *looks up sharply. The **Stern-faced Woman** has still not taken her eyes off him. Her gaze is unflinching. For a moment we see **Callum** wondering what to do.*

He shuts the file.

CALLUM

I'm afraid it's not here.

*The **Stern-faced Woman** gets up.*

But the meeting definitely took place on this week . . . I couldn't have a look at the file for Saturday could I?

STERN-FACED WOMAN

Saturday? There are very few meetings ever held here on a Saturday.

CALLUM

Please. (*He stares straight at her.*) If you could have a look, just in case. It is rather important . . .

The woman hesitates.

I won't touch anything . . .

*The **Stern-faced Woman** leaves the room.*

As soon as she is gone, he tries to get the vital pages out of the file. It is bound like a book and the only way is to tear them out. He tries to get them out with a sharp tug, but after repeated attempts they won't come.

He has to stand up and really pull at the page.

*We cut outside to the passage, to see the **Stern-faced Woman** coming back, her footsteps ringing out.*

*We cut back to **Callum** tearing the pages out with one last really fierce tug. They seem to have come away cleanly. He is just slipping them into his jacket pocket with his back to the door, when the woman re-enters. He turns to face her with a smile.*

CALLUM

Any luck?

STERN-FACED WOMAN

There were no meetings on that Saturday.

INT. BASEMENT BALLROOM. DAY

Rachel *is standing staring at the basement ballroom's decor.* **Eva** *is watching her.*

EVA

So what is going to happen here? You're going to change everything . . . people spouting poetry?!

RACHEL

Hopefully not spouting . . . but I thought I could try something different here once a week. Take a risk! And you'll be part of it Eva, please?

EVA

I will, good . . . But they'll be fighting for the exit, there'll be a stampede to get out of here you know.

RACHEL

Almost certainly. (*She smiles.*) Do you think the hotel would let me do anything to this room?

INT. STOREROOM. LATE AFTERNOON

We cut to **Rachel** *approaching the storeroom door. The* **Minder** *standing outside lets her in. She moves into the room, to find herself in a maze of forgotten luggage.* **Victor** *has now arranged all the objects in neat lines, piled high.* **Rachel** *moves along one of these corridors of lost property to find* **Victor** *sitting at the far end.*

RACHEL

Hello, Victor . . . I'd heard you were sorting this stuff out . . .

Victor *hardly seems to register her for a second. She looks at him concerned.*

Are you alright?

VICTOR

Yes, I'm sorry . . . (*He smiles at her.*) I'm honoured to have a visitor here . . . especially you. I rarely see anyone!

RACHEL

I was told there was an old chandelier somewhere here – which I might be able to use. I just wanted to take a look . . . I'm planning a sort of gala event in the basement –

VICTOR

It's over there . . . it's rather beautiful.

He indicates the chandelier heaped on the floor in a corner. **Rachel** *walks over to it.*

RACHEL

You sure you're alright, Victor?

She looks across – he hasn't moved.

It must be really difficult being here on your own.

VICTOR

No, no, I can do this job . . . (*He doesn't move.*) It's just sometimes I have these memories, when it comes back, the fighting I'm sure everybody has them, it's nothing special. I was caught up in the merry show in Monte Cassino, which was quite a battle! And sometimes it . . .

He stands up, grins.

It's nothing . . . it's gone for the moment! (*Looks at her.*) Callum has them too you know . . .

RACHEL
(*surprised*)

Does he?

VICTOR

I'm sure he'll tell you one day. And so will I. (*He smiles.*) But right now I have this vital job to do as you can see . . .

INT. HAROLD'S LIBRARY. DAY

Harold *is standing by the window in his library reading the Foreign Office document.* **Callum** *is watching him from across the room.*

HAROLD

Extraordinary . . . It's all here, yes. The plan to overthrow Hitler before the war . . . Did you read it?

CALLUM

I didn't no. I wanted to – but I thought I shouldn't till you had.

HAROLD

Quite right. Thank you. (*His tone changes.*) And you really got it just by strolling into the Foreign Office with your ridiculous story about aeroplanes?

CALLUM

I did.

HAROLD

And you did this in person? You didn't send somebody else?

CALLUM

I couldn't send somebody else. I had to do it myself.

HAROLD
(*suddenly*)

I wish you hadn't done that! I told you to wait didn't I?! I told you to wait and discuss it with me. And you promised to do that –

CALLUM
(*startled by his vehemence*)
I saw a way to get it . . . and I just decided to do it.

HAROLD
Well you shouldn't have done that, Callum! That was completely irresponsible and reckless – and stupid. Why on earth did you do it?

CALLUM
You wanted the file. I got it for you. I don't know why you're so angry – it's my neck on the line, not yours?!

HAROLD
Exactly, that is what I'm so worried about. I can't bear the idea that you may get into some really appalling trouble because of this . . . I couldn't forgive myself.

CALLUM
That's not going to happen, Harold. I'm absolutely certain.

Harold *has turned away. We move in on his face; we see there are tears in his eyes. With his back to* **Callum** *he regains his composure. He turns and faces him.*

HAROLD
I'm sorry . . . I just so hope you're right. (*His tone changes.*) I haven't forgotten we have a deal of course, I'm a man of my word – I will definitely keep my side of it.

INT. THE WAR CRIMES UNIT. EVENING

We are close on **Kathy**'s *face. She is turning the pages of a file; we see the fierce determination in her eyes. We cut wide and see she is surrounded by pages covered with dirt spread all over her desk.*

INT. MELBURY SUITE. DAY

We see a close-up of a scent bottle being put down in front of **Frau Bellinghausen** *in the Melbury Suite.* **Harold** *is standing in front of her.*

HAROLD

Callum gave me this bottle of perfume . . .

He takes off the top.

FRAU BELLINGHAUSEN

Oh one of them was for you was it? He asked me for a couple of bottles, I wondered who they were for. (*She smiles.*) You must have been surprised to be given it?!

HAROLD

I was. It is a delightful smell.

FRAU BELLINGHAUSEN

It is. (*Suddenly.*) Do you want to know what's in it . . .? How it's made?

Their eyes meet.

HAROLD

I would be fascinated to hear.

FRAU BELLINGHAUSEN

I'm certain you would! Why don't you try to guess?

HAROLD

Guess? (*He smiles.*) It's not exactly my field, perfume . . . (*He sniffs the bottle.*) Orange possibly . . .? Peach . . .?

FRAU BELLINGHAUSEN

No, no, no! No peach or orange. Let me give you a little help . . . Eau de Cologne for instance contains, amongst other things, lemon, tangerine, lime, orange, grapefruit, lavender, rosemary, jasmine and tobacco. (*She indicates the bottle.*) None of those are in there.

HAROLD

How interesting . . . (*He sniffs the bottle.*) So no tobacco in this glorious smell then?

FRAU BELLINGHAUSEN

You know it's sad Captain Ferguson sent you to do his work for him . . . because it complicates our teas together doesn't it?

HAROLD

Only if we let it.

INT. BASEMENT BALLROOM. DAY

Callum *appears in the doorway of the ballroom. He is startled to see* **Rachel**, *in overalls and up a ladder, painting the wall at the far end – a new backdrop to the stage.*

CALLUM

I never thought . . .

RACHEL

You'd ever see me painting a wall?!

CALLUM

Exactly. (*Moving over to her.*) I could have sent somebody to do that for you . . .

RACHEL

Would that be somebody from the army or the hotel? Or do you run both now . . .? (*She comes down the ladder.*) I can paint a wall myself for Christ's sake! (*She kisses him.*)

CALLUM

So I see. (*Grins.*) It's still a surprise though –

RACHEL

I can do all sorts of things you don't know about as it happens . . . Well I hope I can anyway. We'll soon find out – when it's time for the gala. (*She looks straight at him.*) And maybe we'll see what you can do too . . .?

Callum *looks surprised. At that very moment a phone starts ringing at the bar which is at the other end of the room. They both stare across at the phone.*

RACHEL

It's going to be for you.

CALLUM

It's not, it can't be . . . (*But he moves towards it.*)

RACHEL

It always is.

Callum *picks up the phone. We hear reception say 'A call for Captain Ferguson'.*

INT. WAR CRIMES UNIT/INTERCUT WITH BASEMENT BALLROOOM. DAY

We see **Kathy** *at her desk surrounded by files. She is holding one near to the phone.*

KATHY

Captain Ferguson? I've found somebody I want in the files you gave me.

CALLUM

Good . . . I'm glad they were of use.

KATHY

Yes, they were. (*Rather formally.*) And thank you.

Her tone then urgent.

She's called Birgit Mentz, she worked with Kleinow, they interrogated many of our agents together and tortured them . . . before they were executed. She is therefore a crucial witness . . . and you're holding her at a place in Colchester.

CALLUM

That's not us – that'll be MI19.

KATHY

(*sharply*)

So there's nothing you can do then?

CALLUM

Did I say that? . . . I think I've shown I like to help when I can. So how about this – I get her brought to London so you can see her?

A close-up of **Kathy**, *surprised, pleased.*

KATHY

Will they let you do that?

CALLUM

If she is proving not much use to anybody, I expect they will . . .

INT. POLICE STATION BASEMENT PASSAGE/CELLS. LATE AFTERNOON

Kathy *is moving along the cell passage in the basement of the London police station. She is being escorted by a uniformed policeman who indicates the right cell. She stares through the grille for a moment at a young woman sitting in a plain prison tunic. We see* **Kathy** *willing herself to banish all emotion. She steels herself and nods for the door to be unlocked. She enters the cell. The young woman hardly looks up.*

KATHY

Fräulein Mentz . . . I'm Kathy Griffiths.

Mentz *avoids her gaze.*

I realise you only have been here in London a few hours . . . but they are treating you alright are they?

Mentz *doesn't look at her.*

I would try to say it in German, but I know you speak good English. So you understand me . . . ?

Mentz *gives a very small nod.* **Kathy** *sits opposite her.*

I have come to see you because I have a proposition to put to you . . .

INT. GOVERNMENT RESEARCH FACILITY. THE HANGAR. DAY

We cut to a low shot, at **Lotte**'s *height, tracking into the huge hangar at the government research facility.* **Lotte** *is moving towards the desks. Everybody is working, concentrating hard. She is moving fast across the space. A voice calls out.*

RITA

Lotte . . . ! Not sure you should be here, this is a restricted area now?! (*She comes up to her.*) But I think we'll make an exception for you . . . Come on I'll show you round. It's changed a lot hasn't it?!

They start to go up the metal stairs.

Of course you know your father is a genius . . .

Dieter *is standing on the landing.*

DIETER

Who is a genius?

RITA

You are a genius . . . (*To* **Lotte**, *her tone exuberant.*) He knows it of course, but he likes to hear it said once a day.

DIETER
(*grins*)

At least . . . (*To* **Lotte** *in German.*) Come on let me show you what we're doing.

RITA

We're getting nearer every day. Lotte!

INT. POLICE STATION. CELL/PASSAGE. LATE AFTERNOON

Kathy *is coming out of the prison cell.* **Mentz** *is sitting, her face turned away. The cell door is shut and locked.* **Kathy** *turns and is startled to see* **Callum**.

CALLUM

How did that go?

KATHY

Not well at all.

The policeman with the keys moves off down the passage, leaving them alone.

She wouldn't talk to me or even look at me really. Thank you for getting her here though.

CALLUM

You don't need to keep thanking me. (*He moves.*) Let me take a look at her . . .

He stares through the grille at the motionless young woman. Then he turns to **Kathy**.

You won't get anywhere with her locked up in this place, she's never going to agree to give evidence like this. You've got to get to know her . . . take her out for the evening.

KATHY

Take her out?!

CALLUM

Yes, for a drink, a night on the town.

KATHY

A night on the town! That's a ridiculous idea! It'd be a total disaster –

CALLUM

Not necessarily. You've got to take a chance. (*His tone sharply serious.*) Is this what I do or not?

KATHY

What if I lost her? If she ran away?

CALLUM

Then we'll catch her again. Anyway you won't lose her. I'll see to that. Bring her to the hotel . . . (*He moves off.*) And get her some new clothes.

INT. STOREROOM. EVENING

We cut to a track along a line of elegant evening footwear, of both sexes. Some single shoes, some pairs. We cut to **Victor** *staring down at them. The door opens, the light stabbing in –* **Callum** *is standing in the doorway with a glass of beer.*

CALLUM

I brought you a drink.

VICTOR

Thanks . . . Feeling guilty are you?

CALLUM

About what?

VICTOR

Keeping me guarded like this . . . (*Takes a gulp of beer.*) Punishing me for finding the file about Dieter.

CALLUM

I'm not punishing you, Victor, not in the slightest. I'm trying to keep you out of trouble.

VICTOR

And this is the best you can do is it?

CALLUM

For the moment, yes . . . (*Indicates shoes.*) And it looks like it's going rather well –

VICTOR

I'm working for you really . . . since you're running the hotel now!

CALLUM

(*smiles, moving off*)

By the way I've given the files you pulled out of the rubbish back to Miss Griffiths, and they're proving useful. So what you did paid off after all . . .

We stay on **Victor**, *very intrigued by the news.*

EXT. CONNINGTON MAIN ENTRANCE. NIGHT

Kathy *is approaching the hotel main entrance in evening dress and coat. It is bitterly cold; the steps of the entrance are covered in ice. The hotel porters are trying to clear them in a flurry of activity, as guests creep down them holding tightly on to the handrail.*

INT. CONNINGTON. THE MAIN LOBBY. NIGHT

We cut to **Kathy** *crossing the lobby.* **Callum** *is standing waiting for her dressed in a dinner jacket.* **Julia** *is standing next to him; she is wearing a skimpy cocktail dress.*

CALLUM

Good evening, Kathy . . . looking forward to this?

KATHY

Not exactly. It feels very strange, taking her out.

CALLUM

I thought it might – so Julia here is kindly going to lend a hand.

JULIA

Hello, good evening. It's bloody freezing isn't it?! I shouldn't be wearing this . . . (*She laughs.*) As always!

CALLUM

I thought it'd be easier with the two of you, not just you alone.

KATHY
(*startled*)
So you're not going to be here? Even at the beginning?!

CALLUM

No, I've got an engagement. Don't worry, Julia is thoroughly briefed . . . (*Moving off.*) and you'll get much further without me. (*He disappears among the guests.*)

KATHY

Thank you for being here. God knows what's going to happen?!

JULIA

Yes, we'll just plunge in . . . not sure there's a right way of doing this! (*She smiles.*) Callum seems to think I've got a talent for entertaining Nazis . . .

We see **Mentz** *approaching across the lobby. She is wearing a simple blue dress and a new coat, and is being escorted by a* **Minder**, *a large woman in* *her forties.* **Kathy** *stares at the approaching young woman, trying very hard to stop her hatred showing.*

JULIA

Well here goes!

As **Mentz** *reaches them,* **Julia** *greets her with a warm smile.*

Welcome to the Connington Hotel, Fräulein Mentz – where nowadays everybody has a good time . . . !

INT. HAROLD'S CLUB. NIGHT

Harold *and* **Callum** *are sitting opposite each other in the dimly lit dining room of* **Harold***'s club. It is sparsely attended and so cold some of the older members are wearing their overcoats as they eat.* **Harold** *and* **Callum** *are tucking in to steaming plates of oysters.*

HAROLD

They've got the heating on full blast – and it's making no difference at all! (*Looking across at* **Callum**.) I'm so glad you agreed to have this meal . . .

CALLUM

Of course I was going to agree . . . why wouldn't I have?

HAROLD

I must apologise for my extraordinary outburst . . . you managed to take me completely by surprise.

CALLUM

I'm sorry, it's just my favourite way of working, always seems to get me results. So it was really useful was it, the document?

HAROLD

It is dynamite, everything is there – the people that turned down the chance, or at least the very real possibility, of getting rid of Hitler in 1938. If that military coup had actually happened –

CALLUM

There might have been no war!

HAROLD
Exactly. They are all named, those that were present at the crucial meeting . . . and the evidence they were given.

It absolutely confirms that these German generals who were going to launch the coup – the only thing they wanted was for us to announce we'd definitely go to war with Germany if Hitler invaded Czechoslovakia, that's all they required to trigger the coup. Because they felt the German people had no appetite for war at that moment – and therefore they would be able to justify their action.

CALLUM
Are you going to make this all public?

HAROLD
Yes . . . but how I do it needs very careful thought – so as not to implicate you. The best chance I may have, I think, is at a Foreign Office dinner they are giving in my honour, which is happening sometime soon . . . if I reveal it suddenly, in a seemingly spontaneous way in my speech, then the information could have come from any number of people couldn't it?

CALLUM
Yes!

HAROLD
And I have a journalist friend I trust – who I will make sure is there that night to hear it . . .

CALLUM
It's exciting . . . I love the idea of shaming those responsible, putting a bomb under them, not letting the guilty men get away with it! They won't know what's hit them . . .

HAROLD
They won't.

CALLUM
You could cause a sensation, Harold!

HAROLD
A sensation would be good, even a small one. I am pretty sure I have never caused one before . . . (*He smiles.*) On that note let's order more oysters!

INT. CONSERVATORY BAR. NIGHT

Julia, **Kathy** *and* **Mentz** *are sitting drinking in the conservatory bar. There is a bottle of wine on the table and* **Julia** *leans over and fills up* **Mentz**'s *glass.*

JULIA
Do you like the movies, Fräulein Mentz?

MENTZ
A little . . . (*Her voice is barely audible.*) I haven't been to one for a long time of course.

KATHY
We must try to do something about that . . .

JULIA
I'm in the movies . . . ! Well after a fashion, I've just made my first one. I had a dressing room all to myself. It had very thin walls – I could hear everything the actress did next door, including having sex very loudly during nearly every lunch break!

Kathy *immediately looks at* **Mentz**. *She is watching* **Julia** *impassively.*

It made me quite jealous! Isn't that awful? But I admit it . . . ! During the war I had so many lovers. (*She laughs.*) It's much harder now of course . . .

Mentz *is listening to her.*

We cut to the edge of the bar. We see **Victor** *being escorted along the passage by a minder. He stops for a second to peer into the bar. He sees* **Kathy**, **Julia** *and* **Mentz** *sharing a bottle of wine. He tries to catch* **Kathy**'s *attention but she is concentrating intently on* **Mentz** *and doesn't notice him.*

We stay on **Victor** *for a moment, before the minder moves him on.*

INT. HAROLD'S CLUB. DINING ROOM. NIGHT

We cut back to **Callum** *and* **Harold** *just finishing two even bigger plates of oysters.* **Harold** *tucking in vigorously.*

> HAROLD
>
> Marvellous aren't they? Thank God seafood isn't rationed!

> CALLUM
>
> And you've got an excuse to gorge yourself tonight . . . the plan.

> HAROLD
>
> Yes . . . (*Looking at* **Callum** *anxiously.*) But you know I would never do anything that would endanger you in any way . . .

> CALLUM
>
> Of course, I know that.

> HAROLD
>
> I hope it's obvious . . . I have grown very fond of you and your brother. You both have such energy, imagination – (*Smiles.*) and anger too of course . . .

> CALLUM
> (*grins*)
>
> Yes . . . rage more like!

> HAROLD
>
> Hopefully not rage . . . that can get one into serious trouble.
>
> You know the strange thing about me, Callum, and I would never say this to anyone else because it can be misinterpreted, but I have a great capacity for love . . . for parental love in particular. If one is allowed to say that about one's self.

> CALLUM
>
> Of course one is.

> HAROLD
>
> I have no children as you know, but there is Lucy thank goodness, my brother's child. He and his wife were killed in

the war . . . we came off very badly as a family . . . My wife too of course . . . Three deaths . . .

He pauses.

So I have this talent for loving people . . . and the need to use it. (*He looks at* **Callum**.) I have never told anybody that . . .

CALLUM
I'm glad you've told me.

INT. CONSERVATORY BAR. NIGHT

Two more bottles are on **Julia**, **Kathy** *and* **Mentz**'s *table.* **Julia** *is emptying the last drops of wine into* **Mentz**'s *glass.*

JULIA
Might as well finish this . . . (*As she pours the wine.*) Men betray us, don't they?

MENTZ
Do they?

Julia *looks at* **Kathy**.

KATHY
Always.

JULIA
They do . . . and they get away with it nearly every time. Because they think we're not going to do anything about it . . . something will always stop us. But it doesn't need to –

MENTZ
I have to go now . . . (*She suddenly stands up.*) Thank you.

She moves towards her **Minder** *who is sitting near the bar.*

JULIA
It was a bit clumsy wasn't it?! I was a bit loud . . . I didn't get her to say much at all really!

KATHY
No, you did brilliantly, thank you.

JULIA
Well, it's good preparation for me at least – I'm going on a tour up north tomorrow, in a funny old play called *Daggers Drawn* . . . I play a murderess.

Kathy *watches* **Mentz** *leave.*

INT./EXT. HALL OF HAROLD'S CLUB. NIGHT

Harold *and* **Callum** *moving towards the front door of the club. They can see thick fog through the open door and club members in their coats and hats, waiting for taxis.*

HAROLD
My God fog now . . . ! Ice and fog, what more can they throw at us tonight?! We'll never get a cab, Callum . . .

CALLUM
Oh yes we will . . . you forget how competitive I am . . .

He pushes through the crowd towards the street.

Come on, let's get ahead of this lot . . .

EXT. LONDON STREET. NIGHT

Callum *and* **Harold** *are moving along the street in a thick fog, yellow headlights passing them and disappearing.* **Callum** *stands out in the road trying to flag down a cab, but they all drive past.*

Suddenly he turns. He sees **Harold** *crumple down in a heap on the pavement. He runs towards him.*

CALLUM
Harold . . .? Harold!

He kneels beside him.

What's happened Harold . . .?!

He pulls him up in his arms.

Harold?!

Harold *seems to be breathing with difficulty.*

HAROLD
It's just . . . just . . . Get me home . . . please . . .

Callum *rushes into the middle of the road and stands in the path of oncoming vehicles. A cab is coming straight towards him. He refuses to move; the taxi is forced to break sharply. We hear a voice say, 'Get the hell out of the way, I'm booked, mate.'*

CALLUM
No you're fucking not, you're free. This is an emergency!

INT. THE CAB. NIGHT

We cut inside the cab as it rattles along. **Callum** *and* **Harold** *on the back seat.* **Harold** *gulping for air, looking ashen.*

CALLUM
(*to driver*)
We need to get to the nearest hospital . . . come on. As quick as you can!

HAROLD
No, no, it's just the oysters . . . Get me home, Callum . . . It's just the bloody oysters!!

INT. HAROLD'S BEDROOM. NIGHT

Harold *is lying in bed in the darkened bedroom in his house.* **Callum** *is sitting on the edge of the bed, looking down at him.* **Mrs Gorton** *is standing in the doorway.* **Harold** *is already breathing much more easily.*

CALLUM
I thought you were dying, Harold . . . that you were having a heart attack . . . or else the Intelligence Service had poisoned you because of your plan!

HAROLD
You would think that. It's because you're one of them! It was the oysters . . . I over-indulged massively – it's all my fault.

He touches **Callum**'s *sleeve.*

Thank you for being so good to me.

CALLUM

Don't be stupid . . .

HAROLD

And I promise I'm not going to conk out yet, not a bit of it! I have too much to do – both of us have.

INT. THE TUNNEL. DAY

There are now arc lights fixed in a stretch of the tunnel. Workmen are constructing a viewing platform. **Dieter**, **Rita** *and* **Callum** *are watching the preparations.*

DIETER

So we're getting closer to the big day as you can see. First we do a test for ourselves of course . . .

CALLUM

Well it's been getting close for quite a while now . . . what are we talking about? When can we see something?

RITA

A few weeks . . . a couple of months.

CALLUM

A couple of months?!

DIETER

You're getting impatient now are you, Callum?

CALLUM

A little, yes. I need results just like anybody else. And we have to beat the Americans and the Russians.

DIETER

Of course . . . and we will . . . And with an engine that is so small, so light, the plane will be able to go faster than the speed of sound.

CALLUM

Definitely?

DIETER

Definitely.

He moves close, his tone excited.

Now I have something else, very special, to tell you, Callum.

EXT. THE SECRET VILLAGE. OUTSIDE TUNNEL. DAY

Callum *and* **Dieter** *are standing facing each other just outside the tunnel entrance.* **Rita** *is smoking on a bench some distance away.*

DIETER

Before I tell you, I need to know something . . . do you believe me? About my work at Nordhausen?

CALLUM

(*fractional pause*)

I'm doing my best to believe you.

DIETER

As I said, of course in one way it doesn't make such a difference, because I was undoubtedly there . . . and that can't be changed. But it is important to me you believe me, that I didn't cause people to be executed. I hope you check the facts in any way you can.

CALLUM

We are. In Germany. I haven't received any information back yet.

DIETER

Then hurry them up! The reason it's so important you believe me is – I like to think we're almost friends . . . if there is such a thing as 'almost friends'?

CALLUM

I'm not sure there is . . . , but it doesn't matter, because we are, friends . . . (*He sees* **Rita** *watching them.*)

DIETER

Then I can tell you . . . (*He lowers his voice.*) Nobody must know this . . . it's a total secret . . . but I'm getting married.

CALLUM

Married?!

We move in on **Callum**.

DIETER

Yes, married! We've not told anybody so far . . . not even Lotte knows yet!

CALLUM
(*watching* **Rita**)
I knew you liked each other, but marriage?! That is a surprise, Dieter . . .

Dieter *follows his glance towards* **Rita**.

DIETER

No, no, no! Not to her . . . I'm not marrying her, Callum! (*He smiles.*) Much as I like her!

CALLUM
(*truly startled*)
It's not her?! Then who the hell are you marrying, Dieter?!

INT. BASEMENT BALLROOM. AFTERNOON

We cut to a close-up of **Anna** *in her waitress uniform arranging flowers in the basement ballroom, smiling as she does so. We see her through a half-opened door,* **Callum** *and* **Dieter** *are just outside the ballroom.* **Callum** *watches* **Anna**, *her young face; she seems to exude a new poise.*

DIETER

Doesn't she look enchanting . . .?!

CALLUM

She does.

DIETER

My friend . . . another thing I haven't told anybody. (*He*

smiles.) Except her of course, I love her so much. It's the most amazing feeling. It's still a secret of course, I will tell Lotte nearer the time . . .

Callum *and* **Dieter** *enter the ballroom. We see it is transformed: it is full of flowers, different furnishings and colours.* **Rachel** *is in the middle of the room supervising the hanging of the chandelier.* **Eva** *is watching from the edge of the stage.*

RACHEL

Come to help, you two? Not before time – we open in two hours!

The chandelier lights up, glowing beautifully.

And though I say it myself, I think things are looking pretty good!

CALLUM

They are. (*He stares at her under the chandelier.*)

EVA

Honey, I didn't think this room was about chandeliers! Are you going to start talking with an English accent next?!

RACHEL

Is Victor coming?

CALLUM

No, no, he's not here. I let him have the day off.

RACHEL

That's a pity . . . And are *you* ready, Callum, for what you're going to do? (*He just smiles.*)

EVA

The big question is – will anybody show up?

HAROLD

Well I'm here, and very early too!

He is standing in the doorway in full evening dress and wearing a flower in his buttonhole.

I'm feeling fully restored as you can see . . .

EXT. MRS TOOLEY'S GARDEN. SUNSET

Victor *is in* **Mrs Tooley**'s *garden. He is digging up the files he buried there with a vigorous burst of energy. He is partially hidden from the house by trees.*

We cut to him moving towards the house, cradling the files in his arms.

INT. VICTOR'S BEDROOM. EVENING

We then cut inside **Victor**'s *bedroom: the files all over the room, woodlice crawling out of some of them.* **Victor** *is sitting on the floor, a file on his lap, beginning to read.*

INT. BASEMENT BALLROOM. NIGHT

We are in the ballroom, the opening of the gala. The room glitters with candles. The audience is a mixture of the hotel clientele, more glamorous society figures, and intellectuals, members of the avant-garde. The room is packed. **Eva** *and the musicians are on stage. We see* **Rachel** *moving up to a microphone in a spotlight. She faces the audience. She is obviously extremely nervous but determined to do well.*

RACHEL
So I want to welcome you all here . . .

There is a drum roll from the stage.

Thank you! I don't think I've made a speech after a drum roll before, in fact I've hardly ever made a speech at all . . . But I just wanted to say a word about the purpose of this evening – and I sincerely hope this won't be the last one. It is a mixture of music and poetry, some old, a lot of it new.

It is, if you like, like jazz and classical all muddled up together. There are no boundaries here, no categories. We're calling it 'Feast' – which I hope is what it will prove to be! It is an experiment . . . and a celebration – (*She smiles.*) for the beginning of spring! But we're going to start with the familiar, to make you feel at home — the wonderful Eva and her musicians . . .

EVA

But with something new! Hold on tight everybody!

The band burst into a jazz number with **Richie** *drumming vigorously. We see* **Rachel** *standing close to the stage.* **Alex** *and* **Callum** *are watching her confidence, her natural authority.* **Anna**, *in a new dress, is sitting next to* **Dieter** *and* **Lotte**. **Anna** *exchanges a secret look with* **Dieter**.

INT. MELBURY SUITE/INTERCUT WITH BASEMENT BALLROOM. NIGHT

Harold *is standing in front of* **Frau Bellinghausen** *in her suite. We can hear the music as a distant throb.*

HAROLD

I'm going to be very bold, Frau Bellinghausen.

FRAU BELLINGHAUSEN

Bold? Do you think that's a good idea?

HAROLD

Probably not, and this may be the last conversation we ever have . . . but I think you should leave this room tonight, and sample a little of what's happening —

FRAU BELLINGHAUSEN

Go downstairs? To see this event?! I couldn't possibly do that. I find it so difficult to be with other people at the moment, in a crowd of any sort . . . And they are just playing the same sort of music —

HAROLD

But you don't need to go downstairs . . . (*Their eyes meet.*)

We cut back to the basement ballroom, the number reaching its percussive climax.

INT. MAIN STAIRCASE/LANDING. NIGHT

We cut to **Frau Bellinghausen** *coming down the main staircase with* **Harold**. *We can hear the music now much more clearly.*

> FRAU BELLINGHAUSEN
> I thought you said I didn't need to come downstairs . . .

> HAROLD
> You're almost there.

On the landing below them, **Harold** *has prepared an area for her. A chair and a table with a candle on it, food and drink and flowers. A waiter is standing in attendance.*

> FRAU BELLINGHAUSEN
> Goodness! Is this for me?

> HAROLD
> Yes, I had it prepared this evening.

He moves the chair for her.

> If you sit here . . . you can hear everything that's going on, the sound comes straight up the stairwell.

> FRAU BELLINGHAUSEN
> It's like being in a box in the theatre! That is very kind, extremely touching of you . . . and the food too. I don't think I've ever perched on the stairs before and had a meal.

The jazz ringing out.

> But why should I want to listen to this?

> HAROLD
> Just wait for a moment and see.

INT./EXT. MRS TOOLEY'S HOUSE/STREET/BOMBED HOUSES. NIGHT

We see **Victor** *push open the front door of* **Mrs Tooley**'s *house and stare out into the night street, checking to see if anybody is watching him.*

We then see him moving along the street past the ruined bombed houses.

INT. BASEMENT BALLROOM. NIGHT

We cut to a young opera singer standing next to a black trumpet player.

RACHEL

And now an aria by Handel, accompanied by Jack here, who usually plays jazz trumpet as you've seen . . . (*She smiles.*) And he has never done this before . . . two sides of music coming together.

The Handel aria begins with the jazz trumpet accompaniment. **Eva** *is on the piano; the band has been augmented by some string players.*

INT. STAIRCASE LANDING/BASEMENT BALLROOM. NIGHT

Frau Bellinghausen *sitting at her table on the landing,* **Harold** *watching her.*

FRAU BELLINGHAUSEN

This is surprise . . . that's Handel! (*As the music soars towards her.*) A German in London . . . and I was an Englishwoman in Germany.

HAROLD

Yes, that trumpet playing is marvellous isn't it?!

FRAU BELLINGHAUSEN

Yes . . . (*Her tone serious; we move in on her.*) Music is such a strong force, isn't it . . . provokes such thoughts inside one . . .

We cut down to the basement ballroom, and the opera singer and the jazz trumpet player in unison. The sound is very powerful.

We cut back to **Frau Bellinghausen** *and* **Harold**, *listening to the music.*

FRAU BELLINGHAUSEN

Go, go, go down there please . . . Don't miss it all because of me . . . that would be ridiculous.

HAROLD
I don't need to leave yet.

FRAU BELLINGHAUSEN
Please, I have my own waiter here and everything . . . What luxury, it's unforgivable really! Please don't miss it . . .

Harold *nods and starts to go down the stairs as the aria continues. We stay on* **Frau Bellinghausen**.

EXT./INT. WAR CRIMES UNIT STREET AND BUILDING/HALL. NIGHT

Victor *is moving along the street towards the War Crimes Unit building, past parked cars. He glances behind him to see if anybody is following him. He then rushes across the road and into the entrance hall of the War Crimes Unit. At that very moment* **Kathy** *is coming down the stairs with* **Mentz** *and her* **Minder**. *They are in their hats and coats and are clearly going out for the evening.*

KATHY
Victor! What are you doing here?!

VICTOR
That's not much of a greeting! I need to talk to you urgently –

Kathy *indicates to the* **Minder** *to take* **Mentz** *out into the road.* **Mentz**'s *manner is still very chilly and self-contained.* **Kathy** *and* **Victor** *are in the hall entrance; the door is open into the street and they can see* **Mentz**.

KATHY
Victor, I only have a second.

VICTOR
Yes, yes, I wanted to tell you this, because it's very important. I've got some more files! I buried some in the garden –

KATHY
You buried some in the garden? (*She tries to hide her disbelief.*)

VICTOR
Yes, and I've just dug them up, and I haven't had a real chance to read them yet . . . but I think there may be some really good new information there. I thought we could go through them together! We're a team now aren't we?! And it works best together –

KATHY
Victor . . . I can't at the moment –

VICTOR
You're too busy for that? You can't be!

KATHY
I have made an important contact, Callum helped me meet her . . . (*She indicates* **Mentz**.) She worked with Kleinow . . . I'm seeing if there's any way I can get her to give evidence at his trial . . . I'm spending some time with her –

VICTOR
Ah I see . . . taking her out for the evening are you for a few drinks? Giving Nazis a whale of a time?! Everybody's doing it aren't they?! You and Callum –

KATHY
Yes, I'm using his methods, because they might just work!

A shot of **Mentz** *and the* **Minder** *in the street.*

Listen, Victor, I really appreciate you wanting to help, but I've got everything I need at the moment, more than enough for me to do, and I have to concentrate on this. Now I must go –

VICTOR
You don't want the files? Is that what you're saying?

He takes her by the sleeve.

You're not interested?!

KATHY
I'm not saying that of course . . . but, Victor, I have to go!

She sees **Mentz** *staring at her, intrigued by the altercation.*

I don't want trouble, please, it's the last thing I need tonight.

She begins to move off. **Victor** *catches her by the arm.*

> VICTOR
> So I've become trouble now? That's so easy to say about me isn't it?!

> KATHY
> No, no, I didn't mean . . . I will phone you.

She pulls free of him.

Victor, I have to go.

She moves off. We stay on **Victor***'s face.*

INT. BASEMENT BALLROOM. NIGHT

We cut to the basement ballroom. **Rachel** *is in the spotlight, in front of the stage, with a book in her hand. She swallows hard to overcome her nerves.*

> RACHEL
> Now I'm doing this because I know it's terrifying reading in public . . . (*She smiles.*) I am in fact terrified, because I don't make a habit of doing this . . . performing. But I know if I do it, however badly, others of you will come up and read your poetry to us. I'm not a poet of course myself, but I wanted to read a poem by a fellow American, Emily Dickinson, who is not nearly as well known here in London as she should be. (*Smiles warmly.*) In my opinion . . .

She starts to seem to read, but she knows the poem and she aims it out into the audience, looking directly at **Callum.** **Alex** *is next to him. She meets* **Callum***'s look.*

> RACHEL
> I taste a liquor never brewed
> From tankards scooped in pearl
> Not all the vats upon the Rhine
> Yield such an alcohol!

We move in on **Callum** *and* **Alex** *watching her.*

> Inebriate of air am I
> And debauchee of dew
> Reeling, through endless summer days
> From inns of molten blue.

EXT. CONNINGTON. NIGHT

Victor *is moving fast, purposefully across the bombsite towards the Connington.*

INT. BASEMENT BALLROOM. NIGHT

A **Portly Young Poet** *is sitting on the stage, with his legs dangling down, proclaiming his poem:*

> Dead shore that lies beyond the cottage walls
> Crunching under my feet in moonlight, scaly cold.

INT. CONNINGTON LOBBY/PASSAGES/BACK STAIRS. NIGHT

We see **Victor** *dodging fast across the Connington lobby, making sure he is not spotted by the* **Desk Clerk***. He then hurtles along the passage and up the back staircase.*

INT. ATTIC ROOM. NIGHT

We see **Victor** *slamming through the door into the attic office. The room is deserted except for the* **Chubby Minder***, who looks very startled to see him.*

VICTOR
Just thought I'd drop by to say hello!

CHUBBY MINDER
Mr Ferguson! Your brother is not here –

VICTOR
I can see that . . . I thought I'd show you I can get back into this hotel without anybody at all noticing! (*He looks straight at*

him.) But I also thought it was time I told the world about what's going on – how we're giving Nazis a night out on the town . . . and lovely new lives if we think they're worth it! I'm pretty sure people would be very interested to hear all about that don't you?!

He bangs out of the room. We stay on the **Chubby Minder**.

INT. STAIRCASE HOTEL. NIGHT

We see **Victor** *running down the back stairs of the hotel, glancing over his shoulder as he goes to see if anybody is following. We can hear the opera singer beginning another Handel aria, the sound very faintly floating up the stairwell.*

INT. SALTER'S BASEMENT ROOM. NIGHT

With a sharp cut we see the spools of a tape recorder turning in a dimly lit room. We cut wide to see we are in **Salter**'s *basement office, the one* **Callum** *evicted him from.* **Salter** *is sitting with headphones on, listening to a recording of what* **Victor** *has just said in the attic office.*

VICTOR
(*voice-over*)
But I also thought it was time I told the world about what's going on – how we're giving Nazis a night on the town . . . and lovely new lives if we think they're worth it!

We move in on **Salter**'s *face as he listens to* **Victor** *saying this.*

INT. BASEMENT BALLROOM. NIGHT

We cut back to the Handel aria ringing out in the basement ballroom. We see **Callum** *staring over towards* **Rachel**.

We see **Dieter** *sitting with* **Anna**.

We move in on **Dieter**'s *face as the music rings out.*

CREDITS

Part Six

INT. PASSAGE/BASEMENT BALLROOM. NIGHT

We cut to the camera moving along the passage that leads to the basement ballroom. We can see in the distance the entrance to the ballroom is now packed with guests. There is standing room only as people crowd in to watch **Rachel***'s evening.*

We cut to **Rachel** *approaching the microphone glimpsed through the standing people.*

INT. BASEMENT BALLROOM. NIGHT

Rachel *reaches the microphone. We have now cut inside the ballroom.*

RACHEL
And now we have a chance to hear some more music . . . a world premiere in fact. Mr Callum Ferguson is going to play his latest composition.

Callum *stands up reluctantly and walks up to the piano. He whispers to* **Rachel***.*

CALLUM
I've never been so terrified . . .

His hand is shaking. **Rachel** *helps him place the music.*

Fighting in Normandy was nothing compared to this . . . !

He starts to play a fuller version of the piece he played to her in his bedroom; it is intensely romantic. The string section and the band are accompanying him. **Alex**, **Dieter** *watching with rapt attention. We move in on* **Harold** *as he watches* **Callum** *play. And then we cut to* **Rachel** *as she sees him conquer his nerves.*

As the piece unfolds the credits play.

INT. CONNINGTON PASSAGE/STAIRCASE. NIGHT

We cut to **Victor** *moving along the second-floor passage and then dodging into a doorway. The* **Chubby Minder** *is at the other end of the passage, looking for him; he now turns the wrong way. As soon as he is out of sight,* **Victor** *moves off fast, taking the main staircase. He starts rushing down it* *and comes across* **Frau Bellinghausen** *sitting at her table on the landing. He just avoids crashing into her.*

VICTOR

I'm so sorry . . .

FRAU BELLINGHAUSEN

No need to apologise. I am rather in the way.

Callum's *music is flowing up the stairs.* **Victor**'s *face is flushed, agitated.*

VICTOR

Ah I might have guessed it'd happen – that's my brother playing . . . !

FRAU BELLINGHAUSEN

You can tell from up here?

VICTOR

Oh yes, I know that tune. Callum always tries out his new pieces on me . . . since we were little.

FRAU BELLINGHAUSEN

Ah, so you're the policeman's brother . . .?! (*Seeing his agitation, her tone genuine.*) I'm very interested to meet you.

VICTOR

Yes I'm Victor . . . and I guess you're the perfume lady?

FRAU BELLINGHAUSEN

I am yes. Very definitely the perfume lady.

VICTOR

(*glancing back up the stairs*)

I won't stop though!

FRAU BELLINGHAUSEN

Can't you? Not even for a moment?

VICTOR

No, there are people looking for me . . . and I have much to do. What's more I've just realised something . . .

FRAU BELLINGHAUSEN
What have you realised?

VICTOR
That everybody is moving on . . . and that's how it's going to be now. And I'm not sure where I fit in at all really . . .

FRAU BELLINGHAUSEN
(*struck by his vulnerability.*)
Well if it is any comfort . . . that makes two of us!

He looks at her.

Absolutely. Me sitting here on the landing, too nervous to go downstairs –

VICTOR
And me charging about . . . yes.

FRAU BELLINGHAUSEN
Won't you pause here just a moment longer? (*Indicating food.*) We could share some of this – there's plenty left . . .

VICTOR
I can't, no, I'm sorry. (*He moves off fast down the stairs.*)

INT. BASEMENT BALLROOM. NIGHT

We cut to **Callum** *at the piano reaching the emotional climax of his piece.* **Harold** *watching fascinated, impressed. A close-up of* **Dieter** *surprised by* **Callum**'s *performance.* **Rachel**'s *eyes are shining.* **Callum** *finishes with a flourish and leaps up almost too quickly to take his bow, as the applause rings out.* **Eva** *announces loudly.*

EVA
I take it all back – this man has a use after all! And the other thing I take back – I thought this evening was going to be a disaster! And so far . . . it hasn't been has it?! It's getting dangerously close to being a success!

INT. GROUND-FLOOR PASSAGE/STAIRS/BALLROOM/DINING
ROOM. NIGHT

We cut to **Victor** *moving fast along the ground-floor passage, glancing over his shoulder, sweat on his face. We can hear some more music, very loud now, from the basement ballroom, a fast rhythmic piece. He follows the music.*

We cut to him moving along the basement passage towards the lights and music of the ballroom. There are people now crowded in the doorway. Like **Lotte** *in Part One,* **Victor** *is forced to move around to get even a glimpse of what is happening.*

When he manages to get a place near the front of the doorway he is greeted by the sight of **Eva** *and* **Callum** *playing a duet on the piano with the rest of the band joining in. He sees* **Rachel** *laughing and clapping as the music gets faster and faster. He sees* **Dieter** *and* **Anna** *and* **Lotte** *getting to their feet and clapping in rhythm, immediately followed by other members of the audience. He sees* **Harold** *watching delightedly and* **Alex** *getting to his feet now, riveted by the whole performance.*

We move in **Victor's** *face.* **Rachel** *turns for a moment to glance at the audience and sees* **Victor** *standing there looking agitated and vulnerable. A member of the audience masks her view for a second, and when she has moved she sees* **Victor** *has vanished. We see the concern on her face; she hesitates, then decides to go after him.*

We cut to **Victor** *moving fast up the stairs, sweat glistening on his face. He throws off his jacket without looking back. He is now heading straight towards the formal dining room, knocking into trolleys and chairs as he goes. He starts to unbutton his shirt, lets it drop behind him. When he gets to the door of the dining room he is totally bare-chested.*

Suddenly his movements become very controlled. He surveys the dining room. People begin to notice, heads turn in astonishment. **Victor** *moves purposefully across the dining room towards a vacant table. Waiters converge on him but he sidesteps them, gets to the table and sits down. He picks up the menu and puts a napkin on his lap.*

We cut to **Rachel** *heading for the dining room down the main passage.*

We cut back to the dining room. **Victor** *is now surrounded by waiters and the* **Maître d'**, *trying to screen him from the fellow diners and move him* *from the table. But* **Victor** *suddenly stands up and moves fast across the dining room. And then he sits on the floor, right against the wall. The* **Maître d'** *and waiters surround him again, but* **Rachel** *waves them away indicating she will handle it. She moves towards* **Victor** *as he sits in the corner. She addresses him softly, as if they are alone.*

RACHEL

Victor, what's the matter?

VICTOR

You shouldn't be here . . . You're missing your evening.

RACHEL

Don't worry, they can manage without me. (*She crouches down next to him.*)

VICTOR

I don't think I can manage though, not tonight, not any more . . .

RACHEL

That's alright, Victor . . . (*She takes his arm.*)

VICTOR

I don't want to cry all over you again . . . and I'm not going to . . .

We are now on **Victor**'s *eyes. We see his point of view of the room, from down on the floor: all the legs moving towards him or standing watching him. The legs of the* **Maître d'**, *the waiters and waitresses, some of the diners, the hotel porters. We move in on his eyes as* **Rachel** *holds him tight. We cut back to the legs and fade to black.*

INT. PSYCHIATRIC WARD. LONDON HOSPITAL. DAY

We see a fade-up, gradually coming into focus, of women's legs in dark stockings and sensible shoes walking towards us down a passage.

And then we cut to **Victor**'s *face, upside down, watching the nurses approach in the psychiatric wing of a London hospital. He suddenly moves, sits up sharply and smiles. He is in pyjamas in bed. It is a hot summer day.*

Callum *is sitting by the bed.*

VICTOR

It's always a much better view like that!

CALLUM

So you say each time . . .

VICTOR

Really? How many times have you been this week?

CALLUM

I've been almost every day this week – almost every day for six weeks actually!

VICTOR

What dedication! . . . It's been a bit of a blur with all the pills . . . (*Suddenly.*) Aren't you neglecting the German then?!

CALLUM

No, no, his work's nearly there, and there's a plastics man I've been dealing with and the perfume lady of course. I'm going to get results with all of them, hopefully . . .

VICTOR

You always do . . . you look fantastically smart today! Do you always look like this when you visit the loony ward?

CALLUM

You're not in a loony ward, you're in a psychiatric ward, and you're going to be able to leave soon –

VICTOR

I'm locked up, Callum! But at least I've not got electrodes poking out of my head, thanks to you. And I'm grateful. And today my mind is wonderfully clear.

CALLUM

That's good . . . (*He waves over to the door*) Because there's a surprise today. I brought visitors.

VICTOR

Visitors? Marvellous!

Rachel, *in a summer dress, and* **Alex**, *in a smart summer suit, move towards him.*

RACHEL
Hello, Victor . . . you look so much better!

ALEX
Very good to see you, Victor.

VICTOR
Blimey! You all look amazing!

RACHEL
I've brought you some chocolate. Really good dark chocolate, don't ask me how I got it!

VICTOR
Thank you. (*Staring at them.*) This can't be all for me? You looking like this?

RACHEL
It's not entirely for you I admit, we're going to a rather formal cricket match – to watch Alex play.

ALEX
The Foreign Office versus the Home Office.

VICTOR
That explains it . . . I thought you were going to a wedding or something!

RACHEL
Ah . . . talking of weddings, have you heard the news?! The German is getting married!

VICTOR
He's getting married?!

Callum *is looking edgy – he was not expecting this to be mentioned.*

RACHEL
Yes, he's just announced it . . . he's marrying that young waitress at the hotel, Anna, isn't that amazing?!

We see a concerned look in **Victor**'s *eyes.*

We're going to the engagement party very soon.

EXT. THE CRICKET MATCH. AFTERNOON

We see a wide shot of a cricket match played out in front of a big house. It is surrounded by a steep hill on which there is a pavilion staring down at the view. Cakes and tea are laid out in the pavilion. There is an audience of Foreign Office and Home Office grandees watching the match. The Foreign Office is batting. **Alex** *is all padded up ready to go in. He is sitting with* **Callum** *and* **Harold.** **Rachel** *is just collecting soft drinks from a table beneath the pavilion.* **Callum** *turns to* **Alex.**

CALLUM
You are very calm for somebody about to go in!

ALEX
I'm totally calm, yes . . . altogether in fact.

Looks across to **Rachel.**

It makes such a difference she's happy . . . I had no idea what an avalanche of work was going to hit me at the FO, all these worries about if the Russians get the Bomb, and whether we should strike at them first . . .? (*He smiles.*) So I'm so pleased her evenings of music and poetry have proved such a success . . .

CALLUM
It was your idea, Alex.

ALEX
It was, but you've encouraged her. (*He looks straight at him.*) And for that I am grateful . . .

In the background a wicket has fallen. **Alex** *is still looking at him, smiling.*

Callum *cannot work out if he knows something.*

CALLUM
I think you're in, Alex!

Alex *gets up and marches towards the wicket.* **Rachel** *has just reached them with the drinks, and waves to him.*

RACHEL

So he's off!

HAROLD

Talking of bombs going off . . .

Callum *looks at him sharply.*

I have just been given a date for my dinner . . . my party at the FO . . .

CALLUM

At last. Terrific!

Alex *receives his first ball, and smashes it like a rifle shot to the boundary.*

RACHEL

What a start that was! (*She smiles.*) I knew he'd be good.

CALLUM
(*watching Alex*)

It's only just occurred to me.

Alex *plays another brilliant shot.*

I don't know why I never thought of this before . . . (*He lowers his voice to* **Harold**.) But Alex . . . he's not involved, is he?!

HAROLD

No, no, not Alex . . .

He indicates the important-looking men watching.

But there are people here who were very involved . . .

Alex *sends another ball racing to the boundary.*

Rachel *and* **Callum** *watch him putting on a masterful display.*

INT. PSYCHIATRIC WARD. LONDON HOSPITAL. AFTERNOON

Victor *is sitting at the the end of his bed in his pyjamas in the strong sunlight.*

He is muttering to himself. A **Nurse** *is nearby.*

> VICTOR
> The German is getting married.
>
> NURSE
> What is it, Victor? Don't you start working yourself up.
>
> VICTOR
> The German is getting married . . . That's not right.

EXT. CRICKET MATCH. AFTERNOON

We cut to **Alex** *smashing another ball to the boundary. We see from the scoreboard he's just scored fifty. He raises his bat to the applause, to the grandees, to* **Harold**, *and to* **Rachel** *and* **Callum** *who are now standing on the balcony of the pavilion.* **Harold** *turns to one of the grandees next to him.*

> HAROLD
> Good Lord, this is some innings . . . Who would have thought he had it in him?!

We cut to **Rachel** *and* **Callum** *withdrawing into the pavilion where the cakes are all laid out.*

> RACHEL
> It's amazing . . . I think he's going to score a hundred runs!
>
> CALLUM
> I hope he's not trying to prove something to us . . . (*He grins.*) Because I can't play cricket.
>
> RACHEL
> So there's something you can't do . . . !

She stares down at the cakes.

> Alex is going back to Washington for a few weeks on Saturday . . .
>
> CALLUM
> He is . . . ?

Watching **Alex** *delicately hit another boundary.*

He's definitely batting as if he knows about us . . . !

RACHEL
He doesn't know. I would be able to tell if he did. I thought . . . (*She looks at* **Callum**.) We might go away somewhere . . .? As a last sort of –

CALLUM
Last? Why last?

RACHEL
Because if we don't stop . . . he will find out. And I don't want that . . . not at all.

Callum *moves.*

Don't argue with me, Callum . . . Very soon you and I will have to start new lives . . . very different to this. And we can't keep putting it off.

CALLUM
(*sharp*)
We better not miss his century . . .

Alex *cracks another glorious shot. They move back onto the balcony.*

INT. HOSPITAL. PSYCHIATRIC WARD. NIGHT

Victor *is in bed. The ward is in semi-darkness. A* **Nurse** *is just giving him his medication. As he takes it he stares into her face, in a sudden unmistakably sexual way.*

NURSE
Now, Victor, it is way past bedtime. Time for you –

VICTOR
(*suddenly catching her arm*)
The German is getting married.

He pulls her close and kisses her on the lips.

NURSE

Victor!

She pulls away from him.

VICTOR

I'm so sorry . . . (*Immediately struck by remorse.*) I shouldn't have done that . . . (*We move close.*) I'm so very sorry . . .

INT. WAR CRIMES UNIT. EARLY EVENING

Kathy *is sitting working alone in the War Crimes Unit office.*

Callum *is standing in the doorway; she has not seen him.*

CALLUM

You've got a picture up, of the bastard . . .

He indicates **Kleinow** *on the wall.*

KATHY

Captain Ferguson! (*Looking at photo.*) I have, yes . . . I like to have photographs of my targets . . . I used to have a picture of you up there.

CALLUM

So I've dropped off the wall have I? (*Moving into the room.*) I've never been allowed in here before.

KATHY

You've never bothered to come before.

CALLUM

So how is your drinking companion? The torturer?

KATHY

She is still very quiet . . . Sometimes it seems I'm making progress, but I'm not really. Maybe it's because I can't stop myself thinking about what she's done! And time is running out, the trial is very soon –

CALLUM

Have you thought of taking her home for a meal?

KATHY

No! No I haven't thought of that, surprisingly! And it's not a good idea . . . Cooking is not my strong suit.

CALLUM

She won't be thinking about your cooking . . . (*He stares at* **Kleinow**.) she'll be so startled to be in somebody's home again. It's just a thought . . .

KATHY

I'm grateful for your interest. (*He looks around sharply.*) No, I mean it . . . After all you helped me catch him.

CALLUM

I did.

KATHY

How is your friend doing, the jet plane man?

CALLUM

Ah . . . (*Quiet.*) he's tremendously happy . . . starting a new life in fact.

INT. CONSERVATORY BAR/SURROUNDING ROOMS. DAY

We see flowers being arranged in the conservatory bar. We see **Anna** *standing in the doorway watching the preparations for the party. She smiles excitedly.*

INT. PSYCHIATRIC WARD. LONDON HOSPITAL. MORNING

We cut to **Victor** *in his pyjamas sitting on a chair next to his bed. He is wearing gloves.* **Callum** *is sitting on the edge of the bed.*

CALLUM

You okay? Why are you wearing those gloves?

VICTOR

Because they won't let us wear anything with our pyjamas – unless we say we're cold. Of course I'm boiling now! (*Lowers his voice.*) I know where they keep the clothes hidden though.

CALLUM
Now listen, Victor . . . (*Very firm.*) The German is having his party this evening to celebrate his engagement to Anna. And I'm going to have to go. But I want you to know –

VICTOR
It's not right, Callum . . . that he should have a lovely new life.

CALLUM
I wanted you to know that I've now had his records checked in Germany, and there is no evidence of war crimes, of him ordering people to be executed –

VICTOR
They haven't looked. You haven't looked.

CALLUM
You must stop worrying about this, Victor . . . (*Gently.*) And work hard to get better.

INT. THE CONSERVATORY BAR/SURROUNDING ROOMS. AFTERNOON

We see a string of fairy lights being laced through the plants in the party area.

INT. MELBURY SUITE. DAY

Frau Bellinghausen *is watching* **Harold** *cut a very appetising-looking cake.*

HAROLD
I 'borrowed' one of the cakes they've made for the party this evening. It's not too early for cake today is it?

FRAU BELLINGHAUSEN
Well looking at that, I think I can certainly make an exception . . . (*She takes a piece.*) Tell me, Mr Lindsay-Jones, why are you helping the policeman?

HAROLD
Because I like him . . .

She gives him a searching look.

And because he did me a very big favour.

FRAU BELLINGHAUSEN
Yes. I see. Because of the war we all have to conceal our real reasons don't we? Just in case . . .

HAROLD
That is very true . . . (*Close on him.*) True of me anyway.

FRAU BELLINGHAUSEN
(*suddenly*)
I'm ready to sign the deal, Mr Lindsay-Jones – and give them the formula. (*Picking up scent bottle.*) How this is made! Tell anybody who's interested I want to do it.

HAROLD
I will. That's splendid news. I'll tell Callum at once.

FRAU BELLINGHAUSEN
Yes . . . I wish he'd come and see me. I met his brother . . . and he's an extraordinary boy too.

HAROLD
Victor? Yes he is.

FRAU BELLINGHAUSEN
I only met him for a few seconds, but even in that time, he seemed so intelligent . . . but so unhappy.

*We see **Harold**'s eyes.*

I do hope he's alright.

INT. PSYCHIATRIC WARD/PASSAGE/STOREROOM. EARLY EVENING

*We see **Victor** waiting, like a coiled spring, as the nurses gather round a patient who is moaning and crying. **Victor** is watching the barred door to the ward that has been left ajar. As soon as the nurses are all at the other end of the room, he seizes his chance and slips out of the ward.*

He then runs really fast down the passage. We cut to him in the storeroom going through all the patients' clothes. He is pulling them down frantically off the rack. He can't find his own, but he stops at a beautiful grey suit.

EXT. HOSPITAL CAR PARK. EARLY EVENING

*We cut to **Victor** emerging out of the front door of the hospital, acting very confidently in his grey suit which is too big for him. Medical staff and hospital visitors are moving past him. He walks along the parked cars. As soon as he realises he is alone in the car park, he jumps into an open-topped car that is parked under a sign saying* DOCTORS ONLY PARKING *and roars off.*

MONTAGE: COUNTRY ROADS/CONSERVATORY BAR/KATHY'S FLAT/MRS TOOLEY'S HOUSE AND ROAD

*As **Victor** drives off fast in the open-top car we intercut with the beginning of the party. The guests are gathering in the conservatory bar. **Jack**, the jazz trumpeter, appears in the entrance to the party. He plays a jazz fanfare. Then **Dieter** and **Anna** appear in the doorway to applause from the guests. **Anna** is laughing, not expecting such a grand entrance. The music on the soundtrack develops from the fanfare as it pulses under the montage.*

*We cut to **Victor** driving fast down country roads.*

*We cut to **Kathy** lighting a single candle on the table she has laid in the front room for **Mentz**, as there is a knock on the door. She opens the door to **Mentz** and the **Minder**, who indicates she will wait in a car outside. **Mentz** enters **Kathy**'s front room.*

*We cut back to the party in full swing. We see **Dieter** and **Anna** moving among the guests, looking a glittering couple. We see **Rita** and other colleagues from the hangar there, and **Ringwood** and the **Chubby Minder** and other workers from the attic office. We see **Harold** and **Lucy**, **Eva**, and **Rachel** and **Callum**. And we see **Lotte**, in another dress from the fashion show, staring at her father. Her face is a mask as she watches **Dieter** and **Anna** together. **Rita** whispers to her.*

RITA
Don't they look so romantic?!

We cut to **Victor** *stopping near the bombed houses and leaving the car parked in the shadows. He walks the last bit of the journey, the wrecked buildings towering above him. He stares behind him to see if anybody is following, the street seems deserted.*

We see him let himself into **Mrs Tooley**'s *house and run up the stairs.*

We cut back to the party and the joyous celebration, with **Eva** *moving among the guests brandishing a bottle of pink champagne.*

We see **Victor** *sitting on the floor of his room, reading a file intently, turning the pages fast. We get closer and closer; his eyes are gleaming.*

We cut back to **Kathy** *and* **Mentz** *sitting at the small table together, eating.*

MENTZ
(*suddenly*)
You look at me all the time, those little looks . . .

KATHY
Do I? I'm sorry.

MENTZ
What if I did that to you?

KATHY
You're quite right. Forgive me.

MENTZ
The food is good. Let us just eat the food.

A wide shot of them sitting together eating in silence.

We cut back to **Rachel** *and* **Callum** *together at the party.*

RACHEL
Tomorrow? We'll go?

CALLUM
We will.

Eva *goes up to* **Lotte** *as she is watching the party.*

EVA
Your dad has surprised us all, honey – and I think it's

wonderful. Everybody coming together . . . That's how it should be.

We cut back to **Victor** *hunched over the files. There is a loud knocking on* **Mrs Tooley**'s *front door; the pulsating music cuts out suddenly.*

INT. VICTOR'S ROOM/STAIRCASE. NIGHT

We cut to **Victor** *looking through a crack in the door, down into the hall. He can see a half-obscured figure talking to* **Mrs Tooley**. *He rushes back into his room, furiously kicking the files under his bed. He gets down on the floor, pushing one last file under a chair. Just at that moment there is a knock on his door. We see, from his low angle,* **Salter** *enter the room.*

SALTER
Victor? I'm Geoffrey Salter.

Victor *jumps up.*

I'm a colleague of your brother's.

VICTOR
Mr Salter?! Ah yes, he doesn't like you.

SALTER
I'm sure that's true. (*He sits calmly as if it's his room.*) On the other hand I'm surprisingly fond of your brother . . . and that is why I've come.

VICTOR
You're here because you like my brother? I don't think so!

He is trying not to look at the file, just sticking out under the chair.

SALTER
I know a lot about your brother. (*He smiles.*) Everything there is to know in fact . . . and whatever else you say about him, he is a patriot. That is why I like him, that is why I'm here.

VICTOR
You will have to explain that to me.

SALTER

You've taken some files that don't belong to you, Victor, which Miss Griffiths now has . . . You have also escaped from the psychiatric ward where you were being held for your own safety . . .

VICTOR

Yes I'm surprised they haven't come after me . . . unless you –

SALTER

No, no, that's not my business! In fact I want to give you a chance to consider what I have to say all on your own. Victor, you've gone round boasting you will tell the world about what's happening to the ex-Nazis who are helping us, how we're giving them new identities.

Victor *looks surprised.*

Yes I have heard about that . . .

He gets up, his face very close.

You mustn't do that, Victor, any more, ever again. It will make all our lives more difficult. But shall I tell you what it really means? – It will destroy your brother, his career, his prospects. Even endanger his life . . . for failing to control you.

He stares straight into **Victor**'*s eyes.*

And if that happens, there will be only one person to blame.

INT. KATHY'S FRONT ROOM. NIGHT

We cut to **Mentz** *and* **Kathy** *sitting opposite each other at the table.*

KATHY

Oh the candle's gone out . . . (*She gets up to re-light it.*)

MENTZ

I couldn't . . .?

                                KATHY
Yes?

                                MENTZ
I couldn't stay a little longer?

We see a look of alarm in **Kathy**'s *eyes.*

Not for the night of course . . . but just sit here . . . for a
moment longer?

                                KATHY
Of course?

                                MENTZ
We don't need to talk . . .

EXT. RACHEL AND ALEX'S HOUSE. MORNING

We see **Callum** *drive up to* **Rachel**'s *house in a jeep in early morning
light.* **Rachel** *is in the doorway waiting. She gets into the jeep with one
suitcase and they drive off fast.*

EXT. BOMBED STREET. NEAR MRS TOOLEY'S. MORNING

We see **Victor** *walking with* **Mrs Tooley** *past the bombed houses. He is
holding the files. He stares about him to see if anybody is following.*

                                VICTOR
It's so kind of you to walk me to the bus stop, Mrs Tooley . . .

As they walk.

I'm going to miss your dog you know, Bella.

They reach the bus stop.

I'm going back to the hospital I promise. As soon as I'm on
the bus I'll be okay . . .

                                MRS TOOLEY
That's alright, Victor, I believe you.

VICTOR
We're not so different you and me. Not really. I hear you crying at night sometimes.

Their eyes meet. There is sadness in **Mrs Tooley**'s *eyes.*

INT. HAROLD'S LIBRARY. MORNING

Harold *is sitting at his desk.* **Lucy** *is in the doorway.*

LUCY
Good morning, Harold . . . (*He hardly responds.*) Is everything alright?

HAROLD
I've been very remiss, Lucy . . . I neglected the other brother. I don't know how I could have made such a mistake.

EXT. CONNINGTON FRONT ENTRANCE. DAY

We cut to **Victor**, *clutching his files, standing in front of the Connington's main entrance. His way is barred by the hotel's commissionaires. There are several expensive cars parked. He sees* **Ringwood** *about to enter the hotel. He moves up to him.*

RINGWOOD
What are doing here, Mr Ferguson?! Your brother's not here . . . (*Sharply.*) And no I don't know where he's gone!

Victor *makes as if he is moving off. But as soon as* **Ringwood** *enters the hotel, he moves over to the group of chauffeurs who are waiting near their cars, chatting in a cluster. They watch* **Victor** *approach, in his too large suit, with amusement.*

VICTOR
Morning, gentlemen! Tell me, who is the worst tipper amongst all the people you drive?

One of the chauffeurs involuntarily looks over to a blue Rolls-Royce. **Victor** *smiles, waves and moves off. We stay on the chauffeurs chatting together. Suddenly they turn in astonishment –* **Victor** *is in the blue Rolls-Royce and* *trying to start it. Several of them run towards him, yelling.* **Victor** *manages to get it started just in time and drives off.*

INT. MELBURY SUITE. DAY

Ringwood *is by the door,* **Frau Bellinghausen** *is by the window.*

> FRAU BELLINGHAUSEN
> (*urgent*)
> There was a commotion just now outside . . . lots of people shouting?

> RINGWOOD
> Yes, I will find out more details, but it could have been something to do with Captain Ferguson's brother, Victor, I saw him near the entrance

> FRAU BELLINGHAUSEN
> I knew it! I knew he'd try to come back here. You must find Callum immediately.

> RINGWOOD
> I don't know where he is this weekend I'm afraid!

> FRAU BELLINGHAUSEN
> You have to find out! You must find him.

EXT. ROAD APPROACHING GOVERNMENT RESEARCH FACILITY. DAY

We see **Rachel** *and* **Callum** *in the jeep passing the front gates of the Research Facility.*

> CALLUM
> That's where Dieter does his work . . . I can't take you in I'm afraid. It's like a whole secret village in there!

Rachel *stares fascinated.*

> But we're staying nearby . . .

EXT. SMALL COUNTRY HOTEL. DAY

We see **Callum** *and* **Rachel** *drive up to the front of a small country hotel. Some of the guests, elderly faces, come to the window, seeing a military jeep roar up to the front.*

INT. COUNTRY HOTEL RECEPTION. DAY

We see **Callum** *and* **Rachel** *at the reception of the hotel. The interior is chintzy and claustrophobic. The elderly clientele, men with large moustaches, prim looking women, are blatantly staring at them as they book in. It is as if they immediately sense they are not married.* **Rachel** *stares back at them and smiles warmly but she is only met with frosty looks. We see* **Callum***'s hand hovering over the page he has to sign in the hotel register. He writes 'Mr and Mrs Ferguson' with a flourish.*

INT. BEDROOM. COUNTRY HOTEL. DAY

We cut to **Callum** *and* **Rachel** *in the cramped hotel bedroom, which is dominated by a very high four-poster bed.*

RACHEL

They seem to hate us!

CALLUM

They sense danger . . .

He kisses her.

And love.

RACHEL

You signed your real name?!

CALLUM

I had to . . . I might be called by somebody from the base.

RACHEL

No, you're not answering any calls here! None at all. You've got to let your work go for a moment, Callum . . .

She puts her arms round him.

You're like one of your machines, those engines, that can never be . . .

CALLUM
Can't be stopped?

He kisses her.

EXT. ROAD/ENTRANCE OF GOVERNMENT RESEARCH FACILITY. DAY

Victor *is driving the blue Rolls-Royce very fast along country roads. We see through the windscreen it approaching the gates of the government research facility.* **Victor** *stops the Rolls about fifty yards from the gates, but in full view of the guards.*

He gets out, and approaches the guards, calling out to them.

VICTOR
I'm Captain Ferguson's brother . . . I need to see him! I need to see him now!

The guards stare back at this strange figure in a baggy suit, getting out of a Rolls.

GUARD
We haven't seen him today . . . He's not here.

VICTOR
Then get Mr Dieter Koehler! It's extremely urgent!

INT. COUNTRY HOTEL BEDROOM. DAY

Rachel *and* **Callum** *fall fully clothed on to the bed, which creaks loudly.*

RACHEL
God, it makes a noise! (*She laughs.*) They will all be listening. There'll be a queue in the passage!

EXT. GATES OF RESEARCH FACILITY. DAY

We see **Dieter** *approaching the gates.* **Victor** *is pacing in the road, with the blue Rolls behind him.* **Dieter** *watching this incongruous agitated figure.*

VICTOR
I need my brother! I've got something to tell him!

Victor *stares at* **Dieter**, *right into his eyes, as if he knows something.*

DIETER
I don't have an address for where he is.

VICTOR
But you must be able to contact him in some way? In case there was an emergency? You must?!

Dieter *hesitates.*

DIETER
I have just a telephone number.

INT. COUNTRY HOTEL BEDROOM. DAY

Rachel *and* **Callum** *are on the bed kissing passionately. She is in her slip and he is bare-chested. A voice is calling urgently 'Mr Ferguson! A telephone call!'*

RACHEL
You are not answering that.

EXT. VILLAGE/INTERCUT HOTEL RECEPTION. DAY

We cut to **Victor** *in a phone box in a picturesque village with a duck pond and green. He is swaying backwards and forwards as he waits on the phone.*

VICTOR
Come on . . . come on!

He looks round; he sees the seemingly deserted village green. Then he notices faces staring at him from behind laced curtains and figures in their gardens, half obscured by trees. He sees a man in a dark suit watching him from under a tree.

We see a look of fear in **Victor***'s eyes. Then he hears* **Callum***'s voice.*

VICTOR
Cal, there you are! I need to say something to you . . .

CALLUM

Victor? What is it? Where are you? Are you at the hospital?

VICTOR

I'm not at the hospital . . . I couldn't stay, there was a nurse, I did something wrong . . . but I've done worse things, bad things . . . I know I shouldn't have said what I did about your work . . . (*His voice breaking.*) You must forgive me.

CALLUM

Victor, what is this? Where are you?

Callum *is instantly alarmed. He is on the phone at reception. His shirt is barely done up; the elderly clientele are watching from the lounge, fascinated and shocked.* **Rachel** *appears at the top of the stairs.*

VICTOR

I found some evidence . . . the real evidence now. You must read it, it was all true about Dieter, what I said! I knew it was . . . but that doesn't matter now.

CALLUM

Victor, you must tell me exactly where you are?! (*His voice rising in urgency despite everybody watching.*) I will come and find you –

VICTOR

They wouldn't like that! . . . They came to see me, I know I've done the wrong thing. I'm not worth it Cal, I'm really not. (*Tears in his eyes.*) Not worth destroying everything for you . . .

CALLUM

Who came to see you?! (*Tries to lower his voice.*) If they threatened you – I will kill them, I will fucking kill them.

Faces staring from the lounge. There is alarm in **Rachel**'s *eyes.*

WHERE ARE YOU VICTOR?!

VICTOR

Somewhere with a pond . . . Little Rooting or Great Rooting or Tiny Rooting. I stole a blue Rolls, Cal . . . If you're going to steal a car, what a car to steal don't you think?! A great car! I've got to go now, Cal, there are people watching . . .

CALLUM
Victor, don't move, stay there. Whatever you do don't move. I'm coming to get you.

VICTOR
Better you don't, Cal . . . I don't need you to come . . . I don't want to spoil anything any more.

EXT. HOTEL/ROADS/VILLAGE GREEN/WOODS. DAY

We cut to **Callum** *rushing out of the hotel and jumping into the jeep.*

Rachel *is standing in the door, guests crowding at the windows.*

RACHEL
I'll come with you, Cal . . . !

But **Callum** *waves to her to stay as he roars off in the jeep.*

We see him arrive at the village, past a sign saying 'Little Rooting'. He draws up at the village green, where the receiver is dangling in the phone box. There is no sign of **Victor**. *As he walks towards the phone box he sees movement in the windows of the cottages, faces staring at him, and people watching from the shadow of their gardens.*

He gets back into the jeep and we see his point of view as he drives fast around the village searching for **Victor**. *He swings the jeep round and heads back to the green to ask somebody, but the place now appears deserted – the faces have gone from the windows. He hesitates for a second. We see sharp cuts from his point of view; the village green, the church and the road leading towards some woods. He suddenly puts his foot down and starts driving really fast towards the woods. We see his point of view, scouring both sides of the road. Suddenly he brakes and reverses really fast.*

He has caught a glimpse of blue through the trees. Just off the road there is the blue Rolls-Royce. He runs towards the car; the seats are covered by the files, but there is no **Victor**. *He looks around wildly and sees about fifty yards away a figure slumped at the base of a tree. He runs towards* **Victor** *to find him lying in a pool of blood.*

A knife beside him, blood pouring from his throat. **Victor** *is only half conscious.* **Callum** *is crying and shouting at him. He takes him in his arms and carries him towards the vehicles.*

Victor *is staring back at him, his eyes nearly closed. He manages to whisper:*

VICTOR

Take the Rolls!

We cut to **Callum** *driving the Rolls with one hand, trying to hold* **Victor** *on the front seat with the other.* **Victor** *is still bleeding profusely. Blood all over the seat.*

INT. COUNTRY HOSPITAL/OPERATING THEATRE. DAY

We cut to **Victor** *in the operating theatre, surrounded by surgeons and nurses as they try to stop the bleeding.*

We cut to **Callum** *in the hospital passage. Opposite him is a large boy playing with a clockwork toy watched by his parents. The boy stares coldly at* **Callum***'s agitated state.* **Rachel** *appears, running down the passage towards him.*

RACHEL

How is he?! How is he now?!

CALLUM

I'm waiting to hear . . .

RACHEL

Did somebody attack him? What happened Callum?

CALLUM

I think I know exactly what happened . . .

We move in on **Callum***'s eyes. They are incredibly hard.*

INT. OPERATING THEATRE. DAY

We cut back to the operating theatre, the camera circling **Victor** *as the surgeons work on the wound in his neck. We move closer and closer onto his face under the oxygen mask.*

The image fades to black.

INT. THE TUNNEL. DAY

We cut to the jet engine standing alone, in the middle of the tunnel, looking mysterious in the shadowy light.

INT. COUNTY HOSPITAL. DAY

*We see a close-up of one of **Victor**'s eyes, hovering open. We cut to **Callum** staring down at him as he lies in a hospital bed. We move back on to **Victor**'s eyes.*

*Suddenly there is a cut of **Salter** staring straight at him in his bedroom. We cut back to **Victor**'s eyes as he lies in the bed, **Callum** watching him.*

*We cut wide: the hospital ward is splashed in afternoon sun, the nurses moving around in white uniforms. It is very quiet. A nurse is peeling an apple for a patient. It is the only sound. **Callum** is now sitting on a chair near the bed, watching **Victor**.*

VICTOR

Forgive me.

CALLUM

There's nothing to forgive you for.

There is a sudden violent sound on the soundtrack.

INT. THE TUNNEL. SECRET VILLAGE. DAY

The crash on the soundtrack is the arc lights being switched on in the tunnel. We see a whole stretch of the tunnel in brilliant white light. The finished jet engine now dominates the space sitting in the middle of the tunnel. Men in overalls are scurrying around, sweeping the floor, preparing for an important visit.

INT. COUNTY HOSPITAL WARD. DAY

*We cut back to **Callum** by **Victor**'s bed.*

VICTOR

I made such a mess of it . . . I bungled it . . . Trying to cut one's own throat, not the best way . . .

CALLUM
Luckily, probably not. (*He moves close, his voice quiet.*) But you were driven to it . . . they threatened you . . . (*Very hushed.*) Don't worry, I'm going to take care of it.

Victor *looking at him.*

In a way they'll not forget.

EXT. THE SECRET VILLAGE. DAY

We see, through the windscreen, the car of the air vice-marshall driving through the secret village towards the tunnel entrance. We then cut wide and see the main street of the village is full of official cars of the RAF top brass. The senior officers are gathering together near the entrance to the tunnel. **Wainwright** *is standing with* **Callum** *and* **Ringwood**. **Dieter** *and* **Rita** *are watching the top brass arrive.*

INT. COUNTY HOSPITAL WARD. DAY

We cut to **Victor**'s *face turning in the bed.* **Rachel** *is staring down at him.*

RACHEL
How are you, Victor? (*Softly.*) Can you hear me?

INT. THE TUNNEL. DAY

The top brass are all gathered on a viewing platform in the tunnel, some distance from the jet engine which is just being fired up. The noise is building and building.

We see **Wainwright** *watching the RAF high command; we see* **Dieter**'s *confident face. And* **Callum** *is standing a little apart. The noise is getting ear-splitting, the red exhaust fumes pouring out of the engine.*

Suddenly **Callum** *is startled to see* **Salter** *and* **Ruth** *standing in an alcove in the wall, a little closer to the engine than anybody else.*

The engine is reaching its fullest power. At that very moment we see **Dieter** *begin to look agitated. And then we cut to the engine; it is beginning to vibrate.*

As the noise reaches a scream, the engine is vibrating badly.

DIETER

Stop! . . . Stop!

He gesticulates to the men controlling it; the engine begins to die.

It should not be vibrating like that . . .

EXT. THE SECRET VILLAGE. JUST OUTSIDE THE TUNNEL. DAY

We cut to all the top brass clustered in the sunlight outside the tunnel entrance. **Dieter** *and* **Rita** *are standing in front of them.* **Dieter**'s *voice is raised, trying to reassure.*

DIETER

It will just take a little adjustment . . . We need to rebalance the components . . . That is all it will take I promise.

We see **Wainwright** *standing with* **Callum**. *A car drives past them;* **Salter** *and* **Ruth** *are sitting on the back seat.* **Salter** *glances at* **Callum**; *his face is pale, his eyes dull. We see* **Callum** *meeting his look with a piercing stare.*

WAINWRIGHT

You won't be seeing them again . . . they're being reassigned to some godforsaken place in Germany.

Callum *watching them disappear.*

So don't worry about them, worry about this, Ferguson! The engine's not ready yet.

CALLUM

I saw that, sir.

WAINWRIGHT

It's very simple . . . (*He looks straight at* **Callum**.) If we fall behind the Americans and the Russians, if we can't fly as fast, we lose the next war.

INT. COUNTY HOSPITAL WARD. DAY

We cut back to **Rachel** *sitting next to* **Victor**'s *bed. Her head turns –* **Harold** *is in the entrance to the ward holding a large bunch of very colourful flowers. He approaches.*

HAROLD
Victor, my dear boy . . . how are you feeling?

Victor *manages a smile; he is extremely pale.*

I brought these because I got it into my head something really colourful would be best . . . (*He stares down at* **Victor**.)

Victor *beckons* **Rachel** *close; his voice is very weak.*

VICTOR
What I really want is another huge bar of chocolate.

INT. THE TUNNEL. DAY

We cut to **Dieter** *and* **Rita** *alone with the technicians in the tunnel. The engine is being fired up again, screaming towards its full power, and vibrating badly.* **Dieter**'s *expression is very determined; tears are pouring down* **Rita**'s *cheeks.*

RITA
I can't believe that just happened . . . in front of all of them.

DIETER
We will take it apart . . . (*Staring at engine.*) And see why it's happening, and then stop it happening. We will be able to do it Rita. We are still going to beat the Americans . . .

We move in on the engine.

INT. MELBURY SUITE. AFTERNOON

We dissolve from the roar of the engine to the silence of the Melbury Suite. **Frau Bellinghausen** *is squinting as the sun blazes through the window.*

Harold *is just drawing the curtains across for her.*

                        HAROLD
Is that how you want it?

                   FRAU BELLINGHAUSEN
Yes, thank you. With so many buildings destroyed round here, the sun is so bright! Too bright sometimes . . . Now tell me, is he better? Is the brother better?

                        HAROLD
It's hard to tell yet, a little I think.

                   FRAU BELLINGHAUSEN
And they're keeping a watch on him? So he doesn't try to do it again?

                        HAROLD
I'm sure they are. Callum is seeing to everything, as he always does.

                   FRAU BELLINGHAUSEN
That boy must not be left alone.

                        HAROLD
He won't be.

INT. COUNTY HOSPTIAL WARD. AFTERNOON

A sharp cut to **Kathy** *and* **Rachel** *by* **Victor**'s *bed. It is some days later.* **Victor** *has a little more colour in his face. There is a bar of plain chocolate next to him.*

                        VICTOR
Ah, the two women together!

                        RACHEL
Yes, you've managed to introduce us Victor . . .

                        KATHY
I brought something for you – well two things actually . . . It took a lot of coupons . . . but here's another, rather smaller bar of chocolate –

VICTOR

Some milk chocolate at last! (*Hastily to* **Rachel**.) Not that the other isn't nice –

KATHY

And I thought this might interest you too? (*She produces a jam jar out of her bag.*) It's a little silly, but I brought it anyway! All the beetles that have crawled out of the files you found.

VICTOR

That's terrific . . .

Taking jar, **Rachel** *looks startled.*

Blimey, that's a lot! You're right. (*He grins.*) It really appeals to me, even if they are all dead. (*Indicating nurses.*) They'll probably take it away though.

KATHY

And, Victor . . . I'm determined to get a result with Fräulein Mentz – who I found out about because of the files! I'm going to do everything I can to try to get her to give evidence against her boss, at his trial.

VICTOR

(*his expression darkens*)

If they let you keep trying of course . . .

There is a momentary pause. **Victor** *looks at* **Rachel**.

Are you in love with Callum? And is he in love with you?

RACHEL

Victor!

KATHY

Excuse me . . . I have to get back to work –

VICTOR

Don't go, please!

KATHY

No, no, it's quite a long journey. I ought to go. I'll be here again very soon.

VICTOR
(*watching her go*)
She's run away just because I asked a perfectly sensible question.

RACHEL
You made her run away.

VICTOR
So aren't you going to give me an answer?

RACHEL
Why do you even ask?

VICTOR
Because I know my brother.

RACHEL
This is not the place, Victor . . .

VICTOR
That's a very disappointing reply. I thought we were friends?

RACHEL
We are friends.

VICTOR
(*beckoning her close*)
Anyway whether you are or you aren't in love with each other – you must promise me you'll keep a close eye on him . . . He blames the Secret Service for me being like this . . . (*He indicates his wound.*) He may try to take certain actions because of that.

RACHEL
What kind of actions?

VICTOR
You must remember the war messed him up just as much as it did me . . . maybe more –

Callum *suddenly appears behind* **Rachel**, *having just arrived in the ward.*

CALLUM

Who's messed up?

VICTOR

Me of course! It's always me.

INT. ANTEROOM. COUNTY HOSPITAL. AFTERNOON

Rachel *is facing* **Callum** *in a small room. Nurses are working in the passage.*

CALLUM

What was he saying to you?

RACHEL

That you are as much scarred by the war as he is.

CALLUM

That's rubbish.

RACHEL

Is it? You've never talked to me about it . . . (*Her tone softens.*) About the fighting in Normandy . . . everything you went through –

CALLUM

So? . . . Who talks about the war?! Nobody does . . . not to people who weren't there anyway . . . Remember Victor is full of medication . . . not everything he says is to be taken literally –

RACHEL

You are totally calm and relaxed are you, Callum?! Is that what you're telling me! Your brother has tried to take his own life . . . but everything is fine?

CALLUM

I'm as calm as I've been for a long time, without a doubt. Somebody has to be . . . (*Close, touches her face.*) Don't believe Victor.

INT. FULLER'S COFFEE SHOP. DAY

We cut to women in hats having afternoon tea at Fuller's. The place is packed; there are voices ringing out. **Callum** *is watching* **Dieter** *approach his table.*

Callum's *manner is very contained.*

DIETER
I'm very sorry I'm so late.

CALLUM
Don't worry, you're very busy I know, getting the engine ready . . . I took the liberty of ordering, I thought we should see if the ice cream had improved here.

DIETER
Excellent. What better way to take time off work than to have a day in London, and eat an ice cream with you?

CALLUM
Yes . . .

The waitress is bringing over two tall glasses containing lumps of grey vanilla ice cream. There are also two smaller plates.

WAITRESS
Your ice cream sir . . . and there's a little fresh fruit, it's an extra on the side. Some people like to mix it in with their vanilla ices . . . There is no additional charge.

There are two saucers containing a couple of strawberries and three raspberries.

DIETER
What a good idea! (*Smiles at waitress.*) How did you think of that?

The waitress nods politely and moves off. **Callum** *watches* **Dieter** *for a second and then reaches down on to the chair next to him and produces one of* **Victor**'s *files.*

He drops it in front of **Dieter**.

CALLUM
I think you'll find this is the file.

DIETER
Another of Victor's files?

The pages are covered with stains from the woods.

CALLUM
Eight different witness statements . . . all identifying you.

Their eyes meet.

INT. WAR CRIMES UNIT. AFTERNOON

Kathy *is looking down at a series of photographs of* **Mentz**, *charting her arrest. A mug shot of her staring straight out, a picture of her outside the police station with a uniformed police escort, a picture of her with* **Kathy** *and her* **Minder** *in the conservatory bar. We are close on* **Kathy**, *and then on the unyielding expression of* **Mentz**.

INT. FULLER'S COFFEE SHOP. AFTERNOON

We cut back to the tea room. The genteel atmosphere: some of the ladies are stirring the fruit into the ice creams; the sound of their chatter. **Dieter** *is staring at the file.*

CALLUM
You're going to tell me they're all a case of mistaken identity?

Dieter *doesn't reply; he turns the pages slowly.*

DIETER
No, I'm not saying that . . . (*He looks up at* **Callum**.) People died . . . there were acts of sabotage which were punishable by death. I saw people executed, yes . . . Did I cause any of those, did I encourage any of them to be carried out? . . . I certainly didn't stop them . . .

He looks down at the ice cream, suddenly very emotional.

It seems extraordinary thinking about this now, with ice cream . . . and the ladies here.

He stares at the file; there are tears in his eyes.

What really went on . . . people were hanging from hooks . . .

His voice cracks slightly. **Callum** *watching him. We move in on* **Dieter**'s *eyes; the sound of the tea room suddenly cuts out.*

For one brief moment there is a flashback:

The camera tracking along a wall; a terrible sound of choking is leading us. We see, in silhouette on the wall, people hanging from hooks, their legs jerking as they fight for breath.

The sound of the tea room comes rushing back. We cut to **Dieter**, *full of emotion.*

DIETER
Sitting here . . . it is almost unimaginable that it happened so recently . . .

He looks down at the file, turning the pages abstractedly. **Callum** *is watching him.*

DIETER
I always knew you would find out in the end. I thought it might be right at the beginning, that is why I was so keen to get back to Germany. And when you did ask . . . I just couldn't tell you.

He looks at **Callum** *for a response.*

But you and I . . . we have come so far in such a short time . . .

Callum *is giving him nothing.*

I'm not going to insult your intelligence by saying we are on the same side now . . . that there's a new enemy that we have to defeat together . . . (*Sharp.*) Except I've just said that –

WAITRESS
(*suddenly at the table*)
Is everything alright, gentlemen? Any teas or coffees to go with your ice creams?

DIETER
No . . . (*Sharp.*) Everything is alright, thank you.

The waitress notices his flushed face, then leaves.

Dieter *looks at* **Callum**; *he tries to brush the tears out of his eyes.*

DIETER
I have no excuse . . . except of course to say that we were at war, which is no excuse . . . and the work was everything . . . I think you of all people may understand how consuming the work can be . . . One is blind. (*Momentary silence.*)

What do we do now, Callum?

Callum *is still just watching him.*

DIETER
I know we like each other . . . did like each other. Which makes it all the more difficult . . .

CALLUM
(*matter of fact*)

Yes, that's true.

DIETER
We were friends.

CALLUM
We *are* friends.

DIETER
Yes, we are . . .

He stares at him.

Right now of course my work is so very close, and naturally I want to finish it if that's at all possible . . . to help protect the West in some way, and the government seems to think the work is of great importance –

CALLUM
It is of great importance.

DIETER

You always have a plan. Callum, something in mind
usually – a way out of things. (*Looks at him; his tone emotional.*)
What is it do you think?

CALLUM

The government will see to it that you can finish your work
and have immunity from prosecution.

DIETER

But you're not saying anything, about what I've just told you?

CALLUM

No.

DIETER

It is ridiculous of me to expect you to say anything . . . what
can you say?

CALLUM

(*impassive*)

That is also true.

The sound of the tea room.

DIETER

I hardly dare ask this . . . but are you still going to come to
the wedding?

CALLUM

Oh absolutely. It will be a very busy few days for me,
Harold's having his party at the Foreign Office, and then
your wedding at the end of the week. (*He stares at* **Dieter**.)
Two occasions I couldn't possibly miss . . .

EXT. MILITARY CAMP. RUINED HOUSE. DAY

The approach to the military camp in the suburbs, seen through the windscreen of a jeep. **Harold** *is sitting on his shooting stick, waiting at the entrance. He is dressed very formally.* **Callum** *draws up.*

CALLUM
Harold! You're all dressed up?!

HAROLD
I am. (*As he gets in.*) Thank you for letting me do this.

CALLUM
Yes, well it's not going to be possible soon, they're moving out.

They drive through the gates and then head towards the bombed ruins of the great house. Military trucks are passing them on the drive, beginning to leave.

EXT. RUINS OF GREAT HOUSE. DAY

We cut to **Callum** *and* **Harold** *alone in the ruins of the house, moving among the charred walls.*

We see them initially from above, two small figures among the shattered building.

CALLUM
All being well they've stopped using this for training . . . sniper training especially! (*Yells.*) Anybody up there?! (*His voice echoes.*)

HAROLD
Well that will be one way of curing my nerves about tomorrow. A bullet between the eyes!

CALLUM
How nervous are you?

HAROLD
Fairly terrified. A room completely packed with people I know, and I'm going to attack them all . . . I've come here to give myself strength.

CALLUM
We both need strength in fact.

HAROLD
You as well? What are you planning to do?

CALLUM

Ah. I can't tell you that.

They both move through the ruined ballroom, and stare out from the terrace at the fountain and the gardens.

HAROLD

This place is so important to me . . . not just because it was the last party I ever went to with my wife, but because I keep coming back here in my dreams . . . nearly every night recently.

We stay on his face.

Flashback:
We see figures in evening dress and ball gowns flowing down the steps in the evening light towards the fountain, which is lit by lanterns. The figure of **Harold**'s *wife, moving down the steps and looking back at him.*

We hear music and see the guests surround the fountain, laughing and drinking.

We cut back to **Harold**.

There was beauty . . . but also terrible ignorance . . .

We see the faces of the guests at the ball.

Our complacency seems so shocking now . . .

Suddenly there is the roar of military trucks and we see soldiers shouting out at them as they drive past the building. **Harold** *watches the military trucks driving away, his manner intense.*

The extraordinary mistakes that nobody has owned up to.

CALLUM

I know! Like letting the bloody jet engine go! I was there, I was working on it before the war, and Mr Whittle needed just five pounds to renew his patent – five fucking pounds and he couldn't afford it – and the government wouldn't give it to him, *wouldn't give him five pounds*, and we lost the jet engine!

What a price we paid for that! It's incredible, the incompetent bastards . . . just like your incompetent bastards who failed to back the coup against Hitler that could have prevented the war . . . Well their fucking moment has come! We are their nemesis, Harold!

HAROLD

Let's hope so . . . (*Watching* **Callum**'s *vehemence, his energy.*) They've certainly gone unpunished so far . . .

CALLUM

And you'll manage fine tomorrow!

INT. MELBURY SUITE. EARLY EVENING

All the bottles of perfume are out of the travelling case, glinting in the evening sunlight. A subjective shot approaching **Frau Bellinghausen** *as* **Callum** *enters the suite.*

FRAU BELLINGHAUSEN

So there you are!

CALLUM

Here I am, yes. I've been neglectful, I'm sorry.

FRAU BELLINGHAUSEN

Don't be stupid . . . Your brother has been very ill, of course you've had better things to do. I just wanted to know how he is?

CALLUM

He's getting better, the wounds are healing. He lost a lot of blood, he needs to get his strength back.

FRAU BELLINGHAUSEN

What really happened to him?

CALLUM

(*hesitates*)

I'm not sure of the facts yet. But whatever it was, it was caused by him being put under terrible pressure by a member of the Secret Service.

FRAU BELLINGHAUSEN
Why would they do that? I'm sorry, I'm asking a lot of questions –

CALLUM
Yes, but that's okay. Because he was proving a nuisance. Of course their action has to be answered.

FRAU BELLINGHAUSEN
How? . . . I'm sorry I'm doing it again. I don't know why I think I have a right to know, because I don't. I only met him for a couple of minutes

CALLUM
It's all Victor needs to make an impression! I have a plan of what to do, but at the moment it's private.

FRAU BELLINGHAUSEN
Of course. (*She looks at him searchingly.*) Quite right.

She indicates the perfume bottles.

FRAU BELLINGHAUSEN
I was going to suggest I gave you the formula today and signed the papers, but clearly this is not the right moment, when you have so much on your mind . . .

CALLUM
I have a little on my mind, yes. (*Smiles.*) We'll do it in the next forty-eight hours.

INT. HAROLD'S CLUB. HALL. NIGHT

All the members of the club, plus grandees from the Foreign Office, are swirling about in the hall ready for the gala dinner. **Callum** *watching the crowd of expectant faces. He sees some of the same people that were present at the cricket match.* **Rachel** *and* **Alex** *are moving through the crowd towards him.* **Rachel** *is wearing a striking evening gown,* **Alex** *is looking more at ease now among his peers.*

ALEX

Callum, I'm here! I made it back from Washington just in time . . . I wasn't going to miss this – Harold being honoured. It's going to be a splendid night!

CALLUM

It is.

Alex *moves off to greet more colleagues.*

So he is back.

RACHEL

Yes. For quite a while anyway.

CALLUM

So that really was our last time together?

RACHEL

I hardly think this is the place, Callum . . .

Callum *stares at her for a moment.*

It's fine. It doesn't matter. I have other plans anyway.

RACHEL
(sharply)

What's that mean?

CALLUM

It means exactly that.

Callum *spots* **Harold**, *glass in hand, surrounded by a group of Foreign Office grandees. He moves up to him.* **Harold** *gives a conspiratorial smile.*

HAROLD

Just thought I'd fortify myself . . . but oddly I find I'm quite calm, and really rather excited! *(Points to man.)* My friend the journalist . . . even he doesn't know what's coming. *(Whispers.)* I'm going to tell the truth about the coup against Hitler that never was . . . and they have no idea!

CALLUM

And no oysters before the speech?

HAROLD
No, definitely not. I will be oyster-free.

INT. THE DINING ROOM. THE GALA MEAL. NIGHT

We cut inside the gala dinner; everybody is now seated at round tables. **Callum** *is sitting with* **Rachel** *and* **Alex** *and some Foreign Office grandees. There is a little dais facing the diners, on which* **Harold** *is sitting with the* **Head of the Foreign Office***, who is in the middle of his introductory speech.*

HEAD OF THE F.O.
. . . It's long overdue of course . . . that we're all gathered here to honour Harold Lindsay-Jones and his many years of service . . . But now we are finally here, we're doing it exactly in the way Harold wants – which is totally appropriate. At his favourite place in the world, his beloved club . . . and having the speeches before the dinner, rather than after as is customary. Harold says he wanted all the suspense out of the way . . .

We are on **Callum***. The* **Head of the F.O.***'s voice dips on the soundtrack.* **Callum** *is studying the faces all staring up at* **Harold***. And then he looks at* **Harold** *waiting; his face seems perfectly calm, but his fingers are tapping on the chair.* **Callum***'s heart is beating fast; he tries to conceal his tension by drinking.*

The **Head of the F.O.***'s voice comes back sharply.*

HEAD OF THE F.O.
And of course Harold was famous to all of us for knowing what people were thinking, even the most inscrutable! His colleagues, the French, the Germans, above all the Americans . . . He invariably had an extraordinary insight into other people's minds – which makes tonight a little alarming! Does he know what we're all thinking now?!

Good-natured laughter erupts.

Well if he does, he will know we're full of admiration, and gratitude . . . and of course friendship. So now Harold I will hand over to you . . . Naturally we have a gift or two to give – which everybody here has contributed to . . . but we're allowed at least a little surprise . . . so that will wait. Harold . . .

There is applause. **Harold** *gets up, moves to the microphone and taps it nervously.*

HAROLD
It's working . . . so that's a very good start!

So my friends, this is a very important moment for me . . . in all sorts of ways . . . and you will have to forgive me, because to help me through these nervous opening moments, I have brought a couple of props . . . (*He produces a small box out of his pocket.*) A golden box . . . with a couple of little stories inside.

So first out, is this – (*He produces a piece of paper.*) A scrap of paper . . . and what is it? It's a film review by Winston Churchill of Mr Orson Welles' *Citizen Kane* . . . and it is exceedingly short! Let me paint the scene, how it happened. There was a film show almost every night at Chequers during the war, certainly every time I was there, often starting after midnight –

We cut out into the hall. **Lucy** *is arriving at the reception desk, running up the stairs. A middle-aged* **Desk Clerk** *is watching her approach.*

LUCY
I'm sorry I'm so late . . . ! I've come for the gala dinner for Mr Lindsay-Jones.

DESK CLERK
Your name? (*His movements are very slow.*)

LUCY
It's Lucy Lindsay-Jones, I'm his niece . . . please hurry!

DESK CLERK
Your name's not here.

LUCY
What do you mean?! It's got to be there . . . I can't miss it, you've got to let me in –

DESK CLERK
Your name is not here. And therefore I cannot let you in.

We cut back inside the gala dinner. **Harold** *is holding up the piece of paper to the diners and then reading it out aloud.*

HAROLD
'Rubbish, rubbish, bloody rubbish'.

There is a ripple of laughter, of recognition.

Winston may have been no film critic, I'm sure he won't mind me saying that . . . but what a man to work for . . . ! Glorious . . . ! He stomped along the corridors of Chequers at night . . . yelling 'this unnecessary war! This completely unnecessary war!' More of that in a moment . . .

He takes a key out of the golden box.

HAROLD
And that brings me now to my next exhibit . . . the key.

Lord Halifax, our old boss, his private key . . . I know, by the way, he's relaxed about me showing you this . . . a key given to him by the Queen – to the garden of Buckingham Palace, to that secret garden. This key opened a special door, and let him use the lovely summer house whenever he wanted . . . for him to retreat to in those terrifying days after the invasion of Norway, when we all thought he would become Prime Minister . . .

We intercut with **Rachel** *during this. She sees* **Lucy** *through the door, surrounded by the club's porters, as she tries to get into the dining room. They are barring her path and remonstrating with her.* **Rachel** *gets up from the table.*

We cut outside into the hall. **Rachel** *approaches them urgently.*

RACHEL
Lucy, there you are . . .

LUCY
They won't let me in!

RACHEL

That's ridiculous.

She turns to the porters.

Her uncle, who also happens to be her guardian, is making an important speech – she can't possibly miss that.

You will let her in immediately. Right now!

*Faced by **Rachel**'s authority the porters back away, giving **Lucy** a surly nod.*

Rachel *and* **Lucy** *enter the dining room just as* **Harold** *is holding up the key.*

HAROLD

How did I end up with this key? (*He smiles.*) It was a gift from His Lordship because it doesn't work any more!

There is laughter.

A memento of that extraordinary time . . . when all of us were holding our breath to see who was going to be the Prime Minister. When so many of us at the Foreign Office, including myself I might add, were saying, 'Let it be anybody but Churchill! Please, whatever happens, don't let it be Winston . . . !' Before we got to know him and love him . . .

As **Harold** *is saying this,* **Rachel** *is finding a chair for* **Lucy**, *so she can sit at their table.* **Harold** *pauses, as* **Lucy** *sits. She beams up at him, her face full of excitement.* **Harold** *stares back at her.*

Then we cut to **Callum**, *drinking, very tense, willing* **Harold** *on.*

HAROLD

Now I come to the heart of what I want to say . . . We fought the 'unnecessary war'. What did Churchill mean by that? How was it 'unnecessary'? He meant of course, there were opportunities in the events leading up to war, when different decisions could have been made . . .

We see **Callum**, *and then* **Lucy**, *staring at* **Harold**.

When maybe the war could have been prevented . . . we know there were many moments like that, some better known than others . . . some still to be uncovered . . .

We see **Harold** *staring at* **Lucy**. *And then at all of his colleagues' faces.*

His hand tightens round the golden box. He stops. He stares at **Lucy**.

Silence. We move in on his face. Everybody is looking at him.

HAROLD
But in the end we all did what we had to . . . we went on a startling momentous journey together, terrifying, sometimes exhilarating . . . and sometimes tragic.

We are moving in on **Callum**, *and then back on* **Harold**.

I want to thank you for your wonderful support during that time . . . and for this dinner tonight of course. Thank you to you all! Thank you so much!

We are on **Callum**; *he is stunned that* **Harold** *did not go through with it.*

Everybody is applauding, standing up, an ovation. **Rachel** *and* **Alex** *clapping loudly.*

Harold *is being presented with a grand portrait of himself by the* **Head of the F.O.** **Harold** *is immediately surrounded by colleagues and well-wishers.*

Lucy *turns to* **Callum**, *tears in her eyes.*

LUCY
Didn't he do brilliantly?! I wish I'd seen all of it!

We move close on **Callum**'s *eyes.*

INT. COUNTY HOSPITAL. DAY

We cut to **Victor** *lying in bed in bright sunlight.* **Kathy** *is sitting near the bed.*

KATHY
You're looking much better, Victor.

VICTOR

I am aren't I . . .?! Not quite rosy cheeks yet, but definitely an improvement.

KATHY

A big improvement.

VICTOR

They've sent for some brain doctors, to interrogate me . . . an inquisition! And if I pass, if they conclude I'm not a lunatic, I might be free to go soon.

KATHY

That would be tremendous, Victor . . . And I'm sure you'll pass.

VICTOR

I intend to! And how are you? Have you got the girl in the green coat to agree to give evidence yet? The Green Torturer?

KATHY

Not yet, no. I've tried everything I can think of – and everything Callum suggested too.

VICTOR

Ah, you've been using Callum's methods . . . well take them even further then! Send all her minders away, get her to feel really free. Let her run away if necessary . . .

KATHY

Now you really do sound like Callum! –

VICTOR

And take her to your favourite place in the world too . . . or in London at any rate. Your special place.

KATHY

I haven't got a favourite place.

VICTOR

You ought to have . . . mine is a bombed church called St Mildred's.

KATHY
(*smiles*)
I'll think about it.

VICTOR
Be even bolder than Callum, Kathy. He is a genius of course at making the enemy feel at home . . . but he's not nearly as good at looking after himself. He thinks he's in control all the time, but he isn't. (*Leans close.*) I'm really quite worried about him.

KATHY
The last person that needs worrying about is Callum!

INT./EXT. HAROLD'S GARDEN. CHICKEN COOP. DAY

Mrs Gorton *is leading* **Callum** *through the French windows and out into the garden where* **Harold** *is standing among the chickens. She lets* **Callum** *into the coop and leaves.* **Harold** *is holding some documents in one hand, and feeding the chickens with the other.*

HAROLD
(*as* **Callum** *approaches*)
Your brother is right, we underestimate chickens, they can be very formidable when they choose . . . to 'chicken' out of something, that is a very unfair expression . . . (*Looking at the birds.*) Unfair on them.

CALLUM
I'm sure it is.

HAROLD
(*suddenly looking at him*)
I am so very sorry, Callum.

CALLUM
You can do it again. It doesn't have to be at your farewell party – we can find an easier moment.

HAROLD
You didn't read this document did you? The document you

'borrowed' from the Foreign Office. The memo of the crucial meeting?

CALLUM

I didn't read it no. Just glanced at it.

HAROLD

So you missed the most vital thing then didn't you?! I'm about to use it to go under their eggs in the hut there . . . but before I do . . .

He hands the document to **Callum**.

Look at the top . . . where it says who was present at the meeting . . .

We see the typed names. 'Herr Theodor Kordt, Lord Halifax, Mr Horace Wilson, Mr Cecil Thurston' and then suddenly it leaps out 'Mr Harold Lindsay-Jones'.

Callum *looks up at* **Harold**, *truly startled, confused.*

HAROLD

It was me, Callum, that told them not to do anything . . . It was my advice that meant we didn't back the coup against Hitler. Not just me of course, but I was, 'the man who knew what foreigners were thinking' . . . My contribution was crucial.

Silence.

CALLUM

So this whole plan . . .?

Phrases jump out of the document at him in sharp cuts, 'Mr Lindsay-Jones advised that no action should be taken' . . . 'Mr Lindsay-Jones said the proposed coup d'état was not credible'.

CALLUM

You wanted to get hold of the file to –

HAROLD

So I could cover my tracks, yes. So people wouldn't know

about the biggest mistake of my life. That I advised them these senior well-intentioned Germans were not serious people. Posterity would never know it was me. That was my initial idea, Callum, to bury the truth.

Close-up of **Callum**. *His manner very contained.*

CALLUM

I see.

HAROLD

Then over the last few months as I've got to know you well, and you've encouraged me, made me bolder – I decided I was going to make all this public . . . my contribution, the dramatic failure of the Foreign Office to seize the chance, the whole story. I really meant to.

He stares at **Callum**.

I just wasn't brave enough . . . and seeing Lucy there especially, I thought she was away with friends . . . I didn't expect her to come. But it was all those faces looking at me . . . I was afraid. (*Momentary pause.*) I hate to think what you must feel about me, Callum . . .

There is just the sound of the chickens. **Callum** *watching him.*

CALLUM

Don't worry yourself so much . . . that still leaves me – I can do something. (*Sharp smile.*) I just have a little matter to take care of first.

INT. THIRD-FLOOR PASSAGE. CONNINGTON. DAY

We cut to **Lotte** *in her school uniform, looking rather solemn. She is following* **Dieter** *and his entourage down the third-floor passage of the Connington towards their old bedroom.* **Dieter** *is surrounded by three of his colleagues from the base.*

Suddenly both **Lotte** *and* **Dieter** *notice* **Callum** *watching them from the other end of the passage.*

DIETER
Ah, we're back staying here, my friend, and two days early! But there's the rehearsal tomorrow . . . (*He smiles.*) And of course we wanted to make sure we were on time for the ceremony!

LOTTE
And to see the hotel again.

DIETER
Yes, she's grown to love it here. I promised she could play outside for once on the bombsite. (*Indicating his colleagues.*) Meanwhile I'm continuing to work right up to the last minute . . .

Dieter *moves with his colleagues into the room*

We stay on **Callum** *watching them.*

Lotte *follows her father into the room. She turns to see* **Callum** *still standing in the passage watching them.*

Their eyes meet. It is as if **Lotte** *senses something.*

We cut back to **Callum**.

And then to **Lotte** *as she slowly shuts the bedroom door, never taking her eyes off* **Callum**.

We fade to black.

CREDITS

Part Seven

EXT. BOMBSITE. DAY

CREDIT SEQUENCE

*We see **Lotte**, now out of her school uniform, going through a door of the hotel and out into the daylight and dust.*

Then we see her skirting along the edge of the bombsite. She can see kids playing in the crater below her.

*We then cut down into the crater itself, where the kids are whooping and running, ambushing and chasing each other. **Lotte** is down there amongst them.*

She breaks into a run and charges across the crater, in an explosion of energy and freedom.

*We then see in a high shot **Lotte** crossing the length of the bombsite, running and shouting exuberantly, playing with the other kids.*

END OF CREDIT SEQUENCE

INT. DINING ROOM. CONNINGTON. DAY

Callum *is entering the dining room of the hotel when he stops in total surprise.*

The room is already hung with large Union Jacks and RAF banners. Moreover there is a cluster of smaller Union Jacks on the side, ready to be put on the tables.

Rachel *is standing in the middle of the room, and **Eva** is sitting on the edge of the stage. She calls over to **Callum**.*

EVA
You didn't realise this wedding was in fact a military parade did you?!

RACHEL
It is ridiculous isn't it . . . and this is only the start apparently!

CALLUM
It is ridiculous.

RACHEL
I'm going to see what I can do to change things by tomorrow, but I'm not that hopeful. It's your boss that has arranged all this –

CALLUM
Of course. They see the wedding as a chance for some good propaganda for them – to say we're still very much in the race to break the sound barrier. They want to make Dieter a bit famous . . .

EVA
Well all I can say is, the Soviets might even be shy about doing something like this!

CALLUM
That's true.

EVA
I thought it was going to be a nice small wedding . . . how's Anna going to manage with all this?!

Rachel *is watching him, his contained, preoccupied mood.*

RACHEL
Have you not been getting enough sleep? What's the matter with you, Callum?

CALLUM
I'm absolutely fine. It must be just all those speeches I had to listen to at Harold's do . . .

RACHEL
And what about your speech? You're a sort of best man aren't you? Or is somebody from the base doing it?

CALLUM
No, no, I'm the nearest thing to the best man . . . (*Smiles.*) And my contribution will surprise everybody.

INT. COUNTY HOSPITAL WARD/PASSAGE. AFTERNOON

Victor *is in his pyjamas and dressing gown standing in the middle of the ward.* **Callum** *is approaching down the passage.*

CALLUM

You've got out of bed . . .

VICTOR

That is allowed! I'm not chained to it you know. Anyway, I'm rehearsing for my interrogation – when I have to show them how normal I am . . . !

CALLUM
(smiles)
Well that's going to prove difficult. *(More serious.)* So you're really on the mend, Victor?

VICTOR

I am. And what about you?

CALLUM

What's that meant to mean?

VICTOR

You know perfectly well. You're going to behave yourself are you?

CALLUM

At the wedding? Of course!

VICTOR

So there are no schemes? No hatching of plots?

CALLUM

I will be the perfect guest . . .

We stay on **Victor**.

EXT. LONDON PARK. AFTERNOON

Kathy *and* **Mentz** *are walking in the London park along a broad promenade. They are both holding toffee apples.* **Kathy** *is eating hers,* **Mentz** *is not touching hers.*

*The **Minder** is walking a few paces behind. They are walking in silence.*

Kathy *suddenly turns to the **Minder**.*

KATHY
You can go. We don't need you. Thank you.

*The **Minder** looks very surprised.*

MINDER
Are you sure, Miss Griffiths?

KATHY
I'm perfectly sure. Will you leave the park please.

*She glances at **Mentz** who is looking very startled.*

We will be absolutely fine. The two of us together . . .

*The **Minder** begins to walk off, glancing behind her as she does so.*

Mentz *watches her go.*

MENTZ
She is not really leaving?

KATHY
Oh yes she is.

MENTZ
Then there are others you have?

She stares around at the people sitting on benches, or walking past them.

Some of these . . .?

KATHY
None of those, no. You're alone with me. There's nobody else to worry about. Eat your toffee apple.

MENTZ
Not now . . . maybe later . . .

KATHY
It's a rare treat at the moment, toffee . . . as I'm sure you know.

Children running past, looking at them.

Be a pity to waste it . . .

They move on. **Mentz** *is deeply unsettled. She keeps looking at people in the park, studying their faces. She stops suddenly and looks back along the path.*

KATHY

There's nobody there . . . I told you.

MENTZ

Yes . . .

They begin to move again. **Mentz** *can't stop looking at the people in the park.*

You say there's nobody working for you here . . . but I feel these people . . . some of them are looking at me.

KATHY

You think it's the toffee apple? Because it's so special? We can solve that . . .

She takes **Mentz***'s apple from her and holds it.*

But maybe it isn't that at all . . .

Mentz *keeps glancing at the people.*

You think they know what you did? Some of them are looking at you . . . because they know all the things you did . . .? Is that what you're wondering?

MENTZ

(very disconcerted)

I am not thinking anything like that . . . these people know nothing about either of us. Of course they don't, how could they?

KATHY

But you feel like they're looking at you all the same? You feel as if you're naked . . .?

Faces turning towards them.

Totally naked?

*Mentz is startled by **Kathy**'s sudden directness, her controlled hostility.*

MENTZ
It's not very easy to be amongst people . . . It's a shock . . . It's been a long time.

KATHY
We'll go where there'll probably be nobody then shall we?

She stops on the path. Three boys are watching them.

Kathy *holds up* **Mentz**'s *toffee apple.*

KATHY
Does anybody want this?

The boys come running up.

You'll have to work out how to share it won't you?!

EXT. BOMBED CHURCH. AFTERNOON

The bombed church. **Kathy** *and* **Mentz** *are sitting side by side in the ruined nave.*

MENTZ
Why did you bring me here?

KATHY
Because you don't want people staring at you.

MENTZ
You brought me here so you could say to me, 'You did this, your air force'?

KATHY
No, that is not the reason. We came here because it is peaceful.

MENTZ
We could have gone to a church that wasn't ruined . . . a normal church.

KATHY

We could . . . (*Suddenly her tone very direct.*) But what would you have done in a normal church, Birgit? . . . Light candles? . . . Ask to speak to God?

Mentz *staring at her, startled by her tone.*

That would be an interesting conversation wouldn't it? Do you think he really wants to hear from you, Birgit? You kneeling on a cushion, telling him all the things you've done? You listing things to God?

Mentz *staring at her.*

So maybe a normal church isn't such a good idea . . .

We hear the sound of birds flapping in the ruins.

MENTZ

It would be quiet there. Quieter than here, in a church with a roof.

They suddenly see a homeless man watching them from the shadows of the ruins. He is behind them. He runs off as they look at him, disappearing away from the church. **Mentz** *watches him go through the ruined windows.*

KATHY

Not one of ours, no! Just somebody with nowhere to sleep . . . Now we really are alone.

She is staring straight at **Mentz**, *who is increasingly unsettled by her look.*

Why don't you go?

Mentz *looks very surprised, confused.*

Go on – you're free to go. Go! There are no doors, nothing to stop you . . . this is not a trick . . .

Mentz *glances about her.*

Why wouldn't you go?

A momentary pause.

KATHY

Of course maybe the Russians will pick you up by the end of the day . . . or maybe it will be sooner . . . and perhaps we'll take bets on it back at the office.

Suddenly **Kathy** *is very close.*

You tortured friends of mine, and of course you saw them die. I have no interest in what happens to you now, none at all. You had your chance and you didn't take it. You pretended to think about giving evidence at the trial, to consider it . . . but you were never going to do it were you?!

So now you're on your own, Birgit, and you should go. I advise you to take this opportunity for all sorts of reasons . . . but especially because I will enjoy thinking about what the Russians will do to you when they get you.

Kathy *indicates the view through the ruined windows.*

Go on . . . there's the whole of London out there – surely there's somewhere you can go where they won't find you?

Mentz *follows her look.*

Why don't you put it to the test?

Kathy *gets up.*

You're going to have to anyway . . . because we're not going to protect you any more.

Mentz *stares out of the windows.*

I wonder how far you'll get . . .?

Mentz *looks back at* **Kathy**.

MENTZ

Don't go . . .

INT. THE STORE ROOM. DAY OF THE WEDDING. EARLY MORNING

The door of the hotel storeroom is opening and **Anna** *in her wedding dress enters the room, which has been prepared with three large full-length mirrors.* **Victor**'s *work, tidying all the objects, lies unfinished all around.*

Anna *is followed by* **Julia** *and two dressers.*

JULIA
We thought this was a good place . . . no chance of Dieter coming in here by mistake and seeing the dress.

ANNA
Yes, because that would mean a whole life of bad luck wouldn't it?!

She stares into the mirror at herself in her surprisingly lavish wedding dress.

Doesn't it look good?! It does look good doesn't it?

JULIA
Of course, it's amazing, Anna! You look like a film star preparing for the wedding of the year.

INT. SECOND-FLOOR PASSAGE. CONNINGTON. EARLY MORNING

We cut to **Julia** *moving along the second-floor passage. She sees the door of* **Callum**'s *bedroom fractionally ajar. She pushes it open.* **Callum** *is standing by his dressing table in his smart suit for the wedding, loading a pistol. He looks up as* **Julia** *appears and calmly continues loading the bullets.*

CALLUM
Hello, stranger . . .

JULIA
Hello, Callum.

She tries not to show how startled she is to see him with a gun.

I was just making sure the coast was clear, that there was no Dieter around . . . when Anna comes back to her room – so he doesn't see the dress.

CALLUM
Well he's not hiding in here.

He goes on loading the gun.

JULIA
You need to be armed for the wedding?

CALLUM
I'm always armed . . . didn't you know that?

JULIA
I didn't. You expect the Russians to jump out of the wedding cake and grab the groom do you . . . and whisk him off?!

CALLUM
It's not very likely, no . . . but I'm always prepared for anything, Julia.

He flicks the magazine of the gun.

JULIA
Right . . . (*She watches him.*) It's funny being back here. My career is not going too badly at the moment since you were kind enough to ask.

Callum *smiles at this.*

I'm going to play the Nurse in *Romeo and Juliet* – I'm going to make her an exceptionally young nurse!

Callum *puts the gun in his jacket.*

And your career, Callum?

CALLUM
What about it?

JULIA
You're going to leave the army very soon aren't you? How is everything working out for you?

CALLUM
I'm about to find out.

INT. LOTTE'S BEDROOM. MORNING

Lotte *is standing in her old bedroom, staring at herself in the mirror. She is dressed in her bridesmaid's clothes, a rich apricot-coloured dress with bows. Her appearance has a doll-like prettiness compared to the wildness and freedom when she was playing on the bombsite.*

Her face is gravely serious.

INT. PASSAGE/KLEINOW'S SUITE. DAY

Frau Bellinghausen *is walking with* **Callum** *down a short stretch of passage that leads to the* **Kleinow** *suite.*

> FRAU BELLINGHAUSEN
> (*lightly*)
> This is a dangerous development . . . me venturing down the passage with you. It's not necessary.

> CALLUM
> It is necessary.

> FRAU BELLINGHAUSEN
> I've already signed the papers, with a whole group of lawyers crammed into my room – why do we have to do the handover somewhere else?

> CALLUM
> Because it seemed the right thing to do.

He opens the door of the **Kleinow** *suite and ushers* **Frau Bellinghausen** *inside.*

She is greeted with the two rooms, the bedroom and its adjoining room, filled with flowers and other party decorations. In the sitting room there is a table laid out as if for a solo banquet, with fine china, candles and a large silver bowl of fruit.

> FRAU BELLINGHAUSEN
> My goodness, Callum, what have you done?!

> CALLUM
> I thought you shouldn't miss out on the wedding.

Harold mentioned you had a meal on the stairs listening to the music . . . so I thought I would go one better, and provide your own private banquet. Since you refuse to come down.

FRAU BELLINGHAUSEN
I have never met your German scientist, so how could I possibly come to his wedding?

CALLUM
Precisely . . . but now you can feast like the rest of us, be as greedy as you want and nobody will see!

FRAU BELLINGHAUSEN
I do not plan to be greedy, Callum, whether people can see or not. But thank you for the extremely generous gesture.

She glances around the bedroom and at the huge bed.

Have you used this room yourself for any reason?

CALLUM
(*hesitates, smiles*)
On occasions . . . why do you ask?

FRAU BELLINGHAUSEN
No reason. (*Gives him a knowing look, then smiles.*) I don't think I should pry further . . .

CALLUM
It was in fact being used by a top Nazi . . . the Secret Service had him holed up here, while he pretended to be dying.

FRAU BELLINGHAUSEN
Did they indeed?! I wish you hadn't told me that, now I will feel his presence all around . . . while I'm tucking in.

CALLUM
No you won't. I helped get him arrested. He is now in a prison cell in Germany, awaiting trial.

FRAU BELLINGHAUSEN
Good for you. (*With feeling.*) Making him pay for what he did.

She looks at him, takes out an envelope.

> So, Callum, here it is – the formula. What you've been waiting for! (*She turns the envelope in her hand.*) I never thought I'd agree to this . . . but they sent the right policeman.

She hands it to him.

> And so it's yours.

CALLUM

> Thanks.

Frau Bellinghausen *is startled by his obvious preoccupation; he doesn't even glance down at the envelope.*

FRAU BELLINGHAUSEN
Aren't you going to open it? See what the formula is?

CALLUM
I don't need to. This is not for me.

FRAU BELLINGHAUSEN
There are some surprises in our secret ingredients . . . completely unguessable, what really goes into our perfume . . .

CALLUM
I will study it later then, when I'm able to give it my full attention.

He moves to the door, then turns.

> Goodbye.

FRAU BELLINGHAUSEN
Goodbye? What do you mean 'goodbye'?

CALLUM
I meant au revoir, sorry.

FRAU BELLINGHAUSEN
You will come and see me during the meal?

CALLUM
Of course. I promise.

We stay on **Frau Bellinghausen** *after* **Callum** *leaves.*

INT. RAF CHAPEL. DAY

The wedding. The congregation is gathered in a large chapel decorated with RAF memorial banners and a great many flowers.

Harold *is sitting with* **Lucy**. *We see all the congregation through his eyes –* **Rachel** *sitting with* **Alex** *and* **Eva** *together,* **Rita** *and many of her colleagues from the base. They are all in their wedding finery.* **Wainwright** *is sitting near the front, flanked by several members of the RAF top brass.* **Ringwood** *is near the back with the* **Chubby Minder** *and other workers from the attic room.*

Harold *is looking for* **Callum**. *Then just as the organ music begins, filling the chapel with a burst of Bach,* **Callum** *slips in at the back. He stands for a moment then makes his way down the aisle.* **Harold** *looks straight at him, but* **Callum** *does not acknowledge him. Then* **Callum** *takes up his position as best man beneath the altar.*

INT. COUNTY HOSPITAL. CONSULTING ROOM. DAY

Victor *is entering a consulting room in the county hospital. He is in his pyjamas but wearing a dressing gown. There is a panel of three doctors facing him. A middle-aged* **Psychiatrist**, *a doctor of the same age and a third rather younger man.*

> VICTOR
>
> Hello gentlemen!

> PSYCHIATRIST
>
> Hello, Mr Ferguson. Please take a seat.

Victor *sits in front of them.*

> Now before we begin, I just want to explain –

> VICTOR
>
> But we began as I came through the door didn't we?! You were all watching to see how normal my entrance was . . . but that's okay – everything I do is being measured I realise on a thermometer . . . the bonkers thermometer, and I quite

understand. (*He grins.*) I rehearsed how to come into the room anyway . . .

> PSYCHIATRIST
>
> Well, Mr Ferguson, I'm glad you say you understand. We just have a few questions to start off with, covering both the state of your health and the state of your mind. And then you will be able to add anything that you feel is relevant.

> VICTOR
>
> Okay, I'm ready for all of it . . .

The **Psychiatrist** *looks down at his notes.*

But before you start, I just want to say – of course I've been through a very difficult phase, my moods have been very hard to predict I know, and often they've become quite extreme. But I feel now much more stable, much more normal. (*Smiles.*) And I will steal no more cars I promise, even though I seem to have a great facility for it.

I realise I still could be locked up for what I've done . . .

> PSYCHIATRIST
>
> Thank you, Mr Ferguson . . . that's very clear. We've made a good start.

INT. CHAPEL/COUNTY HOSPITAL. DAY

We begin intercutting between the consulting room and the chapel as the wedding service begins.

We see **Dieter** *enter the chapel, walking down the aisle, looking confident.*

Wainwright *gives him a warm smile.* **Dieter** *joins* **Callum** *beneath the altar, watched over by the vicar.*

We see **Harold**'s *head turn, and the organ music changes to a trumpet voluntary as* **Anna** *comes down the aisle in her splendid dress with a long train. She is escorted by eight bridesmaids, one of whom is* **Lotte**. *Accompanying her down the aisle is her father, a working-class man in his forties.* **Anna** *looks radiant.*

We cut back to the consulting room.

> PSYCHIATRIST
> And I understand you are sleeping much better, Mr Ferguson?

> VICTOR
> Indeed. I've had oceans of sleep recently, and very vivid dreams. (*He smiles.*) Some extremely sexual, amazingly realistic! . . . but then I'm not alone doing that am I?

The **Psychiatrist** *is making notes.*

We cut back to the vicar beginning the ceremony. **Callum** *standing with the couple, fingering the wedding ring he has to hand over.*

We move in on **Harold** *watching the bride, who is looking nervous but incredibly excited. He watches* **Callum** *and* **Dieter** *standing together.*

Lucy *notices how intensely* **Harold** *is watching.*

> LUCY
> Is everything alright?

> HAROLD
> Yes my dear . . . I always get emotional at weddings, and for some reason it gets worse . . .

He is watching **Callum** *closely, noticing his abstracted manner.*

We cut back to **Victor** *facing the doctors.*

> PSYCHIATRIST
> And now I just want to turn to another matter . . . (*He looks down at his notes.*) One moment, I seem to have mislaid a piece of paper –

> VICTOR
> Please ask about my brother.

The doctors all look up.

> My brother is the most important thing we need to talk about . . .

We cut back to the chapel as **Dieter** *and* **Anna** *are in the middle of their marriage vows.* **Callum** *hands over the ring.*

We cut back to **Victor** *in the consulting room.*

VICTOR
My brother has had the most extraordinary time serving this country . . . far more than me. He saw some of the worst fighting on D-Day, he then became an integral part of T-Force, grabbing important German scientists before anybody else could get them, and then befriending some of them, and making them work brilliantly for us! He has taken on the bungling idiots from the Secret Service and stopped them wrecking everything . . .

The doctors are staring at him.

I know my problems are not entirely due to the war, but Callum's are . . . He is fuelled – that's the right word! – he is fuelled like the jet planes he loves so much, by a tremendous desire to do the best for this country . . . but now he's like a missile himself. Because he has seen crimes ignored, crimes committed by these people, these ex-Nazis who are now our closest friends. He tried to reconcile these things . . . what's best for the country and for justice to be done . . . but it's breaking down now!

We cut to the wedding, the procession moving down the aisle as the organ music plays.

We cut back to **Victor**.

VICTOR
And you have to realise this . . . that it's reached a breaking point.

He looks up at them; they are staring at him blankly.

I have a talent for piecing things together . . . putting books in the right order . . . sorting out lost property . . . and I have pieced this together.

He stares pleadingly at them.

You have to listen!

INT. MAIN PASSAGE/DINING ROOM. CONNINGTON. DAY

We cut to the hotel, the passage just outside the main dining room. The guests are swirling around, about to enter the wedding banquet. **Dieter** *is standing in the doorway to the dining room, greeting the guests.* **Rachel** *spots* **Callum** *standing in a corner, staring at* **Dieter**. *She sees how focused* **Callum** *looks, completely detached from all the other guests. We see concern in her eyes. She moves up to him.*

RACHEL

That was a lovely service wasn't it?! It all went very smoothly.

CALLUM

It's not over yet . . .

He moves off. We stay on **Rachel**.

INT. MAIN GENTS CLOAKROOM AND LAVATORY. DAY

We cut to the gentlemen's cloakroom and lavatory, next to the dining room. An RAF officer is washing his hands. **Callum** *is standing at the other end of the basins; he calmly takes the gun out and spins the chamber. The RAF man glances at him, watching this idly, as if it was not unusual. The officer dries his hands and leaves.*

Callum *is alone. For a moment he stares at himself in the mirror.*

Alex *enters the cloakroom,* **Callum** *doesn't see him.*

ALEX

Are you alright?

CALLUM

Of course I'm alright. Are you alright?

ALEX

We'll see . . .

He moves over to the basin, starts washing his hands.

I know you don't think I'm an idiot.

CALLUM
(*surprised*)
I don't think you're an idiot, no, Alex.

ALEX
So of course I realise you and Rachel have become great friends – especially since I've been away.

CALLUM
We are great friends, yes.

ALEX
Great, great friends. You may wonder what I think of that? . . . Perhaps you don't wonder?

CALLUM
This is hardly the time, Alex –

ALEX
This isn't the time . . . no. But maybe we won't get another opportunity in a hurry.

Two guests enter and go through the cloakroom to the lavatory.

CALLUM
Don't be stupid, we can have a drink together next week.

ALEX
But you won't do that will you, Callum? (Moving closer.) I am going to say it anyway . . . (*For a second he stares at Callum.*) She was still in grief of course when I met her, her husband dying suddenly . . . I adored her . . . but we clearly had nothing in common – That was obvious to you I know . . .

CALLUM
Alex, this is a wedding –

A large man comes out of the lavatory and moves into the cloakroom to wash his hands. **Alex** *half lowers his voice.*

ALEX
I know it's a wedding, Callum! But I've got your attention now, which is something I rarely have nowadays. And I'm telling the truth aren't I?

CALLUM

About what?

The large man is drying his hands, clearly listening. He then nods at them and leaves.

ALEX

That it was obvious about me and Rachel . . . it was obvious to me anyway, that we were two people who should not be together. But . . . I didn't want her to leave so much, not yet, not just after a few months.

He stares straight at **Callum**.

I didn't want the shame of it – what people would say, especially after my cushy war in Washington, how it would look . . . What a terrible reason I know . . . (*His tone emotional.*) It is a terrible reason isn't it? (*Looking at* **Callum**.) But in a way understandable? We're not the only marriage like that . . .

CALLUM

Alex, I've got to get back in there . . .

ALEX

You see I so wanted her to be happy, so she'd stay. And she is happy spending time with you . . . I know she's never going to leave me for you, Callum . . . and goodness knows what will happen soon? – I mean we could be all blown to smithereens in a few months, if the Russians manage to get the Bomb, couldn't we?!

CALLUM

That is possible, yes.

Suddenly **Alex** *is very close, intense.*

ALEX

You're not planning on changing anything are you, Callum?

Callum *staring at him.*

I just want you to know, and please take notice of this, you don't need to. Because if she's happy, I'm happy, and so that makes three of us . . . doesn't it?

Callum *is staring at him with a hard stare.*

A group of men enter the cloakroom talking loudly.

CALLUM

Excuse me . . .

INT. THE BANQUET. THE DINING ROOM, DAY

Callum *moves into the dining room. The room now looks extraordinary, with its RAF banners, Union Jacks, and clusters of flowers and table arrangements which are clearly influenced by* **Rachel**. *There are many men in uniform and a few women too. Not just the RAF but also representatives from the Army and T-Force. There are also all the wives of the top brass, dressed as if at the most fashionable society wedding.*

We see **Callum** *stare at all the officers wearing their medals and ceremonial uniforms and* **Dieter** *at the high table with* **Anna**, *looking radiant. And* **Wainwright** *next to them, beaming proudly. We see there is a spare chair at the high table, but* **Callum** *moves over to a table at the edge of the room, where* **Ringwood** *is sitting with the* **Chubby Minder** *and other workers from the attic office.*

RINGWOOD

Sir? Aren't you meant to be on the high table, sir, with the bride and groom?

CALLUM

I'm just going to perch here a moment . . . (*Sharp smile.*) Prepare my speech.

We see **Callum** *watching* **Alex** *join* **Rachel** *on another table. They whisper to each other, and then* **Rachel** *looks straight in* **Callum**'s *direction.*

We cut to **Eva** *sitting at a table with some of her musicians, including the drummer* **Richie**, *and* **Julia**. **Eva** *stares around at all the top brass.*

                    EVA
It's like having a wedding at the Pentagon! I hope it's not all
over the papers tomorrow . . .

She looks around.

Have they got some reporters here? We ought to smell them
out oughtn't we?

We cut to **Dieter** *and* **Anna** *at the high table.* **Dieter** *looks relaxed talking to* **Wainwright** *and* **Anna**'s *parents.* **Callum** *is watching him.*

We cut to **Harold** *with* **Lucy** *at another table.* **Harold** *has a little parcel with him.*

                    HAROLD
I brought this as a wedding gift, Lucy, it is very old, from the
late eighteenth century, an edition of German fairy stories.

                    LUCY
I'm sure he will love that . . . both of them will.

But she sees **Harold** *is not listening; he is looking over in* **Callum**'s *direction, who avoids meeting his gaze.*

We cut back to **Harold***; we see the emotion in his eyes as* **Callum** *ignores him.*

                    HAROLD
Excuse me my dear . . . I will be back shortly.

INT. KLEINOW SUITE. DAY

We cut to **Frau Bellinghausen** *eating on her own in the* **Kleinow** *suite. There is a knock on the door in the far room. The waiter, who is in attendance, opens the door to the bedroom;* **Harold** *is standing there. He moves towards* **Frau Bellinghausen** *in the sitting room.*

                    HAROLD
Ah, there you are.

                FRAU BELLINGHAUSEN
Mr Lindsay-Jones!

HAROLD
It took a little detective work to find you . . . I hope you don't mind me intruding?

FRAU BELLINGHAUSEN
Not at all! I feel distinctly foolish having a banquet all on my own. Please come and share some of this with me.

HAROLD
No, no, I've not come to take your food –

FRAU BELLINGHAUSEN
Well at least – (*She lifts bottle of wine.*) you must have some of this. Now you are here I can drink something – one can't really drink happily on one's own.

She starts pouring two glasses, waving the waiter away.

But I don't want you to miss any of the banquet.

HAROLD
I won't miss anything, and they won't miss me.

He sits with her, drinking.

FRAU BELLINGHAUSEN
Why do you say that? Who won't miss you? The policeman?

HAROLD
Yes. I have disappointed him.

FRAU BELLINGHAUSEN
I'm sure that's not possible.

HAROLD
Yes. I have disappointed him deeply. Downstairs he would hardly look at me . . . It makes one feel like a rejected parent, which is absurd of course, because I'm nothing like a father to him . . . But I'm not ashamed to say I have grown extremely fond of him.

FRAU BELLINGHAUSEN
Me too, I have to admit.

HAROLD
And his brother as well of course. They have brought such life, such colour into my house, into this place . . .

FRAU BELLINGHAUSEN
And didn't we need it!

HAROLD
Yes . . . ! And I wanted so much to live up to expectations . . . I owed it not just to Callum, but to the memory of my family.

Why is not possible to be as brave as one wants to be . . . at the moment you most need it?

FRAU BELLINGHAUSEN
It's funny you should say that . . . I've asked myself that so much recently. Could I have been braver? Could I have been stronger?

HAROLD
I'm sorry, I am very successfully ruining your meal!

FRAU BELLINGHAUSEN
You are doing no such thing.

INT. WEDDING BANQUET. DAY

We cut to **Rita** *moving on to the stage, which is flanked by RAF banners and Union Jacks. The guests are finishing their main course. She taps the microphone.*

RITA
So this is an early warning . . .

The conversation dips.

Very soon the dessert will be served, and we will be beginning the speeches quite quickly after that. So for those of you that are coming up here, your ordeal is not far off now.

She looks at **Callum**, *sitting on his distant table.*

I hope everybody is aware of their duties . . .

INT. KLEINOW SUITE. DAY

Frau Bellinghausen *and* **Harold** *together at the table in the suite. There is another bottle open now, and both of them are holding their glasses and drinking.*

FRAU BELLINGHAUSEN

I know whatever you did or didn't do, it can never be as serious as what I did or didn't do. I did nothing, Harold.

She looks at him.

When people were disappearing, people who had worked for us for years . . . suddenly they were taken away. My husband had been dead for some time by then, I was head of the family business, a woman of consequence . . . a big local employer, living in a house which of course always smelt beautiful.

HAROLD

I can imagine.

FRAU BELLINGHAUSEN

I hated the regime . . . but like so many others I turned away, I drew the curtains in my house . . . I told myself I was a foreigner, I couldn't criticise somebody else's country. These horrors one hears about, they must be exaggerated! And it's just a phase that will pass surely . . . How can I make a difference anyway? . . . Of course so many other people were saying exactly the same thing.

Her eyes are shining.

I looked away . . . (*Suddenly with vehemence.*) I will never look away again . . . It must be strange hearing me say this when I've been hiding away from the world in my hotel room . . . but I will never let myself look away again, Harold.

HAROLD

That I can believe. (*He clinks her glass.*)

INT. THE BANQUET. THE DINING ROOM. DAY

We cut to **Callum**, *his eyes sharp, intense, staring at the high table. And then we cut to* **Rachel**: *we see her point of view of* **Callum**, *and then she follows* **Callum**'s *stare towards* **Dieter**.

Then she sees **Callum** *suddenly get up and leave the room.*

We are close on **Rachel**. *She gets up and follows him.*

INT. GROUND-FLOOR PASSAGE/ANTE ROOM CONNINGTON. DAY

We cut to **Rachel** *moving down the passage next to the dining room,* **Callum** *is standing in the shadows at the far end, with his back to her.*

RACHEL
Callum! (*He turns.*) Where are you going?

CALLUM
Where am I going? I'm getting ready – (*Their eyes meet.*) for my speech.

RACHEL
Right. I just wanted a moment to –

CALLUM
To see if your message had worked?

RACHEL
My message?

Waiters are passing them with trays and trolleys.

CALLUM
Come here . . .

He takes her by the arm and pulls her into an adjoining room full of stacked chairs.

CALLUM
Did you send Alex to see me? To give me that message?

RACHEL
What are you talking about? What message?

CALLUM
Asking me not to disrupt the convenient arrangement that makes everybody happy? That you both are so relaxed about?!

RACHEL
You think I'm mad? I wouldn't send Alex with a message like that . . . I wouldn't send him with any kind of message! You really think that's something I would do?

CALLUM
I don't know . . . I think it's more than possible though . . . It's a sort of rich person's game isn't it, having a marriage where everything is so completely open –

RACHEL
Don't you dare talk like that! (*Truly furious.*) Don't you dare try to reduce what we've had to that . . . what we've felt for each other! What I've felt for you . . . (*She stares at him.*) What's happened, Callum? Why on earth do you think you can talk to me like that?

Their eyes meet.

CALLUM
Because you sent Alex to give me that message.

INT. DINING ROOM. THE BANQUET. DAY

We cut back to the banquet. **Rita** *is moving on to the stage.*

She stands in front of the microphone.

RITA
So attention, everybody!

The noise begins to reduce.

Yes, we have got to the moment I warned you about . . .

> Blimey! (*She stares out.*) That's a terrifying sight! All these senior officers staring at me . . . I am being almost blinded up here by all those medals . . .
>
> Now before we reach the really important business, let's get the purely trivial out of the way which is of course, 'What is our current progress on the famous engine?!'

She stops. The top brass are staring at her with frozen looks.

> Sorry, I was joking! The latest news is, I'm delighted to say, it will just take a couple more weeks of Dieter's work, his brilliant work, after he's had a few days' honeymoon of course! And then we will be ready to show it to you again . . . and this time we will be triumphant!

Loud applause.

> Now to the serious business, and the best man's speech . . . so Callum can you come up here? Callum?

Everybody peering to see where **Callum** *is.*

INT. ADJOINNG ROOM/INTERCUT WITH BANQUET. DAY

We cut back to **Rachel** *and* **Callum** *among all the stacked chairs.*

Rachel *is staring straight at him.*

RACHEL
Callum, you're not planning something are you?

CALLUM
Like what? I was of course trying to plan my speech until I was interrupted.

RACHEL
I know how close you are to your brother, of course I do! And I know how angry you are about what happened – and how you want to do something about it . . .

Callum *is just staring at her.*

I care about you, Callum, I really care. I don't want you to do anything that will –

CALLUM
You think I'd be crazy enough to do something during a wedding banquet?! What on earth would that be anyway?

RACHEL
I don't know . . . I just think you want to do something that will hurt them.

CALLUM
There are lots of ways of doing that –

RACHEL
So you *are* planning on doing something?

CALLUM
I didn't say that.

He tries to go. **Rachel** *catches hold of his arm.*

RACHEL
Callum, please . . . I promise you I didn't involve Alex. I just want you to listen for one more second . . . These last few months, our time together, I have been so happy –

CALLUM
Alex's words exactly.

RACHEL
I don't care what he said to you?! . . . *This is me speaking . . . me here* . . . and I want you to listen to me.

CALLUM
So? I'm listening . . .

He is staring at her, his eyes hard, his tone very sharp.

RACHEL
Right –

CALLUM
What do you want to say? I'm late –

RACHEL

Callum, when we are together . . .

She pauses for a moment.

CALLUM

When we are together, what?!

RACHEL

Stop hurrying me for Christ's sake! . . . *I'm going to say this* . . . when we are together . . . it all seems, the future seems so much less frightening. For me anyway.

She looks straight at him.

And for you too I think . . .

Callum *staring back at her impassively.*

CALLUM

So don't do *anything* to mess that up? Is that what you want to say?

We cut back to **Rita** *at the microphone.*

RITA

Well since nobody seems to know where the best man is . . . I can't believe he's flunked it by the way, Callum never flunks anything . . . but we must move on! So, Dieter, we will come straight to you.

We cut back to **Rachel** *and* **Callum**.

RACHEL

Please let's find a moment after the meal, I don't want to keep trying to say things in such a rush . . . let's go somewhere quiet and –

CALLUM

Of course. (*Impassive.*) When have I ever refused that? Now, they are going to be sending out search parties for me . . .

He leaves.

We cut back to the banquet. **Dieter** *is at the microphone staring out at all the top brass.*

DIETER
So facing all of you now . . . which is certainly a truly impressive sight! And seeing my beautiful wife sitting there, and my daughter looking such a tremendous young lady . . . It is hard to believe when we first arrived here, how frightened we were . . . and what a difference one helping of specially cooked cabbage made!

So I would first like to tell you the story of that cabbage . . .

Callum *is entering the dining room from a side door.*

CALLUM
I'm here, very late for my cue, but I've made it back!

DIETER
Ah, the best man . . . I knew he wouldn't let us down!

Harold *is re-entering at the back just in time to see* **Callum** *join* **Dieter** *on stage.*

DIETER
So I will give way now, and resume later.

CALLUM
No, no, you don't need to leave . . . We will do a duet.

Staring at the top brass; **Wainwright** *watching him.*

It is only fitting . . . it has been a partnership after all hasn't it?! This far anyway . . .

We see **Rachel** *re-enter the dining room.*

DIETER
Indeed, a partnership. (*Next to* **Callum**.) Putting the past behind us and looking into the future . . . (*Smiles, loud.*) And being ready for whatever the Russians have in store for us!

CALLUM
Absolutely . . .

He stares out; **Rachel** *watching.*

> Let us not let the past get in the way . . . what use would that be?

Harold *is staring at him from the back of the room.* **Callum** *pauses as if he is about to say something different. The audience wait. A close-up of* **Rachel**.

> How counterproductive that would be . . . if we let what happened . . . haunt all our actions.

He puts his hand inside his jacket. We see **Harold** *watching.*

EVA
(*whispering to Julia*)
Do you think he means that?

JULIA
I'm the actress . . . and I can tell you he's acting . . . better than me of course, but he's acting.

EVA
(*watching* **Callum**)
Time he realised his job is over . . . he was told to make Dieter one of us, and he has!

Callum's *hand is inside his jacket. There is a pause. Everybody is watching him.*

CALLUM
Yes.

Producing a piece of paper out of his jacket. A close-up of **Rachel**.

> I have managed to find my speech! . . . (*He smiles.*) And I was also going to start with the cabbage . . .

INT. KLEINOW SUITE. AFTERNOON

We cut to **Frau Bellinghausen** *sitting in the* **Kleinow** *suite, alone with the waiter who is pouring her a glass of champagne.*

FRAU BELLINGHAUSEN
Thank you. Thank you very much. But I have decided, I must never be alone at a banquet again. A feast for one person . . . It makes me feel very strange.

INT. COUNTY HOSPITAL. PASSAGE/CONSULTING ROOM. AFTERNOON

We see **Victor**, *sitting in his dressing gown and slippers, in the passage outside the consulting room. Next to him is the ward matron. It is now very late afternoon. The door opens: the* **Psychiatrist** *is standing there; behind him the other two men are smoking and drinking tea. The* **Psychiatrist** *calls out to the matron.*

PSYCHIATRIST
Can you come in here for a moment?

The matron gets up.

VICTOR
What's the verdict then? . . . How normal am I?

PSYCHIATRIST
(*sharply*)
We'll be ready for you in a moment, Mr Ferguson.

VICTOR
You ought to know by now oughtn't you? Blimey! You've had a long enough lunch break . . . !

The **Psychiatrist** *turns.*

Making a day trip of it are you? The government must be paying you mustn't they . . . And told you to be very thorough? Is that how big a nuisance they consider me?

PSYCHIATRIST
Mr Ferguson, we will discuss our findings with you shortly.

VICTOR
Your findings? That sounds ominous . . . And what about the other matter, my brother? You should get somebody sent to him now – in the morning at the very latest . . .

PSYCHIATRIST
One matter at a time, Mr Ferguson . . . it is you that we are interested in today.

The **Psychiatrist** *closes the door. We move in on* **Victor**; *he realises what their findings will be. He gets up sharply, and then notices some doctors' overcoats hanging on hooks outside the consulting room. He moves up to them, watching the nurses pass him in the passage.*

As soon as the passage is momentarily empty, he quickly takes one of the overcoats and puts it on. He also grabs a hat. He then moves off along the passage, the hat tilted down; he is looking straight ahead.

EXT. COUNTY HOSPITAL. AFTERNOON

We cut to **Victor** *striding down the short drive of the county hospital. The coat doesn't completely cover his pyjama trousers, and he still has a bandage over his neck wound. But he is close now to the gates. A couple of nurses are walking past him, and immediately turn to have a second look.* **Victor** *begins to run; he sprints down the rest of the drive towards the main road.*

EXT. COUNTRY ROADS. AFTERNOON

We cut to **Victor** *running fast along a country road. He sees a car approaching; he tries desperately to flag it down, but it roars past. He keeps running. A second car appears; he moves further out into the road to make it stop, but it swerves round him, sounding its horn, and drives on.*

Victor *continues running, looking over his shoulder all the time to see if there is any sign of pursuers from the hospital. A truck is now approaching. He decides to stand right in the middle of the road this time, directly in its path, holding up his hand. The truck thunders towards him. But then it begins to slow, pulling up a few yards short of him.* **Victor** *approaches, waving politely.*

VICTOR
Thank you so much for stopping, very considerate. (*He climbs into the cab.*) I need to get to the middle of London in rather a hurry . . . They won't listen to me!

INT. WAR CRIMES UNIT. EARLY EVENING

Kathy *and* **Miss Clarkson** *are at one end of the office,* **Mentz** *is at the other. She is in her green coat, and holding a suitcase. Her* **Minder** *is in the doorway.*

KATHY

Have you got everything?

MENTZ

I have everything, yes, I think.

MISS CLARKSON

You are ready for the journey then?

MENTZ

I am. (*Suddenly looking straight at her.*) Are you coming too?

MISS CLARKSON

Yes, I am.

There is silence, **Mentz** *staring at them.*

KATHY

Why don't you go and wait for the car downstairs . . . (*She indicates to the* **Minder**.) We'll be with you in a moment.

The **Minder** *leads* **Mentz** *down the passage; they watch her go.*

MISS CLARKSON

I don't know how you did it, Kathy?!

KATHY

Don't speak too soon, she may change her mind . . .

Miss Clarkson *watches them disappear round the corner of the passage.*

MISS CLARKSON

I wonder what she thinks about at night? Does she see the faces of some of the people she tortured do you think?

KATHY

I'm sure she doesn't. I doubt she has any imagination at all . . . or memories really.

MISS CLARKSON
To be without memories . . . how is that possible?

EXT. STREET OUTSIDE WAR CRIMES UNIT/CAR. EVENING

We cut to **Kathy**, **Mentz** *and* **Miss Clarkson** *getting into a large black car outside the War Crimes Unit.* **Mentz** *sits between them on the back seat. The driver is a military policeman, the* **Minder** *sits in the front.*

Kathy *looks at* **Mentz** *as the car starts.* **Mentz** *meets her look.*

MENTZ
Don't worry . . . I'm not going to try to jump out of the car.

As the car moves off, **Kathy** *can't stop staring at* **Mentz**'*s pale face.*

KATHY
There's a radio . . . maybe we should have some music.

The radio crackles into life.

INT. BASEMENT BALLROOM NIGHT

We cut from the sound of a waltz coming out of the car radio, to the full blast of **Eva**'*s band playing in the basement ballroom. It is the party after the wedding. We are on* **Callum** *standing in the doorway staring at the packed dance floor. Many of the wedding guests are dancing, including senior RAF officers and their wives.* **Wainwright** *is having a drink in a corner, looking on with satisfaction.*

We move closer on **Callum**, *as he watches the top brass dancing.*

Harold *is sitting with* **Lucy**; *he is watching* **Callum** *who still does not acknowledge him.*

Dieter *is suddenly by* **Callum**'*s side; he smiles at* **Callum**.

DIETER
This music . . . It was what brought us together wasn't it really? It was the music?

CALLUM
It was. Yes. Partly.

DIETER

I want to thank you so very much for being here and doing the speech. I know it was difficult. The circumstances were not ideal. We have a lot still to talk about, I am not forgetting that . . .

Callum *looks at him but says nothing.*

Harold *is watching them both from across the room.*

But I want you to know that I'm truly grateful.

He smiles at **Callum** *with genuine warmth.*

EVA
(*calling to* **Callum**)

We should get you to play soon . . . now we know what you can do! He is not at all bad! We're going to get you up here, Callum.

Callum *moves away, walking among the dancers. We are very close on his eyes.*

We cut to **Harold** *and* **Lucy**.

HAROLD

I'm going to miss this place . . . It's the last time I will ever be here.

LUCY
(*startled*)

Why do you say that? You love coming here!

Harold *sees* **Lucy**'s *concerned expression, anxious about his darkness, sadness.*

HAROLD

I think it's being sold, because the Army and Secret Service are stopping using it . . . Somebody will probably knock it down. I won't be here again anyway.

Lucy *watching him.*

You must go and dance, Lucy! Come on . . . (*She hesitates.*) I will be alright.

Just after she has moved off, **Dieter** *appears by* **Harold**'s *side. He is holding the wedding gift.*

DIETER
I must thank you so much for this wonderful book, so generous . . . these beautiful old fairy stories.

HAROLD
I'm so glad you like it.

DIETER
It must be priceless.

HAROLD
Not priceless exactly, but valuable! I have a second volume like that at home, I couldn't decide which one to give you.

DIETER
You chose the right one. Thank you.

HAROLD
(*suddenly*)
Callum? . . . I was just wondering . . . is he alright?

DIETER
Absolutely.

He is about to move on.

HAROLD
Nothing has happened between the two of you?

Dieter *turns.*

A difference of a opinion? It's not about the work? (*He gives him a penetrating look.*) Or anything else . . .?

DIETER
No . . . I can assure you, there's nothing.

Balloons are suddenly pouring down from the ceiling on to the dance floor.

There are exuberant shouts. **Dieter** *claps delightedly.*

EXT. RUINED CHURCH. NIGHT

We cut to **Victor** *running across some waste ground towards the ruined church. He is still in the coat and pyjamas. He is glancing over his shoulder, scouring the night city, to see if anybody is following him. There doesn't seem to be anyone.*

He arrives at the ruined church, where three or four people are sleeping rough, including the man we saw in Part Three. **Victor** *calls out to him across the ruined nave.*

VICTOR

Hello, Pete, still keeping this place warm I see.

PETE

I knew you'd be back!

VICTOR

Well it's the only place they won't think of looking for me . . . I can't go back to the hotel, they'll be waiting for me! I can't get to anybody till the morning, because they'll all be there . . .

He sits next to **Pete**.

I only have a few hours to do anything . . . and then it will be too late.

INT. BASEMENT BALLROOM. NIGHT

We cut to everybody on the dance floor, standing poised, waiting for the music. **Lotte** *is by the jukebox; she presses one of the buttons. We cut to a high shot of the guests dancing, the floor covered in balloons.* **Eva** *is at a corner table arguing very loudly with* **Alex**. **Dieter** *is dancing with* **Anna**. *We move in on* **Callum**.

Rachel *is suddenly by his side. We hear* **Eva***'s voice punching through the music.*

EVA
(*indicating* **Alex**)
This man is completely wrong about absolutely *everything* . . .

he thinks he can make the world safer if we all have a nuclear bomb! None of us should have the Bomb do you hear?! *None of us*! Not one single fucking country!

RACHEL
(*to* **Callum**)
They are arguing about the future of the world.

CALLUM
So I can see . . .

We cut back to **Eva** *and* **Alex**.

ALEX
It's not as simple as that. The Russians are very dangerous —

EVA
And if we say we're going to bomb them they become less dangerous?! . . . That's crazy! I'm telling you . . . we're either going to blow ourselves up . . . or we get rid of the Bomb completely. There's nothing in between!

We cut back to **Rachel** *and* **Callum**.

RACHEL
A world free of *the Bomb*!

CALLUM
It's not going to happen.

RACHEL
Not just after we've invented it, no! But you never know . . .

She smiles; she is full of drink, but not drunk.

Talking about the future . . .

CALLUM
Yes?

Momentary pause, the music playing. She looks at him.

RACHEL
I want to spend the rest of my life with you.

CALLUM

What?

RACHEL
(*laughs*)
You're not going to make me repeat it are you?! Whatever's going to happen . . . whether we're all going to blow ourselves up . . . or have to fight the Russians quite soon, or even in the morning . . . or maybe we manage to avoid doing any of those things . . . Whatever it is, I want to be with you when it happens.

CALLUM
I don't even know what I'm going to be doing next week, Rachel, let alone –

RACHEL
The rest of your life, no! (*She is close, warm.*) But I want you to know – I think we should do that. Can't put it more simply than that.

We stay on **Callum**. *He stares at her. His manner is very detached.*

INT./EXT. ROADSIDE CAFÉ. NIGHT

We cut to the night café near the port; travellers with luggage eating and drinking. **Mentz** *is sitting at the table near the window staring into a milky cup of tea, watched by* **Kathy**, **Miss Clarkson** *and the* **Minder**. *Trucks and cars are moving in the car park, their headlights stabbing towards them.* **Mentz** *turns to look.*

KATHY
That's not them yet . . .

Mentz *takes a sip of tea.*

I thought doing it here was better than doing it at the port . . . a little more private.

MENTZ
Thank you for thinking of that.

KATHY
We were here with him you know, in this very café . . . here with Kleinow.

MENTZ
Were you? (*She looks straight at* **Kathy**.) I have decided to do this, I will give evidence at the trial, you don't have to worry yourself.

Kathy *nods.*

I just need to go now . . .

She indicates the lavatories. The **Minder** *stands to accompany her.*

KATHY
No that's fine . . .

The **Minder** *looks startled.* **Kathy** *to* **Mentz**:

You can go . . . on your own.

MENTZ
I can go? Thank you. (*She moves across the café.*)

KATHY
We've got to show we trust her.

MISS CLARKSON
Captain Ferguson? . . . What he would have done?

KATHY
Not sure he would have taken this risk! . . . But we couldn't have done it without him. (*Close on her.*)

Victor was worried about him . . . I must find out why.

MISS CLARKSON
Here they are . . .

Three military jeeps are driving into the car park, containing the armed escort for **Mentz**. **Kathy** *suddenly looks towards the lavatories realising* **Mentz** *has not come back. The* **Minder** *immediately jumps up and moves fast across the café.*

*We are on **Kathy**: now she is alarmed; she looks around the other tables.*

*The **Minder** comes out of the lavatories, shaking her head.*

***Kathy** rushes out into the car park.*

EXT. CAR PARK. NIGHT

***Kathy** is staring around her, at the military police, at families getting into a coach.*

*Then she sees **Mentz** standing at the other end of the car park.*

*A huge low loader is moving behind her with armoured trucks on it. It totally dwarfs **Mentz**, a young woman in a green coat looking very scared. The military police converge on her and move her across to the jeeps.*

*The **Minder** is running towards her to give her the suitcase.*

>MISS CLARKSON
>
>We've done it . . . !

***Kathy** nods. She watches **Mentz** being driven away.*

INT. BASEMENT BALLROOM. NIGHT

*The ballroom is now entirely empty except for **Callum** and **Eva**. **Callum** is at the piano, playing a few phrases. The floor is covered in balloons and party litter.*

>EVA
>
>You don't know whether to do it?

***Callum** looks up very sharply.*

>CALLUM
>
>What?

>EVA
>
>Whatever you're thinking about . . . You don't know whether to do it.

>CALLUM
>
>You can't *always* tell what I'm thinking.

EVA

Can't I . . .?! (*She smiles.*) When have I ever been wrong?

CALLUM

I'm sure there have been times. Anyway you're wrong tonight, because I have decided.

EVA

Right . . . is that good?

CALLUM

Yes . . . (*We move in on him.*)

EVA

I'm going to try to go back to the US . . . see if they'll have me . . . Maybe they won't let me back! It's not going to be easy, I don't know how much work I'll get . . . I had dreams once of having my own radio show, Callum, and the other night I thought why the hell should I give up on all that?! . . . I ought to have the courage to give it a go . . .

CALLUM

You must, Eva, yes.

EVA

You're right, I must. I had all sorts of dreams when I was little, I didn't realise what the world was like then . . . How many people there are out there who want to stop you, how difficult it is to make them think differently about anything, even the most obvious things, like being allowed to sit in the same restaurant with them. But you know, there's no reason that we in our tiny ways, our really tiny ways, can't try to change one bit of it! What do you think?

CALLUM

That sounds like a good idea, Eva.

EVA

Because both of us have a lot of energy to spare don't we, you and me. Why shouldn't we use it? Make some people angry with it?!

CALLUM

I think you should.

EVA

And what about you? Now you are no longer a soldier, what will you do?

CALLUM

Who knows . . . we'll see.

EVA

You've got a knack for making people do things you know, Callum, you should use it. I hope *that's* what you've decided to do . . . what you're not telling me . . .

Callum *looks up from the piano but does not answer her.*

Well I'm going to miss this place . . . I never thought I'd ever say that! And I'm going to miss you too I expect.

CALLUM
(*quiet*)

I'll miss you.

Eva *watches him at the piano for a moment.*

EVA

You ought to do something with your music too you know . . .

INT. HAROLD'S BEDROOM. EARLY MORNING

Early morning light, a close-up of **Harold** *in bed. His eyes open, the sound of church bells in the distance. We move even closer, we see the darkness and intensity in his eyes.*

EXT. RUINED CHURCH. DAY

We cut to the ruined church. In the distance we can hear the same bells. **Victor** *wakes with a start. For a moment he is disorientated. The other rough sleepers are still asleep.*

VICTOR

It's morning! I'm late!

He sits up. Suddenly he sees across the nave, sitting watching him is **Salter**. *Immediately there is fear in* **Victor**'*s eyes.*

He stands up. **Salter** *is staring at him.*

> SALTER
> Don't worry yourself... I'm banished! There's nothing I can do to you and your brother now... I'm going somewhere horrible and very remote... I'm being sent into exile, Victor.

Now he gets up and moves towards **Victor**.

> I just wanted to show you, I could still find you... still capable of that −

> VICTOR
> I'm impressed... (*Watching him very carefully.*)

> SALTER
> So you'd remember me...

Victor *begins to move, to try to get out of the church.*

> I'm surprised your brother hasn't come after me...?!

> VICTOR
> That's because you're not important enough...

He is near the exit; he turns and calls back.

> He wants to hit them where it'll hurt much more...

We cut to **Salter**, *watching* **Victor** *running away across the waste ground.*

INT. CALLUM'S BEDROOM. THE HOTEL. EARLY MORNING

A high shot of **Callum** *lying in bed, his eyes wide open. There is a knock on the door.*

> CALLUM
> Who is it?

The knocking is insistent. He pulls his jacket over his bare chest and goes to the door.

> Who the hell is it?

A voice says 'Room Service'.

I didn't order any room service, and don't you know what time it is?!

He opens the door. **Kathy** *is standing there.*

KATHY
I do know what time it is, yes. It's 6.45. I'm sorry about the subterfuge, I just wanted you to open the door.

CALLUM
I didn't get to bed till four in the morning. (*Sharply.*) But I need to be up now anyway as it happens . . . What do you want?

KATHY
Birgit Mentz has just gone back to Germany. She has agreed to give evidence at the trial. I wanted to tell you that and to thank you for your help.

CALLUM
And you needed to do that first thing in the morning?

KATHY
Yes, I was excited! She will get a lower sentence of course, but what he did was much, much worse, so many people died because of him – and now he can't be slipped back into our Secret Service! And what's more it'll help make sure we don't use torture. It's a real achievement I think, Callum, for both of us.

CALLUM
Right . . . (*He turns.*) Somewhere here . . . I have one orange. I have been saving it for just such a moment . . . you must have some. (*He finds the orange.*) It's not very fresh, but –

KATHY
Still worth its weight in gold?! Can't think of a better way of celebrating!

Callum *begins to peel the orange.*

I followed your instructions . . . and they worked. Naturally.

CALLUM

Did they . . .? You know what I'm beginning to think . . .? I've been wrong about everything.

He hands her some orange.

KATHY

You're never wrong, Callum, remember?!

Callum's *tone matter of fact, but his eyes very serious.*

CALLUM

That is true of course . . . but I was wrong about not going after these people until we had seen off the Russians. That was a very bad decision.

You were right, those that are guilty of these crimes . . . we should be pursuing them to the ends of the earth.

KATHY

Well we got one of them! And I assure you I'm not stopping now. We got Kleinow, Callum!

CALLUM

And Dieter got married. (*Quiet.*) Victor found more evidence about him you know . . .

KATHY

Did he? About Dieter? (*Watching him, seeing his tension.*) But we were never going to be able to do anything about him, in the end he was too important to people. There will always be those who are untouchable, terrible though that is . . . But it doesn't take away from our victory.

CALLUM

No . . .

KATHY

It really doesn't, Callum!

He doesn't look at her.

Was the wedding difficult?

CALLUM

No, as it happens . . . (*Not looking at her.*) I sailed through it. Resisted disrupting it in any way.

KATHY

And where are the happy couple now?

CALLUM

They are about to leave the hotel and go off on their honeymoon . . .

He looks straight at her.

Don't expect I'll ever set eyes on them again . . .

EXT./INT. HAROLD'S HOUSE/HALL. EARLY MORNING

Victor *is rushing across the road towards* **Harold**'s *house. He rings the doorbell frantically, looking over his shoulder between rings.*

Lucy *opens the door; she is in an elegant coat and hat.*

LUCY

Victor?! (*Looking at his coat and pyjamas.*) Are you alright? Shouldn't you be in hospital, Victor?!

VICTOR

I need to see Mr Lindsay-Jones urgently!

Harold *and* **Miss Gorton** *are now in the hall,* **Victor** *moves towards them.*

HAROLD

Victor?! This is a very early time to call? Fortunately we're all up, because Lucy is going on holiday.

VICTOR

I have something extremely important to tell you, Mr Lindsay-Jones . . .

HAROLD

Just one moment, Victor!

A taxi is drawing up outside.

There it is my dear . . . have a terrific time.

Lucy *kisses him. Then she moves to go.*

Lucy . . .

His voice more intense. She turns in the doorway, the light behind her.

What a marvellous young woman you look this morning.

She looks back at him and smiles.

INT. HAROLD'S LIBRARY. EARLY MORNING

Harold *is facing* **Victor** *in the library with the coloured glass catching the light.*

HAROLD
So, Victor, you've escaped from hospital again I see.

VICTOR
I have . . . it's something I've got very good at. But the brain doctors weren't listening to me . . . (*His tone intense.*) Harold, you're the only person who can help now!

HAROLD
Help in what way, Victor?

VICTOR
My brother is going to try to do something and I need you to stop him, because I don't think I can.

HAROLD
What do I have to stop him doing?

VICTOR
You're not going to believe me . . . because I'm standing here in pyjamas looking ridiculous – but you've got to listen . . . I'm not crazy, Harold, and certainly not about this . . . I found some files that prove Dieter was involved in war crimes . . . the execution of workers –

HAROLD

He was, was he?

We are close on **Harold**.

So that's why he got married . . . (*He moves.*) I saw Callum and him together last night, I thought something was going on, something was wrong –

VICTOR

Harold . . .

He pauses, momentarily.

Callum is going to assassinate him.

HAROLD

Victor . . . (*We move close on him.*)

VICTOR

I told you you wouldn't believe me! He is going to do it . . . and then use his trial as some big, hopeless gesture, which of course will fail . . . trying to tell the world, and –

HAROLD

Victor!

Victor *stops.*

Even if it was true . . . (*Pause, we are close on him.*) And I'm willing to believe it just might be true . . . how could I possibly do anything?

VICTOR

You can. Because you're the only person of authority Callum respects.

HAROLD

Not any more. I can assure you of that.

VICTOR

You've got to do something, Harold! (*He starts to pace.*) It's only you that can –

We are close on **Harold**.

> HAROLD
> Stopping Callum doing anything is not easy, let alone –

> VICTOR
> PLEASE! I know you want to help him . . . because you care about him. (*Looks straight at him.*) We both care about him so much.

INT. HOTEL. GROUND-FLOOR PASSAGE. DAY

We cut to **Dieter**, **Anna** *and* **Lotte** *walking along the ground-floor passage of the hotel.* **Dieter** *is in a fine new overcoat and hat and carrying an umbrella.*

We cut close to **Lotte**. *She suddenly senses something and looks behind her, as if somebody was following them. But she sees nobody.*

EXT./INT. BOMBSITE/HOTEL DOOR. DAY

We see **Dieter**, **Anna** *and* **Lotte** *framed in a doorway, about to go out to the bombsite.* **Ringwood** *is now with them.* **Dieter** *is giving him instructions.*

> DIETER
> If you get me a taxi please, to leave in ten minutes precisely. We're just going across the bombsite, I promised her one last helping of toffee . . . then I have just one more errand.

> RINGWOOD
> Of course, sir. I'll do that for you. And congratulations, sir, to you both.

Dieter *smiles at him, indicating the umbrella.*

> DIETER
> Don't I look the perfect Englishman today?!

Then we cut close to **Callum** *in the shadows, watching them in the doorway.*

Dieter, **Anna** *and* **Lotte** *now move off and begin to cross the bombsite.*

Callum *lets them get ahead for a few seconds. We are close on his eyes, then he begins to tail them along the duckboard walkways that cross the bombsite. The air is thick with dust, and the figures ahead of him are blurred shapes. The tall* **Dieter** *striding ahead,* **Anna** *and* **Lotte** *talking together, moving animatedly behind him.*

Callum *is getting close; he reaches inside his jacket and takes out the gun. He lines up* **Dieter**. *The girls keep masking the target, through the thick haze of dust.*

Suddenly they stop two-thirds of the way across the bombsite, **Lotte** *is gesticulating, wanting to go down into the crater one last time.* **Anna** *agrees to go with her.* **Dieter** *gives a quick wave and lets them go down into the crater. He then sets off along the diagonal path that leads to the far end of the back of the hotel, where in the distance a taxi is waiting.*

Now **Callum** *has a clear target. We are close on his eyes, as* **Dieter** *is striding quickly towards the distant taxi.*

The dust is clearing a bit, and **Callum** *has got close enough. It is the right moment.* **Callum** *stops walking and aims to shoot.*

At that very moment his name is being called from a distance. He looks behind him. Right across the bombsite, but coming towards him quickly, is **Victor**.

Callum *moves on fast after* **Dieter**, *who is now much closer to the taxi. The dust is thick again. Then for one brief moment there is a clear target.*

VICTOR
Cal! . . . Cal!

Dieter *gets into the taxi and it drives off. We cut inside the taxi;* **Dieter** *looking immaculate as he settles back. He glances out at the dusty ruined street as the taxi moves*

We cut back to **Callum** *just as* **Victor** *is reaching him, his coat flapping in the dust.*

Callum's *tone is coldly furious, his eyes hard.*

CALLUM
Victor?! What are you doing here?!

VICTOR
Looking after you.

CALLUM
No you're not. You're not going to. You shouldn't be here.

Callum *turns and moves off rapidly.*

INT. HAROLD'S HOUSE/HALL/GARDEN. DAY

We cut to **Dieter** *ringing the doorbell of* **Harold**'s *house.* **Harold** *opens the door.*

DIETER
Here I am, Mr Lindsay-Jones. I got your message.

HAROLD
Come in, come in . . . it's just here . . .

Dieter *enters the hall.* **Harold** *picks up a book, gift-wrapped, from the hall table.*

HAROLD
This is the other book of fairy tales I told you about. I thought I just had to give it to you too . . . it belongs with the other one, so you must have it.

DIETER
That is extremely kind . . . that is far too generous.

HAROLD
No, no, not a bit of it . . . a gesture, just a small gesture . . . (*He turns.*) I have one little favour to ask in return now you are here. Mrs Gorton is out, and I need to feed the chickens, if you could just come into the garden with me and help me with the gate? Otherwise some of them always escape!

DIETER
Of course.

We move with them into the garden.

Dieter *holds the gate open for* **Harold** *as he goes into the coop.*

HAROLD
Please come in too, that's the best way.

Dieter enters the chicken coop, as Harold moves towards the hut.

HAROLD
The neighbours will be so pleased when I decide to get rid of them, which I'm sure is pretty soon. I must show you what I keep in here . . .

We see inside the little hut the Foreign Office documents spread under the hens.

So here we have, not just some secret Foreign Office documents for them to lay their eggs on –

DIETER
So I see!

HAROLD
But also this . . .

He picks up an old pre-war pistol from inside the hut.

I keep it here for shooting rats . . . but I've only managed to get one so far.

DIETER
So it's loaded?

HAROLD
Oh yes.

He turns and stares at Dieter, holding the pistol loosely by his side. But there is a moment of realisation in Dieter's eyes that Harold's mood has changed.

HAROLD
I don't know what else I can do? I have no idea what else there is . . . Because I care about him . . . I love Callum, like a son. A stupid thing to think I know . . .

He turns and shoots Dieter.

There is the sound of the birds screeching.

We cut to a very high shot of the body lying surrounded by the chickens and with **Harold** *standing over it.*

We then dissolve into an even higher shot. There is now no **Harold** *in the garden.* **Dieter***'s body is still lying there, with the chickens milling around it.*

EXT./INT. WINTER. THE HOTEL. PASSAGES/ATTIC ROOM/ COURTYARD/MELBURY SUITE/BASEMENT BALLROOM. DAY

We cut to snow falling in the courtyard at the hotel.

At first we see it through windows and through open doors.

In a series of cuts we see the hotel is almost closed down, the last luggage being wheeled away, the jukebox standing outside in a yard with snow falling on it.

The passages are full of boxes.

We then see in a high shot the figures of **Lotte**, **Anna**, **Lucy** *and* **Rachel**, *all in dark clothes out in the snow in the courtyard. They are building a strange-shaped snowman as the hotel is being packed up around them.*

Their faces are pale, serious, very focused.

The camera is now moving fast along the upstairs passages. We begin to hear in the distance, echoing half heard on the soundtrack, like a memory, one of **Eva***'s songs from the basement ballroom. In a series of dissolves we travel upstairs into the attic room which is now completely empty except for one notice board.*

On it is pinned the front page of a newspaper with the headline:
US AIR FORCE BREAKS THE SOUND BARRIER.

We dissolve down to the passage that leads towards the Melbury Suite.

Victor *is moving ahead of us. He is dressed in a suit. He knocks on the door and then enters the suite.*

Frau Bellinghausen *is sitting surrounded by suitcases and large trunks.*

                FRAU BELLINGHAUSEN
There you are, Victor.

Her tone is warm. Then we see **Callum** *is standing in the shadows.*

FRAU BELLINGHAUSEN

You're late.

VICTOR

I'm always late, yes.

FRAU BELLINGHAUSEN

And I'm the last one to leave, as you can see . . .

The echoing sound of the music is getting stronger. We cut down to the courtyard; the snowman is growing. **Rachel**, **Anna**, **Lucy** *and* **Lotte** *working in silence, their faces severe as the snow falls.*

We dissolve back to the Melbury Suite.

FRAU BELLINGHAUSEN

I have received this letter from Harold –

VICTOR

So he's alive?! All the press and everybody said him vanishing completely like that . . . must mean he'd killed himself . . .

CALLUM

Does he say where he is?

FRAU BELLINGHAUSEN

Not so we can find him, no . . . Most of the letter is to me . . . but there is a passage which he says, 'Please show this to the boys.' So of course –

She hands **Callum** *the letter.* **Victor** *peers over his shoulder. We move in on* **Callum***'s eyes and begin to hear* **Harold***'s voice.*

HAROLD

(*voice-over*)

I'm somewhere in France . . . I think it is better I'm not too exact . . . and I will post this many miles away from where I am . . .

INT. FRENCH LIBRARY. EVENING

We see, in long shot, **Harold** *sitting in a large library that could be in a great house or a French municipal building. He is surrounded by books in chaotic piles. We hear his voice-over as the camera travels towards him, and we dissolve between him,* **Callum**, **Victor** *and* **Frau Bellinghausen**.

HAROLD
(voice-over)

I'm trying to be like Victor, and sort this library I'm sitting in now. The nice gentleman that is in charge is allowing me to have a go. All the books are in chaos after the war, in completely the wrong order . . . but I'm not nearly as good at it as Victor is . . .

Maybe they will find me here . . . and I will never get to see either of you again . . . in fact I'm expecting one of those Secret Service men to come through the door at any time . . . I would also appreciate it, if you didn't tell Lucy yet. Soon I will find the words to tell her myself about what happened.

We are close on **Callum**.

HAROLD

I just wanted you to know what I did was a desperate act . . . and of course a very imperfect act . . . leaving such a trail of mess and grief, a little girl without a father and all the rest . . . But it was the only thing I could do. It was an act of love.

We are on **Harold**'s *face among the books and then on* **Callum** *and* **Victor**.

The music is getting stronger all the time. We dissolve down to the courtyard. The misshapen snowman is almost finished, tilting at an odd angle. We see **Lotte**'s *grave face as she works on it. We see the closeness between her and* **Anna**.

Kathy *is just arriving in the courtyard; she approaches* **Rachel**.

KATHY

I got an invitation from Callum. The last day of the hotel . . .

We dissolve back to the Melbury Suite.

Frau Bellinghausen *is carefully folding the letter.*

> FRAU BELLINGHAUSEN
> He was so wrong to blame himself for everything, what he thought he should have done before the war . . . How could it all be his fault?

We move in on her, tears in her eyes.

> A good man . . . I miss him terribly.

> CALLUM
> Yes . . .

He moves towards her.

> We're going to look at the ballroom, this being the last day of the hotel . . . and see it before they knock it down. I wanted to suggest something revolutionary.

Frau Bellinghausen *looks at him surprised.*

> That you come down with us . . . ?

We dissolve to the snow-covered courtyard. A piano piece is beginning on the soundtrack. It is snowing more lightly now. **Callum** *is crossing towards the group as they are putting the final touches to the snowman, which is tilting at an angle.*

Rachel *comes towards* **Callum.**

> RACHEL
> Look who's here! (*Indicating* **Kathy**.)

> KATHY
> I wasn't going to miss this! (*To* **Callum**.) And I brought you something . . .

She pulls out of her bag a framed photo. **Callum** *stares at it. It is of* **Kleinow**, *bent forwards, moving along a wall almost crouching, his hand held up against the photographers, trying to hide.*

KATHY

It is Kleinow being led away . . . just after being sentenced to spend the rest of his life in jail.

CALLUM

Thank you. (*He smiles.*) It'll be on my mantelpiece.

RACHEL
(*to* **Kathy**)

You're going to come downstairs aren't you? There are some drinks . . . (*She smiles.*) No food though . . . but Callum is going to play a new piece . . . ! (*She takes his arm.*) It's not bad, I've heard it already . . .

The piano piece is getting louder. We see **Rachel** *and* **Callum** *framed in the doorway, the snow falling behind them, their faces close.*

CALLUM

Not bad? The new piece? (*Staring at her.*) Is that all . . .?

RACHEL
(*softly*)

No . . .

Their eyes meet.

I love it . . .

She kisses him.

We dissolve to **Callum** *in the basement ballroom; all the tables have gone now, just the piano and some chairs.*

He is sitting at the piano playing. He is being watched by **Anna** *and* **Lotte** *sitting close together,* **Lucy**, **Rachel**, *and* **Kathy**.

The door suddenly opens and there is **Victor** *escorting* **Frau Bellinghausen** *into the ballroom. She sits in pride of place.*

FRAU BELLINGHAUSEN

I made it downstairs, at last!

We dissolve to the faces, as **Callum** *plays. We see* **Anna**, *in mourning, but staring out calmly. We are close on* **Kathy**.

We move in on **Lotte**, *we get very close on her eyes. For one brief moment we see her running freely by herself across the crater of the bombsite.*

We cut back to her eyes, clear, determined, strong.

We see **Victor** *sitting perfectly still for once.*

We cut to **Rachel** *watching* **Callum** *at the piano.*

We move in on **Callum** *as he plays.*

Fade to black.

CREDITS